THE MOTIVATED AMATEUR'S GUIDE TO WINTER CAMPING

Essential Winter Camping Tips to Make Your Cold Outdoor Experience Safe and Enjoyable

AARON LINSDAU

Sastrugi Press
Jackson, WY

©2025 Aaron Linsdau
The Motivated Amateur's Guide to Winter Camping: Essential Winter Camping Tips to Make Your Cold Outdoor Experience Safe and Enjoyable

Interior image copyrights © Aaron Linsdau unless otherwise noted
All rights reserved. No part of this book may be reproduced or transmitted in any form or by any means, electronic or mechanical, including photocopying, recording, or by any information storage and retrieval system without the written permission of the author, except where permitted by law.

Sastrugi Press / Published by arrangement with the author
Sastrugi Press: PO Box 1297, Jackson, WY 83001, United States
www.sastrugipress.com
The activities described in this book are inherently dangerous. The publisher does not have any control over and does not assume any responsibility for author or third-party websites or their content. No content in this book is to be construed as legal advice. Seek out a qualified and licensed legal advisor.

Modern medical treatment is a constantly evolving field—recommended treatment and drug therapy are always changing. All medical treatment discussed in this book must be evaluated using the most current product information provided by the manufacturer to verify the recommended dose, the proper administration, and contraindications. It is always the responsibility of the licensed practitioner, relying on training and knowledge of the patient, to determine the best treatment and proper dosages for each individual. Neither the publisher nor the author assume any liability for any injury, illness, or death related to the medical discussions in this publication.

Any person participating in the activities described in this work is personally responsible for learning the proper techniques and using good judgment. You are responsible for your own actions and decisions. The information contained in this work is subjective and based solely on opinions. No book can advise you of all potential hazards or anticipate the limitations of any reader. Participation in the described activities can result in severe injury or death. Neither the publisher nor the author assume any liability for anyone participating in the activities described in this work.

Library of Congress Cataloging-in-Publication Data

Names: Linsdau, Aaron author
  http://id.loc.gov/authorities/names/no2018033681
  http://id.loc.gov/rwo/agents/no2018033681
Title: The motivated amateur's guide to winter camping : essential winter
  camping tips to make your cold outdoor experience safe and enjoyable /
  Aaron Linsdau.
Description: Jackson, WY : Sastrugi Press, [2025]
Identifiers: LCCN 2025012230 | ISBN 9781649220998 paperback
Subjects: LCSH: Snow camping
  http://id.loc.gov/authorities/subjects/sh85123778 | Snow
  camping--Equipment and supplies | Outdoor recreation
  http://id.loc.gov/authorities/subjects/sh85096148
Classification: LCC GV198.9 .L58 2025 | DDC 796.9--dc23/eng/20250510
LC record available at https://lccn.loc.gov/2025012230

ISBN-13: 978-1-64922-099-8 (paperback LS)

613.6—dc23

15 14 13 12 11 10 9 8 7 6 5 4 3

Dedication

For my dad, Timothy, who led by example—introducing me to adventure through the Boy Scouts, shaping my character with his unwavering faith, and showing me how to navigate both the wild and life with courage, integrity, and wisdom.

Timothy snowshoeing away from camp in the morning at 15°F (-9°C) in Sequoia National Park. This was our coldest winter camping trip together.

Camping at the South Pole with a sense of humor.

Contents

Preface	vii
Introduction	x
Part 1 Equipment	**1**
1 Winter Clothing Layers	3
2 Winter Camping Footwear	35
3 Choosing the Right Winter Shelter	55
4 Sleeping Bags and Staying Warm at Night	66
5 Selecting Snow Travel Gear	80
6 Stove Selection and Accesories	100
7 Communications, Electronics, Accessories	111
Part 2 Winter Camping Techniques and Strategies	**124**
8 Choosing the Best Campsite	125
9 Staying Warm and Dry	149
10 Managing Body Heat, Exposure, Travel	160
11 Maintaining Electronics in the Winter	171
12 Winter Camping Efficiency	180
13 Avalanche Safety for Winter Campers	196
14 Winter Weather	201
15 Planning for Short vs. Long Winter Trips	209
16 Solo vs. Team Camping	216
17 Dealing with Wildlife in Winter	227
18 First Aid	238
19 Training and Fitness	250
Part 3 Stoves, Cooking, and Water Management in Winter	**254**
20 Stove Use in the Winter	255
21 Food for Winter Camping	274
22 Water Management in Winter Camping	284
23 Specialized Diets	288
24 Shopping and Packaging Food	298

Part 4 Terrain and Environmental Considerations — 301
- 25 Navigating Winter Terrain — 302
- 26 Dealing with Altitude — 314
- 27 Reducing Impact — 318

Part 5 Planning and Executing Your Winter Adventure — 322
- 28 Preparing for Your Trip — 323
- 29 Long Trips — 327
- 30 Polar Camping — 333

Part 6 The Daily Experience of Winter Camping — 339
- 31 Expedition Experience: Greenland and Denali — 341
- 32 Conclusion — 348

Appendices — 351
- Appendix 1 Author Resources for Winter Camping — 351
- Appendix 2 Training and Education — 352
- Appendix 3 Online Resources and Reading — 355
- Appendix 4 Author Gear: Winter Overnight — 356

Free Downloads — 360
Author's Review Note — 361
Other Books by the Author — 362
About the Author — 364

Winter tarp camping in Sequoia National Park.

Preface

Experiencing the outdoors in winter wasn't how I originally started camping. I grew up in San Diego, where snow was rare, only appearing occasionally in the local mountains. It might seem odd to think of a kid from Southern California as someone who would later embrace winter camping.

However, my appreciation for the outdoors didn't begin there. My family was from the Rocky Mountains, where they spent much of their lives fishing, hunting, camping, and enjoying nature. That love of the outdoors was passed down to me through my father and the Boy Scout program. He encouraged me to join, and after seven years, I earned my Eagle Scout award—an honor I've carried with me throughout my life. I deeply appreciate everything the program taught me.

One thing I didn't learn in my San Diego Scout troop, however, was how to camp in the winter.

During college, my brother and I took a winter camping trip into the Laguna Mountains. We froze our collective backsides off. It was so cold that we couldn't stand on the ground—our feet were numb and aching. We spent an hour standing on the picnic bench at our campsite, trying to warm up. Our desperate attempt to generate heat with a Chevy Sprint idling for half an hour was a complete failure. At midnight, we finally crawled into our sleeping bags.

Somehow, we made it through the night without frostbite.

The next morning, we drove to Julian for a hot breakfast. Our food had frozen solid overnight, and there was no way we were going to cook anything. It was a valuable learning experience.

A couple of years passed before I decided to challenge myself with a cold-weather trip to the Sierras. For my thirtieth birthday, I chose Sequoia National Park as my test site. I knew that if things got bad, I could retreat to the Wuksachi Lodge to warm up. This time, I was better prepared. It was still brutally cold, but I made it through the night and even managed to cook breakfast. I had advanced my skills and learned important lessons along the way.

I began my winter camping journey before the internet was widely accessible. There were no YouTube tutorials, few books on the subject, and not many people to ask for advice. Today, people—including myself—make entire careers out of teaching others how to enjoy the outdoors. A small number of us specialize in the snowy, cold months.

Since that first trip with my brother and my initial adventure in the Sierras, I have spent over a year of my life camping in winter conditions. I hiked over 100 miles (160 km) across the Greenland tundra alone in October, enduring sub-zero temperatures. In hindsight, that probably wasn't the wisest time of year to hike the Arctic Circle Trail, but it gave me valuable exposure to international Arctic expeditions.

I have snowshoed and skied across Yellowstone in the dead of winter. On my first trip, I camped in -45°F (-43°C) temperatures—20 degrees colder than I had anticipated. Fortunately, I avoided frostbite, but my toes were numb for a month afterward.

To put that cold into perspective, your home freezer typically sits at 0°F (-18°C). Camping inside your freezer would have been 40 degrees warmer than my first Yellowstone trip. While I had the right gear, I lacked the mental framework to handle those conditions. That experience taught me a lot and led me to start writing about and filming my winter camping adventures.

Since then, I've set records and taken on extreme challenges. I hold the record for the longest-duration solo expedition to the South Pole in history. My friend, Dr. Terry Williams, and I are among the oldest teams to have crossed the Greenland ice cap alone. Together, we've written two books about our expeditions: *Adventure Expedition One* and *Two Friends and a Polar Bear*.

I have also climbed high-altitude peaks such as Mount Elbrus in Russia and Mount Kilimanjaro in Tanzania. I've solo-climbed Denali five times, and my experiences on the mountain are chronicled in my book *Lost at Windy Corner*.

Now, I'm writing this book to consolidate everything I've learned about winter camping into a single resource. My YouTube channel has tens of thousands of subscribers, and my primary focus is outdoor adventure—particularly expeditions and winter camping. Many people have asked me about my experiences, eager to learn more in-depth details about what I do.

I wrote this book not only to share my love of the outdoors but, more importantly, to make winter camping safer and more accessible for others. Millions of people visit Yellowstone National Park in the summer, but only a few thousand experience it in the winter—and just a few dozen attempt overnight camping.

For me, winter camping is both a challenge and an escape. It requires focus and planning—without both, accidents can happen. Venturing into freezing conditions forces me to stay present, paying attention to what I'm doing rather than worrying about everyday life.

As of the date of this writing, I am not sponsored by any of the brands mentioned in this book. All product names, titles, and trademarks referenced in this book are the property of their respective owners and are used for identification purposes only.

Some people think I'm reckless for camping in the winter—especially when I go solo, which is often. Perhaps they're right. But in my experience, mindful winter camping is far safer than commuting several hours a day. Are there risks beyond my control in the backcountry?

Absolutely.

I'll take my chances with the snow, weather, and the occasional animal.

My hope is that you, too, will be inspired to experience the outdoors in the snowy months. Enjoy what we've been blessed with on this planet.

Take my advice to heart. I share all my gear choices in this book—yes, even my underwear. Over time, certain products may become unavailable. My goal isn't for you to use the exact brands I do, but to find your own versions of the gear that will serve you best.

Winter camping carries more risks than summer camping. If something doesn't feel right, turn back. Avoid unnecessary risks whenever possible. The most important goal isn't reaching the summit or hitting a distance milestone—it's making it home safely, just as you left, with your body unharmed. The only change should be the confidence and experience you gain from facing nature in its rawest form.

Enjoy the journey. Stay safe out there.

Introduction

Camping in the winter is at once one of the most satisfying outdoor experiences and one of the riskiest. Except for the ski slopes, you'll have the outdoors pretty much to yourself. Only a fraction of people venture out in the winter compared to the other three seasons.

Snow gives you the opportunity to create shelters where none would exist. You can do things that wouldn't be possible in summer. What may be an impassable forest due to deadfall can become completely navigable. You can camp in places you wouldn't otherwise.

However, weather is always a factor. Even though forecasts are generally accurate, storms can come out of nowhere. Temperatures can drop 20 degrees lower than predicted. This has happened to even the most experienced winter campers. A minor mistake can cascade into a life-threatening situation.

The goal of this book is to prepare you for winter camping so you can enjoy yourself. Sure, you will be cold. But with the proper gear and preparation, you can have a great time. There's an old Northern European saying: *The weather isn't too cold—you just have the wrong clothing.*

How This Book is Structured

The first part of this book focuses on the gear necessary for a successful winter camping trip. While some summer camping gear can be repurposed, there are extra items you'll need. Clothing, stoves, tents, and sleeping bags are just a few of the many pieces of equipment required for a safe and enjoyable trip. On flat ground, you can get away without too much technical gear. However, once you head into hills and mountains, additional equipment becomes necessary for a safe journey.

One challenge for many people is the cost of winter camping. Throughout this book, references are made to various gear brands. The manufacturers mentioned are simply suggestions. Availability depends on where in the world you're reading this book. Since this book was written in the United

States, most of the manufacturers mentioned are from the U.S. All you need to do is find the equivalent piece of gear in your country.

After covering equipment, the book moves on to winter camping techniques. All the gear in the world won't do you any good if you don't know how to use it. This section focuses on efficiency, safety, and experience. One of the challenges of winter camping is that it's difficult to test your skills if you live in a warm place. You'll learn in-depth techniques for using your equipment effectively for speed and comfort.

In Part Three, you'll learn about food, cooking, and water management. Staying hydrated in extremely cold temperatures is a challenge. It's easy to become dehydrated and run out of water. Managing food is also tricky since everything you bring will freeze. How do you deal with that? This part of the book explores those challenges.

Part Four covers terrain and environmental considerations. In some parts of the world, winter travel is relatively simple. There are no mountains or other major obstacles to worry about. However, rivers and lakes may pose risks. In other regions, mountains dominate the landscape, creating their own unique hazards.

By Part Five, you'll be ready to tackle planning and advanced topics. This section covers everything from developing a trip plan to dealing with unexpected situations. Navigation in whiteouts, handling emergencies, and camping in areas with little to no natural shelter are just a few of the topics discussed. Whether you're planning a local overnight trip or a multi-week expedition, this section will help you prepare and adapt.

Part Six features two excerpts from my books *Two Friends and a Polar Bear* and *Lost at Windy Corner*. These accounts provide firsthand insight into real winter expeditions, giving you a deeper understanding of the challenges and rewards of extreme cold-weather travel. It also includes the conclusion, bringing together all the lessons covered in the book.

Finally, an Additional Resources section is included at the end. Here, you'll find recommendations for further reading, gear suppliers, training programs, and organizations that can help you continue developing your winter camping skills. You'll also find a winter camping checklist.

The Purpose of This Book

The ultimate goal of this book is to prepare you for all the considerations that go into winter camping. It's a completely different experience from simply living in a cold climate. Many parts of the U.S. and Europe experience winter conditions, providing great test beds to see if you're ready for true winter camping.

Running from a warm house to a car and then into work in subzero temperatures does not prepare you for the realities of being in the wilderness during winter. Only through careful preparation and an understanding of consequences can you truly be ready. Even with the best preparation and gear, things can go wrong. Being ready for the unexpected can mean the difference between returning home with a great story and ending up in a bad situation.

Hopefully, you're excited to learn about winter camping and the joys it brings. One of the best parts of snow-covered landscapes is that they tell a story of passage and survival. While plants go dormant, animals continue moving through their environment, leaving behind tracks and signs of life. By learning to read these tracks, you'll realize that you and your camping friends aren't as alone as you might think. After a heavy snowfall, those stories disappear, creating a completely different experience from other seasons.

Understanding the Risks

This book covers all levels of winter camping. If you're planning your first foray into the cold, take the advice contained here to heart. Evaluate your situation as you go, and be willing to adapt. If conditions don't match what you expected, consider turning back. There's no shame in retreat—regroup, reassess, and try again.

Winter camping carries higher risks than summer camping. Mistakes can quickly escalate into dangerous situations. In warm-weather conditions, there's simply less that can go wrong. Avalanches, crevasses, unexpected weather—these elements make winter camping fascinating but also risky. If an unexpected blizzard is forecast for your first trip, stay home. Being smart is what separates those who become experienced winter campers from those who don't come home.

The Scope of This Book

This book primarily focuses on tent-based camping without external heating sources. There are excellent resources available on *hot tent* camping, where a tent includes a built-in stove for warmth. While hot tent camping is a fantastic option, it falls outside the scope of this book.

Introduction

One of the most important aspects of winter camping is understanding the *why*. This means knowing *why* a certain piece of gear is used instead of something else. It explains *why* certain approaches work in winter but wouldn't make sense in summer. It also covers *why* layers are stacked in a specific way and why certain fabrics are chosen. Simply reading a gear list won't teach you the reasoning or the experience behind these choices.

Once you understand *why* each item and technique matters, you'll be able to make smarter decisions based on your situation. This knowledge will help you see how everything works together and why it's valuable.

The *how* is less important than the *why*, though both are critical. Understanding the *why* behind the *how* gives you a complete picture of winter camping. It helps you adapt to different conditions and make better choices for your specific needs.

Even if you have years of experience, this book contains details that may challenge your thinking. Each small piece of knowledge offers a new perspective. The journey of learning never ends, and there's always something new to pick up.

A Final Note on Safety

This book does not cover the mountaineering aspects of winter travel. Mountaineering presents its own unique challenges and rewards. It's a deeply enriching experience, but it falls beyond the scope of this book. There are excellent resources available through professional organizations and books that cover mountaineering in depth. If you're interested, consider hiring a professional guide or joining a professionally led expedition. Whenever possible, avoid going into the mountains alone to minimize risk.

This book is not a substitute for professional training from certified guides or medical professionals. Everything included here is based on real-world experience. However, if you're venturing into challenging or potentially dangerous conditions, it's best to go with someone more experienced or join a guided group. If something feels dangerous, it probably is—trust your instincts. Returning home safely is always more important than reaching a summit or pushing on.

Now, get ready to begin your journey into winter camping!

Digging out after a pitteraq (blizzard) in Greenland.

Melting snow for water in the Hilleberg Nammatj 2 tent with the vestibule open in calm weather for better ventilation.

Part 1
Equipment

Gear Introduction

It's all about the right gear. Combine the right skill set with the right equipment, and you can have an amazingly comfortable experience in the winter. Away from the trappings of home, the winter experience is partly about the kit, partly about skill, and wholly about mentality.

That doesn't mean you need the most expensive gear. Outdoor retailers may tell you otherwise, but this is the truth. Every winter camper has their cherished piece of gear that cost a lot to purchase. Some have piles of equipment worth tens of thousands of dollars or euros. Others get by with used gear from thrift stores—and they enjoy themselves just as much as the well-financed camper.

Some things can be found at very reasonable prices. However, with winter camping, certain expenses simply cannot be avoided. Gear needs to be heavier and more robust to insulate against the cold.

The equipment mentioned in this book is based on the author's experience, but your experience may vary. Vendors go out of business, and new suppliers appear constantly. The goal is to find something equivalent to what's listed in the text. Don't waste time scouring the internet or asking store clerks for the exact model mentioned here.

The key is to find equivalent gear with the proper temperature rating and strength. Shoes that fit one person might not fit another. The same goes for jackets. Some people prefer specific fabrics or colors. Men's equipment differs from women's, too. Physiologically, men and women are different, so simply buying a smaller men's jacket may not fit a woman properly.

Fabric choices are another significant consideration. There are both synthetic and natural fibers to choose from. Make sure the base layer fabric of your clothing doesn't irritate your skin. Some people find fine natural fibers, like wool, irritating. Others feel that synthetic fabrics trap bacteria and odors. Each option has trade-offs to consider.

Testing your equipment before you leave home is one of the most important things to remember. Test it in the coldest and toughest conditions you can manage. You don't want to be in the wilderness and discover that something you purchased simply doesn't work. It happens all the time.

This is especially true with footwear. Many people end up with terrible blisters or foot problems because they buy boots but never try them out beforehand. Reality television is full of stories like this—someone buys boots the day before leaving, only to end up with painful blisters and foot injuries. It's more common than you might think.

All your gear, clothing, and equipment (or "kit," as they say in the UK) will be highly personal. The suggestions in this book are just a starting point. You don't have to purchase everything at once—in fact, doing so can be overwhelming and discouraging. There is a minimum level of gear necessary to safely make it through the night. You'll find three gear lists in the back of the book to help guide your choices. Everything else expands your ability to travel farther and deeper into the field.

As you read through the gear section, think about what you will wear and what you might enjoy using. If this is your first time winter camping and you live in a warm climate, this equipment list may surprise you. For those with experience, it can help fine-tune your gear to improve your overall experience.

Whichever the case, enjoy the process. Don't feel overwhelmed—winter camping is a long game. It's something you grow into, and if you enjoy it, you'll never get enough of it.

Finishing camp before being visited at midnight by the Wapiti Lake Pack wolves in Yellowstone National Park.

Chapter 1
Winter Clothing Layers

To successfully navigate the highly variable climate of winter, you'll need multiple layers of clothing. Gone are the days of wearing just a regular shirt with an ultra-heavy jacket and nothing in between. One day may be sunny and relatively comfortable, while the next could bring a blizzard with life-threatening conditions.

The concept of layering allows you to adapt to different temperatures and precipitation levels. On some days, you may only need a shirt and a shell jacket. On others, you'll wear every piece of clothing you brought—and you may still feel chilly. This does mean you'll need more clothing than you would on a summer trip. It can be tempting to leave certain items at home based on the forecast, but that can be a mistake.

Winter and mountain forecasts are frequently wrong. Having multiple layers of clothing reduces the likelihood of problems. It gives you flexibility that one or two layers simply cannot provide.

Layering works by stacking clothing from the skin outward. Below is a breakdown of the different layers in a proper winter clothing system, followed by a discussion of their functions:

Base layer: Worn next to the skin, this layer provides warmth and wicks moisture away.
Mid layer: An insulating layer worn over the base layer and under the outer layer.
Outer layer: The protective shell that shields you from wind, snow, and rain.

Base Layer

The base layer consists of your undergarments, shirt, and leg coverings. It also includes thin head coverings, socks, and liner gloves. These are the clothing items you'll be wearing all day—anything less, and you'll be exposing bare skin to the cold.

The base layer is a key component of a cold-weather layering system. Its primary job is to wick sweat away from your skin, keeping you dry and preventing chills. It also provides a thin layer of insulation by trapping body heat close to the skin. Staying dry is especially important in cold conditions, where moisture can quickly lead to discomfort or even danger.

Material choice is critical for an effective base layer. Merino wool is an excellent option because it wicks moisture, resists odors naturally, and retains warmth even when damp. Synthetic fabrics like polyester and nylon are also popular—they dry quickly and are lightweight, making them ideal for high-activity situations where you might sweat more. Choosing the right material can make a big difference in staying comfortable and warm during cold weather.

Base Layer: Fabrics

The two fundamental choices for base layer fabrics are synthetic and natural. Each has its advantages and disadvantages, and costs can vary widely.

Before the advent of synthetic fibers, natural fabrics were the only option. The classic example is the scratchy red wool underwear, often featured in old movies. While not particularly comfortable, it got the job done. Today's wool, however, is vastly improved—not because the sheep have changed, but due to better selection and weaving techniques. Modern wool is an excellent choice for a base layer. It's no longer scratchy, and it doesn't irritate the skin.

Unlike other fabrics, wool comes in different weights. Merino wool base layers are often available in 100, 150, 200, and 260 weights, with higher numbers indicating greater thickness and insulation. For extremely cold camping, 260-weight shirts and long underwear provide excellent warmth. On some climbs and expeditions, layering a 150-weight base with a 260-weight layer can be a useful strategy. Wearing both together isn't particularly comfortable, but it's another tool in your winter gear arsenal.

One major benefit of wool is that it doesn't develop odors as quickly as synthetic fabrics. On a weeklong or longer trip, bacteria buildup and odor can become a real issue. Avoiding skin irritation is crucial for maintaining overall comfort and body health.

However, wool does have downsides. It's not as durable as synthetic fabrics and tends to develop small holes over time. While wool is more fire-resistant than synthetics, it isn't as tough when compared at the same fabric thickness.

Another drawback is cost. Wool clothing tends to be significantly more expensive than synthetic alternatives. Much of the high-end wool used for base layers comes from New Zealand and other premium sources. Additionally, wool isn't as widely available as synthetic or cotton fabrics. Finding wool base layers often requires shopping at specialty stores, though some large retailers carry them online. It pays to shop around.

Silk is another natural fiber worth considering for a base layer. Like wool, silk resists bacterial buildup, reducing odor and skin irritation compared to synthetics. However, silk has limited stretch, making it less flexible than wool or synthetic options. It has high tensile strength but lacks wool's abrasion resistance, making it more prone to wear in rugged use. Some enthusiasts swear by silk shirts and socks, but silk long underwear is uncommon due to its lack of stretch.

The One Fabric to Avoid: Cotton

For winter camping, avoid cotton at all costs. In the *NOLS* (National Outdoor Leadership School) training program, the phrase "cotton kills" is a well-known truism.

Cotton is by far the most popular fabric for clothing in the United States—denim jeans, T-shirts, and hoodies are all made from cotton. It's durable and comfortable, but it poses serious risks in cold environments.

The biggest problem with cotton is that once it gets wet, it stays wet. Unlike wool, silk, or synthetics, it does not wick moisture away from the skin. Instead, it holds onto moisture—whether from sweat, precipitation, or an accidental fall into a body of water. Without a reliable heat source, drying cotton in cold conditions is extremely difficult.

Try a simple test at home: Wear the same cotton T-shirt for three days straight, engaging in physical activity each day so that you break a sweat. By the end of the third day, you'll likely want to throw that shirt away. Cotton retains moisture, body oils, and dirt much more than wool or synthetics, making it a poor choice for multi-day wear.

Another drawback of cotton is that once it gets wet and stretches out, it doesn't return to its original shape. Wool fibers have microscopic scales that interlock, helping them maintain their structure. Cotton fibers, however, separate and lose their form when wet, causing them to sag and lose insulation.

If you wear cotton in winter and it becomes wet—whether from perspiration, precipitation, or an unexpected plunge into a lake—it may never dry for the entire duration of your trip. There are far better fabric choices for winter camping.

Cotton hoodies (*jumpers* in the UK) can work for low-risk overnight trips where you have an easy exit if needed. A cotton hoodie is fine if you have a warm vehicle or cabin nearby as a backup, but it's still not recommended for prolonged exposure to winter conditions.

Does this mean you need to purchase different fabrics specifically for winter camping?

Yes. Skip the cotton.

Base Layer: Underwear

Underwear is a particularly personal choice. Both style and fit depend on the individual. Boxers, briefs, and various cuts designed for women are all options on the market.

Whichever underwear you choose, make sure it fits well and works for you. For women, synthetic fabrics are a popular choice, but in the crotch area, it's important to have a breathable fabric to reduce the likelihood of developing problems.

The same consideration applies to bras. Choose one that you can wear for multiple days and that is comfortable. Sports bras are by far the most popular option, and extra-padded versions can provide additional comfort. While synthetic fabric bras are the most common, Merino wool bras offer the same advantages as wool underwear compared to synthetic alternatives. A quick internet search will reveal many manufacturers offering wool bras. Modern wool blends and weaves are designed to be comfortable against the skin.

Whichever option you choose, make sure it's something you can wear day after day for a week or more. On long expeditions, you may only have two or three pairs of underwear to rotate through.

Go with your personal preference, but test it at home first. Wear a single pair of underwear for three days. Yes, it may feel a bit gross, but this test will help you discover potential issues before heading into the wilderness. What seems fine at first may become unbearable by day five. As strange as this advice may sound, countless people have suffered through terrible underwear choices.

Getting the underwear layer wrong on a long winter camping trip is a quick path to misery.

Base Layer: Legs (Long Underwear)

In addition to regular underwear, long underwear is a good choice for winter camping. This style of clothing has gained popularity due to the fashion trend of wearing leggings, but long underwear is specifically designed for insulation and moisture management in cold environments.

Long underwear is a form-fitting layer that conforms to your legs. While you don't lose as much heat from your legs as from your torso, wearing long underwear makes a substantial difference in overall comfort. Both wool and synthetic materials work well. Again, wool has the advantage of resisting bacterial buildup and odors far better than synthetic fabrics.

Long underwear also helps prevent chilblains and polar thigh. Chilblains occur when skin reacts to cold exposure, resulting in small to large patches of damage. It's not quite frostbite, but it can cause the skin to deteriorate, exposing underlying layers to injury and infection. Polar thigh occurs when skiing or traveling in extreme cold and strong headwinds, causing large raw spots where the outer epidermis sloughs off, exposing the sensitive skin beneath.

It is not something you want to experience.

One challenge with long underwear is that it is difficult to remove if conditions become too warm. If you're overheating and have already stripped down to just your shirt, how do you regulate your temperature? If overheating is even a remote possibility, make sure your shell pants have full-length side zippers. Most shell pants allow for side ventilation without requiring complete removal, helping regulate heat while keeping your long underwear on.

One of the most important functions of long underwear isn't just warmth—it's preventing muscle cramping. If your legs become too cold, your muscles won't function as well. This is something you'll need to experiment with. Some people tolerate overheating without issue, while others struggle with heat retention and slow down. Humans are highly adaptable, but we are also sensitive to body temperature. There's a fine line between staying slightly cool—so you can move efficiently and warm up naturally—and being uncomfortably hot. Long underwear is part of the layering system, but it's also the most difficult to manage.

Consider three-quarter length long underwear as an alternative. Depending on the type of boots and socks you plan to wear, shorter long underwear can be more convenient. The problem with full-length long underwear is that they have to be tucked into your boots, which can create discomfort.

This setup works fine with long-distance ski boots or mountaineering boots. However, with traditional downhill or free-ski boots, stuffing anything thicker than the thinnest long underwear into the boot around your ankle is a recipe for discomfort.

This is definitely something to test out at home before heading into the wilderness.

Base Layer: Torso

The standard winter camping shirt is a long-sleeve pullover with no buttons. Your base layer shirt should be form-fitting without being too tight. It shouldn't be so short that it rides up and exposes your midsection or so constricting that it limits movement under your arms. At the same time, a shirt that's too loose can bunch up under your mid-layer, creating discomfort. A long-sleeve base layer also absorbs oils from your skin, keeping your mid-layer cleaner for longer.

A button-down synthetic shirt can also be a viable option. These shirts offer more adaptability to changing weather conditions. However, they are not as warm per unit weight as shirts designed specifically for cold conditions. They are useful when you need to ventilate heat, especially on trips that involve long-distance travel at lower elevations before heading into higher, colder terrain. Button-down shirts also work well as a camp shirt when conditions are warm. You can unbutton them or roll up the sleeves much more easily than a non-adjustable pullover. They aren't ideal for cold weather, but you can layer a lightweight base layer wool or synthetic shirt underneath to retain warmth while maintaining the versatility of a button-down.

For longer trips, you may also want to consider bringing a very light wool or synthetic T-shirt as an additional base layer. In calm, sunny conditions, even in the mountains, it can become uncomfortably hot inside a tent or during midday travel. If your only base layer is a long-sleeve shirt, you won't be able to roll up the sleeves for cooling.

The downside of a light T-shirt layer is that if it's your only layer outdoors, your skin will be exposed to the sun. Sunburn and dehydration are risks when any skin is left uncovered in mountainous or winter conditions, where sunlight can be intense due to reflection off snow.

Author's Note

On every climbing expedition I've been on to Denali (the tallest mountain in North America, located in Alaska at 20,310 ft / 6,190 m), I've had uncomfortably hot days. The first time I was at 11,300-foot camp (3,444 m), the inside temperature of my tent reached 100°F (38°C). This particular camp is incredibly warm due to the surrounding ice walls, which act like a solar oven.

At lower elevations on the Kahiltna Glacier, the air temperature can get so hot that the snow starts turning to mild slush in the middle of the day. I and other climbers have taken our shirts off and rubbed snow over our bodies to cool off.

However, in just eight hours, the temperature can drop below 0°F (-18°C). The temperature swings on cold mountains like Denali are similar to those in a desert—scorching in the middle of the day, then plummeting as soon as the sun disappears.

I've taken to wearing a synthetic Eddie Bauer or ExOfficio button-down shirt for the first couple of days of the trip. If I'm traveling on the lower Kahiltna Glacier when it's hot, I unbutton the shirt and roll up the sleeves under my shell jacket to cool off. Higher on the mountain, I use the long-sleeve button-down as my camp shirt when conditions are warm. Since climbing Denali is a heavyweight activity, bringing an extra shirt provides a significant comfort advantage.

I've had people joke that I look like I'm on the mountain for an interview—right up until the heat hits and they're struggling with their pullover shirts while I've unbuttoned mine. I roll up the sleeves and use my shell jacket to protect myself from the sun. It's a surprisingly comfortable experience.

Do not underestimate how hot the mountains can be on a clear, still day. It's a surreal experience.

Base Layer: Socks

In mountaineering and cold-weather expeditions, layering socks is a standard practice to ensure warmth. Multiple layers create extra insulation, helping to keep feet warmer in extreme conditions. However, this approach doesn't always apply to skiing.

Ski boots are designed for a single, longer sock and rely on the boot's insulation to keep feet warm. Layering socks in ski boots can backfire—too much bulk compresses the foot, cutting off circulation, which can actually make your feet colder. This is true for most types of ski boots, including hybrid, downhill, and touring models.

Polar ski boots or heavy-duty double- and triple-layer mountaineering boots are often fit to accommodate a double-layer sock system—or even a triple-layer setup in extreme cases. Typically, this includes a thin liner sock under a heavier wool or synthetic sock, providing insulation without compromising comfort or circulation.

Circulation is key to keeping your feet warm. If your boots are packed with too many socks or socks that are too thick, they'll compress your feet, reducing circulation. This can quickly lead to cold feet—or even frostbite. With looser hiking or mountaineering boots, you may have some flexibility, but ski touring and similar types of ski boots generally require thinner socks. Thick mountaineering socks can be a poor choice if your boots weren't fitted with them in mind.

When people get ski boots fitted at a shop, they're typically wearing thin socks, either provided by the store or whatever they happened to have on that day. If you later switch to bulkier socks, the thermal shaping of the boots can create pressure points, reducing circulation. That's why adding more layers to your feet often creates more problems than it solves.

In cold conditions, compressing your feet too much is a mistake to avoid.

Base Layer: Hands

Liner gloves are one of the secret weapons for staying warm in cold climates and during cold-weather camping. They serve multiple purposes, with the most important being that you can wear them continuously while performing tasks. This may require adjusting the sizing of your outer shell gloves to accommodate them.

First, when you remove your outer gloves for any reason, liner gloves stay on, protecting your hands and fingers from direct exposure to the cold. They also help regulate moisture, reducing evaporation—a critical factor in preventing heat loss. Sweat evaporating from your hands draws away heat, making your fingers colder. Every small effort to protect your hands counts.

That said, liner gloves aren't suitable for everything. When handling toilet activities involving toilet paper, it's better to wear nothing or use disposable nitrile gloves to avoid contamination. Developing frostbite while defecating is something you definitely want to avoid. That's where nitrile gloves can come in handy.

Liner gloves have downsides. Most are made from synthetic materials, making them prone to heat damage from stoves, hot pots, or rising flames. Wool gloves fare better against heat but develop holes more quickly. The durability of liner gloves varies widely—some last years, while others fall apart after a single trip.

It's wise to test them at home before heading out and to bring multiple pairs for longer trips. Damaged or dirty liner gloves lose insulation, and greasy gloves can leave your hands feeling colder. Keep a pair specifically for sleeping—clean, lightweight gloves will make a significant difference during cold nights.

During high-intensity activities like climbing or skiing, liner gloves can quickly become sweaty, greasy, and uncomfortable. They're tough to clean in camp, but reserving a fresh pair for sleeping will help you rest warmer and more comfortably.

Even small changes like this can make a big difference in the cold.

Base Layer: Neck and Head

A head and neck buff is one of the most versatile pieces of equipment you can bring on a winter camping trip. Though small and seemingly simple, this stretchable fabric has countless practical uses, making it an essential item for outdoor adventures.

One of its primary purposes is wind protection. Wrapped around your neck or pulled over your head, it shields sensitive areas like your ears, neck, and face from harsh, biting winds. It also provides a thin but effective layer of insulation, keeping you warm without causing overheating during active pursuits like hiking or skiing. On sunny, snowy days, buffs offer another advantage: UV protection. By reducing exposure to reflected sunlight, they help prevent sunburn on exposed skin.

In emergencies, buffs become even more valuable. They can be improvised as bandages or slings in a pinch, offering quick solutions when first-aid supplies are limited. For non-emergency uses, they also function as headbands, hair ties, or even as a makeshift tube top for smaller individuals. Their adaptability makes them indispensable for unexpected situations.

For extreme cold conditions, the Arctic buff is an excellent option. This specialized version combines a thicker fleece buff with a thin, stretchable buff in a single tube. The fleece section provides enhanced insulation for your neck and lower face, while the thinner portion allows for better breathability when pulled over your mouth or nose. This design makes it particularly effective in super-cold environments, where warmth and moisture management are critical.

The thick fabric of the Arctic buff tends to be too warm unless you're standing around in camp or facing particularly severe wind.

Author's note

One of the most interesting uses I've seen for a buff is in mountaineering and ultraviolet protection. When I was climbing Mount Elbrus in Russia, one of my guides used a unique setup. He wore a buff over his neck and mouth, pulling it up to cover his nose. Then he used a second buff to cover his entire head, leaving only a slit for his eyes. He placed his glasses over the slit to shield himself from ultraviolet radiation. Since he spent the entire climbing season living in the mountains, he needed additional protection beyond that setup.

He also applied a generous amount of sunscreen before putting on the buffs. The layers gave him excellent protection from ultraviolet rays and wind, allowing him to use lighter clothing and gear. The style made him look like a colorful ninja, but the protection was unmatched. The downside to this method was the difficulty of breathing through the buffs. I tried it myself and found it too uncomfortable. I've thought about cutting a slit for the mouth and reinforcing the edges to make breathing easier. That might be a good solution for anyone trying this setup.

My guide and other Russian guides were also concerned about the long-term effects of high ultraviolet exposure and the risk of developing cancer. This setup isn't just about preventing sunburn and windburn in the short term but also about protecting your long-term health. It's worth considering if you spend a lot of time at high altitudes.

Mid-Layer

Worn over the base layer, the mid layer is the first essential layer in the clothing system designed to provide insulation and warmth. This layer can range from light to moderately heavy, depending on activity level and conditions. It's the primary layer responsible for warmth, rather than just supplementing insulation.

The mid layer covers the head, torso, and legs. Typically, this includes a fleece cap or buff on your head. For the torso, you might wear a jacket or a combination of a vest and jacket. On the legs, this layer could be regular synthetic pants, climbing pants, or insulated pants, depending on the conditions.

Sometimes, the mid layer is combined with the outer layer into a single piece, especially if the weather is mild and comfortable. As weather worsens and conditions become more difficult, your layering system will change.

In many cases, mid layers can be stacked together. For example, some climbers add a vest over a fleece jacket or wear a lightweight down jacket as part of their mid-layer system. In polar exploration, it's common to wear multiple mid layers to provide adequate insulation.

In high-activity environments like mountaineering, sled towing, or cross-country skiing, the mid layer is often quite light unless the weather is particularly severe. A thin fleece pullover or zip-up fleece works well here. Down jackets are also suitable mid layers, though they can cause overheating when activity levels are high. If using a down jacket as a mid layer, it must be thin enough to avoid overheating during exertion.

Mid-Layer: Head Covering

The mid-layer is where you'll wear your insulating hat. The most commonly used option is a fleece watch cap that fits snugly and covers the ears. Ideally, the hat should also be windproof. This item doesn't have to be expensive, and no particular brand is necessary as long as it's made of quality, windproof polar fleece.

Some climbers bring a knitted wool hat, whether handmade or machine-made. If you have someone in your life who can make hats, this can be a nice, personalized addition to your otherwise commercially purchased gear. You'll be wearing this often, in almost any condition.

The only time you won't wear a hat is when you're in camp and it's warm with no wind. At any other time, expect to be wearing a hat during your winter sojourn.

Another incredibly handy piece of equipment is a windproof fleece headband. This is worn in addition to a hat and is an inexpensive yet effective way to add flexibility to your layering system.

The headband provides additional warmth and wind resistance in extreme wind events. One of the biggest issues in windy conditions is cold wind cutting through your layering system, especially around your ears. If your setup isn't completely windproof, this can cause earaches and discomfort.

One of the best uses for headbands is during relatively warm winter conditions while traveling. In polar exploration or mountaineering, there are times when a light breeze combines with fairly warm temperatures, and you start overheating. What do you do in this situation? Put on a fleece headband. This protects your ears while still allowing heat to escape from your head.

These light breeze conditions on warm, sunny days can be challenging. Often, your body feels comfortable, but your ears start to hurt from the wind. Without a headband, this discomfort can be hard to manage. While some headbands are less common than other gear, an online search or a visit to an outdoor store should help you find one.

There are two main types of headbands:
- A thin headband, like the 66° North version, designed solely for wind protection.
- A windproof fleece headband, which provides both insulation and wind resistance.

Deciding whether to bring one or both on your next expedition or winter camping trip depends on your style of camping and how prone you are to overheating. Experiment to see what works best for you, but including a headband in your kit is incredibly useful for staying warm, preventing earaches, and avoiding cold-related injuries. A good headband can make a noticeable difference in your winter camping experience.

Mid-Layer: Vests

The vest is an often-overlooked layer in cold-weather layering systems. Since it doesn't cover the arms, many people dismiss it as less effective. However, this can be a mistake. Keeping your torso and core warm is crucial for overall warmth, and a vest is an efficient way to achieve that.

When you're active and generating heat, the vest provides a good balance by warming your core while allowing some heat to escape from your arms. This might sound counterintuitive at first, as the initial ten minutes of activity can feel chilly and uncomfortable. But as you continue moving and generating heat, you'll appreciate the vest's role in regulating temperature. By keeping your core warm while allowing some heat to escape from your arms, it prevents overheating and keeps you comfortable.

A vest doesn't have to be heavy or bulky to be effective. Instead of a thick down vest, consider a thin fleece vest. It offers just enough warmth to maintain core temperature while still allowing your arms to cool, striking a comfortable balance between warmth and ventilation.

The advantage of a thin vest is that it provides enough warmth to keep the cold at bay, reducing the need for a heavier mid-layer or even an outer layer. This should be one of the weapons in your quiver against the cold while active.

Mid-Layer: Torso

The mid-layer jacket can consist of one or more jackets, made of fleece, down, or another insulating fabric. The primary goal of this layer is to provide insulation.

One of the challenges with the mid-layer is balancing insulation between activity and rest. In camp, the mid-layer can be lighter, as you'll typically wear a heavier outer shell jacket for warmth. However, when climbing, backpacking, or sledding, the choice of mid-layer jackets depends heavily on your level of exertion and weather conditions.

One significant advantage of a fleece jacket over a down jacket as a mid-layer is its versatility, especially when used as a pillow. Fleece is excellent for comfort, as it doesn't feel cold against the skin, even in temperatures as low as -40°F (-40°C). The textured, wavy nature of fleece prevents heat from being drawn away from the skin, unlike smooth nylon fabrics.

This difference is particularly noticeable with down jackets, which require a nylon or synthetic shell to contain the insulation. Pressing your face or skin against a down jacket in cold temperatures can feel uncomfortably cold. Additionally, the nylon shell on down jackets often makes rustling or rubbing noises, which can be distracting and uncomfortable while trying to sleep.

Fleece, on the other hand, is virtually silent when rubbed against itself or your skin. There's no sound transfer, making it a better option for doubling as a pillow at night. This extra functionality makes a fleece jacket or pullover more valuable than a lightweight down vest or sweater as a mid-layer.

Consider using a hoodie (British English: jumper) or a similar mid-layer insulation piece. The added hood provides extra protection for your neck and enhances warmth while still allowing flexibility to ventilate heat when needed.

Although hoodies are not typically considered a technical mid-layer, they offer excellent versatility. They allow you to maintain warmth without relying too heavily on external layers, giving you more control over your layering system.

One drawback is managing multiple hoods, but this is balanced by the ability to stay warm without carrying or wearing excessive gear. This makes a hoodie a practical and adaptable option for mid-layer insulation.

As with long underwear, wool sweaters are an excellent choice for mid-layer insulation. One of the best features of wool is its ability to retain insulation even when wet. This can be especially helpful if the sweater gets damp from sweating in warmer conditions.

A wool sweater can also double as a pillow. It doesn't make much noise when used this way, though certain types of wool may feel a bit scratchy to sleep on. Another advantage of wool is its fire resistance. Around a campfire, wool only gets small burn holes from embers, unlike synthetic fabrics, which can be easily destroyed by sparks.

Anytime you can use a single piece of gear for insulation, comfort, and another purpose like a pillow, it's a huge benefit. It saves both weight and volume in your packed sled or backpack.

Mid-Layer: Legs

Choosing the right pants for your mid-layer in a layering system can be one of the most challenging decisions. You might opt for insulated pants made of thick fabric, woven material, or fleece-lined options. Alternatively, you can choose pants made of technical fabric that prioritize breathability and mobility over insulation.

While trekking, climbing, or winter camping, pants often don't get as much attention as the upper body because the legs have a lower surface area and lose less heat overall. However, when the wind picks up or your legs start to feel chilly while the rest of your body remains warm, it can impact your efficiency. Cold legs can lead to muscle stiffness and reduced efficiency, making walking, climbing, and hiking more difficult.

One major drawback of wearing insulated pants is how difficult they are to remove or modify during the day. Changing pants often means removing your boots, sitting down, and fiddling with layers, which can be inconvenient or impossible during an active day. Some climbers have no problem wearing insulated pants, even while trekking up mountains in variable conditions.

They might sweat heavily but still manage without issues. Others, however, can overheat, struggle to regulate their temperature, and slow down, even with their outer shell layers unzipped for ventilation. For those who tend to overheat, insulated pants may not be the best option during high-exertion activities.

In camp, however, insulated pants are a game-changer. They can keep your entire body warm, preventing the discomfort of a warm torso paired with cold legs. Additionally, having cold legs can lead to cold feet since cooler blood from your legs circulates down, chilling your feet.

If you struggle with cold feet, consider insulated pants or thicker mid-layer pants over your base layer of long underwear. Keep in mind that mid-layer pants are not waterproof; waterproofing is handled by your outer shell pants. These outer pants protect you from wet and snowy conditions while sitting or moving in icy terrain.

Insulated pants with fleece lining are a great option. They provide enough warmth while allowing the flexibility of wearing lighter long underwear underneath. Fleece-lined pants are also breathable and comfortable, even without long underwear, as the fleece feels soft against the skin and doesn't feel cold immediately.

When you compare fleece-lined pants to regular technical shell fabrics, such as nylon blends, the difference is noticeable. In extremely cold temperatures, nylon can create a cold-soaking effect, similar to putting cold metal against your skin. This can be uncomfortable and make it harder to stay warm, even if you're wearing long underwear underneath.

A thin fleece lining can make a significant difference in warmth and comfort. Even at temperatures as low as -40°F (-40°C), fleece doesn't feel cold against the skin. This is the major advantage of fleece—it provides immediate comfort and helps maintain warmth more effectively than cold-sinking nylon fabrics.

Outer Layer

The outer layer is your weather protection and second layer of insulation. This layer will cover your feet, legs, torso, hands, and head. As the final defense against the elements, the outer shell is arguably the most important part of the layering system in clothing.

What you need to know is that this is where you're going to have to spend more money compared to other layers. You can get away with less expensive gear on the inside, but for the outer layer, the best gear tends to be quite expensive and sometimes difficult to find.

Managing breathability versus weatherproofing in the outer layer is a balancing act. You need enough weatherproofing to block wind, rain, and snow, but too much can trap sweat, leaving you cold and damp. Features like vents or pit zips help regulate airflow while keeping out the elements.

Waterproof-breathable fabrics like eVent and Gore-Tex work well for finding this balance. Test your outer layer with your full system to make sure it keeps you dry but still allows ventilation when you're active.

An additional part of the outer layer can provide significant insulation against the cold. This is often achieved with a large down parka. These substantial jackets offer excellent protection and serve as the final insulating layer in cold weather. However, they need to be carefully managed to avoid getting wet, which can be a challenge in milder winter conditions.

Outer layer: Head covering

The outer layer of head coverings can consist of multiple components. One commonly used option is a balaclava. These fleece hoods cover your head, lower face, and neck, and their design is reminiscent of medieval coifs or knightly hoods. Balaclavas are popular because they provide excellent protection for your head, neck, and ears, which is essential in windy conditions. The hood from your shell jacket or parka provides an additional layer of protection. In harsh weather, you'll often need to use every hood and covering available to shield yourself effectively. Face masks are another valuable option for protecting against extreme cold and wind. Brands like Sirius produce masks that are especially popular for polar travel, as they offer reliable defense against strong winds. These masks are particularly useful when your jacket lacks a fur ruff. However, one drawback is that they can accumulate ice and restrict breathability crucial to test a mask before your trip to ensure you can breathe easily. Some designs have holes that are too small, which can make breathing difficult. Ice buildup is another issue that typically only occurs in extremely cold conditions. Neoprene masks, for example, are prone to accumulating ice. Silicone masks, such as the Darth Avenger model, solve this problem and are less likely to freeze up compared to neoprene options.

Outer layer: Hands

Hand coverings are an essential part of your layering system. Over your liner gloves, you'll need to add gloves or mittens. Gloves have individual spaces for each finger, while mittens group your four fingers together with a separate space for the thumb.

Gloves provide better dexterity, but they are less warm. In extremely cold conditions, where frostbite is a concern, mittens are the best option to protect your fingers. One thing to avoid with gloves is wearing them too tight. Though you want gloves to fit well, you don't want them compressing your fingers at all. This is a sure way to develop frostbite.

Many mittens and gloves are designed to be used with an inner liner and an outer shell. Adding a liner glove creates a triple-layer system for maximum protection in harsh conditions.

Mittens can make it harder to use your hands. A helpful trick is to pull your thumb out of the thumb hole and use your hand inside the mitten like a sock, which helps retain warmth while performing simpler tasks.

When possible, choose a glove or mitten with a security cord. In expedition parlance, they're called "idiot cords" for their purpose. These cords attach to the glove and have some sort of drawstring design to tighten around the wrist. They prevent the wearer from dropping the glove, which can be especially important in windy conditions. Many a mountaineer and polar explorer have watched their dropped glove disappear over the horizon.

Outer layer: Torso

Part of the outer layering system depends on providing a final insulation layer against precipitation and wind, as well as heat retention. The outer shell is most commonly known as a rain jacket or parka. These items can be categorized as either hard shell or soft shell. In extreme conditions or extremely cold camps, people sometimes pair the hard shell with a large down jacket to provide additional insulation. High-altitude mountain camps and polar exploration are the typical places where people use this combination.

One of the best aspects of a down-insulated jacket is its effectiveness once you reach camp. You can put it on when you're no longer generating as much body heat, such as after setting up camp and preparing to settle into your tent. However, in severe weather, you may need every piece of insulation and protection you have.

One drawback of using a down jacket as the final insulation layer is its vulnerability to driving snow. If temperatures are moderate or you're warm enough to cause some melting, the snow can start soaking into the outer down jacket. Since wet down does not insulate, this is a critical consideration.

Typically, heavy down jackets are not designed to fit under a shell jacket. This makes it essential to carefully evaluate what to wear, both under and over the shell. There are two types of shell jacket materials: hard shell and soft shell. People most commonly use hard shells made from coated fabrics, like Gore-Tex or eVent fabric. You are likely already familiar with them.

Soft shell fabrics are water-resistant but not as water-repellent or waterproof. Depending on the conditions, soft shell jackets can be advantageous because they are less noisy and distracting compared to hard shell jackets. Hard shell jackets sound like a potato chip bag when you move around. While effective, this noise can detract from the experience. For moderate conditions, soft shell jackets can actually be a good choice.

Another style of outer layer to consider is an anorak or an ultra-long parka. These jackets are designed to be oversized, often several sizes larger than your regular fit. They are meant to go over every layer of clothing, including super-heavy down jackets. Their sleeves are loose, and the jacket typically falls well below the seat of the pants. The primary purpose of this style is to serve as the ultimate outer layer of protection against extreme conditions.

Anoraks and ultra-long parkas are very common in polar exploration, both in the Arctic and Antarctica. While they might appear a bit bulky or sloppy, there is no substitute for the loose-fitting design when it comes to trapping heat and blocking the elements. Despite lacking built-in insulation, these jackets provide incredible warmth due to their ability to shield you from harsh weather.

To further enhance insulation, many anoraks include Velcro or drawcord adjustments around the wrist cuffs to seal out cold air and snow. Additionally, they often have neck drawcords and other drawstrings around the hood and waist, allowing you to seal the jacket completely against the environment.

Brands like Wintergreen are known for producing quality anoraks and parkas. They often feature very large pockets, allowing you to easily store thick mittens or other bulky items. Many also include adjustable hoods with drawcords. Most anoraks extend to mid-thigh length, offering excellent coverage and shielding against snow and wind.

Outer layer: Legs

The outer layer of your leg layering system has two main components.

The most common is the waterproof layer, which protects your legs from wind and precipitation. Zippered side pants are often used in winter. These allow you to adjust clothing, put on boots, or fit pants over crampons. This feature is essential because forgetting to put on crampons before your pants can create unnecessary hassle. Side zippers are also helpful for ventilation, allowing excess heat to escape—especially if your base layers facilitate airflow.

The second component is a secondary insulating layer worn over shell pants. This layer is typically used in extreme cold on high-altitude mountains like Denali. It's added only at the highest elevations, where temperatures are dangerously low. While it does add complexity, this extra insulation is often the only way to stay warm in such conditions.

Using both layers together creates a system that protects against harsh weather and freezing temperatures. Although managing multiple layers can take extra effort, the flexibility and warmth they provide make them essential for winter and high-altitude environments.

Consider how bathroom access will work with your shell pants and overpants. This can be a real challenge if you have too many layers or if the buttons and zippers are too complicated to operate while wearing gloves. It's important to test this in the store to ensure your layering system is manageable. Try operating the closures and zippers while wearing gloves or mittens to ensure they function smoothly and won't cause problems in the field.

When choosing shell pants, you'll often need to decide between hard shell and soft shell options. Hard shell pants offer maximum protection against wind, rain, and snow, making them ideal for harsh or extreme conditions. However, they can feel less breathable and may be restrictive when you're active for long periods. Soft shell pants, by contrast, are more breathable and flexible, which makes them better suited for activities involving high mobility or in milder winter conditions.

Both hard shell and soft shell pants should be tested with your full layering system to ensure they work well together and allow unrestricted movement. Pay close attention to how they fit and how easy they are to use with gloves or mittens. The right choice will depend on the specific conditions you'll face, but comfort and functionality should always be the priority.

Outer layer: Gaiters

Gaiters are an additional layer for your lower leg system. They create a barrier against snow, wind, and debris, protecting the space between your pants and boots. Some boots, like the La Sportiva Olympus Mons and Millet Everest, come with built-in gaiter systems that cover your pants and provide excellent weather protection. However, for most other boots, you'll need to use separate gaiters to prevent snow and debris from getting inside.

The Outdoor Research Crocodile is a popular choice and works well for most conditions. Be sure to size your gaiters appropriately for your mountaineering or winter boots. Gaiters that fit lightweight boots may not work with larger boots, especially double mountaineering boots. Ensuring a slightly looser fit helps them secure properly over heavy-duty footwear without excess bulk.

For colder conditions, you can opt for insulated gaiters. Some models, often called Supergaiters, integrate directly with boots for maximum warmth. These are available at specialty stores like Mountain Tools. While they can be challenging to put on, they offer excellent warmth and are worth the effort.

Author's note
I custom-designed my own insulated gaiters. I use them every winter. The difference in warmth and comfort is incredible.

Outer layer: Feet

Boots are the final layer that protect your feet. In winter conditions, they are essential, as there aren't any other practical options. The type of boot you choose can make a big difference in your experience. Simple boots, like leather or synthetic ones, work well in moderate temperatures. But for colder conditions, you will need insulated boots. Thinsulate is a common insulation material found in many mountaineering boots, such as the La Sportiva Cube. These are ideal for mountains like Mount Hood, where cold temperatures can occur even during the summer.

For colder mountains or true winter conditions, double boots are often the best choice. These boots have a plastic outer shell and a removable inner liner, which provides extra insulation and protection. Ski boots are a type of double boot and work well in snowy environments. They are a solid option when you need more warmth and durability than standard insulated boots can offer.

In extreme cold, triple boots become necessary. These are designed for the harshest environments, where freezing temperatures can be life-threatening. Models like the Millet Everest or La Sportiva Olympus Mons provide unmatched insulation and warmth. They are the ultimate choice for mountaineering in the coldest climates and are often used on expeditions to high-altitude peaks.

Choosing the right boots is crucial for winter and mountaineering adventures. Each layer of protection, from the material to the insulation, contributes to keeping your feet warm and functional. Take the time to assess your needs and select the right boot for the conditions you will face.

One of the tools you can use to insulate non-insulated boots is toe caps. These are custom-designed for specific boots and include an insulated layer to provide extra warmth in cold conditions. They are designed to attach securely to your boots, adding extra warmth in cold conditions.

On mountains like Kilimanjaro, you usually only need regular hiking boots for most of the climb. However, at the summit, conditions are much colder. Even so, the top of the mountain doesn't usually require single mountaineering boots and certainly not double boots during the climbing season.

Toe caps are a great solution for this. They let you adapt your boots for colder temperatures without needing to buy specialized mountaineering boots. They bridge the gap between comfortable walking boots and stiff mountaineering boots.

See the chapter on winter camping boots for an in-depth explanation of the different types of footwear, when to use them, and how to select the best option for your needs.

Choosing the Right Clothing Materials: Benefits of Wool, Synthetics, and Down

There are multiple types of fabrics used for insulation and shell layers in winter gear. Outer layers are typically made of synthetic materials. Gone are the days of heavy wool parkas, mainstream cotton anoraks, or seal-skin outfits; synthetic fabrics have become the standard in winter climates worldwide. However, some traditional materials, like windproof cotton anoraks, are still used in specialized Arctic expeditions.

Synthetic fabrics repel water, are durable, and last a long time. However, they are not fire-resistant. If you are near a campfire or heat source, including a small stove, the fabric can melt or catch fire rapidly. Additionally, synthetic fabrics can be noisy, especially when they rub together. If you plan to use your jacket as a pillow, keep in mind it might be loud against your ears.

Wool fabrics are excellent insulators. While they aren't waterproof, they retain warmth even when wet. For instance, even if your wool socks are drenched, wringing them out will still leave them capable of providing some heat. This ability makes wool a reliable insulating layer.

Synthetic fabrics also perform well in damp conditions. This is why synthetic sleeping bags are often preferred in humid, coastal Arctic climates, where moisture is a persistent challenge. In cold, dry Arctic regions, however, down sleeping bags remain the top choice due to their superior warmth-to-weight ratio.

Down, however, remains unmatched for insulation. While not a fabric, down provides the best warmth-to-weight ratio, and no synthetic alternative has fully replicated its performance.

That said, down has a critical drawback: it loses its insulating ability when soaked. Wet down absorbs water, clumps together, and loses the air gaps that trap heat. In contrast, synthetic fibers don't absorb water and maintain their structure even when damp. Drying down in winter conditions can be extremely challenging, though body heat inside a tent or sleeping bag can help evaporate light moisture. However, if your down jacket or sleeping bag becomes completely soaked, it can create a serious problem.

Adjusting Layers for Different Conditions: How to manage warmth and stay dry

One of the biggest challenges in winter camping is the high variability of temperatures during the day. At night, temperatures can plummet to sub-zero levels, making even a freezer seem warm by comparison. However, during the day, temperatures can rise significantly depending on sun and cloud cover. If the sky is clear and the sun is out, you might completely overheat in the same winter camping gear that kept you warm overnight.

A critical factor in winter camping is moisture management. One of your most important goals is to avoid becoming wet, whether from perspiration, precipitation, or an accidental spill. Many shell jackets are designed with features like "pit zips"—zippers located under the arms and along the sides of the jacket. These allow you to ventilate while maintaining protection against snow and rain, preventing moisture from reaching your inner layers.

Some campers worry about becoming too cool, but when you're highly active, staying slightly cool can be an advantage. Overheating leads to sweating, which can cause moisture buildup and discomfort.

Managing the balance between cool, warm, and hot is essential to avoid these issues.

Footwear moisture management is another critical consideration. Keeping your feet dry is vital, as sweaty feet increase friction between your skin and socks, leading to blisters or other debilitating injuries. Chilblains—a skin condition caused by prolonged exposure to cold and damp conditions—can also occur, especially when wind presses fabric against exposed skin. Chilblains will be discussed further in the first aid section, but keeping yourself cool while protecting against wind and cold is essential.

When your feet are wet, the risk of frostbite increases significantly. Since feet are farther from the core of the body, they are more prone to chilling. If your feet get damp from sweat or soaked from snow or rain, the moment you stop moving, your body will cool rapidly. What was manageable while active can quickly escalate into severe frostbite.

As long as you're moving, you can likely keep warm. However, if your feet are wet, staying warm when you stop becomes much harder. This is why monitoring moisture levels throughout the day is critical.

When conditions are variable, you may need to remove outer layers to adjust inner ones. Early in the morning, whether climbing or trekking, you might start off too cold to remove layers. However, after 10 to 40 minutes of activity, you may begin to overheat and will need to start unzipping your jacket or adjusting layers. A small adjustment—such as opening a zipper by an inch or a few centimeters—can make a big difference, keeping you from becoming uncomfortably warm or overly chilly. Windy conditions make zipper adjustments even more critical, as they help you fine-tune your comfort level.

If you're wearing an outer down parka and the wind starts driving snow onto your jacket, causing it to get wet, you'll need to act quickly. You may have to remove the down layer to adjust your shell jacket. This can be uncomfortable, but it's far better to endure a few minutes of discomfort than to risk soaking your down layer and losing its insulating properties, which could put you in a dangerous situation.

The key takeaway is to stay flexible and adapt to the conditions. Avoid relying on preconceived notions or outdated advice. If an adjustment is needed, make it. The ability to adapt quickly ensures safety and comfort during winter camping.

Specialty Gear for Extreme Conditions

Fur Ruffs

One of the most useful accessories to add to your outer shell jacket or parka is a fur ruff. While not typically used in mountaineering, a fur ruff is invaluable for windy, polar exploration or exposed winter camping conditions. Though often regarded as a fashion accessory by some, the fur ruff is the best way to prevent windburn and frostbite on your face.

Many fur ruffs are made from coyote fur due to its affordability and wide availability. While it's not the most premium option, coyote fur is still effective at blocking wind and providing protection in harsh conditions. Synthetic fur ruffs are available as an alternative, but they don't perform nearly as well. Unlike natural fur, synthetic fibers lack the hollow guard hairs that break up airflow and reduce wind penetration, making them less effective at shielding your face in extreme conditions. The best type of fur ruff is made from wolverine fur. While significantly more expensive, wolverine fur has natural antifreeze properties that reduce icing, and its longer hairs provide superior insulation. Premium fur ruffs often also feature a soft lining, such as beaver fur, for additional comfort.

If you plan to travel with a fur ruff, it's important to note that some countries enforce regulations under the CITES treaty, which restricts the transportation and even possession of certain furs. In many cases, if the fur ruff is attached to the jacket, you won't encounter issues, but some locations have stricter rules. Always check the regulations of your destination in advance. In most cold climates, fur is considered a practical necessity rather than a luxury.

In extremely windy conditions, a fur ruff is essential. When you raise the fur ruff on your hood, it can block the wind so effectively that it feels as though the wind has stopped entirely. This happens because the hollow hairs of natural fur disrupt turbulence and break up the airflow before it reaches your face. Lowering the fur ruff will immediately remind you of the harsh conditions, almost as if stepping into a windstorm again.

There are two main styles for attaching fur ruffs to a jacket. The first is sewing the fur ruff directly to the hood. While this method is simple, it doesn't offer adequate protection against wind being driven into your face. The better option is a specialized flap design, such as those made by Alaska Raw Fur in Fairbanks. This design places the fur on heavy-duty nylon, which is then attached to a zipper on the hood. This allows you to remove the fur for cleaning or adjustments and also provides the structure needed to create a fur tunnel. A fur tunnel enables you to face winds of 50 to 70 mph (80 to 110+ km/h) head-on while maintaining protection.

Make sure to have your fur ruff professionally attached unless you are an experienced seamstress. Fur ruffs have specific attachment requirements, and if done improperly, they can fall apart. You don't want to be halfway through a trip only to have your fur ruff detach.

Additionally, if you have a removable (unzippable) fur ruff, improper sewing can render it unusable. It's best to send your jacket to the provider you are purchasing the fur ruff from and have them handle the sewing work. This is definitely a task to leave to the professionals.

For those traveling in extreme winter environments, a properly attached fur ruff is an invaluable addition. It provides an unmatched level of protection against wind, frostbite, and snow buildup, making it a key piece of gear for any serious cold-weather expedition.

Balaclavas and Face Masks

Two pieces of equipment you definitely want to consider are balaclavas and face masks. A balaclava is a specialized piece of clothing that covers your head and neck, providing continuous protection against harsh weather conditions. Unlike hats and scarves, it offers coverage without gaps, making it highly effective in extreme cold. Typically, balaclavas are made of synthetic fleece, though wool and other fabrics are also available. Choose one that is comfortable to the touch, even in sub-freezing conditions, and allows for adequate breathability. Neoprene is another option, but it tends to be less breathable and can feel stiff in very cold temperatures.

Face masks, on the other hand, are often made of neoprene, sometimes with a silicone "muzzle." Some face masks have a fabric blend, such as fleece on the inside for comfort and loosely woven nylon on the outside for durability. Many models feature a removable section around the mouth, allowing for easier eating, drinking, and reducing ice buildup from breath condensation. One challenge with face masks is maintaining hygiene. Over time, breathing into the mask, sneezing, coughing, or other activities can lead to bacterial buildup. Silicone muzzle face masks are easier to clean, making them a practical choice.

Neoprene-style face masks, however, accumulate bacteria much faster and are difficult, if not impossible, to clean properly in the field. This is an important consideration when choosing a mask. Additionally, ensure the face mask allows you to breathe without restriction. Some face masks have holes that are too small, making breathing uncomfortable and even causing restricted airflow. Always test the mask before extended use to ensure it meets your needs.

Neck Gaiters and Scarves

Neck gaiters and scarves are also excellent options to add to your arsenal of winter camping clothing. Neck gaiters are essentially longer and typically thicker versions of buffs, often made of fleece or other insulating fabrics. Like buffs, they provide a snug covering that can be pulled up over your mouth and nose in harsh conditions. Neck gaiters are more flexible than balaclavas, as they allow you to adjust ventilation or remove them while keeping your hat on.

Another option is the classic scarf. Although less common for mountaineering, some flatland travelers enjoy using scarves because they are highly adjustable. You can wrap the scarf more or less around your neck, head, and ears depending on the conditions, temperatures, and your comfort level. Plus, scarves also double as a stylish accessory.

Protecting Your Eyes in Harsh Conditions: Choosing the Right Eyewear

Choosing the right eyewear for winter camping is critical. You can survive many problems, but snow blindness will leave you helpless.

There aren't many options for eyewear, but selecting the right pair requires considering several factors, including fit, protection, and durability.

Proper eyewear protects your eyes from bright sunlight, wind, driving snow, and ultraviolet light common in high-altitude winter travel.

Glacier Glasses vs. Regular Glasses

When traveling in snowy conditions, especially in the mountains or on glaciers, it's crucial to use glacier glasses. These are typically equipped with Category 4 lenses, allowing only 3–8% of visible light to pass through, providing maximum protection against intense sunlight and glare. This level of darkness is significantly higher than standard sunglasses, making glacier glasses unsuitable and unsafe for driving, as they can impair visibility.

Some models come with interchangeable lenses, allowing adjustments for different lighting conditions. Glacier glasses come in various styles, but the wrap-around design with side shields—either removable or built-in—is essential. Standard flat glasses, like those used for everyday wear, are inadequate because they allow light to enter from the sides and bottom, which can harm your eyes over time. Some climbers and trekkers prefer UV-protective eyewear with lighter lenses, such as Category 3, which transmit 8–18% of visible light. These may suffice in overcast conditions or lower-altitude snow travel, where glare is less intense. However, individuals who are highly sensitive to light or are in extremely bright environments should use Category 4 lenses for optimal protection. It's advisable to test different lens categories before heading out to determine which provides the best comfort and protection for your specific needs.

Photochromatic Lenses

One of the great advances in 20th-century technology was the development of photochromatic lenses. These lenses darken in intense UV light and then return to being somewhat clear, if not completely clear, when you move indoors or out of bright light.

Photochromatic glasses typically range from Grade 1, the lightest tint, to Grade 4, the absolute darkest. However, for winter conditions, Grade 2 to Grade 4 is the most practical range, as Grade 1 doesn't provide enough tint for snowy environments.

Photochromatic lenses work through a chemical reaction inside the lens. Photoreactive molecules react to UV light by changing their structure, which causes the lenses to darken. When the UV light decreases, these molecules revert to their original state, and the lenses clear up. This process can take 30–60 seconds to darken and 2–3 minutes to clear, depending on conditions.

One thing to be aware of is temperature sensitivity. In colder conditions, photochromatic lenses often darken more effectively but can take longer to clear. In warmer temperatures, they may not darken as much and will typically clear faster. This variability can make them a little unpredictable in extreme environments.

Another limitation is that photochromatic lenses might not work well inside vehicles. Many car windshields block a significant amount of UV light, which is needed for the lenses to darken. That means they may stay clear even if it's bright outside.

Author's note

I've noticed that my old photochromatic glasses stopped darkening entirely. I'm not exactly sure why this happened. It's possible that being stored away and not exposed to light for a long time caused the photochromatic chemicals in the lenses to fail. While this might be rare, it's something to keep in mind—don't leave these glasses in a drawer for extended periods.

Despite these factors, photochromatic lenses provide excellent UV protection by blocking both UVA and UVB rays, which helps protect your eyes from long-term sun damage. Once you start using them, you'll never want to go back. They're incredibly convenient for adapting to variable light conditions. They adjust in just a few minutes, making it much easier to handle transitions between bright and dark environments.

This convenience is especially noticeable when you step out of a dark tent and are immediately hit with the glaring sunlight on a glacier. Photochromatic lenses handle this transition seamlessly and are a great option for such conditions.

Terry used tinted safety glasses for UV protection on particularly bright days. He has blue eyes, whereas I need the darkest lenses available, even though I have brown eyes.

Goggles

When trekking into the wilderness during winter, it's important to bring a pair of goggles. Goggles are similar to ski goggles in that they completely cover the upper part of your face. They have foam that seals around your eyes, and the lens is large for maximum visibility.

These are far better than regular glacier glasses in blasting wind conditions because they protect your eyes and prevent swirling snow from impairing your vision. Regular glasses and glacier glasses simply don't offer the same level of protection. Goggles create a full seal around your eyes, blocking out snow and cold air. This can be a huge advantage in severe weather.

Polar explorers often rely on goggles because they provide more complete protection, shielding a larger portion of the face from the elements. However, if you're wearing goggles with a balaclava, be mindful of the small gap that can expose your forehead between the goggles and your hood or hat. This gap, sometimes called the "Gaper Gap," can leave the upper forehead exposed to UV rays, leading to a severe sunburn. It's a small detail but one worth addressing to avoid unnecessary discomfort.

Author's note

One of my climbing friends from Australia was making his final push to the summit when his eyes started burning. By the time Felix reached the summit, he had developed snow blindness and could no longer see. He was stuck on the summit.

It was a calm day, so he was able to relax and take in the moment, even though he had lost his vision. Soon, a couple of climbers arrived, enjoyed their summit moment, and started to walk away. Once they realized Felix was in real trouble, they took pity on him, roped him in, and climbed back down with him to high camp.

It was an incredibly risky and dangerous task. Descending from high camp to Denali Pass with a blind climber is extremely dangerous due to the steep slopes. It's amazing that Felix made it back at all.

He later said that his goggles simply weren't dark enough. It's odd because all goggles should have UV protection to prevent snow blindness. However, his goggles weren't dark enough to limit visible light exposure, causing his pupils to stay too dilated. The intensity of the light led to snow blindness. He admitted that he should have used his glacier glasses under his goggles to provide enough protection.

Fortunately, he made it back, but this was an unexpected event. It's definitely something to think about as you plan your own wilderness adventures.

Backup eyewear—Bring spares

It is critical for your safety to always bring backup eyewear. One pair of glasses or goggles isn't enough. If you drop, step on, or accidentally sit on them, you'll have serious trouble traveling and seeing in bright light.

You don't want to end up scavenging for birch bark to make a slit mask, like the Indigenous peoples of North America and the Arctic used to do. That's not a situation you want to face.

Consider the example of Todd Carmichael, the first American to complete a solo ski trip to the South Pole. During his journey, a tent pole got out of control in windy conditions and struck him across the face, shattering his goggles. Despite being made of impact-resistant polycarbonate, the force was enough to break them.

Fortunately, Carmichael found a way to improvise a backup and managed to continue, but it was an incredible challenge. His story, as recounted in *Reader's Digest*, highlights the dangers of being alone and having an accident in extreme environments. Damaging your eyewear in such conditions could leave you without a way to continue safely.

In his case, the weather was so severe that one of his eyelids froze shut, and he struggled for a long time to thaw it open. Always bring backup glasses and goggles when heading out for extended trips. It's a small step that can save you from enormous trouble.

Eyewear maintenance, fogging, and icing over

For people who use corrective lenses—whether glasses or contacts—winter conditions can be especially challenging. If you wear contacts, consider bringing eyeglasses as a backup. Keeping your hands clean in the field can be difficult, and touching your contacts with dirty hands can lead to eye irritation and, over time, infections that could cause more serious problems. In extreme conditions, contact solution might freeze or thicken, so store it close to your body to prevent this.

Eyeglass wearers should think about a spare pair, especially if losing or breaking them would leave you essentially blind or unable to navigate. Cold weather can cause glasses to fog up due to condensation from body heat and breath. If exposed to freezing temperatures, any moisture buildup can turn into ice, making visibility even worse. While anti-fog wipes or sprays can help, not all formulas work in extreme cold—some may freeze in the bottle or form a thin layer of ice on the lenses instead of preventing fogging. Choosing the right formula is important.

Metal frames can also become uncomfortably cold or irritate your skin, making plastic frames a better choice for extreme conditions.

Don't forget about UV exposure—snow can reflect up to 80% of sunlight, significantly increasing the risk of snow blindness. Wearing sunglasses or goggles with 100% UV protection over your glasses or contacts is essential. These are all critical factors to consider before heading into winter conditions.

One of the most difficult challenges in cold conditions is dealing with glasses or goggles fogging up and then icing over. When the temperature difference between the inside of your goggles and the outside becomes too great, the moisture from your breath or body heat begins to condense and freeze on the inside of the lenses. This creates fogging, which can be extremely frustrating to manage because it's hard to remove without taking off your glasses and exposing yourself to the cold.

Ice buildup can become so thick that it's a real struggle to get rid of it, especially when you're winter camping or trekking. Glacier glasses are even more prone to this issue because they are more exposed. When skiing, hiking, or climbing, the moisture in your breath naturally rises and begins fogging your lenses.

One trick to mitigate this is to slightly lift your glasses off your face—about an inch or a couple of centimeters. This keeps your eyes protected while reducing fogging. However, it's awkward and not always practical. Goggles face the same issue. Once they are sealed against your face with foam, the humidity from your skin begins to freeze on the inside of the lenses.

Manufacturers often make goggles with a double-layered lens to help reduce fogging. These goggles are more expensive, but when you're struggling to see, they suddenly seem worth every penny.

The only realistic way to prevent goggle fogging is to keep your body temperature cool while traveling. While goggles and glasses often come with vents to help reduce fogging, they don't work incredibly well. Instead, you need to manage your body temperature deliberately—staying just cool enough to minimize perspiration and moisture buildup. It's not the most comfortable way to move, but it helps prevent your goggles or glasses from fogging up. The moment you start feeling too warm, your body begins perspiring, and the extra moisture will fog your lenses.

Some anti-fogging solutions are marketed to address this issue, but certain formulations can freeze in extreme cold, while others may damage the optical coating on your goggles. Always test any product before relying on it in the field.

Managing fogging in extreme winter conditions is a challenge you're almost guaranteed to face. Knowing how to minimize it and planning ahead will make all the difference.

Breathing techniques, face masks cause fogging and icing

If you can adjust your breathing to direct the warm, moist air downward or to the side, it will reduce the fogging on your glasses. This can be more challenging when wearing a face mask, as the air tends to float upward. You may need to modify your glasses, such as attaching a fleece skirt or a similar barrier, to prevent the air from rising and fogging your eyewear. Another method of reducing fogging on glasses and goggles is to adjust your breathing. Typically, when you exhale, the moist air rises directly into your glasses. It only takes a few breaths to obscure your vision. The same issue can happen with goggles.

Icicles form on face masks with surprisingly regularity.

Chapter 2
Winter Camping Footwear

Choosing Winter Footwear

One of the biggest challenges in winter outdoor adventures is selecting the proper footwear. With a wide variety of options available, your choice will depend on the conditions you'll encounter, the mode of transport (such as walking, skiing, or snowshoeing), and how cold it will be.

Some decisions are best made based on experience. If you live in a warm climate and are preparing for a winter adventure, be cautious when choosing boots in a retail store. While well-meaning clerks may offer advice, their information could sometimes be incomplete if they lack personal experience with extreme winter conditions.

That said, experience suggests that visiting a shop specializing in cold-weather equipment may be a better choice to ensure you get the right footwear for your needs.

Types of Winter Boots

A wide variety of winter boots are available for traveling in snowy and cold conditions. With so many options, it can be difficult to decide which one is best for a specific situation. Below is a list of boot types and their basic functions in winter climates. Don't be overwhelmed by this list—you'll likely end up using only a few types. However, it's important to know that different options exist depending on your travel style and what you plan to do on your winter trip.

Here's a comprehensive list of winter boot styles that covers many categories:

General Winter Boots

Insulated Hiking Boots
  Use: Moderate winter conditions, hiking, and snow trekking.
  Features: Waterproof uppers (leather or synthetic), insulated lining (e.g., Thinsulate), and rugged soles.

Pac Boots
  Use: Extreme cold and deep snow.
  Features: Rubber lower, leather upper, removable insulated liners (e.g., felt or wool). Examples: Sorel, Kamik.

Mukluks
  Use: Arctic and subarctic climates.
  Features: Soft leather uppers, fur or felt insulation, lightweight flexibility. Traditionally made by Indigenous Arctic peoples.

Felt-Lined Winter Boots
  Use: Cold, dry conditions (e.g., Russia, Mongolia).
  Features: Wool or felt construction with optional rubber soles. Known as "valenki" in Russia.

Moon Boots
  Use: Casual snowy urban areas or après-ski.
  Features: Puffy, insulated nylon or polyester exterior with a thick flat sole. Iconic retro look.

Wool-Lined Rubber Boots
  Use: Wet, cold climates (e.g., Scandinavia).
  Features: Waterproof rubber exteriors with wool or synthetic liners. Excellent for slushy conditions.

UGG-Style Boots
  Use: Casual wear in cold, dry climates.
  Features: Sheepskin exterior with plush fleece interior. Not ideal for wet conditions.

Traditional Leather Winter Boots
  Use: Urban settings and moderate snow.
  Features: Treated leather uppers, insulated linings, fashionable designs.

Steel-Toe Winter Work Boots
  Use: Industrial or outdoor work in snow/ice.
  Features: Safety toe caps, waterproofing, heavy insulation, slip-resistant soles.

Caribou or Inuit Boots
  Use: Traditional Arctic footwear.
  Features: Handmade with seal or caribou hide, fur linings, lightweight for mobility in extreme cold.

Baffin-Style Arctic Boots
  Use: Extreme polar expeditions or hunting.
  Features: Multi-layer systems with rubber exteriors and heavy insulation, rated for -70°C or lower.

Military Winter Boots
  Use: Military operations in cold regions.
  Features: Rugged materials, waterproofing, heavy-duty soles, and removable liners.

Gaiter-Compatible Boots
  Use: Snow trekking and mountaineering.
  Features: Durable waterproof uppers, insulated interiors, designed to pair with gaiters for deep snow protection.

Specialized Mountaineering Boots

Single-Layer Mountaineering Boots
  Use: Summer alpine climbing or moderate winter conditions.
  Features: Lightweight, rigid soles, basic insulation, crampon-compatible.

Double-Layer Mountaineering Boots
  Use: High-altitude climbing or extreme winter trips.
  Features: Outer shell with removable insulated liners, durable for prolonged exposure.

Triple-Layer Mountaineering Boots
  Use: Extreme expeditions (e.g., Everest).
  Features: Outer shell, thick removable liner, ultimate insulation for severe cold.

Ski Boots

Traditional Alpine Ski Boots
  Use: Downhill skiing.
  Features: Rigid plastic shells, thick insulated liners, no flexibility for walking.

Free-Heel Ski Boots (Telemark Ski Boots)

Use: Telemark skiing (a mix of downhill and cross-country).
Features: Flexible bindings at the toe, free heel, reinforced plastic uppers.

Alpine Touring (AT) Ski Boots
Use: Backcountry skiing and ski mountaineering.
Features: Hybrid boots with a walk mode for climbing and rigidity for downhill skiing.

Hybrid Ski Boots (Crossover Boots)
Use: Versatile skiing (resort and backcountry).
Features: Comfort and adaptability, compatible with various binding systems.

Overboots

Use: Extreme cold environments and mountaineering expeditions.
Features: Lightweight outer covers worn over standard mountaineering boots to add insulation and protect against snow and ice. Used to extend the temperature rating of existing boots.
Examples: Forty Below Overboots, Outdoor Research Crocodile Gaiters.

Crampon-Compatible Boots
Use: Technical ice climbing and glacier travel.
Features: Insulated mountaineering boots with integrated toe and heel welts for step-in or hybrid crampons.
Examples: Scarpa Mont Blanc Pro GTX.

High-Altitude Expedition Boots
Use: Extreme altitudes (e.g., Himalayas, Denali).
Features: Similar to triple-layer boots but with additional gaiters integrated into the boot design for extreme weatherproofing and insulation.
Examples: Millet Everest Summit GTX.

Ice Fishing Boots
Use: Static winter activities like ice fishing or stationary camping.
Features: Heavy-duty insulation (often with liners), waterproof materials, and extremely thick soles with insulation against ground chill.
Examples: Muck Arctic Pro, Baffin Impact.

Pullover Snow Boots (Temporary Boots)
  Use: Camp setup or emergency use in the snow.
  Features: Lightweight, packable nylon or rubber uppers with basic insulation and waterproofing. Designed for temporary use to keep feet warm and dry around camp.
  Examples: Forty Below Overboots.

Cold Weather Hunting Boots
  Use: Hunting and stationary activities in cold weather.
  Features: Insulated with waterproof leather or synthetic uppers, camouflaged exteriors, and robust soles for traction.
  Examples: Danner Insulated, LaCrosse AlphaBurly Pro, Irish Setter Elk Tracker.

Arctic Winter Muck Boots
  Use: Expeditions in wet, snowy environments.
  Features: Heavy-duty waterproof rubber lowers with neoprene uppers and thick insulation. Often used for slushy, mixed conditions.
  Examples: Muck Arctic Ice, Kamik Icebreaker.

Minimalist Winter Boots
  Use: Lightweight expeditions or survival situations.
  Features: Thin, flexible soles with basic waterproofing and insulation, prioritizing mobility over extensive insulation.
  Examples: Vivobarefoot Tracker FG, Xero Alpine Boots.

Author's Note

During a climbing trip to Mexico, I met a group of climbers from the East Coast—ranging from the Mid-Atlantic to New England—that I hadn't known before the trip. It was one of those group-combine expeditions where a leader assembles a mix of climbers for a larger adventure. The group stopped at an outdoor outfitter to buy boots for the climb, hoping to find footwear that would work with their new crampons. The enthusiastic clerk walked them through several options, and while the boots fit fine, it wasn't until we got to the climbing camp in Mexico and did a gear review that we realized the boots were completely unsuitable for mountaineering. They lacked any shank, making them completely flexible—perfect for hiking but useless for crampons and climbing.

Despite the clerk's best efforts, he didn't fully understand the requirements for crampon compatibility, and the group ended up renting boots and crampons once we arrived in Mexico. This experience was a reminder that, while store staff may be well-meaning, they might not always understand the specific needs for extreme conditions. It's crucial to do your own research and ensure you're properly prepared.

Details of the Most Commonly Used Winter Camping Boots

Traditional Leather Boot Non-Insulated

Traditional leather boots without insulation can be viable in winter conditions, but they come with notable risks. These boots offer durability, comfort, and flexibility, making them a popular choice for outdoor activities in cold weather. However, without added insulation, leather boots can struggle to retain warmth, especially in extremely cold temperatures. They can handle moderately low temperatures for short durations, particularly if you're active and generating body heat. In conditions where you're frequently moving, such as winter trekking or moderate cold weather, these boots may provide enough warmth, as long as you manage other aspects of your layering system, such as thick wool socks.

The real risk with uninsulated leather boots lies in prolonged exposure to cold temperatures. Leather is not an effective insulator, and without added lining or insulation, the boots are prone to allowing cold air to seep in. If you're standing still for extended periods or in very cold conditions, the lack of insulation can lead to a rapid loss of body heat, increasing the risk of frostbite or other cold-related injuries. Additionally, leather boots without proper waterproofing can absorb moisture, which further compromises warmth. While they can be used successfully in milder winter conditions, uninsulated leather boots become a risky choice when temperatures drop significantly or during more static activities like ice fishing or snowshoeing.

Traditional Insulated Leather Boot and Hunting Boot

Insulated hunting boots are a good option for winter travel because they often cover more than half your calf, providing significant insulation. These boots are designed for chilly to cold conditions, as hunting typically takes place during the fall and winter in North America.

Hunting boots often come with 200, 400, 600, or 800 grams of Thinsulate, with some models offering up to 1,200 grams or more for extreme cold. The more insulation a boot has, the warmer your feet will be. However, added insulation also makes the boots heavier, which can make travel more difficult.

Standard insulated hunting boots usually feature flexible soles, making them unsuitable for traditional crampons, which require stiffer soles for proper attachment. Some flexible strap-on crampons may work, but compatibility should always be checked. Microspikes are a good alternative and work well with these boots for added traction on icy surfaces.

Hunting boots also pair nicely with snowshoes, as long as the snowshoe bindings fit securely. It's important to ensure the snowshoes are compatible with the boot size and design to maintain stability and comfort during use.

Pack Boots

Pack boots are a classic option for camping when you're not traveling far from your vehicle. These rubberized, insulated boots are great for short-distance camping and activities like hunting, ice fishing, snowmobiling, and more. They are designed for cold, wet conditions and are perfect for wandering around in harsh winter environments.

While pack boots are quite thick and can feel a bit bulky—especially older models—many modern versions have improved flexibility and comfort, making them easier to walk in than before. They are incredibly warm and protective, keeping your feet safe in severe winter conditions.

Pack boots are typically taller than standard insulated boots, providing better coverage in deep snow. They're very common in northern snowy climates and are often used for short trips, like going from your house to your vehicle, heading to work, or walking to the post office. Their versatility and warmth make them a staple in cold-weather footwear.

Single-Layer Mountaineering Boots

Single-layer mountaineering boots are an excellent choice for those starting with winter expeditions. Boots like the La Sportiva Nepal Cube GTX are perfect for conditions down to about 0°F (-18°C). However, without thicker socks or overboots, your feet may start to feel chilled, depending on your activity level and personal tolerance to the cold.

These boots are commonly used by ice climbers because they offer excellent protection and have extremely stiff soles, making them fully compatible with crampons. They're often seen on climbers tackling the Cascade volcanoes in Washington and Oregon. For extra-cold, challenging peaks like Mount Rainier, double-layer mountaineering boots may be a better choice.

Single-layer mountaineering boots come with insulation throughout, including the toe box, though the insulation in the toe area may be thinner. In very cold or variable conditions, overboots or additional protection are recommended for extra warmth.

These boots are not particularly comfortable for walking on hard surfaces, as the soles are completely stiff. While the ankle area is more flexible, providing some comfort, walking in them on flat or hard terrain can still feel awkward.

Double Mountaineering Boots

Double mountaineering boots are the gold standard for mountain climbing, cold camping, and adventuring in extreme conditions. Similar to ski boots, the outer design often features a durable synthetic or plastic shell, with a removable liner. Some models offer thermally molded liners that can be customized to better fit your foot, reducing hotspots and improving comfort. However, not all liners are designed for thermal molding, so it's essential to check the manufacturer's specifications.

When molding the liner, make sure to wear the same socks you plan to use during your expedition. Socks that are too thick can compress your feet, cutting off circulation and defeating the purpose of double boots, which are meant to keep your feet warm and safe from frostbite. Choosing socks that balance warmth with a proper fit is critical.

Some climbers also use overboots, such as Forty Below models, for additional insulation in extreme conditions like those on Denali. Overboots can be worn over double boots or even ski boots to add warmth and protection, making them a versatile option for high-altitude climbs.

Popular double mountaineering boots include models like the La Sportiva Spantik, known for its lightweight design and excellent insulation, and the Scarpa Phantom 6000, favored for technical climbs in cold weather. The La Sportiva Baruntse is another excellent option, offering durability and comfort for a variety of cold-weather expeditions.

While double boots provide superior warmth and protection, they can feel bulky due to their stiff soles, which are designed for compatibility with crampons and to support technical climbing. Despite this stiffness, their performance in extreme environments makes them an essential piece of gear for serious climbers and adventurers.

Triple Mountaineering Boots

Triple mountaineering boots are the ultimate solution for keeping your feet warm and comfortable in extreme cold and high-altitude conditions. Like single and double mountaineering boots, the soles of triple boots are completely rigid, making them compatible with all types of crampons.

These boots have a shell similar to double mountaineering boots but are often made of durable fabric rather than plastic. They also feature an integrated gaiter system with reflective foil on the inside to enhance insulation. The gaiter typically extends up to the calf, offering excellent protection against snow and cold.

The removable liners allow you to dry them out at night, just like double mountaineering boots. Triple boots are considered the pinnacle of performance for extreme environments. They are quite expensive, typically ranging from $1000USD to $1200USD, with the La Sportiva Olympus Mons Cube being one of the most popular models. Another option is the Millet Everest Summit GTX boots, which are heavier than the Olympus Mons but feature a more durable sole that can handle tougher terrain. For climbs like Denali, where there are fewer rocks to contend with, the lighter Olympus Mons is often a better choice.

Some of the newer Olympus Mons Cube models include front inserts compatible with tech ski bindings, allowing you to traverse glaciers with skis and skins. This versatility combines the capabilities of a mountaineering boot with those of a ski boot, making it an excellent option for glacier travel and high-altitude expeditions.

Alpine Touring and Hybrid Ski Boots (Including Telemark Boots)

Alpine touring and hybrid ski boots are excellent for covering long distances while still allowing for the comfort and control of skiing. However, one of the main drawbacks of alpine touring boots is that they are expensive and relatively heavy. While they can be climbed in, some people find them less comfortable than classic mountaineering boots.

These boots are ideal for backcountry touring in winter, enabling skiers to travel long distances in a climbing mode. When conditions allow for downhill skiing, the boot can be locked into a tech binding (pin binding) for a secure descent. Hybrid boots may include both alpine touring and telemark features, so checking compatibility with your binding system is important.

For extreme cold, upgrading to Intuition Liners is a good option, as they are the industry standard for warmer boot liners. Not all alpine touring or hybrid ski boots come with them, and they often need to be purchased separately as an aftermarket upgrade.

Alpine touring and hybrid boots use a pin connection in the toe, which allows the heel to lift for climbing but does not provide the same natural walking gait as a true cross-country ski boot. These pins can be released, allowing skiers to step out of the ski without requiring a bulky alpine-style binding. This design enables much lighter ski bindings, making them ideal for backcountry use.

Telemark Boots

Telemark ski boots are designed for free-heel skiing, where the heel is never fully locked down. Unlike alpine touring boots, telemark boots flex at the ball of the foot, allowing a distinctive lunging turn style. Telemark bindings come in different styles, including traditional three-pin bindings, cable bindings (such as the 75mm Voilé 3-pin cable system), and the New Telemark Norm (NTN) system, which provides better lateral control and power transfer. NTN bindings are not compatible with older three-pin setups but offer improved performance for aggressive skiing.

Three-Pin Style Cold-Weather Cross-Country Boots

Three-pin ski bindings are the old-school classic for cross-country travel. Also known as the 75mm Nordic Norm (NN), these bindings feature a large toe welt or tongue on the boot, which fits onto a metal plate with three pins. To secure the boot, you step onto the plate, aligning the toe holes with the pins, then lower a bale or clamp to press the toe into place, locking it to the ski.

These bindings are primarily designed for cross-country skiing and moderate backcountry use. They aren't ideal for downhill skiing due to minimal ankle support and limited lateral control, making descents more challenging. However, three-pin bindings remain a gold standard for polar exploration and long-distance skiing in extreme environments like the Arctic, Greenland, and Antarctica.

One of their biggest advantages is their simplicity and durability. If something breaks in the field, repairs can often be made with basic materials like bailing wire. Several brands manufacture compatible boots, including Alpina and Fischer, while Alfa in Norway produces highly efficient models specifically designed for extreme cold and long-distance travel.

Author's Note

My original boots were Rossignol BC X11s. They worked well down to -10°F (-23°C), but they weren't warm enough below that. I was lucky not to freeze my toes when I camped in Yellowstone at -40°F (-40°C). I bought the boots without being able to test them fully and found that the width was too narrow. They pinched the sides of my feet and hurt badly in the cold. My feet went numb for about a month, but I didn't get frostbite.

The three-pin bindings felt reliable, but I often struggled with ice and snow getting stuck in the pinholes, making it difficult to mount the boots onto the bindings. I had to kneel down and dig the ice out by hand. Some skiers carry a small tool or use the tip of a ski pole to clear out the pinholes, but I didn't have that at the time. My buddy Terry, on one of our expeditions, never had this problem. He could kick the ice off his boots, and the pinholes stayed clear. Maybe it was because he was lighter, or maybe his boot soles flexed just enough to break the ice free. I'll never know.

It's important to research the boots you're considering. Some brands reportedly have issues with the soles separating from the boot, especially those that rely on glue rather than stitching or a stronger bond. I've seen pictures where this turned into a total disaster for people. Definitely do some reading before heading into a store and making a purchase.

NNN-Style Cold-Weather Cross-Country Boots

The modern standard for cross-country ski boots is the NNN (New Nordic Norm) binding system. These bindings use a metal bar embedded in the toe of the ski boot that attaches to a rail on the ski. The bar fits into a latching mechanism on the rail, allowing the heel to float freely for cross-country skiing, similar to the three-pin binding system.

NNN bindings are not ideal for downhill skiing. While some designs allow for limited turning, the boots can pop out of the binding under stress, so caution is necessary. For ultra-cold weather travel, NNN-compatible boots are available from brands like Alfa, which specialize in high-performance models designed for extreme conditions.

One of the biggest risks with NNN bindings is ice or water infiltration. If water gets into the mechanism and freezes, it can be extremely difficult to chisel the ice out and reattach your boots to the skis. A common workaround is keeping the bindings dry before clipping in or warming them slightly with body heat if they freeze. Some skiers also carry a small plastic scraper or the tip of a ski pole to clear ice buildup before stepping in.

There is also a Backcountry NNN (NNN BC) variant, which is wider and more robust than standard NNN bindings, making it more durable for off-trail conditions. However, even NNN BC bindings do not provide the lateral stability needed for steep downhill skiing.

Another potential failure point is the bar ripping out of the toe of the boot. While rare, it does happen, especially under extreme stress. In the "Old Camp" lodging in Kangerlussuaq, Greenland, there is a collection of damaged ski bindings, including torn-out boot bars and broken NNN bindings, showing the kind of failures that can occur during long, hard ski expeditions. NNN bindings are more prone to failure in such conditions than the classic three-pin bindings, something to consider when choosing equipment for extreme environments.

Baffin-Style Polar Boots

Baffin-style polar boots are the gold standard for Arctic expeditions, built for extreme cold with ratings as low as -148°F (-100°C). However, these survival ratings may not reflect comfort levels for long durations. In real-world conditions, these boots are typically used for sustained activity down to -70°F (-57°C), offering reliable warmth for extended periods. Always verify the manufacturer's claims before committing to a long journey in an extremely cold location.

These boots are not typically used for long-distance expeditions because only one type of binding is compatible with them, limiting their efficiency for ski travel. Their incredible thickness also makes them incompatible with many snowshoes, though if you find a model that fits, they provide unmatched warmth in extreme cold.

While they can feel bulky and awkward, they excel at keeping your feet warm in the most severe Arctic conditions, making them a staple for those working in or traveling through extreme environments.

Overboots

If you want to use a lighter boot for warmer conditions but need to handle extremely cold temperatures later in your trip, consider using overboots. One of the best manufacturers in the world for overboots, and the gold standard, is Forty Below. They produce high-quality overboots that extend the temperature range of double mountaineering boots or ski boots. These overboots are also crampon-compatible, but they typically work best with strap-on crampons rather than semi-automatic or step-in models. The thick insulation can interfere with heel and toe bails, so you'll need to test your specific crampons to ensure a secure fit. Adjustments or modifications may be necessary to get them working properly.

Overboots like these are commonly used from high camp to the summit of Denali on cold days. A related option is super gaiters. Unlike full overboots, super gaiters cover the upper boot and lower leg while integrating with the boot's sole using an adhesive or Velcro skirt. This creates a weatherproof barrier while keeping them compatible with crampons and bindings, but they don't provide the same full insulation as overboots.

Both overboots and super gaiters can be challenging to put on, especially at high altitudes and in subzero temperatures when the materials stiffen. Practice putting them on at home with gloves before your trip. This will help you manage them more easily when conditions are uncomfortable. Without proper preparation, you'll likely struggle when it matters most.

Camp Booties

Camp booties are an excellent addition to your extended camping trip gear list. They allow you to take off your day boots, mountaineering boots, or insulated boots, giving your feet a chance to recover and breathe while also reducing pressure points from tighter-fitting boots.

The extra weight in your gear may seem like a drawback, but the comfort of loose, insulated footwear in snowy conditions or on a glacier provides significant psychological benefits. While camp booties won't dry out your main boots in extreme cold—since moisture inside frozen boots tends to stay frozen—they do allow you to store boot liners inside your sleeping bag overnight, preventing them from freezing solid.

A popular choice for extreme cold is the Forty Below Camp Booties, which provide excellent insulation and warmth for use inside a tent or around camp. Having warm, comfortable feet at camp can greatly improve your mood and overall outdoor experience.

Flexible vs. Rigid Boots

When choosing boots, you need to consider whether you need flexible, semi-rigid, or completely rigid boots. The type of activity and the nature of your trip will determine which is best. There's also a classification system (B0 to B3) that helps determine crampon compatibility.

Flexible Boots (B0)

Examples include Baffin boots or bunny boots. These are highly adaptable and great for walking or snowshoeing, but they aren't designed for crampons. Their flexibility can cause crampons to pop off, making them unsuitable for technical activities or long-distance travel with crampons.

Semi-Rigid Boots (B1)

These boots have a ¾ nylon or steel shank in the sole, making them better for longer distances and tougher hikes. They are widely used for hiking and backpacking. Flexible (C1) crampons are compatible with these boots, but because the toe can still flex, crampons may loosen if used aggressively on steep slopes or technical terrain. Using crampons with flexible center bars can help mitigate this issue.

Rigid Boots (B2 & B3)

B2 Boots: Designed for mountaineering, these work best with semi-automatic (C2) crampons.

B3 Boots: Fully rigid, meant for technical climbs, and designed for use with automatic (C3) crampons, which provide a secure fit on steep, icy terrain. While they are uncomfortable for walking on flat or hard terrain, they are designed to be more efficient in steep, icy conditions, where a flexible boot would be less stable.

An alternative option is alpine touring ski boots, which allow uphill walking with a flexible ankle for climbing and lock into place for downhill skiing. While many modern AT boots have toe and heel welts for semi-automatic crampons, not all are crampon-compatible. Lighter ski mountaineering boots may lack the necessary sole rigidity or welts for proper attachment, so compatibility should always be checked. These boots provide versatility for those needing both mobility and technical performance in alpine environments.

Waterproof Boot Downsides

One of the challenges with waterproof boots is that, although they are designed to breathe, moisture from your feet can still have trouble escaping. Many manufacturers use Gore-Tex or similar waterproof membranes, which allow moisture vapor to escape. However, if the outer boot is wet or frozen, moisture can become trapped inside because the pressure gradient isn't sufficient to push it out.

If water or snow soaks the exterior of your boots, especially if they have a synthetic outer surface, the material can remain wet and cold, further trapping moisture inside. This means that if your feet overheat, they will likely become damp, increasing the risk of chilled feet, frostbite, or blisters.

While waterproof boots are essential in many conditions, they have limitations. They keep water out, but they aren't perfect at managing internal moisture. Being prepared for the potential for wet feet—by using moisture-wicking socks, foot powder, or drying methods—is essential for staying comfortable in extreme conditions.

Boot Fit and Comfort

Making sure your boots fit properly is absolutely essential for a positive experience in winter mountain conditions. If your boots are too tight, they will restrict circulation, leading to cold feet or even frostbite. Tight boots can also press on the width of your feet, causing intense pain. On the other hand, boots that are too large will flop around and feel sloppy. While you can stack socks to make up for extra space, too many socks can compress your toes and reduce circulation, which can cause the same problems as boots that are too small. Use a combination of liner socks and insulating socks to avoid over-layering.

When trying on boots, do fit testing in the late afternoon or evening, when your feet have swollen from walking or standing. This mimics the natural swelling that happens during long hikes or expeditions. When lacing up boots, press your toes on a ledge and flex your foot upward. This helps check for heel lift and fit, which can indicate whether the boot will cause Achilles tendon irritation or blisters over time.

Make sure to perform the kick test. Put the boots on, lace them up completely, stand up, and flex your foot slightly forward. Then lift your foot and kick it against the ground or floor:

First kick: Your toe should not touch the front of the boot.
Second kick: Your toe might just barely touch.
Third kick: Your toe will likely hit the front more noticeably.

If your toe strikes the front of the boot on the first kick, the boot is too short. Also, check for heel lift and walk on an incline or stairs if possible. Walking upstairs helps check for heel lift and pressure points, while walking downstairs helps identify toe bang and forward foot movement.

This is crucial because as you climb uphill, your toes won't usually press forward. However, when descending, you could experience "toe bang", where your toes repeatedly hit the front of the boot. This can lead to blackened toes, lost toenails, and serious discomfort.

The advantage of testing and purchasing boots in a store rather than online cannot be overstated. Some boots fit certain feet well while others don't, even if they are popular among other users. Feet come in many shapes, and it's important to find the right match for yours. Winter boots are expensive and a significant investment, so trying them on first is ideal.

If you must buy boots online, consider a service like Mountain Tools (mtntools.com). They've been in the business for a long time and offer a foot tracing service. You send them a tracing of your foot, and they help you choose the correct boot size. However, foot tracing only accounts for length and basic width—it doesn't measure arch height, volume, or instep shape, which are equally important. If possible, try on a similar boot model in person before ordering online to help ensure a better fit.

When you receive your boots, test them indoors. Don't take them outside until you are sure they fit, as you may not be able to return them once they show signs of use. Walk around, perform the kick test, and simulate uneven terrain if possible. Wear the same socks you plan to use on your trip to ensure a proper fit. Testing thoroughly before use can save you from discomfort and injury in harsh winter conditions.

Insulation Materials

The insulation materials used in boots have evolved over the years, starting with wool and shearling and advancing to modern high-tech materials like Aerogel. The most popular insulation in many boots today is Thinsulate, though other options like PrimaLoft are also common. These materials provide excellent warmth but are permanently integrated into the boot—whatever insulation your boots come with is what you'll have.

Unlike clothing layers, boot insulation cannot be adjusted at all unless the boots have removable liners. Some boots—not just ski boots—are designed with removable liners, allowing you to swap liners to change the level of insulation. This provides more flexibility in varying conditions and has the added benefit of allowing liners to dry separately overnight, which is crucial for extended winter expeditions to prevent moisture buildup inside the boots.

The outer material of the boot plays an important role as well. In extreme conditions, double mountaineering boots address this with standardized, layered designs that optimize insulation and protection. For single-layer boots, such as traditional leather hiking or winter camping boots, the outer material varies significantly.

Leather Boots

Durable, flexible, and naturally breathable, leather remains a popular choice for cold-weather boots. However, untreated leather absorbs moisture, which can lead to stiffening and heat loss in wet conditions. Regular treatment with wax or waterproofing agents is necessary to maintain its water resistance. Even waterproof leather boots often include a Gore-Tex liner for added protection.

Synthetic Boots

Lighter and generally requiring less upkeep, modern synthetic materials have improved durability and waterproofing. In some conditions, they offer a strong alternative to leather, particularly in wet or high-exposure environments where moisture resistance is critical.

Choosing the right combination of insulation and outer material is crucial for maintaining warmth, comfort, and durability in winter conditions.

Boot Waterproofing & Maintenance

Waterproofing Leather and Synthetic Winter Boots

Enhancing the waterproofing of your winter boots is essential, even if they come with a Gore-Tex liner. Most waterproof membranes provide water resistance rather than absolute waterproofing. Over time, the outer material absorbs moisture, making the boots heavier and increasing heat loss from evaporative cooling. Adding extra waterproofing treatment helps prevent this absorption and keeps your boots functioning properly in harsh conditions.

For leather boots, applying Obenauf's Heavy Duty LP or Obenauf's Water Shield provides extra protection:

Obenauf's Water Shield – A silicone-based spray that is easy to apply and doesn't change the color of the boot.

Obenauf's Heavy Duty LP – A wax-based sealant that lasts longer but requires more effort to apply and will darken leather.

Even with waterproof treatments, the outer material of boots can still freeze if it gets wet and temperatures drop. However, wax-based treatments like Obenauf's Heavy Duty LP help prevent water absorption, making freezing less likely than with untreated boots.

For synthetic boots, water does not soak into the material like it does with leather, but it can cling to the surface and freeze, making the boots stiff and less flexible. Some synthetic boots come with factory-applied water-repellent coatings, but these wear down over time and need to be re-applied. Using Obenauf's Water Shield on synthetic boots can improve water resistance and extend their lifespan.

While manufacturers may claim their boots are waterproof, adding extra protection makes a big difference in real-world conditions. In sub-freezing temperatures, when your boots stay dry instead of accumulating moisture, you'll be glad you took the extra step.

Author's Note

From personal experience, combining Obenauf's Heavy Duty LP with Obenauf's Water Shield has made my boots significantly more water-repellent than relying solely on the Gore-Tex liner. Obenauf's Water Shield is applied using a hand-pump sprayer, while Obenauf's Heavy Duty LP comes in a jar and is applied by hand. This combination has worked well for me in keeping my boots dry.

Enhancing Warmth with Gaiters and Socks

Gaiters

Gaiters are essential for winter camping, providing a fabric covering that wraps around your ankle and extends up toward your knee, covering the top of your boot. They prevent water, snow, and debris from entering your boots, helping keep your feet dry and comfortable.

Beyond keeping out snow and debris, gaiters help reduce heat loss by blocking wind and preventing snow from entering the boots. While standard gaiters don't provide insulation like super gaiters, they still improve protection in winter camping conditions by keeping your lower legs and boots drier.

Super gaiters, such as those made by Forty Below and Mountain Tools, fully cover your boot and extend up your lower leg. These provide excellent insulation and are designed for extreme cold environments. Unlike standard gaiters, super gaiters seal tightly to your boot, offering superior protection against snow and freezing temperatures. These are ideal for mountaineering or extreme cold camping, where standard gaiters might not be enough.

For added warmth without excessive bulk, custom-designed insulated gaiters are another option. They help extend the range of your boots in cold conditions while keeping weight minimal. Similarly, custom-made insulated toe caps can improve warmth in the toe area, though they may affect crampon compatibility or snowshoe fit if they add too much bulk. These modifications are especially useful for treks like Kilimanjaro, where warmer boots are only needed for summit day.

Although Outdoor Research's X-Gaiters are no longer in production, they may still be available through secondary reseller markets. Other similar products can provide additional insulation. By combining standard gaiters, super gaiters, or custom options, you can adapt to varying temperatures without carrying overly bulky or specialized boots. This setup is ideal for those who need warmth in specific conditions but prefer lighter footwear for the rest of the trek.

Sock Layering

Layering your socks is crucial for protecting your feet from blisters, friction, and cold-related injuries. Using a double sock system is an effective way to maintain warmth and comfort in extreme conditions, but layering beyond that can reduce breathability and circulation, leading to cold feet rather than added warmth.

For liner socks, Wrightsock is an excellent choice. These synthetic, double-layer socks are woven together to function as a single sock, making them easier to use in cold temperatures. A Wrightsock-style liner reduces friction, helps prevent blisters, and wicks moisture away from the skin, keeping your feet dry and warm—critical for avoiding chilling and discomfort.

For outer socks, choose high-quality wool socks like Smartwool or Darn Tough. Wool provides superior insulation, retains warmth even when damp, and is a reliable material for winter trekking.

If your boots fit slightly loose due to foot shape—such as a large toe box combined with a narrow heel—mountaineering-weight socks can help fill the space and stabilize your foot. However, be careful not to over-layer, as too many sock layers can restrict circulation, leading to cold feet instead of added warmth. A properly balanced sock system ensures warmth, dryness, and reduced foot movement inside your boots, enhancing overall comfort in winter conditions.

Clothing layers stack up for a variety of conditions on Denali.

Chapter 3
Choosing the Right Winter Shelter

Choosing a Winter Shelter
The variety of winter shelter types is vast. Throughout history, people have created igloos, tepees, wigwams, and longhouses to survive harsh winters.

As a modern winter camper, you're unlikely to build a large, fixed structure, but there are many approaches to creating or carrying a shelter that will keep you safe and comfortable in winter conditions.

Base Camping vs. Mobile Camping
There are two fundamental styles of winter camping and adventuring: base camping and mobile camping.

Key Differences
Base camping supports heavier gear and equipment, offering greater comfort and more food options.

Mobile camping prioritizes lightweight efficiency, limiting food and gear choices due to weight restrictions.

Your choice between these two approaches will directly impact your gear selection, food supply, and shelter decisions for a successful winter camping experience.

Base Camping
Base camping involves establishing a camp in the wilderness and using it as a hub for exploration. Typically, the camp remains in one location, unless there's a specific reason to move it. You set up camp and then venture out for a day or several days, always returning to the same spot.

A classic example of base camping is Mount Everest, where base camp serves as the starting point for expeditions. On mountains like Denali, base camp is also the starting point, but climbers establish multiple higher camps as they ascend. They move between these camps during the climb and typically do not return to base camp until the expedition is complete. However, climbers often descend to lower camps to recover and acclimate before pushing higher, following the "climb high, sleep low" strategy. Some expeditions cache supplies at lower camps and return to them strategically.

Base camping can also involve a more mobile approach, such as skiing or snowshoeing into a location and camping for multiple days while making excursions to nearby areas. Hunters often use this method to set up a semi-permanent camp while tracking game.

Mobile Camping

Mobile camping focuses on constant movement, setting up camp only when necessary. You establish a new campsite each night, do your camp chores, then break down camp in the morning and move on.

On mountains like Denali and Aconcagua, mobile camping is the norm, but movement is often staggered rather than continuous. Climbers may spend multiple nights at a camp before moving up, especially for high-altitude acclimatization. On Aconcagua, climbers use the "carry high, sleep low" method, moving gear to a higher camp and then descending to sleep at a lower altitude before making a final move upward. Kilimanjaro follows a similar approach, with trekkers continuously moving to higher camps without returning to previous ones.

Hot Tent vs. Cold Tent Camping

Hot tent camping and cold tent camping are two distinct styles of winter camping, each with its own set of advantages and challenges. Hot tent camping involves using a tent with a small wood stove or other heat source, providing warmth and comfort even in freezing conditions. This setup allows for extended stays in harsh weather by maintaining a livable environment inside the tent.

In contrast, cold tent camping involves relying on insulated gear and natural body heat to keep warm, with no additional heat source inside the tent. This style demands more preparation and resilience, as campers must rely on their gear and layering systems to stay warm in harsher exposed environments.

Hot Tent Camping

Hot tent camping involves bringing a heat source, such as a small stove powered by wood, petroleum products, or electricity. This setup significantly increases comfort by warming your tent, making it a preferred choice for long-term base camps in cold environments.

Modern lightweight hot tents, made from materials like silnylon or Dyneema, are designed for backpacking and easier transport. Traditional hot tents, usually made from canvas, require more effort to move, but they can still be transported using a pulk (sled), toboggan, or a dog team in certain conditions. However, over long distances, motorized transport like a snowmobile is often necessary. Hot tent camping is commonly used in places like Canada and Russia, where campers set up long-term shelters in remote winter environments.

A properly heated hot tent can reach temperatures of 70°F (21°C), creating a warm and comfortable space, even in extreme cold. This makes it ideal for extended stays when mobility isn't a priority.

Cold Tent Camping

Cold tent camping, which is the focus of this book, relies on insulation and gear design rather than an external heat source. Instead of heating the tent, you depend on your sleeping bag, insulated sleeping pad, and layered clothing to retain body heat. Unlike hot tent camping, this method does not generate warmth—it only prevents heat loss.

Natural materials, such as snow walls, can be used to block wind and provide extra insulation. Mobility is a key aspect of cold-weather camping, allowing you to adapt to changing conditions. Proper site selection is essential for staying safe and comfortable, making use of windbreaks, tree cover, and terrain features.

This book emphasizes cold tent camping for those seeking a mobile, lightweight approach to winter adventures. It requires careful planning and reliance on gear insulation to thrive in harsh conditions.

Winter Camping Shelter Types

Winter camping shelters vary widely in design, from ultra-minimalist bivy sacks to fully enclosed huts. Below is a list of different winter shelter with their fundamental differences.

Snow Shelters: Built entirely from ice and snow, these shelters eliminate the need to carry a tent but require significant time and effort to construct. In very cold conditions, hard-packed snow must be cut into blocks or compacted before excavation, making this a labor-intensive but highly effective shelter option.

Bivy Sacks: The ultra-minimalist approach to winter camping, consisting of a large, weatherproof sleeve that slides over your sleeping bag. They offer basic protection but limited space and ventilation.

Tarp Shelters: Lightweight and simple, these shelters provide a covered space for cooking and gear maintenance but offer minimal insulation and wind resistance.

Three-Season Tents: Single-layer tents designed for milder conditions. They often have mesh interiors, making them unsuitable for extreme winter camping.

Four-Season Tents: The gold standard for winter camping. These double-layer tents provide superior insulation, wind resistance, and durability, making them suitable for harsh conditions.

Huts: The most comfortable option for winter travel. These hard-shell, permanent structures provide high protection and warmth but usually require prior arrangements for access.

The following section focuses on choosing and selecting tents, while a later part of the book covers tent placement, shelter design, and snow shelters as additional winter camping options.

Selecting the Right Winter Tent Design

The two most popular winter tent designs are the dome tent and the tunnel tent.

Dome Tents

Dome tents are the classic design, typically using two to six flexible poles to create a rounded structure. This shape provides good stability and strength in snowy conditions, though taller dome tents are more susceptible to high winds. A low-profile dome tent will handle strong gusts better than a roomier, taller model.

One of the biggest advantages of dome tents is that they are freestanding, meaning they don't require guy lines to maintain their structure in calm conditions. However, in high winds or heavy snowfall, securing them with guy lines and stakes is recommended for added stability.

Dome tents offer a lot of floor space and are easy to set up with a team when conditions are manageable. Their spacious interior makes them comfortable for winter camping, especially when spending extended time inside due to harsh weather.

Tunnel Tents

Tunnel tents have a completely different design. They are easier for teams to set up under extreme weather conditions and are often preferred for polar exploration and cold mountain environments. While not necessarily better for harsh weather, their hoop-like structure makes them quicker to assemble in tough conditions.

A key advantage of tunnel tents is that their low-profile shape naturally sheds wind better than most dome tents, reducing the need for additional snow walls. However, in exposed environments, building a snow wall around a tunnel tent can still provide added protection. These tents typically use two to four poles arranged in a hoop fashion, similar to a Quonset hut, creating a longer, lower profile shape.

The main disadvantage of tunnel tents is that they are not freestanding and require guy lines and stakes to maintain their shape. However, their simpler pole system avoids the crisscrossing complexity of dome tents, making them easier to assemble in challenging conditions.

Choosing the Right Tent for Your Camping Style & Trip Type

The type of tent you choose depends on your style of travel and whether you opt for a three-season or four-season tent.

If you plan to cover long distances, minimizing weight is a priority. A three-season tent might seem like a good choice, but its structural limitations make it unsuitable for deep snow or high winds. A lightweight four-season tent is a better compromise for long-distance winter trekking since it provides better protection without excessive weight.

If you're car camping, you have more flexibility and can use almost any tent, even an inexpensive model from a big-box store.

Author's Note:
I've slept in a $30USD Coleman tent in sub-zero temperatures

and been just fine. You don't need to spend thousands of dollars to have an excellent winter camping experience. While this isn't a tent I would use on a mountain or an expedition, for car camping, my inexpensive two-pole Coleman three-season tent has served me well over the years.

Three-Season Tents

Three-season tents are designed for spring, summer, and fall, not winter. They have a single layer of synthetic fabric, usually nylon, to form the tent body. Most models include a rain fly, but it typically doesn't extend all the way to the ground, which limits wind and snow protection.

These tents are built with lighter fabric, stitching, and poles. They are not designed to handle heavy snow or extreme winds. While higher-end three-season models can withstand moderate wind if properly guyed out, they still lack the reinforced pole structure and durability of four-season tents. If snow accumulates, it can collapse a three-season tent, sometimes snapping the poles. While four-season tents can also fail under extreme loads, they are built with stronger materials to withstand more weight and pressure.

Even though three-season tents aren't made for winter, some people still use them in extreme environments, including on mountains like Denali. However, they require extra care to keep them functional in cold conditions. While they can work in milder winter environments, they are not as durable in harsh weather and should be used with caution in extreme conditions.

Four-Season Tents

Four-season tents are specifically designed to handle winter conditions. They feature a double-layer of nylon or synthetic fabric, with a fully enclosed inner tent body. The rain fly extends all the way to the ground, offering extra insulation and wind protection.

Four-season tents come in dome, tunnel, and other structural designs, but they almost always have a double-wall system consisting of an inner tent and an outer shell. These tents also have stronger poles, reinforced stitching, and heavy-duty materials, making them significantly more durable than three-season tents.

If you plan to do frequent winter camping, especially in stormy conditions, a four-season tent is the best option. While they are more expensive, the investment is worth it when facing high winds and heavy snow. When your budget tent collapses or tears during a storm, those extra few hundred dollars will suddenly seem like a small price to pay for safety and comfort.

Igloos and Snow Shelters

If you have a team, an igloo is an excellent shelter option. While it's possible to build a basic igloo alone, it is typically done with a team due to the intensive construction process. Igloos require hard-packed snow that can be cut into blocks. In some conditions, such as fresh powder, building an igloo may not be possible unless the snow is first compacted and allowed to sinter (harden) before cutting. Skill and experience play a significant role, and teamwork speeds up construction while improving stability.

Other snow shelters, like quinzhees, also offer excellent protection in harsh winter conditions. Unlike igloos, which rely on stacked snow blocks, a quinzhee is made by piling up loose snow and hollowing it out. Quinzees can be built with less ideal snow conditions, but they require more effort and time to construct.

While the insulation and protection of snow shelters make them well worth the effort, they are best built with the right tools and experience to ensure safety and efficiency in extreme conditions.

Author's Note

On one of my first winter camping trips to the Sierras, I decided to sleep in a snow tunnel instead of using my tent. It took three hours to dig, and using a standard shovel made it even tougher, but the effort paid off—it was the best night of sleep I've ever had. The tunnel was warm, silent, and completely sheltered from the wind.

The only downside was that moisture from my breath condensed on the walls, making the tunnel slightly damp. In colder conditions, this can freeze into a thin ice layer, but despite that, the tunnel remained incredibly comfortable.

I learned that a shovel with an adjustable head, where the blade locks at a 90-degree angle to the handle, is far better for digging snow tunnels. These are often called avalanche shovels with a hoe mode. This setup allows you to rake the snow out instead of awkwardly poking at it with a straight-handled shovel.

As the tunnel gets deeper, a traditional shovel becomes harder to maneuver. A collapsible avalanche shovel with a folding function is the best choice—it makes excavating confined spaces much easier and saves time and effort in deep snow.

Emergency Shelter Options for Winter Camping

Snow Trenches

In an absolute emergency, a snow trench can serve as an effective survival shelter. Constructing one requires some knowledge, as they rely on spanning the trench with materials like skis, ski poles, or ropes, then covering it with a tarp or other insulating material. In extreme conditions, piling additional snow on top of the tarp adds insulation and wind resistance, helping retain heat. Once built, they can be surprisingly comfortable with minimal effort, especially in a disaster situation.

To build one, dig a trench perpendicular to the wind direction. If there's not enough time or energy to build a full trench, even digging a pit and stacking snow blocks against the windward side can provide crucial protection and increase survival chances.

Bivy Sacks

A bivy sack is a lightweight, compact emergency shelter that can save your life in a pinch. One option is the Western Mountaineering HotSac, a simple cocoon sleeve that fits over your sleeping bag, designed to keep you alive while you figure out your next move.

If you're using a tent, you typically won't bring a bivy sack for mountaineering, as your tent serves as your primary shelter. However, if you're climbing and get caught in bad weather, a bivy sack can be a lifesaving backup. Some climbers carry a simple bivy sack in case conditions turn bad and they can't make it back to their tent.

Bivy sacks trap heat effectively, but they also trap condensation, which can dampen your sleeping bag over time. In extreme cold, breathable winter models help reduce moisture buildup, making them a better choice for emergency use.

Tarp Shelters

A basic tarp can provide all the protection you need in an emergency situation. By digging a snow pit and using ski equipment or other snow gear to stake down the tarp, you can create a makeshift wind and precipitation barrier.

Setting up a tarp shelter in winter can be challenging, especially in high winds. Using deadman-style stakes (burying anchor points in the snow) helps secure the tarp, preventing flapping or collapse, which can compromise heat retention.

Some winter campers use tarp shelters as their primary shelter. Tom Murphy, a Montana photographer, routinely ventures into Yellowstone in winter with a -40°F (-40°C) sleeping bag and a large tarp instead of a tent. This approach leaves him more exposed to animals and the elements, but he has used it successfully for years. While not for everyone, this minimalist method proves that a well-prepared camper can survive harsh conditions with strategic gear choices.

Author's Note

I've tarp camped in winter many times because I prefer a minimalist approach. Using a tarp requires resourcefulness, but it's a great way to keep your pack lighter. However, you have to accept that you're fully exposed to the elements. That said, as long as I'm under my tarp, I'm warm and comfortable.

The few times I've woken up cold, it's usually because I somehow wriggled out from under the tarp. I typically build a snow berm or pitch my tarp like a classic pup tent and sleep the night away. It's a great way to camp, especially in the forest, as long as you have some natural protection from the wind.

Tent Footprint or Not?

Tent footprints are popular, but they can be an expensive add-on meant to provide a secondary layer of protection for the bottom of your tent. Do you really need one for winter camping? Arguably, no. While a footprint protects your tent from rocks and sticks during three-season camping, it's not as useful in winter, where you'll likely be camping on snow.

Some tents, like the MSR Hubba, come with a footprint included, but many newer models sell them as an extra accessory. Since you'll be lying on packed snow, most footprints won't provide much additional insulation or protection from the cold.

Before heading out, test at home to see if you actually need a footprint. An inexpensive synthetic tarp from a hardware store can work just as well for a fraction of the cost.

Staking Down Your Tent

One of the biggest challenges with winter camping is staking your tent down. Unless you know it's going to be calm and you're well-protected in a forest, you'll need to secure your tent for when the winds pick up—which often happens at 2 A.M.

Regular summer camping stakes are virtually useless in winter conditions. Large, scoop-style snow stakes, like those sold by Hilleberg, are an excellent option because they can be used as either a deadman anchor or a regular stake.

A deadman anchor is a technique for securing your tent when you can't drive stakes into the ground. Instead, you use an object like a log, rock, or even a buried shovel to weigh down your guy lines. To set up a deadman anchor, bury the object in snow or ice, ensuring it's well-covered, then tie your guy lines to it. This method is a lifesaver when the ground is frozen solid or when there's not enough snow for traditional stakes.

If you're camping on frozen ground without snow, you may find that no type of stake will work. If this happens, you'll need to improvise with logs, rocks, or other heavy objects to secure your tent. Planning for this ahead of time is critical, as some areas may not have enough snow for a proper stake setup.

Author's Note

I've experienced frozen ground with thin snow cover. It completely disrupted my camp setup.

The first time, I was camping in mild weather, and my tarp tent was fine. But overnight, the temperature dropped as a storm cleared out, and the ground froze solid. In the morning, I couldn't pull out my stakes—they were completely stuck. My toes and hands were freezing, and I was worried about frostbite. With no other option, I had to cut my guy lines, untie the knots, and abandon the stakes. There was no way I was getting them out without a tent stake mallet or an ice axe.

The second time, I arrived at my site and tried to set up my MSR Hubba tent—but the ground was rock solid. There was minimal snow, so I couldn't use deadman anchors, and no stakes would go in. I had to drag logs and other heavy objects to my campsite to secure the tent. It wasn't ideal, and thank goodness the wind didn't pick up.

These two situations taught me a hard lesson—frozen ground with no snow is a serious problem. If you're not prepared, you might find yourself without a stable shelter when you need it most.

Finishing up camp preparations on the Greenland icecap.

Setting up camp where others have previously built a snow wall saves time. Be mindful of collecting clean snow for water to prevent contamination.

Chapter 4
Sleeping Bags and Staying Warm at Night

Choosing a Sleeping Bag

Selecting the right sleeping bag can mean the difference between warm, restful nights and complete misery. Winter sleeping bags are more expensive, heavier, and bulkier than summer ones because they require additional insulation to handle cold temperatures. Advances in materials like down have improved warmth-to-weight ratios and compressibility, but some bulk is unavoidable if you want to stay comfortable on freezing nights.

You can extend your sleeping bag's range by using liners or wearing extra layers. However, the most critical factor is choosing a bag that's warm enough for the conditions you'll face. A cheap or inadequate bag will leave you cold and regretting your decision. A winter sleeping bag should be viewed as an investment in both comfort and safety.

High-quality sleeping bags, particularly those made with down, can last for many years if properly cared for. They rarely wear out, making them a "buy once, cry once" purchase—spend more upfront, and you'll save money in the long run.

Temperature Rating

Selecting the right temperature rating for a sleeping bag is one of the biggest challenges when purchasing your first winter bag. Ratings, insulation types, and manufacturer specifications can be confusing. The key question is: *What is the effective temperature rating of a sleeping bag?* In other words, at what temperature can you use the bag and still have a comfortable night's sleep?

Unfortunately, no standardized rating system exists across the industry. Each manufacturer uses its own methods, despite a standard for measuring loft—the thickness of a sleeping bag's insulation. Many brands adjust their testing processes for market differentiation, adding to the confusion.

Another complication is how ratings are presented. Some manufacturers list the comfort rating, while others highlight the survival rating, and some use a limit rating—each meaning something different.

Comfort Rating: The lowest temperature at which a standard woman can sleep comfortably. She might not feel particularly warm, but she won't be shivering or uncomfortable.
Limit Rating: The temperature at which a standard man can sleep in a curled position without waking due to cold.
Survival Rating: The absolute minimum temperature at which the bag can prevent frostbite or hypothermia. At this limit, you probably won't sleep at all.

For individuals with lower metabolic rates, such as older adults or women, relying on a bag's survival rating is risky. At the survival limit, toes may become extremely cold or even numb—not an ideal situation for winter camping.

Think of the survival rating as the bag's extreme limit, not the temperature you should aim for. If you expect overnight temperatures of 0°F (-18°C), you don't want a bag rated to on that temperature. These ratings assume ideal conditions and optimal metabolism, which don't apply to everyone.

Men typically sleep warmer than women and can often use a bag rated for higher temperatures. Women, however, tend to sleep colder and require a bag rated for lower temperatures. Some brands, like Feathered Friends, provide separate ratings for men and women, but this is uncommon in the industry.

To ensure comfort and safety, choose a sleeping bag rated at least 15 degrees lower than the coldest temperature you expect to encounter. Weather can be unpredictable. A sudden storm clearing the skies can cause temperatures to drop 10 to 15°F (6 to 8°C) lower than the forecast, pushing you into your bag's survival limit.

Yes, this means you may need to invest in a more expensive, bulkier bag. But never push the limits of your gear—this is not the place to cut corners.

Finally, your sleeping pad plays just as critical a role in warmth as your sleeping bag. A high-quality bag won't keep you warm if you lose heat to the frozen ground. Look for a pad with an R-value of 4 or higher for winter conditions, and closer to 6 or above for extreme cold.

Author's Note

I've learned about weather versus sleeping bag ratings the hard way. Once, while camping in Sequoia National Park, the forecast showed average nighttime temperatures of 30°F (-1°C). I used my Western Mountaineering Megalite bag, thinking it would be fine. What a mistake. A snowstorm blew in, and when the skies cleared, the temperature dropped to 5°F (-15°C). I was cold all night and barely managed a few hours of sleep. Relying on the forecast and using a summer bag in winter conditions were both major mistakes.

Another time, I used my Western Mountaineering Antelope bag, rated to 5°F (-15°C), during a winter trip in northwest Wyoming. The forecast predicted 10°F (-12°C), and I assumed I'd be fine. Again, I was wrong. The temperature unexpectedly plummeted to -20°F (-29°C). By morning, my tent stakes were frozen into the ground, and I had to cut the guy lines to escape. My toes were completely numb, and the balls of my feet burned—a sign of early frostbite. Though I avoided permanent damage, my toes remained numb for a month.

Both experiences taught me never to push the limits of a sleeping bag or trust weather forecasts too much. Always plan for colder-than-expected temperatures and choose your sleeping bag accordingly. Learn from my mistakes and don't take unnecessary risks.

Sleeping Bag Insulation Types

One of the most challenging decisions when choosing a sleeping bag is selecting the right insulation. Will you go with down—typically made from goose or duck down in high-end sleeping bags—or synthetic fill?

If you want the lightest and most efficient insulation, high-fill-power down is one of the best options available. Down offers unmatched warmth for its weight and compressibility. No other insulation type comes close in terms of warmth-to-weight efficiency. However, fill power—not just the region it comes from—is the key measure of down quality. Some of the best down comes from northern European geese, but high-fill-power down from other regions can perform just as well.

Synthetic insulation is a great choice for humid or wet conditions, even in winter. Just because it's cold doesn't mean there won't be moisture or humidity. Synthetic fill retains its insulating properties better than untreated down when exposed to moisture, making it ideal for rough conditions. Modern treated downs, like hydrophobic down, have improved moisture resistance, but they still don't match synthetic insulation when completely wet.

The main downside of down is its performance when soaked. While it's light, highly compressible, and the best insulator in dry conditions, it clumps together and loses its insulating properties when wet. This can happen if you're caught in the rain, spill water on the bag, or expose it to other significant moisture sources. Hydrophobic down mitigates this issue, but synthetic still performs better when fully saturated.

In extremely cold and humid environments, such as near the high Arctic Ocean where temperatures can drop below 0°F (-18°C), polar explorers often rely on vapor barrier liners (VBLs) inside high-loft down bags to manage moisture. Some also use hybrid solutions or synthetic bags in particularly damp conditions.

Another factor to consider is cost. Down sleeping bags, especially those made with high-fill-power goose down, are expensive—sometimes prohibitively so. Synthetic bags are generally more affordable, but keep in mind that high-end synthetic bags designed for extreme conditions can approach or even exceed the cost of mid-range down bags. Budget synthetic bags from big-box stores may not be a fair comparison to premium down options, as their performance and durability are often limited.

Temperature ratings also deserve a closer look. While synthetic bags rated to 0°F (-18°C) are available at lower prices, the accuracy of these ratings depends on the manufacturer. Ideally, look for bags tested to EN/ISO standards, which provide more reliable benchmarks. Many budget options have optimistic ratings that may not hold up in real-world conditions.

Synthetic bags don't compress as well as down, though the gap has narrowed. Advanced synthetics like PrimaLoft or Climashield offer better compression and weight than older synthetic fills, but down still has the edge in warmth-to-weight ratio and packability. If minimal weight and maximum compressibility are priorities, down remains the best choice—assuming you're in dry conditions.

Ultimately, both options have strengths and weaknesses. Down is unparalleled for its warmth-to-weight efficiency and compressibility, while synthetic insulation excels in wet conditions and affordability. Your choice depends on your environment, budget, and how much risk you're willing to take with moisture exposure.

Hybrid Sleeping Bag Approach

One effective way to handle cold, humid conditions is to use a hybrid system with a down sleeping bag inside a synthetic sleeping bag. The down sleeping bag stays close to your body, while the synthetic bag covers it.

This setup works because your body heat and moisture pass through the down sleeping bag, keeping it warm and reducing condensation inside. As the moisture moves outward and cools, it may freeze at the outer edges of the synthetic bag in very cold environments. However, in prolonged use, some moisture can freeze inside the down bag if it doesn't escape quickly enough. To prevent this, a vapor barrier liner (VBL) inside the down bag can help reduce internal ice buildup.

Synthetic insulation handles frozen or damp moisture better than down, so the outer layer protects the inner bag and preserves its insulating ability. This method is ideal for extreme cold and damp conditions where managing moisture is critical. However, it's not recommended for mild or dry environments, as it adds unnecessary weight and bulk. Avoid trying to save money by using a low-rated down bag with a synthetic overbag unless you're in a high-risk situation. This technique works well, but it's best suited for specialized use.

Sleeping Bag Shapes and Designs

The most popular sleeping bag shape is the mummy design. These bags are called mummy bags because they resemble a mummy sarcophagus. Mummy sleeping bags are wider at the shoulders and taper down to the legs and feet.

This design has two main advantages:

Minimizes dead air space, making it easier for your body to warm the bag and stay comfortable.

Reduces weight and material by tapering the leg and foot area.

Mummy bags are standard for almost all high-end and winter sleeping bags.

Another option is the hybrid (semi-rectangular) design, which has a wider chest and shoulder area with a moderately tapered lower section. This shape is useful for those who prefer extra room or feel restricted in a traditional mummy bag.

The last design is the classic rectangular sleeping bag, often remembered from childhood camping trips. These are typically the least expensive because they aren't designed for rugged or extreme conditions. While they offer more space and don't feel as claustrophobic, they're not as warm due to excess air space, especially below the hips. This makes them less ideal for cold weather.

For winter camping, a mummy bag is the top recommendation. If you have a broader chest or shoulders, look for a high-end model designed to accommodate your size. Some brands offer wide or long options to ensure a good fit.

Sleeping Bag Features

There are several key design considerations when choosing a sleeping bag that can improve warmth and efficiency. Every added feature increases weight and cost, but the benefits are often worth it over time.

One important feature is the zipper style. High-end sleeping bags typically use three-quarter-length or seven-eighths-length zippers, which run from the neck area down to about three-quarters or seven-eighths of the way, stopping short of the foot section. This design reduces heat loss and minimizes cold air seepage. Rectangular bags often have full-length zippers that extend down the side and around the bottom, but these are less efficient at retaining warmth and are not ideal for winter camping.

Draft collars and hoods are also essential for winter sleeping bags. A draft collar is an insulated baffle around the neck area that prevents cold air from entering and keeps warm air inside. It acts like a built-in scarf and makes a significant difference on cold nights. Mummy-style sleeping bags also include a hood that wraps around your head, providing added warmth compared to rectangular bags, where your head remains exposed.

A zipper baffle is another feature to look for. This insulated strip runs along the zipper to prevent cold air from leaking in and to keep warmth inside. High-end winter sleeping bags often have both an inner and outer baffle, fully sealing the zipper from heat loss. While this feature can make zipping and unzipping slightly harder, it's essential for retaining heat.

Footbox design is another consideration. Some sleeping bags have overfilled footboxes that provide extra insulation for your feet, which is particularly helpful in cold conditions. As a personal tip, I always use down booties inside my sleeping bag to keep my feet warm. Even with excellent bags, my feet tend to get chilly, and this small addition makes a big difference.

Neck collars with a drawcord are common in expedition-style bags. This lets you cinch the collar snugly, sealing your body from outside air while leaving only your head exposed. These cords are typically elastic to prevent discomfort or choking risks.

Zipper stiffeners are in some high-end bags which help prevent snagging and tearing the fabric. These stiffeners add minimal weight but are very effective. To avoid snags, I recommend zipping and unzipping your bag from the outside. It might feel less natural, but it significantly reduces the chance of snagging the fabric.

These features may feel restrictive at first, but when the temperature drops, they can make all the difference between comfort and discomfort during the night.

Another useful feature in some sleeping bags is the inclusion of continuous baffles. These tubes of insulation (typically down) run all the way around the sleeping bag. In some box-baffled cold-weather bags, the down is locked in place in critical areas like the chest and back to prevent shifting. However, in true continuous-baffle designs, the down can be manually shifted, allowing you to adjust how much insulation is covering you. This feature gives you the flexibility to move warmth between the top and bottom of the bag, helping you cool down or warm up as needed.

Sleeping Bag Compression Sacks

For your winter sleeping bag, you'll need a compression sack to reduce its size for packing. These sacks are usually made from water-resistant fabrics, which provide some protection from moisture, but they are not fully waterproof. If you expect wet conditions, consider using a dry bag-style compression sack for full protection. Many compression sacks come with straps to help compress the bag as small as possible, saving space in your gear.

The same goes for air mattresses—you'll want a protective bag to keep it safe from damage. Most sleeping pad manufacturers include a bag that works for this purpose.

The stuff sack that comes with most sleeping bags is usually adequate for storage, but a compression sack with straps, like those from Sea to Summit, can make packing a lot easier. These bags are made with water-resistant eVent fabric, which helps keep moisture out while still allowing the bag to breathe.

If you're unsure which size to get, it's often better to choose one that's slightly bigger. While it may add a tiny bit of weight, it will save you the hassle of struggling with a too-small sack when you're tired and dealing with cold fingers in the morning.

Some compression sacks are designed with breathable fabric to prevent moisture buildup, which helps maintain your sleeping bag's loft and insulation.

Sleeping Bags and Staying Warm at Night

The key is finding a balance between effective compression and avoiding over-stuffing, as excessive compression can damage the insulation over time.

Sleeping Pads

In addition to a sleeping bag, you'll need insulation between your sleeping bag and the ground or snow. Sleeping pads are an absolute requirement for winter camping. While some people can sleep directly on the ground in summer, winter camping requires insulation to prevent heat loss to the frozen ground.

The most reliable type of sleeping pad, with zero chance of failure, is a foam pad. Foam pads provide excellent insulation between your body, the sleeping bag, and the cold ground beneath your tent. Their effectiveness is measured by an R-value, which indicates how well they resist heat loss. For winter camping, look for a pad with an R-value of at least 4.0, but closer to R-5.0 or higher for true winter conditions. The thicker the foam pad, the better its insulation.

There are several styles of foam pads, such as closed-cell foam, egg-crate foam, and the Therm-a-Rest Z Lite style. Each type has pros and cons:

Z Lite-style foam pads fold flat, don't roll up on themselves, and can double as a seat during the day.

Rolled-up closed-cell foam pads are less expensive but harder to manage because they retain their curled shape, making them more difficult to handle at night.

For extreme cold, many campers layer two pads—a closed-cell foam pad and an inflatable pad. Some place the foam pad on the bottom for durability, while others put it on top of the inflatable pad to reduce conductive heat loss from their body. The best setup depends on conditions and personal preference, but this combination provides the durability of foam with the added comfort and insulation of an inflatable pad.

On Arctic expeditions, explorers sometimes use foam pads that are 4 inches (10 cm) thick. These pads eliminate the risks of punctures or leaks associated with inflatable mattresses. While they are incredibly durable and even resistant to knife punctures, their weight and bulk make them impractical for most backpacking trips.

If durability and reliability are critical, foam pads remain the best choice for winter camping. If you need to reduce weight, a winter-rated technical air mat is an excellent choice.

Inflatable Air Pads

Inflatable air pads are popular because they offer a more comfortable night's sleep compared to foam pads. They're lighter per unit of insulation and more enjoyable for side sleepers. Thick, heavy closed-cell foam pads can be uncomfortable for side sleepers, though back sleepers usually manage better.

Insulated air pads are thick enough for side sleepers to sleep comfortably while providing the warmth needed for winter camping. However, basic air mattresses with no insulation can leave you freezing at night. Without insulation, your body constantly warms the cold air inside the mattress, leading to restless and uncomfortable sleep.

To solve this, manufacturers add baffles and insulation to air pads, increasing their R-value (a measure of thermal resistance). For winter camping, you'll want an R-value of at least 4.0, but closer to R-5 or higher for true winter conditions. Insulated air pads cost more than basic ones, but the added warmth is worth it.

Some high-end air pads use down insulation inside, reducing heat loss to the ground and improving warmth. However, they require extra care to stay dry, as moisture from your breath during inflation can reduce the down's effectiveness. Using a pump sack or a dry inflation method can help prevent this issue. Some models also have one-way valves with built-in moisture barriers to reduce internal condensation.

Air pads do have a downside: they're more prone to punctures. Always carry a repair kit, especially in winter. For extreme cold, some campers pair an air pad with a closed-cell foam pad. Some place the foam pad on the bottom for durability, while others put it on top of the inflatable pad to reduce conductive heat loss from their body. The best setup depends on conditions and personal preference, but this combination provides the durability of foam with the added comfort and insulation of an inflatable pad.

Despite the added care they require, insulated air pads are an excellent choice for staying warm and comfortable during winter camping.

Self-Inflating Air Mats

Another option is the hybrid or self-inflating air mattress. These contain compressible foam inside, allowing them to inflate on their own when unrolled and the valve is opened. This saves you the effort of blowing it up after a long, tiring day in winter conditions.

Self-inflating mattresses are useful and comfortable, but they have some downsides. If moisture gets inside, it can stop the foam from expanding fully and lead to mold growth and long-term insulation degradation. If the mattress gets a puncture, it won't hold air and will lose much of its comfort and warmth. While the internal foam provides some support, it won't work as effectively if the pad is deflated.

To avoid problems, store the mattress unrolled with the valve open so it can expand and dry out. These mattresses are a great choice, but they need careful handling. Always protect them from damage and fix any punctures as soon as possible.

Sleeping Mat Combination Approaches

One of the best setups for winter camping is pairing a thin foam pad, like a Therm-a-Rest Z Lite, with your air mattress. This combination improves insulation and provides a backup if your air mattress fails. If the air valve leaks or the mattress becomes damaged and you're unable to repair it, the foam pad can save you from a long, cold night.

With down-filled or other high-end air mats, even a tiny fiber or hair, invisible to the eye, can cause the valve to leak. If this happens and you have no backup, you may end up piling gear and clothing under yourself just to get through the night. Using a foam pad as part of your setup not only provides a secondary mattress but also serves as a versatile tool. The foam pad can protect your air mattress when kneeling on snow inside the tent. It also adds an extra layer of insulation between your body and the ground.

While a thin foam pad alone won't offer the same comfort as an air mattress, especially on snowy ground, it's far better than sleeping directly on snow. This combination provides both comfort and security, ensuring you stay warm and sleep well, even if you need to make repairs to your sleeping setup.

Sleeping Pad R-Value

The insulation rating of a sleeping pad is measured using its R-value, which indicates how much insulation the pad provides between you and the ground. Higher R-values provide better insulation, ensuring a warmer, more comfortable sleep.

Although higher R-values often mean thicker pads, advancements in materials—such as reflective layers or specialized foams—allow some pads to achieve high R-values without extra bulk. Most manufacturers now follow the ASTM F3340-18 industry standard for measuring R-values, making it easier to compare pads across brands.

If a sleeping pad does not list an R-value, its performance is harder to assess. Pads with published R-values provide a clearer understanding of their insulating properties, especially for cold-weather use.

Air Mat Sleeping Pad Features

Sleeping pads may look simple, but there are several features to consider.

One is surface texture—how sticky or grippy is the pad? If you're using a synthetic sleeping bag on a synthetic air mat, you might find yourself sliding off during the night, which can be incredibly frustrating. Some people apply dots of seam grip to the air mat to reduce sliding, while others use a foam pad on top for better grip. Another option is to wrap 550 paracord around the sleeping pad and air mattress to keep them connected and prevent slipping.

Most air mattresses come with some sort of inflation bag. However, summer models typically don't include these, relying instead on manual inflation. In winter conditions, blowing them up manually isn't advisable because your breath introduces moisture, which can freeze inside the air mattress and reduce its insulating effectiveness.

Some air mattresses offer integrated inflation devices, such as a block of expanding foam inside the pad. When uncompressed, the foam expands, drawing air in. You then close the valve with your hand to trap the air inside.

Valve design also matters. Most air mattresses have valves that allow air to flow in and out, but some models feature:
- A dedicated "in" valve to prevent deflation while inflating.
- A separate "out" valve to quickly release air when packing up.

Weight and packability are also important. Foam pads are practically indestructible and can be strapped to the outside of a backpack, but they must be secured properly to avoid falling off or blowing away. However, exposed foam pads can also collect snow, ice, or moisture, which can introduce unwanted dampness inside the tent. Storing the pad inside the pack or using a protective cover can help prevent this issue.

For air mattresses, consider how you'll inflate them in winter. Unless the manufacturer recommends otherwise, avoid using your mouth to blow up an air mat. Each breath contains moisture, and in freezing conditions, this leads to ice buildup inside the pad. Over time, this degrades insulation and makes the mat harder to pack. Some high-end air mats now feature moisture-resistant barriers or antimicrobial coatings to reduce these risks, but using a pump sack or mechanical pump is still the best practice.

Air Mattress Precautions

Air mattresses can significantly improve the quality of your sleep, but they have a major weakness—even the smallest pinhole can cause them to deflate, either slowly or rapidly, leaving them completely useless for sleeping.

Always bring an air mattress repair kit and make sure you know how to use it. A good kit should include patches, adhesive, and possibly a valve cover if your mattress allows for valve repairs. Some models have replaceable valves, but most do not. The middle of a cold, stormy night at 2 A.M. in subzero temperatures is not the time to figure out how to patch a hole.

Be extremely cautious with metal objects or anything sharp that could puncture your mattress. Using a groundsheet or protective layer underneath can help prevent damage from sharp objects on the ground.

It's also smart to have a backup plan in case the mattress becomes unusable. A foam pad serves as a good secondary layer for insulation and support if your air mattress fails. This way, you won't be left without protection from the cold ground, especially in winter conditions.

Some people have had their feet or elbows slide off their sleeping bag or sleeping pad, leaving them in direct contact with the ground all night. There are occasional stories of frostbite developing on heels or elbows because of this. Be aware of this potential issue and set up your tent and sleeping area properly to prevent it from happening.

Proper care and preparation can save you from a cold and uncomfortable night.

Author's Note

In my book, *Two Friends and a Polar Bear*, Terry Williams and I discuss the challenges he faced with his air mattress during an expedition. A couple of days into the trip, Terry's air mattress developed a pinprick leak. Even though we had a repair kit with a valve cover for sealing leaks, we were never able to locate the exact hole in his mattress.

As a result, his expensive air mattress was reduced to little more than a thin sheet of nylon. Our backup plan was to layer clothing and gear beneath him on top of his foam pad so he could get some rest.

Always consider what you'll do if you're relying on an air mattress and it fails. Be prepared with a backup plan in case you can't find or fix a leak.

Sleeping Bag and Mattress Storage Bags

When you're not using your sleeping bag, air mattress, or sleeping pad, store them in a cool, dry place. Avoid keeping your sleeping bag compressed for long periods. While some manufacturers say that a dry sleeping bag won't be damaged by compression, it's still best to store it uncompressed when possible to maintain the insulation's loft and effectiveness.

Down sleeping bags handle compression better than synthetic ones, but long-term compression still reduces loft in both types. To keep your sleeping bag in good shape, spread it out flat—under your bed works well if there are no pets or children around.

The same goes for self-inflating or down-filled air mattresses. Store them unrolled and loose in a safe spot where they won't get compressed or damaged. For self-inflating mattresses, keep the valve open to allow the foam to fully expand and prevent long-term compression damage.

Most sleeping bag manufacturers provide some sort of large, non-compressing laundry sack for storage. If you can't fully stretch out your sleeping bag uncompressed, such as under a bed, these laundry sacks are a great alternative. They protect your sleeping bag while minimally compressing the insulation, helping to extend the life of the bag.

Laundering Your Sleeping Bag

Laundering a sleeping bag is not something most people think to do regularly, but it can make a big difference in comfort, especially in extreme conditions. During my earlier Denali expeditions, I didn't think to launder my Western Mountaineering Puma bag, and I ended up suffering from horrible stuffy noses. It wasn't until my 2024 Denali expedition that I made the change, washing the bag before heading up. The result? Zero stuffy nose, no panic breathing, and far better sleep.

Down sleeping bags aren't easy to wash—down is delicate, and the washing process requires careful attention. Nikwax makes a down wash specifically designed for cleaning sleeping bags and other down-filled items. The bag should be washed in a commercial-sized washer, and it's essential to use a gentle, cold-water cycle. After washing, drying the bag can take a long time.

You'll need to use a dryer on a low heat setting or take it to a dry cleaning service. I tried the dry cleaner once, but I'm not sure how effective it was, as I didn't notice a significant difference in the results. When I laundered it myself, there were no problems, and my bag felt much fresher and more comfortable.

I suspect the unwashed bag had been causing my stuffy nose. I don't have allergies to down, but I believe the bag had accumulated dirt over time, which led to constant congestion that made me feel like I couldn't breathe properly. This feeling of being "claustrophobic" from the stuffy nose led to panicked, shallow breathing at night, which disrupted my sleep. After laundering the bag, all of that went away, and I was able to rest much easier at altitude.

If you're heading out on a demanding expedition, it's worth taking the time to properly launder your sleeping bag. It's a simple maintenance step that can make a huge difference in your overall comfort, ensuring better rest and performance while you're out there in the wilderness.

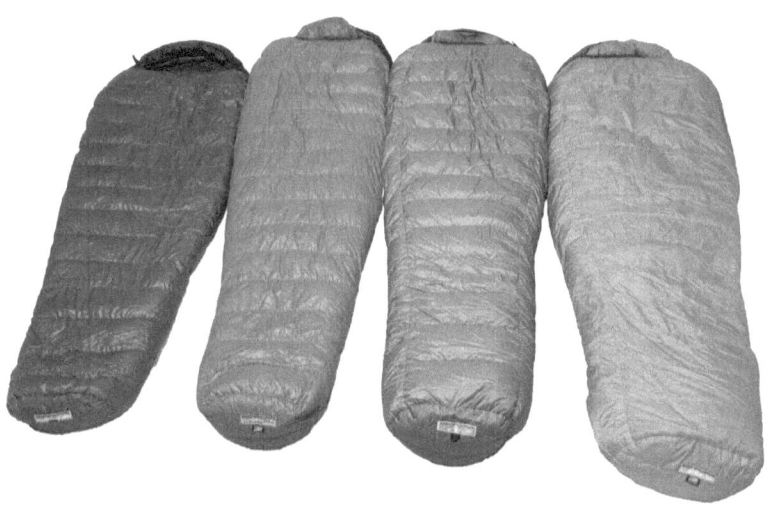

Choosing the right sleeping bag for the job from my collection of Western Mountaineering sleeping bags.
L-R: Megalite (30°F/-1°C), Antelope (5°F/-15°C), Puma (-25°F/-32°C), Bison (-40°F/40°C).

Chapter 5
Selecting Snow Travel Gear

Overview of Skis, Snowshoes, and Crampons

When planning a winter expedition, deciding how to travel on snow is crucial. Options range from walking in regular footwear to using sleds or skis, each with its own challenges. This guide outlines the pros and cons of various methods to help you choose the best approach for your journey.

Walking on Snow (Postholing)

If you're heading out where snow cover is thin, walking can be a solid option. While it might seem unconventional, it often works better than snowshoes or skis, which can be uncomfortable, ineffective, or even get damaged in these conditions.

That said, you'll likely need some kind of traction device to stay safe. For example, in places like Rocky Mountain National Park early in the season, trails can be icy even with minimal snow. Regular boots alone can be slippery, so consider using microspikes or a similar traction device to keep your footing secure.

Snowshoes

The best beginner option for winter camping travel is snowshoes. They're relatively inexpensive, compatible with most footwear, and easy to learn. Once you strap them on, you can walk over the snow with ease and confidence.

Types of Snowshoes

There are as many types of snowshoes as there are traction devices on the market, but they generally fall into three main categories: recreational, backcountry, and racing.

Recreational Snowshoes

Recreational snowshoes are relatively inexpensive and widely available, often found at big box stores. They are designed for casual use on groomed trails or flat terrain but aren't built for carrying heavy loads or tackling rugged backcountry conditions.

These snowshoes are a great option if you're looking to try snowshoeing without making a big upfront investment. If you enjoy the experience, upgrading to durable backcountry snowshoes designed for tougher conditions and longer trips will feel worth it. This way, you avoid the disappointment of buying expensive gear you might never use again.

Some recreational snowshoes come with integrated crampons, and a few kits even include trekking poles, giving you an easy way to get started with minimal effort.

Backcountry Snowshoes

Backcountry snowshoes are built for heavy-duty use and designed to handle tough winter terrain and freezing temperatures. Modern snowshoes typically feature aluminum frames with synthetic decking or composite plastics, making them durable and reliable for rugged conditions. Some high-end models are now fully composite, offering lighter weight and compact storage compared to aluminum-framed versions.

Traditional wooden snowshoes with rawhide lacing are still available but are much less common today, mostly used by enthusiasts who appreciate their classic design and craftsmanship.

Some backcountry snowshoes are lightweight, while others are heavier and more rugged, depending on the materials and design. As features become more technical, the price increases.

Popular options for backcountry use include models like the MSR Evo, the now-discontinued MSR Denali, and various Tubbs snowshoes. The MSR Evo is widely known for its durability and reliability, making it a favorite for rental shops and guiding services. Tubbs snowshoes offer a range of models that balance durability with lightweight performance.

All of these are excellent choices for serious backcountry adventures.

Racing Snowshoes

Snowshoe racing is a real activity, and it uses ultra-light snowshoes designed specifically for speed. These snowshoes are typically paired with lightweight shoes and work best on packed snow or groomed trails. The focus is entirely on speed, with everything else being secondary.

While racing snowshoes are durable enough for their intended purpose, they aren't built for rugged backcountry terrain or carrying heavy loads. They also perform poorly in deep powder due to their minimal surface area, which limits flotation. If your goal is to go ultra-light and fast, they're a great option to consider.

Choosing the Right Snowshoes

How do you choose the right snowshoe for your outdoor activity? The first thing to consider is the type of terrain you'll encounter—not just on your first outing but over time, especially if you're investing in a higher-quality pair.

For flat terrain, like the northern woods, almost any snowshoe that can support your weight will work. However, for mountainous or steep terrain, snowshoes with crampons are essential for safety.

The size of the snowshoe also matters. Larger snowshoes provide more float, which is critical for traveling through light, airy powder, while smaller snowshoes are better for compact, wet snow. Some models include extendable tails, letting you adjust for varying snow conditions. These are great for switching between heavy, compacted snow and deep, fluffy powder.

Snowshoe sizes
Men's models generally need longer and wider snowshoes to match their stride.
Women's models are narrower for a more comfortable gait.
Unisex models snowshoes work for many, but smaller users may find women's models provide a better fit and easier stride.

Integrated crampons are another key feature. These traction devices, built into most snowshoes, help grip icy or uneven surfaces, making them a must for hilly or mountainous terrain. Even budget snowshoes from big box stores often include crampons, though their performance can vary. Some models struggle with side-hilling (walking across slopes), even with crampons. Snowshoes with traction rails or aggressive side crampons dig in much better, preventing slippage on angled terrain and making side-hilling safer.

Another key feature to consider is heel lifts. In flat terrain, like the northern woods of Minnesota, you won't need a heel lift. But if you plan on hiking steep terrain, a heel lift makes all the difference, reducing calf strain by improving your foot angle when climbing steep slopes.

Snowshoe Binding Types

There are many types of snowshoe bindings designed to attach your feet securely. Most snowshoes allow you to use your own boots, as integrated or specialized snowshoe boots are rare these days. If possible, test your boots with your snowshoes in-store to ensure a good fit. If you're ordering online, check the specs to make sure the bindings can handle your boot size.

Bindings come in various styles, including three- or four-strap systems and different heel grips. Some systems are easier to adjust while wearing gloves or mittens, like simple buckle or ratchet designs, which can be helpful in extreme cold.

Be aware that certain materials, like rubber straps, can stiffen or even break in sub-zero conditions. Plastic ratchet bindings may also become brittle or crack in extreme cold, so flexible materials like nylon webbing tend to perform better in severe conditions.

Each binding type has its pros and cons. The key is to find one that:
- Grips your boots confidently.
- Is easy to adjust.
- Doesn't crush the top of your foot.

If you have to over-tighten the bindings to keep your feet secure, you'll compress your boot's insulation, which can lead to cold feet or even injury. A good fit balances comfort, security, and usability, especially in cold weather.

Snowshoe Field Maintenance Tools

When heading out with snowshoes, it's smart to bring a basic repair kit in case something breaks, like crampon pins or bindings.

A reliable multi-tool is a must, along with a small spool of steel or aluminum wire. Duct tape, zip ties, and spare parts specific to your snowshoes, like extra clevis pins or straps, can also be lifesavers.

A multi-tool can help you bend or pry metal parts back into place if they break. Paracord works well for lashing damaged snowshoes together, but zip ties or duct tape can sometimes provide a stronger, more secure fix.

If things get really rough, you can use wire or paracord as stitching material and cut small holes with your multi-tool to lash things back together.

With these tools, you can keep your gear working and avoid a miserable post-holing trek home. A little preparation can mean the difference between a tough walk and confidently making it back.

Skis for Backcountry Travel

Using skis for backcountry travel and winter camping is a great option. You can cover much greater distances compared to snowshoes, without the constant lifting of your feet. While skis require more technical knowledge and skill, once you gain that expertise, their capabilities far exceed those of snowshoes.

However, in dense brush, skis may not be the best choice. Depending on the terrain you plan to travel through, you'll need to weigh the pros and cons of skis versus snowshoes.

Backcountry Ski and Binding Types

There are several types of skis for backcountry travel. The classic Alpine ski, commonly used at ski resorts, isn't practical for backcountry travel because it keeps your foot fixed to the ski.

The next type is the classic cross-country ski, which typically uses either an NNN-BC (New Nordic Norm Backcountry) binding or a 75mm three-pin binding. These are the most common designs for backcountry travel.

NNN-BC bindings provide more support and durability than standard NNN bindings, making them better suited for backcountry conditions.

Standard NNN bindings are lighter but are primarily designed for groomed trails and light touring.

With these bindings, your heel is never attached to the ski, making it difficult to turn or go downhill. Some three-pin bindings include a cable attachment, which improves control, strength, and efficiency.

Another option is Telemark bindings, designed for ski turning. While some Telemark setups can be heavier, modern lightweight models have improved backcountry suitability. However, certain setups remain less ideal for long-distance travel.

A great hybrid option is technical bindings, which provide versatility. These bindings allow you to travel uphill or on flat ground, and when needed, you can lock your heel into the binding for better downhill control and performance.

For denser forest travel, short hybrid Siberian-style skis are an excellent choice. These skis are shorter and wider than traditional cross-country skis, making them more maneuverable in tight brush and wooded areas. They provide better flotation in soft snow and are easier to turn, making them ideal for navigating dense terrain. These skis are often used with free-heel bindings, similar to Telemark bindings, for better control on varied terrain.

Finally, there are skate skis, which are ultra-thin skis designed for speed and long distances. While they aren't typically used for backcountry travel, some ultramarathoners, like those in the Arrowhead 135 in Minnesota, use skate skis with backpacks to cover extreme distances. However, skate skis require packed or firm snow, making them impractical in deep powder or variable terrain.

Backcountry Ski Design

The best way to start when choosing backcountry skis is to visit a local ski shop, as models and techniques evolve regularly, and there are many options to consider.

For most backcountry travel, you'll want a relatively narrow ski for easier tracking. Wider skis are more common in downhill skiing, but they aren't necessarily heavier. The weight of a ski depends more on its construction and materials than on its width. However, wider skis provide better flotation in deep snow, making them a good choice for off-trail skiing. Alpine Touring skis work well for both uphill and downhill, offering great versatility.

Classic backcountry skis typically range around 90mm in width—wider than skate skis but narrower than downhill skis. Factors such as camber and ski flex should also be considered, depending on how much travel you plan to do.

One important factor is whether the ski has a steel edge running along its length. Lighter-duty backcountry skis, like the Rossignol BC 90, have metal edges along the sides but not on the tips or tails.

Norwegian expedition skis also lack steel on the tail to save weight. For rougher conditions, a full metal edge, including on the tips, improves durability and control on icy and hard-packed snow.

However, full metal edges add weight and stiffness, which may not always be beneficial in deep powder. If flotation and maneuverability in soft snow are your primary concerns, a partial steel edge might be a better choice.

Hybrid Short Skis

Another design that has gained popularity in recent years is the hybrid Siberian-style short ski. These skis offer great flotation, giving you the benefits of skiing without the challenges of longer skis—such as getting snagged on undergrowth or stumbling along narrow trails.

Their growing popularity makes them an excellent alternative for those seeking a more maneuverable choice.

Ski Binding Types

Just like skis, new ski bindings are developed every year. The most classic binding types on cross-country skis are the three-pin and NNN-BC (New Nordic Norm Backcountry) designs, which offer more support for off-trail travel. These bindings are great for long-distance travel and carrying heavy loads with your skis. Each design has its advantages and disadvantages, depending on your activity, but they are reliable and can handle the job well.

The technical bindings popularized by the Dynafit brand feature a spring-loaded pin that attaches to the toe of the boot, while the heel locks into the binding. These bindings are lightweight, versatile, and very reliable, especially the all-metal versions, which can withstand a lot of wear. They also offer a unique feature: they can switch between walking mode, where you're locked in, and skiing mode, where the ski pops off in a crash to help prevent injury.

There are also Silvretta bindings and flexible plate bindings, which allow you to use regular boots. While these bindings aren't as common in the backcountry, they let you use different types of boots for travel.

Silvretta bindings allow for the use of mountaineering boots, making them useful for ski-mountaineering, but they are inefficient for ultra-long-distance flatland travel, such as skiing to the South Pole. However, if you find them and they work with your boots, they can be a decent option for short trips or getting into the outdoors without needing specialized gear.

Ski Dimensions and Types

Two important factors to consider when choosing skis are length and width, based on your weight and the type of traction they offer. If you choose skis that are too long for you—designed for a heavier person—you might not be able to properly engage the traction on the bottom.

If possible, head to a dedicated ski shop for advice on choosing the right skis. Staff at specialized shops are more likely to understand the conditions you'll be facing and can help ensure you're selecting the right equipment for your specific needs.

Author's Note

My first pair of skis for backcountry travel were Rossignol BC 90s in a 205 length. I wanted as much float as possible for my Yellowstone expedition. That was a huge mistake. The skis were recommended to me, but they were designed for someone much heavier.

When I arrived in Yellowstone and started skiing, I couldn't press the traction pattern into the snow, making it impossible to pull my sled. I ended up switching to the snowshoes I had brought and snowshoed over 105 miles (170 kilometers) across Yellowstone. It was a tough grind, but it was a valuable lesson in making sure I get the right gear for the job next time.

Ski Traction Types

The variety of traction types on skis is as diverse as the ski types and bindings themselves. One traditional method for cross-country skis is using grip wax, selected based on the temperature you'll be skiing in. There are two main types of wax: glide wax and grip wax.

Glide wax is applied to the areas of the ski that slide over the snow, minimizing friction. Grip wax, when chosen for the right temperature, provides excellent traction without adding extra weight or complexity.

However, grip wax must match the temperature range, and if conditions change dramatically, you'll have to remove and reapply it, which can be a hassle. Because of this, grip wax isn't as popular as it once was.

Another common traction method for cross-country skis is a scale pattern in the kick zone—the area of the ski where you push off the snow. When you lift your foot, the scale pattern doesn't engage, allowing the ski to glide smoothly. But as soon as you step down, the pattern digs into the snow, providing traction.

These scale patterns—whether rounded, rectangular, or another shape—provide traction for moderate inclines and hauling a sled, but they may struggle on steep slopes or icy conditions.

Skins for Ski Traction

Another type of traction device is the skin. Skins are strips of fuzzy fabric that glide in one direction and grip in the other. They are detachable and reattachable, typically full-length, covering from the tip to the tail of the ski. These are commonly used by Alpine touring skiers who need to travel up steep terrain.

For ultra-long treks, kicker skins are often used. Some skiers permanently screw them to the bottom of the skis to prevent them from stripping away. This method is more durable for extended travel, eliminating the risk of skins slipping off or needing to be reattached. However, for long distances on flat ground, full-length skins create significant drag, making them inefficient. This is where kicker skins excel.

Kicker skins are a high-performance replacement for traction or scale patterns. They are only attached to the middle part of the ski, so they don't contact the snow when gliding forward. When you press down, the fibers grip the snow, providing excellent traction.

One downside of skins is that they can accumulate ice and snow, especially when skiing through temperature variations that cause moisture buildup. Applying anti-glop wax helps reduce this issue. Some skins also have sticky, reusable glue, allowing them to stay attached without permanent adhesives.

Skin Care and Material Types

Skins should generally be removed at night, especially if they're removable, to protect the ski base. Leaving them on can cause the adhesive to bond too strongly, making removal difficult and possibly leaving residue behind.

There are two main types of skin materials:
Mohair skins offers superior grip but wears out faster.
Nylon skins provides better glide but is more prone to icing in humid conditions.
Hybrid skins combine mohair and nylon to balance traction and durability.

Author's Note

On Terry's and my expedition across Greenland, Terry used 100% mohair kicker skins and had no issues with snow or ice buildup. I, on the other hand, had a blend of nylon and mohair.

As conditions warmed, my nylon-mohair blend skins began to

retain moisture, leading to snow and ice buildup on the bottom of my skis. At times, 4 inches (10 cm) of snow stuck to the bottom of my skis, making movement exceedingly difficult.

Since then, I no longer use skins with nylon or, if I do, I choose the lowest nylon percentage possible because of that experience.

Ski Maintenance

Regular maintenance—like waxing, edge sharpening, and base repairs—makes a big difference in your skiing experience.

Wax your skis regularly, following the manufacturer's guidelines, to reduce friction and keep the bases in good condition.

Sharp edges are essential for control, especially on icy snow. While a professional tune-up ensures precision, minor edge maintenance can be done at home with a file or diamond stone.

For base repairs, minor dings can be fixed at home, but for bigger damage, it's smart to take your skis to a shop. They can grind the base and make necessary repairs.

Regular maintenance will improve your skiing and extend the life of your skis.

Ski Boots

Choosing the right ski boot depends on the conditions, temperature, terrain, and what you'll be doing. Ski boots can be flexible or stiff and are designed to work with different types of bindings, such as cross-country, backcountry, or alpine touring. The binding type you choose will heavily influence the boot you need, so it's essential to match them up correctly.

Visiting a ski shop and getting professional advice is the best way to go for boot fit and selection.

Ski boots range in price from a few hundred dollars for light-duty cross-country models to over $1,000 for high-performance alpine touring boots or heavy-duty Norwegian designs.

The terrain, temperature, and effort you plan to put in will all impact your boot choice. Make sure to consider what you'll be doing most often to find the right fit.

Ski Poles

Using ski poles is highly recommended whether you're snowshoeing, skiing, or just traveling on foot.

For skiing, poles are practically a necessity for stability and balance. They come in fixed or collapsible designs. You can even use trekking poles for snowshoeing in a pinch.

For long-distance treks with backcountry or expedition skis, longer poles are usually better because they help improve your push. When skiing, you want your pole to be as far back as possible to push forward, not upward.

Short poles are useful for ski mountaineering, where long poles can get in the way. This is where collapsible poles shine.

Many modern poles use twist-lock systems that are lightweight and simple, but they can slip if they get wet or icy. Lever-lock (or clamp-lock) poles allow for easy adjustments—you can shorten them uphill and lengthen them downhill. However, they tend to be a bit heavier than fixed poles.

Choosing the Right Ski Poles

Think about the terrain you'll be covering:

Flat, open areas: Longer poles work best.

Rugged terrain: Long poles can become a hassle, so adjustable poles are ideal.

Make sure the lever-lock mechanisms are working properly—cold temperatures can compress plastic parts, affecting how well they lock. Having a multi-tool handy to make adjustments can save you a lot of trouble in extreme cold.

Snow Baskets and Pogies

Snow baskets are essential. Regular summer baskets aren't designed for snow and will just punch through. The right snow basket will help your poles float on top of the snow, making your trek much easier.

Another tool to add to your skiwear kit is pogies.

Pogies, commonly used in winter cycling and paddling, can also be used for skiing.

These insulated covers slip over the tops of your ski poles, allowing you to insert your hands while wearing gloves, adding an extra layer of warmth.

If you choose commercially made pogies, make sure they are somewhat loose-fitting. Otherwise, inserting your hands with gloves can be awkward and difficult.

Custom pogies are also a great choice. Use windproof fleece to make them, and add an attachment point so you can secure them to your parka, preventing them from flopping off in the wind.

Backcountry Ski Tools and Supplies

A reliable multitool is essential for fixing issues that arise with your skis and boots. A snub-nose or needle-nose multitool can mean the difference between keeping your gear working or walking home.

For long-distance trips, bring a tin of glide wax. In sub-zero temperatures (-18°C and below), snow becomes more crystalline. In polar conditions, it can feel like sand, as it barely melts or doesn't melt at all when you ski across it. This kind of abrasive snow will strip off glide wax over time, gradually adding drag to your skis.

Other Traction Gear

Another traction device to consider when traveling in snowy terrain is a pair of microspikes or crampons.

Microspikes

A micro-spike-style traction device functions like chains for your boots. It consists of a stretchy rubber harness or strap that wraps around your boot, providing traction through stainless steel spikes connected by chains underfoot. Yaktrax models use metal coils or chains for grip on packed snow.

Popular brands include Kahtoola Microspikes and Yaktrax. These are great for most boots and provide solid traction. They might be enough for your first winter outing.

Microspike spikes are short—about half an inch (1.3 cm) tall—and the points are usually dull. There's less risk of damage wearing them. If you step on yourself, you're less likely to tear your clothes or puncture your gear. Proper fit matters—Make sure to check the manufacturer's sizing chart, as some models run small over insulated winter boots, and you may need to size up.

Microspikes are ideal for icy paths, light trails, and beginner-friendly routes. On easier trails in places like Rocky Mountain National Park, they can be a good alternative when snowshoes or skis aren't necessary. They're simple to use, packable, and versatile for light winter hiking.

While microspikes aren't designed for steep or technical terrain, they're an excellent starting point for most people venturing into winter conditions for the first time.

Crampons

By comparison, crampons are built for steeper or more technical terrain. They come in various styles, including lightweight aluminum models for snow travel and heavy-duty steel crampons for ice and mixed terrain.

Crampons provide far better traction than microspikes but are bulkier. They require stiff-soled boots for proper use. For most beginner-level outings, microspikes are more than sufficient. Crampons are best suited for technical climbing, mountaineering, or glacier travel.

As with other equipment, there are multiple types of crampons designed for different uses. They come in 10- and 12-point models, with some specialized 14-point designs. More points generally improve traction on steep terrain, but their effectiveness also depends on the shape and angle of the front points.

10-point crampons are lighter and fine for easier travel but are not suited for heavy-duty mountaineering. For steep or potentially dangerous conditions, 12- or 14-point models are the best choice.

Most crampons are steel, offering high durability, but aluminum models exist for lighter travel. Steel crampons can handle short stretches of walking on rocks, but this dulls the points, reducing their effectiveness on ice.

Binding Types

Crampons have different binding systems, and the right choice depends on your boots. Choosing the right crampons means considering your boots, the terrain, and your planned activity. Universal bindings with horizontal points work for most beginner trips. Hybrid or automatic systems with vertical points are better for technical adventures.

Universal Binding
- Uses straps to secure the crampon.
- Works with most boots, including some flexible hiking models, but performs best with stiff-soled boots for improved stability.
- Most versatile option for general use.

Hybrid Binding
- Combines a strap-on toe with an automatic locking heel.
- Requires boots with a rear welt for the heel lock to engage properly.
- While adjustable, won't work with boots that lack the necessary welt.

Automatic Binding
- Uses a steel toe bail and an automatic locking heel.
- Provides the most secure fit but requires stiff-soled boots with both toe and heel welts.
- Ideal for technical climbs.
- Universal and hybrid crampons rely on straps, while automatic models use a rigid toe bail and heel clip for primary attachment.
- Be aware that soft boots without a shank can flex too much, making it harder for crampons to stay securely attached or maintain traction.

Crampon Point Styles
Crampon points are designed for specific conditions. Each style has its uses and drawbacks.

Glacier Travel Points
- Horizontal points spread weight evenly for stability on snow and softer ice.
- Best for general mountaineering and glacier travel.
- Not the best for substantial vertical ice climbing.

Ice Climbing Points
- Vertical blades designed to bite into hard ice.
- Available in single- or dual-point configurations.
- Some models have removable points to replace worn tips after heavy use.
- While perfect for ice climbing, they're heavier and overkill for basic winter camping.

Crampon Boot Choices
The most important thing to consider with crampons is the type of terrain you'll be traveling on and the boots you're wearing. Not all boots are compatible with crampons.

The stiffness of the boot sole and the presence of a shank (a rigid insert in the sole) play a big role in functionality. Soft-soled boots without a shank aren't suitable for crampons. They flex too much, making it hard for the crampon to stay secure and reducing traction. These boots are better suited for microspikes or light traction devices.

Boot Compatibility by Binding Type

Universal bindings work with boots that have a little flex. Hybrid or automatic crampons require boots with welts—rigid edges at the toe and heel that lock the crampon in place. If you try using hybrid or automatic crampons with boots that lack welts, they won't attach securely which can lead to accidents. For larger boots or double/triple mountaineering boots, some manufacturers sell extension bars to ensure the crampons fit properly. These can be a lifesaver if you're working with bulkier footwear.

Crampon Maintenance

Steel crampons need regular sharpening to stay effective. Focus on sharpening the edges of the front and primary points, as these take the most wear, while secondary points may not need as much maintenance. This method keeps the crampons sharp and functional without weakening the structure. Do not sharpen the outside surface of the points. Thinning the steel can cause the points to dull faster and increase the risk of bending or breaking over time.

Aluminum crampons are designed primarily for snow or glacier travel and will wear down quickly if used frequently on hard ice. They are not suited for repeated sharpening, as the softer metal degrades faster with grinding.

Microspikes do not require sharpening, but their small spikes can wear down over time, so regular inspection is recommended to ensure they still provide adequate traction.

Backpacks and Sleds

For winter travel, you'll need either a backpack, a sled, or both to carry your gear. Winter activities require heavier insulation layers and additional equipment for safe snow travel, which adds weight to your load.

For longer trips or to reduce strain on your back, a sled can be a great option. Sleds are commonly used in areas like Denali, the Boundary Waters in Minnesota, and other northern locations. However, a backpack is essential for nearly all winter camping, even in polar travel, where a harness and sled are typically used, but a small pack may still carry critical items.

Backpack Types

There are several types of backpacks used for winter camping. One of the most important considerations is durability and volume. Due to the increased gear requirements, you'll need a larger backpack than what is typically used for summer trips. Packs in the 60-90 liter range are common, depending on trip length and conditions.

Frameless backpacks are ultralight and have no internal structure. While they've gained popularity in recent years, they typically lack support for heavier loads, though some ultralight models include removable back panels for limited structure. They might work for short trips or specialized ultralight setups but are rarely the best choice for winter travel, where extra insulation and gear are required.
Internal frame backpacks have stiffeners made of aluminum, carbon fiber, plastic, or composite materials built into the pack. From the outside, only the fabric is visible. These are the most popular option for winter camping, offering good support for heavy loads while keeping the frame protected from the cold.
External frame backpacks feature a visible metal or carbon fiber frame with the pack attached. These are useful for base camp setups or carrying heavy expedition loads or irregularly shaped gear that won't fit inside a standard pack. However, they are less practical for long-distance travel due to their heavier weight. The exposed frame on older models can be uncomfortable or even cause skin damage in cold conditions if touched with bare hands, though some modern designs reduce this risk with padding. While still functional, external frames are now more of a niche option, mainly used for hunting, portaging, or hauling heavy loads.

Choosing the Right Backpack

The best backpack depends on your trip and terrain. For long-distance travel, internal frame backpacks are the most versatile, balancing support and comfort. Frameless backpacks might work for short, light trips but generally aren't suited for winter. External frames are great for specific uses like hauling irregular loads but are heavier and less streamlined for longer distances. Winter camping requires careful planning, so match your pack to your needs and destination.

Backpack Features

Modern backpacks come with a wide array of features, but for winter travel, there are a few essentials to focus on: a waist belt, load lifters, sternum strap, attachment points, and pockets.

Waist Belt

A waist belt is critical for carrying substantial loads. Without one, as in frameless, beltless backpacks, all the weight rests on your shoulders. For loads over 10 pounds (5 kilograms), this can quickly become uncomfortable. Additionally, overtightened shoulder straps can compress insulation, creating cold spots.

A good waist belt helps transfer most of the load to your hips and legs, reducing strain on your shoulders and spine. A properly fitted and comfortable waist belt is key to an enjoyable winter backpacking experience.

Load Lifters

Load lifters are straps attached to the top of the shoulder straps. Pulling them slightly shifts the weight forward, reducing pressure on your shoulders while maintaining pack control.

Many retail stores incorrectly recommend fully resting shoulder straps on your shoulders. While this is common advice, it can lead to chafing and discomfort. Proper use of load lifters allows the weight to be balanced more effectively, significantly improving comfort.

Additional Features

Outer Pouches: Useful for water bottles and quick-access gear.
Gear Loops and D-Rings: Found on waist belts and shoulder straps, they're ideal for attaching tools, carabiners, or other essentials.
Weatherproofing: Consider zippers with waterproofing to reduce the chance of them freezing shut. Fully waterproof backpacks are rare and often impractical for winter use. Snow typically slides off, but in conditions where snow might melt, the top and sides of the pack can get wet. A completely sealed waterproof pack limits accessibility, making loading and unloading a challenge.

Rain Covers

Rain covers are less common in winter since they can complicate access to the pack and are prone to snagging on trees or blowing off in high winds. However, in wet snow or mixed conditions, they may provide added protection. Focusing on these features will help ensure your pack is comfortable, functional, and suited to the demands of winter travel.

How Big of a Backpack Do You Need?

There are endless debates online about what size backpack you should buy. The answer depends heavily on your activity and the duration of your trip.

For mountaineering, larger backpacks are essential, and a 100-liter pack for Denali is about right. Even then, you'll likely need to strap additional gear to the outside. For regular winter travel, a 60- to 70-liter pack works well for most people. However, for hardcore mountaineering, these sizes won't carry enough food, fuel, and gear to sustain a longer trip or summit attempt.

Smaller backpacks in the 40- to 60-liter range are excellent for overnight trips. With a lightweight sleeping bag rated to 0°F (-18°C) and compact gear, you can fit everything you need into a smaller pack. These are a great entry point into winter camping, as they reduce expense and load while still allowing you to experience the outdoors.

When in doubt, go with a bigger backpack. It's better to have extra space than to struggle to fit all your winter essentials.

Sleds and Harnesses

Sleds are a popular choice for winter camping, offering a way to carry heavy loads with less strain. Options range from inexpensive children's sleds available at local stores to high-end carbon fiber sleds costing thousands of dollars, designed for polar expeditions.

One of the most commonly used sleds is the orange Paris Expedition sled. These sleds are widely available and great for packed snow or relatively flat terrain, but they may struggle in deep powder or steep slopes without modifications. Other options include toboggans or, for minimalists, a heavy plastic sheet with attachment points. However, plastic sheets only work for very light loads and flat terrain, as they lack stability for bigger gear hauls.

Tub-style sleds can carry more gear but are heavier. Sleds with runners lift the load off the ground, reducing drag and making them easier to pull, but they add weight and are less effective in soft, wet snow. Attaching skis to a sled is another way to reduce drag on flat terrain, making travel easier in places like Minnesota or Yellowstone during winter. However, this setup can make sleds less stable on uneven ground and on hills, an unrestrained sled can slide ahead uncontrollably, potentially colliding with you or causing a fall. Adding brakes, drag ropes, or anchors can help mitigate this issue.

Sleds require a harness for pulling, either a specialized hip or cross-shoulder harness. Attaching a rope directly to your backpack may work for lighter loads but can cause discomfort, throw off balance, and put excessive strain on the pack's frame and straps when hauling heavier gear. The right harness setup makes a big difference in managing the load safely and comfortably.

Connecting the Sled to the Harness

There are two main ways to connect a sled to your harness: using a rope or using poles.

Rope Towing

The simplest setup involves a single 6 mm rope or accessory cord attached to the sled. This method is lightweight and easy to use but has drawbacks. As the rope goes taut with each stride, the shock can transfer to your back and waist, causing discomfort or even injury over time. Adding a coiled bungee cord to the rope helps absorb these shocks and reduce strain.

For downhill control, drag ropes tied to the bottom of the sled can prevent it from overtaking you. Use 6 mm cords loosely attached under the sled to create friction, adding more loops for steeper hills. On extremely steep slopes, such as Squirrel Hill on Denali, maintaining full control of the sled becomes nearly impossible. In these situations, the sled may slide below you, forcing you to hold onto it as you descend. This is a dangerous situation but often unavoidable in such conditions. Maintaining balance and controlling the sled's speed are critical for navigating safely.

Pole Towing

Poles offer more control by keeping the sled from overtaking you and maintaining a safe distance. Some setups use straight poles, while others cross them for added stability depending on the terrain. However, poles can transfer the motion of your hips to the sled, causing it to sway, reducing efficiency over long distances. To counteract this, attach a short rope (about 4 inches or 10 cm) to each end of the poles. This absorbs movement while still keeping the sled under control on hills.

Poles can be tricky in uneven terrain or on side slopes. If the sled tips over, crossed poles may twist, pulling you off balance due to their rigid connection. Be mindful of how to unclip quickly in case of a tumble. In such conditions, ropes may be a better option, as they are less prone to tangling and easier to manage on rough terrain.

Key Considerations for Sled Connections

Each method has its pros and cons. Poles provide better control on downhill sections but require careful handling in uneven terrain. Ropes are simpler and more forgiving, though they rely on drag systems to prevent the sled from overtaking you. On extremely steep terrain, be prepared to manage the sled carefully, as full control may not always be possible. Choose a system that matches your terrain, load, and skill level.

Skiing across the Greenland icecap towing a sled.

(Left) Stepping over a crevasse with crampons.
(Right) That same crevasse a week later. The bottom is not visible.

Chapter 6
Stove Selection and Accesories

For winter camping, a stove serves multiple purposes. Not only is it essential for heating food in the evening and possibly in the morning, but it's also critical for melting snow or ice to produce drinking water. If you can't access an open water source during your trip, your stove becomes your primary tool for hydration.

Melting snow requires significant amounts of fuel, heat, and time to generate enough water for your daily needs. Planning for this is crucial, as it can directly impact the success and safety of your trip.

In this discussion, we'll cover the different stove types available, what to consider when choosing one, and other important factors to keep in mind for winter camping.

Stove Types

There are several types of stoves available for both summer and winter camping. The most common options are liquid fuel, canister fuel, multi-fuel, and wood stoves.

Liquid Fuel Stoves

Liquid fuel stoves are highly popular due to their wide availability and reliability. They are especially useful for heating food and melting snow in winter. These stoves typically use white gas, which burns hot and clean, making it an efficient choice for cold conditions. Some models can also burn unleaded gasoline or kerosene in a pinch, but these produce more soot and require additional maintenance.

Canister Stoves

Canister stoves are another popular option for winter campers. They are clean and convenient, eliminating the mess and risks associated with handling liquid fuel. Common fuels include isobutane, butane, and propane. However, these canisters can struggle in extremely cold temperatures because the fuel loses pressure as the temperature drops. Winter-specific fuel blends help, but performance can still decline in subzero conditions. Keeping the canister warm—such as storing it inside your jacket before use—can improve function.

Multi-Fuel Stoves

Multi-fuel stoves are ideal for international or remote trips where fuel availability is uncertain. These stoves can burn a variety of fuels, including white gas, gasoline, kerosene, and heptane. Their versatility makes them an excellent choice for adventurers traveling to areas with limited fuel options. However, they often require more maintenance, including regular cleaning and jet changes, depending on the fuel used.

Wood Stoves

In certain wilderness settings, a wood stove or wood fire can be an excellent choice for cooking food and melting snow. They require no packed fuel, as they rely on natural wood found in the environment. However, in deep snow or wet conditions, finding dry wood can be difficult, and wet wood burns inefficiently. Always follow local regulations and take precautions to manage fires safely, as wood fires can become dangerous if not properly controlled.

Stove Features to Look For

Choosing the right stove depends on your trip's conditions, the availability of fuel, and your personal preference for convenience versus versatility. Each type has its strengths, and selecting the best option for your needs is critical for a successful winter camping experience.

When you're considering your first stove options for a winter camping trip, there are several factors to take into account:

Cold Resistance: First, consider cold resistance. How well will this stove work in extreme cold? Is it specifically designed for winter conditions, or does it have features such as a fuel line running through the flame to help vaporize the fuel for better efficiency? Keep in mind that canister stoves tend to struggle in very cold temperatures due to pressure drops, unless they are inverted canister stoves or liquid-feed canister stoves, which perform better in extreme cold. Liquid fuel stoves generally offer more reliable performance in freezing conditions.

Ignition style: Next, consider ignition. What type of ignition source will you use? It's not the fuel itself that burns, but the fumes, which must vaporize properly for combustion. Liquid fuel stoves often include a pre-heating loop to facilitate this process. Ignition types vary—manual flint strikers, piezo igniters, or lighters—but piezoelectric igniters often fail in high-altitude or extreme cold due to conductivity issues. Always carry a backup ignition source, such as waterproof matches or a flint striker.

Flame control: Control is another key factor. Some mountaineering stoves are designed for raw power, offering only "blowtorch" or "off." If you need to cook actual food rather than just boiling water, look for a stove with simmering capability to allow finer flame adjustments.

Wind resistance: Wind resistance is equally important. How well can the stove operate in breezy conditions? Some stoves perform better with built-in windshields, while others require an external windscreen. Liquid fuel stoves benefit from windscreens, but using a windscreen around a canister stove can trap heat, causing dangerous pressure buildup. Always follow manufacturer guidelines when adding wind protection.

Fuel efficiency: Fuel efficiency and management are also critical. The more efficient the stove, the less fuel you'll need to bring—especially important when melting snow for water. Heat exchanger pots, such as those found in Jetboil or MSR Reactor systems, significantly improve efficiency by reducing heat loss. Environmental factors like wind and temperature impact efficiency, and the longer your trip, the more fuel-saving features matter.

Packability: Another consideration is how packable and lightweight—or heavy—your stove is. Some stoves are incredibly compact but may sacrifice efficiency when melting snow. Larger expedition-grade stoves are bulkier but often the best choice for extended winter trips where reliability and performance matter most.

Fuel container: Finally, consider the type of fuel container the stove requires. Many liquid fuel stoves use pressurized containers, requiring you to pump air into the fuel bottle for proper operation. Some alcohol and solid fuel stoves don't require pressurization, offering more flexibility in fuel storage and transport. White gas and kerosene stoves almost always require pressurization for consistent output, so understanding the requirements of your chosen stove is essential for safe and efficient use in winter conditions.

Fuel Bottles

The type of fuel bottle your stove requires depends on whether you are using a liquid pressurized stove like white gas, which requires a specialized fuel container. You will need to decide if a small container, like an 11 fl oz (325ml) bottle, a medium 20 fl oz (591ml) bottle, or a large 30 fl oz (887ml) container is suitable. The size you choose depends on whether you're alone or with others, which will also determine how often you need to refill. The fewer times you need to refuel, the fewer risks you incur. Each time you transfer fuel between containers, you risk spillage, fire if there's an open flame nearby, and cold burns from rapid fuel evaporation.

Another consideration is how to store your fuel. Fuels like white gas come in one-gallon or four-liter steel containers. Carrying these into the wilderness can be inconvenient due to their weight, and if damaged, you risk losing your entire fuel supply. A common failure occurs when a sled tips over, denting the container and causing a slow leak that can go unnoticed until fuel has spread over your gear. If this happens, the fuel can degrade certain materials, damage insulation, and pose a fire hazard.

A popular option among Arctic travelers is to decant fuel into multiple one-liter dedicated fuel bottles. These bottles are designed for durability, seal well, and reduce the risk of losing all your fuel if one container fails. As Dixie Dansercoer said in his book *Polar Exploration*, it's better to have a small army of fuel bottles than to rely on one or two large ones.

If you plan to transfer fuel from one container to another, consider how you will do it. The recommended method is to use a white gas funnel specifically designed for fuel transfer. This reduces the likelihood of spilling fuel and helps prevent it from getting on your fingers. At sub-zero temperatures (-18°C), spilled fuel evaporates quickly, drawing heat away from the skin and causing rapid cold burns, which can lead to frostnip or even frostbite if not addressed immediately.

If you are wearing fabric or leather gloves and spill fuel on them, the gloves may retain the smell for the rest of your trip, and the fuel can degrade certain synthetic materials, weakening insulation. If the fuel doesn't fully evaporate, it can ignite when you light your stove. Any spark or open flame nearby could turn fuel-soaked gloves into a fire hazard, leading to severe burns or potentially setting your tent on fire.

Stove Protection

All stoves need some form of wind protection. White gas, alcohol, and canister stoves are particularly susceptible to having air currents carry heat away or extinguish the flame. This can happen very easily. Typically, manufacturers include a thick sheet of aluminum foil that can be wrapped around your stove as a wind barrier. This is essential not only to prevent the stove from going out but also to avoid wasting fuel as heat escapes.

Another item to consider is a heat exchanger. It's a corrugated piece of aluminum that clamps to the outside of your pot, improving heat transfer by trapping more heat close to the pot or kettle. This increases fuel efficiency, helping you melt snow or cook faster while reducing fuel consumption. The added structure may also provide some stability, but its primary function is retaining heat.

Heat from the stove can melt the ground or snow underneath it, causing the stove to sink and tip. Over time, this uneven melting can make the pot or stove overturn, creating a dangerous situation. To avoid this, you need a stove base.

Many people use stove boards made from various materials with reflective metal or aluminum surfaces. These boards are especially useful because if your stove becomes unstable, leaks, or malfunctions, you can pick it up and toss it out of your tent. Yes, in extremely cold conditions, cooking in your tent may be necessary, though it's not ideal. Even with ventilation, carbon monoxide buildup can still be a risk. A small CO detector can provide an extra layer of safety. Severe weather often makes outdoor cooking impossible, especially on mountaineering trips like Denali expeditions.

Dedicated stove holders, such as the MSR XGK or WhisperLite Trillium Base, are another option. The Trillium Base is small and keeps the stove steady, but because the legs conduct heat into the snow, the stove may still slowly sink over time.

A simple and effective solution is using aluminum turkey pans or slightly thicker, reusable cooking trays. These lightweight pans provide an excellent base to prevent snow melting underneath and help stabilize the stove. They also catch spills, stopping fuel from leaking onto the ground. In an emergency, you can grab the pan and stove together and toss them out of the tent. This lightweight option works for both indoor and outdoor cooking, doubling as a container for a windscreen around the stove.

Stove Ignition

The type of ignition source you use to light your stove is crucial, as some options are more reliable than others. Certain ignition methods, like lighters, may struggle at high altitudes or in extremely low temperatures, sometimes requiring pre-warming before they function properly. Standard butane lighters, in particular, can fail due to both temperature and reduced oxygen levels at high elevations.

When relying on matches, it's important to consider how many to bring and whether they are waterproof. Matches can become completely soaked, so storing them in a waterproof container is essential for emergency use. However, over time, matches can absorb humidity and fail to ignite, regardless of what you do. Additionally, they require a reliable striking surface to work effectively.

One ignition method that always functions is a ferro rod. Ferro rods use ferrocerium and steel to generate sparks, making them effective at all altitudes and temperatures—from the desert to -50°F (-46°C) and beyond. The hot sparks can ignite any fuel, yet because they do not produce an open flame, there is minimal risk of damaging technical synthetic fabrics. Unlike a lighter, which may extinguish if dropped, ferro rods remain functional regardless of conditions. That said, disposable lighters still serve as a great backup system.

All ignition methods, including ferro rods, have limitations. If the fuel is too cold, it won't vaporize or evaporate, and only evaporating fuel can ignite. White gas, for example, will not give off flammable fumes if it's below its vaporization point, making ignition impossible.

Author's Note:
In winter camping, I've encountered situations where denatured fuel refused to ignite, even when exposed to a direct flame from a lighter or match. It was simply too cold. I have also faced the same issue with white gas in polar temperatures—no matter what flame source I used, the fuel wouldn't ignite.

In extremely cold conditions, pre-warming the fuel can make a significant difference. Keeping the fuel bottle inside your jacket for a while or warming the stove's fuel bowl by body heat can help. Even a small increase in temperature improves vaporization, making ignition easier. Remember, it's not the liquid fuel that burns, but the vapors it produces.

Fuel pumps are necessary for pressurizing liquid fuel to facilitate vaporization. However, these pumps are delicate and require careful handling. Regular maintenance is essential—not particularly difficult, but crucial to ensure reliable performance in the field.

Some campers use lighter paste or hand sanitizer as an ignition aid. However, hand sanitizer's effectiveness depends on its alcohol content, as some versions contain little to no alcohol and won't ignite reliably. Fuel paste is highly volatile and ignites more easily, but it burns at a lower temperature than liquid fuel. It can be placed in the stove's top cup to help vaporize the fuel, making ignition easier.

One effective method for lighting a white gas stove in extreme cold is to dribble a small amount of white gas onto the flame diffuser, then ignite it with a ferro rod or lighter. This technique works in all but the most severe conditions, where persistence is required to get the vapors ignited and the stove running.

Author's Note

Melting snow for water can be challenging and potentially damaging to your gear if you don't start with a small amount of liquid water. Without it, snow melts unevenly, creating hotspots that can crack or warp your pot. To avoid this, always begin with 2 to 4 ounces (60 to 120 milliliters) of liquid water in the bottom of the pot before adding snow. This ensures even heat distribution and prevents stress from uneven heating.

If you don't have liquid water, the process becomes far more difficult. You'll need to hold the pot several inches (about 8 to 10 centimeters) above the stove, as placing it directly on the burner without water can lead to severe damage, including warping or cracking. Without liquid to buffer the heat, the intense, uneven temperatures will quickly cause thermal stress. Holding the pot higher allows heat to rise and begin melting the snow gradually, but this method is labor-intensive and requires constant attention to prevent overheating.

It's critical to save enough liquid water at the end of each day. Without it, the next time you need to melt snow, you'll struggle to do so safely, putting yourself in an even more difficult situation.

I made this mistake during my first Yellowstone expedition, back when I was just starting out with long-distance winter travel and camping. I ran completely out of water during the day and had to melt snow in my mouth just to stay hydrated. This left me with no water to start melting snow in my pot. I knew the risk of the pot cracking, but I hadn't realized how difficult it would be to manage the process without any liquid to begin with.

I had to carefully add small amounts of snow to the pot and melt it slowly until I could accumulate at least 2 ounces (60 milliliters) of water—enough to start adding more snow in the normal way. The process was mentally exhausting. I sat hunched over my stove, hovering the pot above the heat while already dehydrated, cold, and tired. That experience taught me a hard lesson: I will never, by choice, arrive at camp again without some liquid water.

There's an old adage that says eating snow will make you more dehydrated. This is misleading. On one trip, I ran out of water about three hours before I could stop, and I learned the hard way that swallowing snow can cause significant stomach pain. The issue isn't dehydration but the fact that your body has to expend energy warming the snow, which can lead to discomfort or even mild shock to the digestive system. Instead, I let the snow melt in my mouth before swallowing. While this is a slow and frustrating method of hydration, it can be effective when you're completely out of options.

The myth comes from the idea that consuming cold snow lowers body temperature and can lead to hypothermia. While that could be true in some cases, it wasn't relevant for me—I was pulling a 130-pound (59-kilogram) sled, generating plenty of heat through exertion. My issue was dehydration, not hypothermia, and letting snow melt in my mouth helped me stay functional until I could stop, make camp, and carefully melt snow in my dry pot.

Cooking Gear and Utensils

The type of container you use and the food you plan to prepare are key considerations for backcountry cooking gear. If you're melting snow for water, a two-liter pot is ideal. Many people use an open pot with a lid, either with an integrated handle or a separate pot lifter. If you opt for a lifter, you'll need to keep track of it and maintain it. Titanium pots are popular for their durability and lightweight design, while aluminum is a more affordable but still effective alternative.

If you plan to cook meals, the type of pot or pan you choose depends on weight considerations and whether your stove can simmer. High-output stoves like the MSR XGK don't have a simmer mode and can scorch food, making cleanup difficult. Cleaning cookware in the field requires a scrubber, and waiting too long after cooking can cause food to freeze onto the pan, making cleanup even harder.

You'll also need to plan where to place your hot pot after cooking. Avoid setting it directly on snow, as the snow will melt and refreeze, causing the pot to stick. When you put the pot back on the stove, any snow or ice stuck to the bottom can melt and extinguish the flame, forcing you to reignite the stove and potentially wasting fuel.

Cooking Gear and Utensils

The type of container you use and the food you plan to prepare are key considerations for backcountry cooking gear. If you're melting snow for water, a two-liter pot is ideal. Many people use an open pot with a lid, either with an integrated handle or a separate pot lifter. If you opt for a lifter, you'll need to keep track of it and maintain it. Titanium pots are popular for their durability and lightweight design, while aluminum is a more affordable but still effective alternative.

If you plan to cook meals, the type of pot or pan you choose depends on weight considerations and whether your stove can simmer. High-output stoves like the MSR XGK don't have a simmer mode and can scorch food, making cleanup difficult. Cleaning cookware in the field requires a scrubber, and waiting too long after cooking can cause food to freeze onto the pan, making cleanup even harder.

You'll also need to plan where to place your hot pot after cooking. Avoid setting it directly on snow, as the snow will melt and refreeze, potentially creating an ice layer that makes the pot harder to pick up or causing it to freeze to surfaces like a sled or tarp. When you put the pot back on the stove, any snow or ice stuck to the bottom can melt and extinguish the flame, forcing you to reignite the stove and potentially wasting fuel.

Utensils

The utensils you bring depend on what you plan to eat. If you're just melting snow for water, you may not need utensils at all. A simple cup to scoop snow into your pot works fine, though you can often skip this by using compacted snow, which is denser and melts more efficiently. However, handling snow with gloves can wet them and contaminate your pot. Using a snow shovel to transfer snow is a better option, keeping both your gloves and the snow clean.

If you're eating freeze-dried meals, a spoon or spork is usually all you need. Plastic utensils are lightweight but can break in extreme cold. Titanium or steel utensils are heavier but far more reliable and can double as tools in a pinch. For example, the end of a titanium spoon can work as a makeshift screwdriver or pry bar. The one drawback of metal utensils is that they can freeze to your tongue in very cold weather. It's momentary but unpleasant, so be prepared.

If you're cooking more elaborate meals, you'll need utensils suited to your recipes. Plastic utensils are lightweight but can fail in freezing conditions, so test them by placing them in a freezer for a day or two, then using them quickly to see if they hold up. If they break, they're not the right tools for the job.

Water Containers and Thermos

Water bottles and containers are essential for any outdoor adventure, especially in winter. Primitive-style campers might improvise containers, but most rely on manufactured options. When you need to keep water warm or prevent it from freezing, a thermos is critical.

Thermoses come in a range of styles—wide-mouth, narrow-mouth, snap-top, double-insulated, or glass-insulated. Glass-insulated thermoses work well but are fragile and heavier than other options, making them less ideal for winter camping. Plastic thermoses are lighter but can crack in extreme cold.

Metal containers are durable and safe, but they transfer heat quickly. Without insulation, they lose heat fast and can be uncomfortable to handle in freezing temperatures. In extreme cold, exposed skin can stick to metal surfaces, causing frostbite or injury if pulled away too quickly.

Nalgene Bottles

For winter camping, Nalgene-style bottles are one of the gold standards. These one-liter, highly durable bottles fit well with most gear and withstand significant abuse. The main weak spot is the lid threads, which can get damaged by ice. For long trips, it's smart to bring an extra lid.

Opaque containers make it harder to spot contamination, like bacterial buildup, which can occur if water sits for too long after freezing and thawing repeatedly. Clear containers let you check for cleanliness at a glance, making them more practical.

Water Bladders and Their Limitations

Water bladders work well in warm climates but struggle in cold conditions. The bite valve, hose, and seals freeze easily, even with neoprene insulation. Frozen water inside can render the bladder useless, and trying to flex or squeeze it to break up the ice can cause cracks or leaks.

Nalgene bottles are far better for these conditions, as they handle freezing and impact much more reliably.

Author's Note

On a winter climb of Mount Whitney, I used a water bladder with an insulated tube. It froze solid before I reached camp, making it completely useless. Since then, I've avoided water bladders in cold weather.

Insulating Water Bottles

In very low temperatures, insulated sleeves for Nalgene bottles are essential. Neoprene sleeves provide some protection, but for extreme cold, the Outdoor Research SG Water Bottle Parka adds significant freeze resistance. These sleeves zip around the bottle and help prevent freezing, even in sub-zero conditions.

If a bottle lid freezes shut, warming it under your armpit can help. After drinking, avoid putting your lips directly on the threads, as this leaves bacteria and moisture that can freeze the lid shut. Always shake off excess water before sealing the bottle.

An improvised Whisperlite stove base using an empty steel white gas can on Denali.

Chapter 7
Communications, Electronics, Accessories

Effective communication is crucial in any winter expedition, especially when traveling in remote or challenging environments. This chapter covers communication equipment for staying connected, whether for safety, coordinating with a team, or ensuring help is available in an emergency. From satellite phones to two-way radios, understanding the strengths and limitations of each tool is essential for making informed decisions and maintaining reliable communication throughout the journey.

Comms Equipment

Communication equipment ranges from inexpensive radios to multi-thousand-dollar satellite phones. Your choice depends on how far you're going, your level of preparedness, and the kind of rescue support you might need.

When choosing communication equipment, prioritize reliability and durability. Test your devices before your trip, understand their limitations, and ensure you're equipped with what you need to stay safe in the wilderness.

Satellite Phones

Iridium satellite phones, like the Iridium Extreme 9575, are the gold standard for global communication, providing coverage in nearly every location, including Antarctica and the North Pole. However, like most satellite systems, the Iridium network can struggle under dense tree cover or in mountainous areas due to signal variability. At extreme latitudes, atmospheric conditions can also impact reception.

Satellite phones are invaluable for wilderness travelers, offering direct communication with rescuers or people at home. However, they come with downsides: high initial costs, ongoing subscription fees, and expensive per-minute charges (usually $1–$2). Many satellite plans don't allow unused minutes to roll over, so they must be managed carefully. Additionally, satellite phones are delicate, particularly the antenna, which can break if mishandled. Store them securely in your gear to prevent damage, as a broken antenna renders the phone useless. Check with a satellite phone provider for up-to-date plans and options.

One-Way and Two-Way Messaging Devices

One-way and two-way messaging devices have become increasingly popular. Devices like SPOT and Garmin inReach offer reliable options for staying connected with those at home.

SPOT devices provide one-way communication, ideal for position updates. However, missed check-ins can cause concern and may lead to unnecessary action if misinterpreted. Two-way devices like the Garmin inReach Explorer Plus allow you to confirm message delivery, reducing uncertainty.

Many of these devices pair with smartphones via Bluetooth, expanding their functionality. That said, smartphones can be unreliable in extreme conditions. Batteries drain rapidly in sub-zero temperatures, and touchscreens often fail in cold or wet environments. Avoid depending solely on a smartphone for communication in the backcountry.

Personal Locator Beacons (PLBs)

PLBs are simple and reliable devices designed for emergencies. Operating on the COSPAS-SARSAT satellite network, they transmit a single distress signal to summon help. Unlike other devices, PLBs have no additional features and are strictly for emergencies. They should be registered with the appropriate authority to provide rescuers with critical personal and trip details, improving response efficiency.

Be cautious with the emergency SOS feature on any device. Accidental activations can lead to unnecessary rescue responses and, in some areas, may result in fines or other consequences. Store devices securely to prevent accidental triggers.

Radios

Radios are a practical option for communication within a group or with others nearby. In the United States, FRS (Family Radio Service) radios are popular for team communication, such as among skiers on a mountain. These radios are simple to operate and require no licensing. For more range and capabilities, ham radios are an option, though they require a license in most countries.

When traveling internationally, check local regulations for radio permits. For example, Greenland requires permits for radio and satellite communication equipment. Compliance with local laws is crucial to avoid trouble during your trip.

A major advantage of radios is that anyone listening can respond. This sets them apart from satellite phones or cellular devices, which are point-to-point communication tools. For example, on a sailboat, a radio broadcast on channel 16 can quickly summon help from nearby vessels, while a phone call to someone far away might not be effective.

Marine radios are especially useful, as they connect to standard emergency channels like 16 and 9, as well as other maritime networks. In some locations, carrying a radio capable of these channels is mandatory. Always check local regulations to ensure compliance.

Smartphones and Cellular Networks

Some smartphones now include satellite SOS features, allowing emergency communication via satellite. These services, such as Apple's Emergency SOS via satellite, are typically text-based only and do not allow for full two-way messaging. Test this feature thoroughly before heading out, but don't rely on your smartphone as your only tool. Cell service is often nonexistent in remote areas, and smartphones are prone to damage, battery failure, and touchscreen issues, particularly in extreme conditions. Many accidents have occurred because people relied solely on smartphones for communication. Always have a backup.

Electronic Power Sources

All electronics require power, typically from batteries. While solar power can slowly recharge batteries, it's not generally practical for directly operating active electronics unless paired with efficient panels, consistent sunlight, and proper directionality. Even thin cloud cover or winter's limited daylight hours can render solar panels ineffective. Solar panels are also somewhat delicate—damaged connections or drops can make them unusable. If you plan to use them, secure them properly to your backpack or sled and keep a close eye on them during travel.

Battery Types and Considerations

What type of batteries will you bring? Are they built-in or replaceable? Common options include alkaline, nickel-metal hydride (NiMH), lithium-ion, lithium polymer, and primary lithium batteries. If you're using rechargeable batteries, how will you recharge them in the field?

Portable battery banks are a convenient solution. These typically have USB ports for charging devices and can be recharged themselves. For shorter trips, a couple of battery banks can handle most needs. Test them before your trip by placing your battery bank and electronics in a freezer for two days. This simulates cold conditions and helps you identify any issues. Cold significantly reduces battery performance, so if your gear fails this test, adjust your setup before heading out.

Battery Performance in Cold Conditions

Battery chemistry affects performance in freezing temperatures. Each has its advantages and disadvantages.

Alkaline batteries: Nearly useless in the cold due to rapid power loss.
NiMH batteries: Better than alkaline but still lose some efficiency and capacity.
Lithium-ion rechargeable batteries: Perform well overall, but some types (e.g., camera-specific) can lose power quickly in cold conditions.
Primary lithium batteries: Excellent in extreme cold. Products like Energizer Ultimate Lithium can function at temperatures as low as -40°F (-40°C) or lower.

For extreme cold adventures, primary lithium batteries are ideal. Pair them with a battery bank for recharging devices, but remember that charging efficiency decreases when electronics are cold. To maximize charging, warm your devices first by keeping them in your jacket or sleeping bag, perhaps alongside a hot water bottle.

Solar Power

Solar panels provide theoretically unlimited power but have limitations. In addition to requiring direct sunlight, they become far less efficient in cloudy or low-light conditions, such as during winter or in polar regions. Charging cold electronics is also inefficient, so warming devices before charging is critical.

Solar panels are best suited for longer trips in sunny conditions where they can supplement other power sources. However, they require careful handling—damaged wiring or connectors can render them useless.

Additional Power Source Notes

Battery extenders and range boosters may enhance performance, but test them thoroughly before relying on them in the field. Manufacturer claims don't always match real-world conditions, so preparation is key.

When choosing your power setup, focus on durability, reliability, and suitability for the environment you'll encounter. Proper testing and planning will save you from unpleasant surprises in the wilderness.

Headlamps

One of the most important tools to bring with you is a headlamp—and a backup headlamp. Headlamps can fail at the worst times, whether from battery depletion, switch malfunctions, or cold-induced issues. Winter camping means you'll spend a lot more time in the dark. In the depths of winter, it can get dark as early as 4 P.M., and the sun may not rise until 7 A.M. Make sure your headlamp lasts long enough for your trip, and always have a reliable backup.

There's a wide range of headlamps, from lightweight models to larger, more powerful ones. Keep in mind, heavier headlamps can be less comfortable and may flop down on your head. Simpler designs are often better, especially in extreme cold. Many headlamps have multiple features, but these can be a problem when it's -22°F (-30°C), and you're in a tent trying to figure out how to "tap twice and hold" to get the mode you need. While manufacturers market these features as a selling point, they're often impractical in the field. A simpler headlamp is usually the better choice.

Headlamp Battery Options: USB vs. Single-Use Cells

When choosing a headlamp, consider the type of batteries it uses. USB rechargeable headlamps are convenient, especially for shorter trips or if you have a reliable way to recharge them in the field. However, they lose efficiency in extreme cold and are harder to recharge unless kept warm. Single-use battery headlamps, like those using AA or AAA cells, let you carry spares and replace them easily. For winter conditions, lithium primary batteries are the best choice because they perform reliably in freezing temperatures, unlike alkaline batteries, which are nearly useless in the cold.

For a backup headlamp, choose something simple with a different power source to avoid relying on the same type of batteries or charging system. Redundancy can save you a lot of trouble when your primary headlamp fails.

Must-Have Accessories

Snow shovels are almost an absolute requirement for winter camping. There are a variety of designs and types available, ranging from highly durable models to ultra-light-duty options. Shovels can be made of plastic, aluminum, or steel and come in various sizes, from large grain scoops to small, foldable models that fit easily into a backpack.

Although plastic shovels are popular due to their lightweight construction and low cost, they are not ideal for tough winter camping conditions. When you encounter ice or hard-packed snow, plastic shovels often fail. This is especially critical in an avalanche rescue situation—once snow slides and stops, it compacts into a dense, cement-like consistency, rendering plastic shovels useless.

For serious winter camping, expeditions, and even overnight trips, a metal shovel—especially a hardened aluminum one—is the best choice. They are far more durable and capable.

Author's Note

On my second winter camping trip, I brought a small, snow claw scoop-style plastic shovel. I thought it was great because I had tested it beforehand. However, where I ended up camping, the snow was ultra-hard-packed. The shovel could only scrape the surface, making it impossible to dig effectively. This led to an uncomfortable night of sleep and made it nearly impossible to chisel out enough ice to generate water for drinking the next day. Suffice it to say, I don't bring plastic shovels anymore.

Aluminum shovels are a great choice because they are relatively lightweight, and some models are highly durable. However, some aluminum alloys can become brittle in extreme cold, particularly lower-grade or poorly manufactured models, increasing the risk of breakage.

Author's Note

I broke my aluminum shovel during an Antarctic expedition because I opted for a lightweight model from a low-cost manufacturer. That was a huge mistake. It caused a minor case of frostbite on my knees and made life difficult for weeks. Even though aluminum shovels may look similar, they are not all created equal. It is highly recommended to use an avalanche-rated 6061 aluminum shovel. These shovels can handle all but the hardest ice and chisel through compacted snow without failing. The edges won't compress or fold over.

In contrast, inexpensive, off-brand aluminum shovels from big-box stores or online retailers are far less durable. Under hard conditions, the edges of these shovels can fracture and develop burrs. These burrs can then slice through a tent or damage a sleeping pad without you realizing it.

Author's Note

During my expedition across Greenland with Terry Williams, featured in *Two Friends and a Polar Bear*, Terry chose a lighter, inexpensive shovel. While it was easier to carry, halfway through the expedition, the hard snow and ice we encountered caused the shovel's edge to fold and develop burrs. This made it impossible for him to shovel snow away from the tent because the sharp edges could have sliced through it. We ended up using my Voilé Telepro shovel for most of the hard work because his shovel was too light-duty. Additionally, the head of his shovel began flexing more and more with use because the aluminum wasn't hardened. Lesson learned: avoid cheap shovels—they're simply not worth it.

Steel shovels are another option, particularly for situations where you might encounter ultra-hard snow, such as at high camps on Denali. Even in less extreme locations, steel shovels can handle conditions where aluminum shovels might struggle and plastic shovels would fail completely. Although steel shovels are much heavier, they are capable of chiseling through all but the hardest surfaces.

One significant advantage of steel shovels is that many models have a folding head. This allows the shovel to compact down, reducing the likelihood of damaging your equipment and making it easier to fit into a backpack or sled. Additionally, folding-head shovels can be set at a 90-degree angle, allowing them to function as a rake or scoop. This feature is especially useful for clearing loose snow and shaping snow pits, though a straight shovel is still effective for cutting into firm snow.

Ice Axe

A reliable ice axe is an indispensable item for winter camping, backpacking, or sledding in high-altitude or mountainous terrain. While ice axes are unnecessary in flat regions, such as the Midwest of the United States or low-slung coastal mountains, they become critical in environments with steep slopes or icy conditions. Even in early summer in the Rockies, north-facing slopes can retain snow and ice, making an ice axe a vital safety tool.

Ice axes come in a wide range of styles, from ultralight models to heavy-duty tools specifically designed for ice climbing. Some are tougher than others, with ratings tailored to glacier travel, technical climbing, or emergency use. For most situations, even a lightweight ice axe from brands like Camp or Petzl can be a lifesaver. These ultralight models, often weighing around 8 to 10 ounces (230 to 280 grams), are easy to carry and effective in challenging conditions.

In glaciated environments or areas with significant snow coverage, a longer glacier-style ice axe is recommended. The added length provides better reach for self-belay on moderate slopes, making it easier to maintain control. However, on steep terrain, a shorter ice axe offers better leverage and maneuverability.

Ice axes also serve multiple purposes, such as chiseling through hard snow to overcome barriers. However, be aware that the metal of an ice axe can become extremely cold, posing a risk of frostbite even when wearing gloves. Always ensure you're prepared for these conditions.

Using an ice axe leash is useful for preventing loss in general mountaineering and glacier travel, but it should be used with caution in technical terrain. In steep or self-arrest situations, a leash can become entangled and restrict movement, increasing the risk of injury. Whether you're navigating steep terrain, late-season snow, or icy slopes on trails like the Pacific Crest Trail or the Continental Divide Trail, an ice axe is often the only reliable way to arrest a fall and avoid serious injury.

When in doubt, always bring an ice axe—even a light-duty model can make a significant difference in safety and utility during winter adventures.

Tools

When venturing into cold environments with technical equipment, having a small tool can make the difference between being able to repair your gear and enduring a long, difficult slog home. The most popular tool for this purpose is the multi-tool, which typically includes pliers (either snub-nose or needle-nose), a knife, a saw, a file, and other useful items. Multi-tools are considered an indispensable piece of equipment when dealing with hardware such as skis, snowshoes, sleds, harnesses, or even backpacks.

There is a wide variety of multi-tools on the market, ranging from inexpensive, no-name brands to high-end models from trusted manufacturers like Leatherman. While you don't necessarily need to spend a lot of money, you should invest in a reliable and durable tool. Off-brand multi-tools, particularly those with weak metal or poorly constructed hinges, can break easily under stress. While these cheaper options may seem appealing upfront, their failure in the field can render them useless, making the initial savings irrelevant.

Author's Note
> I once used the file on my multi-tool to create a hole in the blade of my broken shovel during an expedition in Antarctica. That small tool allowed me to reattach the blade of my shovel when it mattered most. It truly made all the difference.

In addition to a multi-tool, consider bringing a small length of aluminum or picture-hanger wire for emergency repairs. While aluminum wire isn't as durable as steel wire, it is much easier to cut and shape in the field. Steel wire requires hardened cutters, which not all multi-tools have, whereas almost any multi-tool can handle aluminum wire. If using picture-hanger wire, opt for the bare metal variety rather than the plastic-coated version, which can be harder to twist and secure in cold conditions.

If you're bringing skis, snowshoes, or other complicated hardware, it's also wise to carry a small bag of short wood screws. If a binding or skin detaches from your skis, you can use the screws to reattach them and keep going.

Repair Kits

Always bring a repair kit tailored to the equipment you're carrying. Include a small multi-tool with screwdrivers (flathead and Phillips), Allen wrenches, or any other tools specific to the screws and fasteners on your gear. For technical equipment—which applies to most outdoor adventurers—patches like Gear Aid are invaluable for quick fixes.

On longer trips, be sure to include outdoor-grade thread, such as upholstery or heavy-duty outdoor thread, along with a couple of easy-to-thread needles. This allows you to sew and repair damaged gear, tents, or equipment in a pinch. If you tear your gaiters or pants with crampons, snowshoes, or skis, you can quickly sew them back together and continue your adventure.

Author's Note

I've had to sew more items in the field than I'd like to admit. During an expedition in Antarctica, I completely sewed an additional piece of fleece insulation onto my pants. On our Greenland expedition, both Terry and I had to make repairs—he tore the crotch of his pants, and I ripped the corner of my jacket. Without a needle and thread, these issues could have caused significant problems.

Your repair kit should also include nail clippers and a small file. On longer trips, your nails will grow and need maintenance, and in cold conditions, the corners of your nails or fingers may crack. Nail clippers can help manage these issues and prevent further discomfort. Additionally, they are useful for small, precise tasks, such as trimming thread or cutting tape.

First Aid Kit

A basic first aid kit is absolutely essential when heading into the wilderness. Even a few bandages can make the difference between managing an injury and having it worsen. Items like gauze pads, adhesive bandages, and Q-tips are recommended. Q-tips can be useful for applying ointment or cleaning wounds but should not be used in the ears, as they can push debris further in. For ear issues, flushing with clean water is a safer alternative.

In cold conditions, not all bandages and tapes work effectively. Many types of medical tape, especially those purchased from big-box stores, lose their adhesive properties in low temperatures. One reliable option is Band-Aid Tough Strips, which adhere well to the skin and are nearly as durable as those used in medical offices—making them an excellent choice for outdoor use.

Include moleskin for blister protection and treatment, and only drain blisters if they interfere with movement. If drainage is necessary, ensure proper sterilization to reduce the risk of infection. Consider seeking additional first aid training or resources from organizations like NOLS (National Outdoor Leadership School) for a more comprehensive understanding of wilderness first aid.

For short trips, a basic kit will suffice, but for longer journeys, a more extensive first aid kit is advisable. While you can improvise certain items, like cutting clothing to create a bandage, having the right supplies on hand can save time and prevent complications.

Other Necessary Items

Duct tape is another essential tool in the wilderness. However, standard inexpensive duct tape often fails in extremely cold temperatures, losing its adhesive properties. Gorilla Tape is a far superior option—it is thicker, tougher, and remains adhesive even at sub-zero temperatures, down to around -40°F (-40°C). In contrast, cheaper duct tape may feel like Teflon, with glue that doesn't activate in the cold. Be cautious when handling Gorilla Tape, as its strong adhesive can strain fingers or cause minor cuts when tearing it by hand. Using scissors or a knife to cut it is safer.

A reliable knife is another key piece of equipment. For longer trips, a small pair of scissors can also be helpful, as there are tasks a knife cannot perform as efficiently. You don't need a large knife unless you're planning specific woodcraft activities. A basic folding pocket knife, such as a $20 Elk Ridge knife, is sufficient for most outdoor adventures. While you can opt for lighter or more expensive models, the goal is generally to avoid using the knife at all unless necessary.

When using a knife, exercise extreme caution, especially around your hands and groin. A deep cut to the artery in your thumb can cause severe bleeding, and the same risk applies to the femoral artery in your groin area. There have been fatal incidents caused by knife injuries in these regions. Always cut away from your body and, when possible, use a cutting board or a flat, stable surface like a log or rock to prevent slips.

Rescue signal mirrors and whistles are invaluable in emergency situations. Your voice can only carry a short distance in the wilderness, but a whistle can be heard much farther away. Additionally, yelling consumes a lot of energy, whereas blowing a whistle is as simple as breathing. Signal mirrors, on the other hand, can be seen from miles away, even in open plains or polar plateaus. However, they require sunlight to function, so they are ineffective at night or in heavy cloud cover. In these cases, a whistle or flashlight is a more reliable backup for signaling.

Vehicle Equipment

When traveling to a snowy climate, especially if you've never lived or driven in snow before, there are a few important considerations to keep in mind. You'll need specific tools to keep yourself safe from snow and potential danger. If your vehicle has been snowed on or iced over while parked, you'll need the right tools and equipment to ensure you can get back on the road safely.

This is particularly crucial when driving on icy roads. People from warm climates often don't have tires that are adequate for snowy or icy conditions, which can lead to serious safety issues. Preparing in advance is key.

Window Scraper

A window scraper and brush is an essential item if you are driving your own vehicle to a snowy location. Trying to scrape a windshield with a credit card is an exercise in frustration. *(I've seen it attempted many times. -AL)* Make sure to purchase this item before leaving on your trip. Sometimes a storm sends residents scurrying, and scrapers sell out the day before you arrive. It happens. Your local automotive store will have this important piece of car hardware, so it's worth picking one up well in advance.

Snow Tires and Snow Chains

Snow chains may be required depending on where you are traveling. Each jurisdiction is different, and rules change. If you have tires with the snow+mountain symbol, dedicated snow tires, or studded tires, you will *usually* be allowed to continue past a checkpoint. However, always verify the current regulations before your trip.

For example, in warm states like California, officers near ski resorts and state or national parks will often stop vehicles to verify they have tire chains or winter-capable tires. If you're not properly equipped, you'll be turned around. In contrast, in northern cold-weather states like Minnesota or Montana, snow chains are rarely used or owned because vehicles are equipped with all-season tires or dedicated snow tires during winter. The clattering sound of studded tires on pavement is common in these regions, where drivers prioritize permanent winter tire setups over chains.

Northern states like Alaska and countries such as Canada, Finland, and Norway often rely on studded tires for extreme conditions. Others may use high-performance, non-studded winter tires, like the Goodyear Blizzak or comparable models.

Windshield Washer Fluid

Regular windshield washer fluid may freeze solid in sub-freezing conditions, rendering it useless when you need it most. Some low-grade fluids contain alcohol that may help prevent freezing but are often only rated to 32°F (0°C), making them unreliable in colder conditions. Before heading into winter terrain, ensure you fill your washer reservoir with a fluid rated for freezing temperatures, often labeled as "winter formula" or rated for temperatures as low as -20°F (-29°C) or colder. This prevents freezing and ensures you can keep your windshield clear of snow, ice, and road grime during your trip. Make sure to top off the reservoir before leaving on your trip.

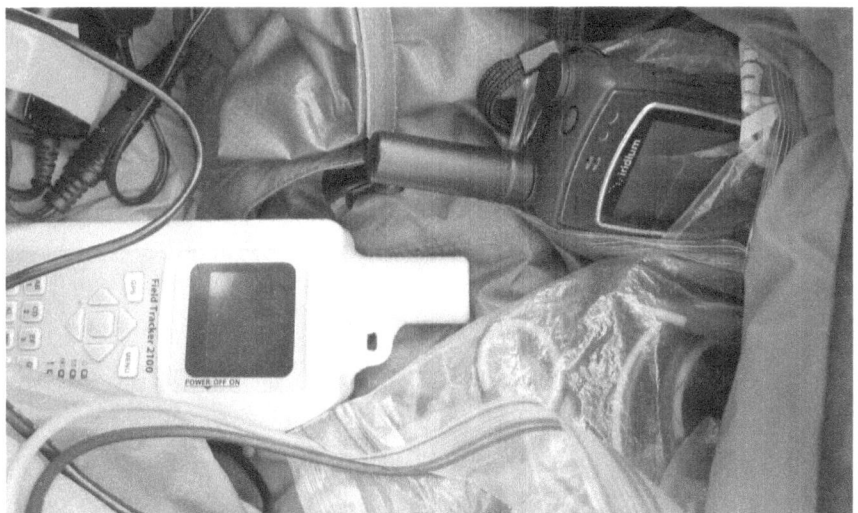

The farther afield you are, the more communication gear you'll likely need to keep you in touch with home.

Part 2
Winter Camping Techniques and Strategies

Winter camping presents a unique set of challenges that require careful planning and specialized techniques. In cold weather conditions, staying warm, dry, and safe is not just about comfort—it's a matter of survival. From choosing the right shelter and gear to understanding how the environment affects your body and equipment, every detail must be considered. This section is designed to equip you with the essential winter camping strategies that will help you face the extreme elements confidently, whether you're setting up camp in a snowstorm or navigating through freezing temperatures.

The techniques outlined here cover the critical aspects of camping in winter, including shelter selection, insulation, stove operation, and food management. By mastering these strategies, you'll learn how to optimize your gear, reduce energy expenditure, and enhance your overall experience. Winter camping is about preparation, adaptability, and awareness—knowing when to adjust your tactics and when to push forward in challenging conditions. This section will ensure a safe, effective, and ultimately rewarding winter adventure.

Having liquid water in the winter is handy if you can safely reach it.

Chapter 8
Choosing the Best Campsite

Choosing a Campsite

Choosing a campsite for winter camping can be one of the simplest parts of your trip—or one of the most challenging, depending on the terrain, weather conditions, and location.

If you're camping on snow, the first step is to establish your campsite in a relatively protected area, if possible. In polar climates or while mountaineering, where there may be no rock cover or natural protection, this might not be feasible. However, the placement of your tent pad can mean the difference between a comfortable night's sleep or an unpleasant experience, such as rolling onto your tent mate or being squashed against the cold tent wall.

Terrain Considerations

Ground Slope: While slightly sloped ground is ideal for drainage in summer camping, it matters less in winter, especially on snow. However, if you're on thin snow cover, a slight slope can help with drainage. In deeper snow, this isn't necessary as you'll typically level out the area.

Cold Sinks

Avoid camping in cold sinks—low-lying areas where cold air naturally collects. These spots can be significantly colder at night. Temperature drops in cold sinks can be significant, sometimes 5°F or more, depending on local conditions.

Author's Note
I once camped in a location forecast at 0°F (-18°C), only to experience temperatures dropping to -15°F (-26°C) due to poor campsite placement in a ground depression. I avoid those spots now.

Wind and Weather
If possible, select a campsite out of the wind, such as behind trees, rocks, or other natural barriers. This not only helps with warmth but also reduces the risk of wind stress damaging your tent. Strong winds can shake the tent violently, causing pole breakage or collapse. Snowfall is an uncontrollable factor, but avoiding wind exposure improves overall comfort.

Safety Concerns
Widowmaker Trees: In forested areas, beware of partially fallen trees (widowmakers) that are leaning on or supported by other trees. Wind or storms can dislodge these, causing them to fall unexpectedly. Even without snow or storms, widowmakers can collapse due to random chance.
Mountain Passes and Saddles: Avoid camping in mountain passes or the saddle between two hills, as these areas are prone to wind funneling. Locations like Windy Corner on Denali or Hurricane Pass on the Teton Crest Trail are infamous for this effect. Wind can shift unexpectedly during storms, exposing your tent to extreme conditions.

Observing Clues
Use natural clues like the direction of drifted snow, the arrangement of trees, or other environmental indicators to deduce the predominant wind direction. Plan your campsite accordingly to minimize exposure.

By carefully choosing your campsite with these factors in mind, you'll set yourself up for a safer, more enjoyable winter camping experience.

Wind Walls
If you find yourself in an exposed location for your campsite, consider putting up a wind wall if there's any possibility of inclement weather. What may seem completely calm during the day can easily turn into a roaring windstorm at night or by morning. Don't be deceived by calm conditions—they don't necessarily guarantee a calm night or following day.

Even a reliable weather forecast isn't a guarantee, and sudden wind shifts can occur without warning. If in doubt, it's better to err on the side of caution and build a wind wall whenever possible.

Adapting a Campsite to Conditions

Adapt your campsite to the local terrain, whether you're in a forest, mountains, valleys, or near rivers. Each environment presents unique challenges and advantages, so tailoring your setup is key to a successful camping experience.

Rivers and Moist Areas

River areas are particularly challenging because the breeze tends to blow more consistently than over land, and the air is usually more humid, which can make you feel colder. If you have a good collection of tall, healthy trees nearby, they can provide significant shelter. You'll often hear the wind in the crowns of the trees, while down below there might be only a slight breeze. This setup can make for a fun evening with plenty of natural sounds but minimal discomfort from the wind.

Rocky or Exposed Areas

In areas with only rocks, such as mountains or high deserts, look for any natural shelters where you can set up your tent. However, be cautious of narrow spaces between rocks that might seem like good spots but could actually create a wind tunnel effect. Wind can also accelerate around large isolated boulders, wrapping around them and increasing exposure. When scouting for a site, avoid these areas to prevent unexpected gusts from disrupting your camp.

No Natural Shelter

If you're forced to camp in an area with no natural protection, you'll need to build your own wind wall or dig a pit to create a barrier for your tent. While this requires significant effort, it will be well worth it if conditions deteriorate. Proper preparation can make all the difference in maintaining comfort and safety during your trip.

Mountainous Terrain

When camping in mountainous terrain, it's crucial to be aware of avalanche hazards. What might appear to be a completely benign area could actually be a death trap. Look for signs such as areas where snow has slid, large blocks of displaced snow, wind-loaded slopes, or fracture lines at the top of slide zones. These are warning signs of potential avalanche danger and should be avoided at all costs. Many have lost their lives to unexpected snow slides they didn't anticipate.

Choosing a Campsite: Ridge Line or Valley?
Ridge Lines: Ridge lines tend to be more exposed and are much more likely to experience bad weather than other parts of a mountain. This is particularly true in saddles and passes, where wind often funnels and intensifies.
Valleys: Valleys, while tranquil and seemingly comfortable, are prone to the cold sink effect. Cold air descends from higher elevations and settles in the valley floor, making these areas significantly colder at night. This effect is especially pronounced on clear, calm nights due to radiative cooling, which causes heat to escape rapidly.

If possible, aim to move your campsite a few hundred yards or meters up the hillside. This small elevation gain can help you avoid cold sink areas and create a safer, more comfortable campsite. Ensure your chosen spot is not in the path of an avalanche or other objective hazards. Even a slight elevation change can make your campsite several degrees warmer and much more enjoyable.

Snowpack Stability and Density
When establishing your camp in a snowy wilderness, it's essential to evaluate snow depth, snowpack density, and stability. These factors can greatly impact both your comfort and safety.

Snow Depth and Access to Water
The depth of the snow is a critical consideration, especially if you need to find water. In areas with deep snow and prolonged cold, it may be difficult to locate liquid water to boil or filter. If a stream is present, digging near exposed rocks or tree wells can sometimes reveal running water, even in subzero conditions. Plan accordingly and prepare for situations where snow might be your only water source. Keep in mind that fresh powder snow has a low water content, meaning you'll need to melt a much larger volume to produce a usable amount.

Snow Depth, Density, and Camp Setup

Hard or Soft Snow

The hardness or softness of the snow determines how easy it will be to establish your campsite. Here are some factors to consider:
- If 1 foot (30 cm) of fresh snow has packed into a firm layer, it can provide a good base for your camp.
- In contrast, areas with a hard crust (formed by cycles of heating and cooling, wind compaction, or freezing rain) over soft, loose snow can make setting up camp difficult. This type of snow, often referred to as "Sierra cement" in the Cascade and Sierra ranges, can lead to unexpected falls. For instance, you might find your campsite stable while using skis but sink waist-deep when stepping off them.
- Compacting the snow by stomping it down with skis, snowshoes, or a shovel before setting up your tent can help create a more stable and insulated surface.

Snow Stability and Safety

Snow stability is another crucial factor. Avoid areas with visible signs of instability, such as:

Snow Slides: Stay clear of slopes with evidence of past slides or cornices hanging above.

Treeless Zones on Hillsides: In mountainous terrain, areas that resemble ski slopes (often devoid of trees) can indicate a higher likelihood of snow slides. However, sparse trees with bent or broken trunks are also strong indicators of past avalanche activity. While terrain without trees can be a warning sign, the steepness of the slope (typically 30-45 degrees) is the most critical factor in assessing avalanche risk.

Avalanche Safety

For mountainous terrain, avalanche training can be invaluable. Learning to identify and avoid avalanche-prone areas is a critical skill. Always consult up-to-date local avalanche forecasts to understand current snowpack conditions. These bulletins provide danger ratings (Low to Extreme), weak layer analysis, and stability test results, helping you assess the risks before heading into the backcountry.

By considering these factors and making informed decisions, you can significantly reduce risks and set up a stable, secure campsite.

Proximity to Resources

When setting up your campsite, consider how close you are to the resources you'll need. This can significantly impact your comfort and safety, especially in winter.

Firewood Availability

If you plan to have a campfire, check for downed, dead wood that complies with local regulations and doesn't require cutting down live trees. However, in winter, this can be challenging because much of the deadfall you'd want to collect for firewood might be buried under several feet or meters of snow.
Digging for Firewood: In deep snow conditions, firewood may require digging to access. Look for dead branches still attached to trees, as these are often drier than those on the ground.
Firewood Alternatives: If gathering wood is impractical, consider bringing a stove or fuel canisters as a backup heat source.
Drying Wet Wood: Wet wood doesn't always dry well near a fire, especially in extreme cold where the outer layer may ice over instead of evaporating. Splitting the wood to expose dry inner layers is the most effective way to make wet wood burnable.

Water Access

If you're not relying on melting snow for water and exposed water sources are unavailable, you'll need a plan. In winter, even areas known for open water can experience sudden freezes during a cold snap, making access difficult and potentially dangerous.
Lakes, Creeks, and Rivers: Snow and ice can obscure the ground beneath you. What appears to be solid ice may be unstable or conceal flowing water beneath a thin crust. Always test the ice before stepping onto it, and avoid areas with visible cracks or weak spots. Clear, blue ice is stronger than white, opaque ice. Carrying an ice chisel or using a trekking pole to check ice thickness before stepping onto it can prevent accidents.
Reliable Springs: Some springs remain unfrozen year-round and can be a great water source if they don't require excessive digging. However, snowdrifts can obscure their exact location, so prior knowledge of the area is helpful.
Ice as a Water Source: Ice contains more water per volume than snow, but

large chunks take longer to melt due to their density. Crushed ice melts faster than solid blocks, and pre-warming snow or ice inside a tent can speed up the melting process.

Building a Shelter

If you're camping in a forested area and there's accessible deadfall, consider using it to create a shelter or wind blockade. This can offer significant protection from the wind and improve your comfort at night. However, keep in mind:

Effort: Gathering and handling wood requires substantial effort, especially in cold conditions when fatigue sets in faster.

Sap: Some types of wood, particularly pine and spruce, can leave sticky sap on your gear, which may be difficult to clean and can cause issues with zippers, gloves, or clothing.

Snow as a Barrier: In some cases, compacted snow walls or snow caves can provide better insulation and wind protection than wooden structures. However, powdery snow won't compact well for walls or caves, whereas wind-packed or consolidated snow is ideal for building effective shelters.

By carefully considering the availability and accessibility of resources near your campsite, you can plan more effectively and ensure a safer, more comfortable camping experience.

Tents vs. Snow Shelters

Deciding between a tent and a snow shelter for winter camping can be a challenge. Each option has distinct advantages and considerations.

Tents

The easiest and most convenient choice is to bring a tent, tarp, or bivy. With a tent, your shelter is always ready to go at a moment's notice, whether during a planned stop or in the event of sudden bad weather. You can quickly set up camp and get yourself out of the elements.

However, tents offer limited insulation. Even the best four-season tents or double-wall designs provide only minimal protection against the cold compared to a well-constructed snow shelter. Heat loss occurs quickly through thin tent walls, and strong winds can increase convective heat loss, rapidly stripping away warmth. Tents with solid fabric walls (instead of mesh-heavy designs) help reduce this effect. Despite their thin walls, tents do provide a psychological barrier against animals, as their visibility is obscured. This minor sense of isolation can make a big difference for your peace of mind.

Tents also offer more ventilation control than many snow shelters, which is essential for reducing condensation buildup. However, if not properly managed, tent condensation can freeze, creating an icy interior and dampening gear. Leaving vents slightly open and shaking off frost buildup in the morning helps minimize this issue.

Snow Shelters

Snow shelters have several advantages, primarily in insulation. They provide vastly superior protection from the cold compared to a thin nylon tent, making them excellent for enduring storms. A well-built snow shelter can offer a comfortable and quiet night's sleep, even in extreme weather conditions.

However, the time and energy required to construct a good snow shelter can be substantial. Building one takes experience and can range from half an hour to several hours, depending on the complexity and materials available. In emergencies, a quick snow hole can suffice to get you out of the weather, but for planned use, you'll need to invest more effort.

Another potential issue with snow shelters is exposure to animals. Unless designed specifically to block entry, animals may be able to access your shelter. While this is rare, rodents and small scavengers might be drawn to food smells inside. Snow shelters also require proper ventilation to prevent excessive carbon dioxide buildup from breathing or stove use. A fist-sized ventilation hole near the highest point of the shelter is essential for safety.

Tents provide ease and immediacy, while snow shelters offer unmatched insulation and storm protection. Weighing the trade-offs between convenience and comfort will help you decide which option best suits your trip and conditions.

Author's Note

Always keep one snow shovel inside the shelter. If there are two entrances to the shelter, keep at least one snow shovel at each end. If only one entrance is available, placing a shovel near the sleeping area ensures quick access in case of heavy snowfall. That way, in severe winds or deep snow accumulation, you can dig yourself out. In extreme conditions, you can also repack snow blocks to protect the vestibule and zippers. That saved Terry and me in Greenland. The wind blew his tent door open, and it was too dangerous to go outside, so I leaned out the window and scraped snow blocks to secure the door.

Styles of Tents

The style of tent chosen for a chilly wilderness trip depends on your approach, experience, and camping style. For winter camping, a double-wall tent or a four-season tent is the most likely choice due to its ability to provide protection from harsh weather.

Freestanding vs. Staked Tents

Freestanding tents have the advantage of being simple to set up; once they are erected, they require no additional staking in favorable conditions. In contrast, tunnel tents or other staked designs absolutely require staking for stability, necessitating more effort and planning. These tents need sufficient space and proper tools for staking, especially in snowy or frozen terrain.

Snow Anchors

In snow, stakes can be substituted with items like skis, snowshoes, or ski poles, but they don't always provide the most secure hold. Deadman anchors—buried tent stakes, sticks, or stuff sacks filled with snow—offer far better stability in deep snow. Dedicated snow stakes, which have a broader surface area, are also effective.

In areas with thin snow cover and frozen ground, driving stakes into the earth may prove difficult or impossible. Carrying a hammer or using the adze of an ice axe can help secure stakes. Stronger aluminum or titanium stakes are more resistant to bending in hard ground than standard stakes.

Preparation and Practice

When selecting a tent, consider how familiar you are with its setup process. Practicing setup in mild conditions, such as your backyard in summer, is very different from managing it in a winter storm. Testing your tent under controlled conditions is essential to ensure you can handle it in severe weather.

Winter conditions require the ability to pitch a tent in driving snow, low visibility, and temperatures well below freezing (e.g., -18°C or colder). Practice setting up your tent while wearing thick gloves, as this simulates what you'll face in extreme conditions. Handling aluminum tent poles with bare hands in subzero temperatures can not only lead to frostbite but also cause skin to stick to the metal, making it painful and dangerous to pull away.

A well-chosen and thoroughly tested tent can make all the difference in your winter camping experience. Becoming familiar with the nuances of a tent—such as zipper function in cold, how guy lines handle ice buildup, and how ventilation works in deep snow—will make you more efficient and confident in challenging conditions.

Snow Shelters

If you plan to use a snow shelter as your primary shelter, be prepared for a significant amount of work, especially if you've never built one before. Starting construction at dusk is a common mistake—temperatures will plummet as you work late into the night, and a half-built shelter offers little protection from the cold. Additionally, snow shelters require time for the snow to sinter (harden), which improves their structural strength and insulation. Allowing at least an hour for the shelter to settle before moving in can make a significant difference in durability and warmth. Always begin early to allow enough time for construction while you still have daylight and warmth.

Types of Snow Shelters

Different types of snow shelters provide varying degrees of insulation, wind resistance, and practicality in winter environments. Snow caves offer excellent thermal retention but require significant effort to construct, while igloos provide long-term durability and structural stability in deep snow conditions. Quinzees, formed by compacting and hollowing out a mound of snow, require settling time before use but offer reliable protection. For rapid shelter in extreme conditions, trench shelters or wind walls can serve as effective emergency solutions. Selecting the appropriate shelter depends on factors such as weather conditions, available time, snow consistency, and the specific demands of the environment.

Do not underestimate the time and energy needed to build a snow shelter. Whether it's a tunnel, mound, or igloo, each type demands significant labor to ensure safety and warmth.

Snow Tunnels
Advantages: Snow tunnels require minimal engineering. Simply dig a tube large enough to fit yourself and your sleeping bag.
Disadvantages: The snowpack must be dense enough to hold its shape. Loose or overly wet snow can make digging difficult or impractical. If the tunnel collapses, it can be hard to dig yourself out, making them riskier without proper reinforcement.
Tips: Position the entrance away from the wind and use the excavated snow to block drafts or create a curved entryway for additional protection. Ensure the tunnel is wide enough to allow movement but compact enough to retain warmth.

Quinzhees (Snow Mounds)
Advantages: Quinzhees are relatively easy to construct, providing excellent insulation and weather protection without specialized tools. The smooth, rounded shape minimizes wind resistance and maximizes heat retention.
Disadvantages: Construction is time-intensive, requiring packed snow to settle before digging, which can be challenging in dry, loose snow. If the walls are too thin, collapse is a serious risk.
Tips: Build walls at least 12–18 inches (30–46cm) thick for insulation, and poke small ventilation holes in the roof to prevent condensation buildup. Let the mound settle for at least 90 minutes, or longer in dry, powdery snow, before digging it out to strengthen the structure.

Igloos
Advantages: Igloos offer unmatched insulation and durability, making them ideal for extreme weather. When properly built, they can withstand powerful winds and maintain an interior temperature well above the outside air.
Disadvantages: Building an igloo is highly labor-intensive, requiring skill and specific tools like a snow saw for cutting blocks. Poor block-cutting technique can lead to structural weakness.
Tips: Practice building igloos beforehand to develop the necessary skills, and use dense, well-bonded snow to ensure stability. When stacking blocks, lean them inward and interlock the edges for maximum strength.

Shelter Cooking and Hygiene
Plan for cooking and hygiene needs in your shelter. With a snow tunnel,

consider how you'll manage ventilation, condensation, and waste disposal to maintain a clean and functional space. In igloos and quinzhees, designate a cooking area and avoid using stoves without proper airflow to prevent carbon monoxide buildup.

By understanding the benefits and challenges of various snow shelters, you can choose the one best suited to your trip and conditions. Proper preparation and planning will ensure your shelter is safe, warm, and functional.

Cutting Snow Blocks

Cutting snow blocks is a valuable skill that can mean the difference between a comfortable night and a miserable one.

A snow saw is the best tool for creating well-shaped, fine-edged blocks, but it requires packed snow with a consistency similar to Styrofoam. Loose, powdery, or blowing snow won't work with a snow saw, making this tool ineffective in such conditions. If the snow is too loose, manually compressing it by stomping or packing before sawing can help.

Another option is to use a wide-bladed avalanche shovel made of hardened T6 aluminum. This allows you to cut wider snow blocks more efficiently and is often the best alternative when snow is too soft for a saw.

However, the effort required to cut blocks with either a snow saw or shovel can be significant. Thousands of precise saw strokes may be necessary to produce enough blocks to build a proper wind wall or snow shelter, so don't underestimate the physical labor involved.

Building Wind Walls

Constructing wind walls requires strategy to balance efficiency and effectiveness. There are different sections of a wall you need to consider. Depending on time and energy, you may opt for different approaches. Whether you use snow saws, shovels, or a combination of methods, adapting your approach to the conditions and available materials is key. Shovels are faster than snow saws, but snow saws create more durable and uniform blocks for long-term structures.

Footing Layer: Begin with a loose pile of rubble snow as a foundation. This wide, unstructured base reduces the need for precise engineering and provides stability for the structure.

Middle and Upper Sections: Place snow blocks on top of the rubble base to build height. This hybrid approach saves effort by combining the simplicity

of a rubble foundation with the sturdiness of properly cut blocks.
Quick Protection: In extremely windy conditions, a simple rubble pile is the fastest solution to get out of the wind. While less elegant, it requires less precision and is easier to construct when time and energy are limited. However, loosely piled rubble can collapse under strong wind gusts. Lightly packing the snow helps improve stability.

Emergency Protection

In an emergency, digging a pit is often the most efficient option. This eliminates the need for complex construction and allows you to create shelter quickly. As you dig, pile the extracted snow on the windward side of the pit. This naturally forms a windbreak, combining the benefits of a pit and a snow barrier with minimal additional effort.

By using the snow you're already displacing, you speed up the process and gain protection from the wind more rapidly, making it an effective and practical solution in harsh conditions. If possible, dig a trench and lie perpendicular to the wind to further reduce exposure and improve insulation.

In extreme situations where a shelter can't be built, simply getting below the surface of the snow can provide critical protection from wind chill and exposure.

Snow Pits vs. Snow Walls

The choice between digging a snow pit for your tent or leaving the tent on the snow's surface and building a snow wall is a common debate among snow campers. Each approach has advantages and challenges, and the decision often depends on the conditions and your preferences.

Snow Pits
Advantages
- Digging a snow pit provides better protection for your tent as you are sheltered from wind and other elements.
- The snow removed from the pit can be repurposed to build a natural wind wall, serving a dual purpose.
- A well-designed pit can provide additional warmth by reducing exposure to moving air and creating a more enclosed space.

Disadvantages
- **Snow Fill:** In windy conditions, snow can swirl and fill the pit around

your tent. This can lead to the snow packing down and potentially squashing the tent. A substantial digging effort may be required in the morning to free your tent without causing damage.
- **Space Constraints:** If the pit is just the size of your tent and heavy snowfall occurs (e.g., 3 feet or 90 cm overnight), you may find it extremely challenging to remove the accumulated snow. Widening the pit by at least a foot (30 cm) on all sides allows easier shoveling and prevents excessive snow buildup against the tent walls.
- **Ventilation Risk:** Waterproof tents are entirely sealed, and if snow completely covers the vents and vestibules, oxygen flow can be cut off. Placing a ski pole or stick near the tent as a vent marker can help maintain airflow by keeping an opening clear.

Tips for Snow Pits

Always leave enough space around the tent to comfortably walk and shovel, even with winter boots. A larger pit allows for better maneuverability and easier snow removal in heavy snowfalls.

If camping for multiple nights, a bigger snow pit improves overall comfort and functionality. A **well-placed step or bench** inside the pit can serve as a convenient sitting or gear storage area.

Snow Walls

Building a snow wall is another approach that requires less digging and can still provide substantial wind protection.

Advantages
- Snow walls are quicker to construct and avoid many of the challenges associated with pits, such as snow accumulation and restricted airflow.
- They can be tailored to shield your tent from the predominant wind direction without the need to dig into the snow.
- If built properly, a well-placed snow wall can redirect drifting snow away from your tent, preventing unwanted accumulation.

Disadvantages
- Snow walls offer less overall protection compared to a well-constructed snow pit. They do not provide the same level of insulation or wind reduction.
- They require compacted snow or snow blocks to be effective, which may take effort depending on the snow conditions. In deep, powdery snow,

snow walls need to be packed or reinforced with cut blocks for structural integrity—otherwise, they may collapse in strong winds.

Balancing Snow Walls and Snow Pits

A hybrid approach can combine the benefits of both methods. For example, Dig a shallow pit to reduce wind exposure and use the extracted snow to build a surrounding wall.

Avoid over-compacting the pit or limiting its size to the exact footprint of your tent. Give yourself enough room to handle unexpected snowfalls and maintain ventilation.

By weighing the pros and cons of each method and considering the specific conditions of your campsite, you can choose the most effective strategy to stay safe, comfortable, and protected during your trip.

Stable Snow Base

Once you reach the location for your campsite, immediately establish where it will be and begin compacting the snow. Use snowshoes or skis for this process. Snowshoes are generally more effective than skis for packing snow, as they sink lower and create a firmer base.

Compacting the snow is crucial because, even if it seems stable while on your skis or snowshoes, stepping off them may cause you to sink up to your waist in loose snow. Attempting to set up a campsite on unpacked, deep snow is nearly impossible.

Methods for Creating a Stable Base

Packing with Snowshoes or Skis: Move in a crisscross pattern over the campsite to ensure the snow is evenly compacted. Repeat the process multiple times to achieve a firm, stable surface.

Digging a Snow Pit: If preferred, dig a snow pit to create a level and protected area for your tent. Be aware that digging a substantial pit can be labor-intensive if you're alone, though much easier with a team. Avoid making the pit too deep unless you have a solid snow wall structure to prevent collapse.

Additional Tips

- Allow the snow to settle after packing. Even with proper compaction, parts of the snow may still break through under pressure, causing knee-deep sinks that can be frustrating during setup. Letting the surface sit

for 30 minutes to an hour before pitching your tent allows for better stabilization.
- Avoid "snow punch-throughs" under your tent. Uneven spots can remain uncomfortable all night, leading to poor sleep and body aches. Using an insulating ground pad on top of the compacted base prevents unwanted sinking.
- Invest time in properly compacting and leveling your campsite before setting up your tent. A firm, stable base will greatly improve your comfort and overall camping experience.

Packing Snow Down

Make every effort to ensure your campsite is as level as possible. What might appear to be level ground on slightly hilly terrain can turn into a frustrating experience once you're inside your tent. A small slope can cause you to roll or slide into your tent mate or press uncomfortably against the tent wall.

- Use a crisscross pattern when packing snow down. This ensures even compaction and helps you identify uneven areas.
- Redistribute snow if necessary—shoveling from one side to another can help achieve a truly level surface. While this may seem excessive during setup, it prevents a tilted sleeping surface that could lead to an uncomfortable night.
- Let the snow settle for at least 30 minutes before setting up your tent. Even after packing, snow can continue to compress under weight, and allowing it to settle can prevent unexpected shifts.

Taking extra time to properly level your campsite during setup will significantly improve your comfort and make the entire camping experience more enjoyable.

Anchoring in the Snow

Anchoring your tent or shelter securely in the snow is essential for stability, especially in harsh conditions. Several methods can be used depending on the tools available and the snow conditions.

Snow Stakes

Snow stakes, typically long (up to 12 inches or 30 cm) and made of aluminum, are a straightforward option. These stakes attach to your tent's guy lines and can be driven into the snow to quickly secure your shelter.

In some conditions, you may be unable to drive the stakes into the snow effectively. Many snow stakes have holes that allow for a "deadman" anchor. A deadman anchor involves placing the stake horizontally in the snow, packing snow over it, and letting it freeze in place for a more secure hold.

Deadman Anchors

A deadman anchor is a reliable method when stakes or natural anchors aren't readily usable. They are highly effective, even in light snow cover. In case of light snow cover, build a small mound of snow to generate artificial snow depth. To create a deadman, do the following:

- Dig a hole in the snow.
- Attach tent guy line to deadman item.
- Place the deadman item (stake, branch, or other object) horizontally in the hole. Use criss-cross sticks to improve the holding power.
- Pack snow firmly over the anchor. The packed snow will bond and refreeze, securing the anchor.
- Allow time for the anchor to freeze. If possible, give it at least 30 minutes before tensioning the guy lines.
- By morning, the anchor may freeze solid. Use a shovel carefully to chisel it out when breaking camp, being mindful not to cut the guy line or damage the anchor or shovel.

Tips for Deadman Anchors

Ensure the guy line extends directly from the anchor to the tent without resting on the snow. If the line rubs against the snow and shifts in the wind, it may loosen the anchor.

Keep the guy line snug but not overly tight. Refer to your tent's manufacturer guidelines for proper tension. Over-tightening can overstretch and damage the tent, while loose lines can allow excessive flapping, causing wear and tear.

Natural Anchors

If stakes are unavailable, use natural objects like rocks, branches, or even a firmly packed stuff sack filled with snow to create anchors. Bury the object in the snow, pack snow over it, and tie the guy line securely. This method works well when traditional stakes are ineffective or unavailable.

Stuff sacks should be tied off before burying to prevent the packed snow from loosening when tension is applied. By using these anchoring techniques and maintaining proper tension on the guy lines, you can ensure your tent stays secure and withstands challenging weather conditions.

Orienting Your Tent

When establishing a campsite, it's important to think about what direction your tent will face. This will impact the ease of your cooking, sleeping, and striking camp in the morning.

Wind Direction

The most critical factor is wind. You want to minimize the exposure of the tent's widest side to the wind by positioning the narrow part toward it.

This reduces resistance and keeps the tent more stable.

For dome tents, this orientation isn't as crucial because of their symmetrical design, but make sure the main entrance faces away from the predominant wind direction.

Opening your tent zipper in the morning and being greeted by 30 mph (45 km/h) winds is something you'll want to avoid.

If the wind is particularly strong, building a snow wall to protect your tent entrance can make a significant difference. The wall should be at least 3 feet (1 meter) away from the tent to prevent turbulence that could push snow back onto the shelter.

Sun Exposure

If you have the flexibility to orient your tent and the weather allows, positioning the broadside of your tent toward the morning sun can help warm it up as the sun rises, improving comfort.

Tunnel tents don't capture as much sunlight when the narrow end faces the sunrise, so positioning them broadside can provide a much brighter and warmer interior in the morning.

While wind protection should always be the primary consideration, orienting your tent to catch the sun's warming rays can make your morning much more pleasant. Balancing these factors can create a more comfortable and enjoyable campsite experience.

Tent Efficiency

When setting up your tent, carefully consider how to organize your gear inside. Avoid creating a mess by throwing everything around; instead, aim for a neat and organized setup that keeps your tent functional and efficient. This is especially important in snow camping, where you'll have more gear to manage. Without a system, you may waste time digging around for black gloves inside a black sleeping bag at midnight—something to avoid at all costs.

Establish designated wet and dry zones inside your tent. Keep wet gear near the door, and try to keep the center of the tent as dry as possible to prevent moisture from soaking your sleeping bag and other essential gear. This approach also keeps dirt and debris out as well.

Bring your boots inside the tent. If left outside or even in the vestibule, boots can freeze solid or fill with snow. Worse, animals could chew on or steal them, leaving you in serious trouble. Place them inside a waterproof bag or at the foot of your sleeping bag to keep them from freezing while protecting the rest of your gear from moisture.

Be cautious with sharp implements like shovels, and think carefully about where you'll place your stove, sleeping gear, and toiletries. Consistency is key. Always put items in the same place so you can find them quickly, even in the dark. Taking a few extra seconds to place something properly can save a lot of time later.

For small items like liner gloves, avoid losing them by tucking them into the neck of your shirt instead of setting them down. This keeps them warm and ensures they're always within reach, preventing the discomfort of putting on cold gloves.

If you need to hang gear to dry, be considerate of your tent mate. No one wants to wake up with wet socks or underwear dangling in their face. Carefully choose where to hang wet gear to avoid it brushing against you or your sleeping bag repeatedly through the night. A bit of planning goes a long way toward maintaining comfort and harmony in your tent.

Keeping Your Tent Warm at Night

Balancing ventilation and warmth is one of the trickiest aspects of winter camping. If there's wind outside and snow is blowing, you may have no choice but to seal the tent completely. The downside is that condensation from your breath and body moisture will collect on the interior surfaces of the tent, leaving you with a frosty wake-up.

The more ventilation you can allow, the better, even if it feels chillier at night. It's tempting to zip everything up tightly, but try to leave the vents open to help draw moisture away from your body.

A drier tent makes for a much better morning. Frost buildup inside the tent can make packing up in the morning a miserable experience. If you must fully seal the tent, briefly vent it in the morning before packing up to reduce interior frost buildup. If you have the option, using reflective materials like Mylar or a foil-lined sleeping pad can make a significant difference in retaining warmth.

Inside the tent

Stay off the snow. Spread out a foam pad or layers of clothing to avoid sitting, kneeling, or lying directly on snow. Snow saps heat over time, and prolonged contact can lead to numbness or even frostbite.

A foam pad helps create a thermal barrier and makes an otherwise cold environment much more comfortable. This is also why bringing a foam pad along with an air mattress is a good idea. Foam pads are quick to set up and let you sit down immediately to deal with boots or gear without messing around with inflating an air mattress first.

This makes entering the tent after a long day much easier. Once you've got your setup in place, try to minimize how often you go in and out of the tent. Every time you open the door, whatever heat you've managed to build up will escape, leaving the interior colder.

If you need to exit frequently, use a designated entry point and brush off boots and gear before entering to keep snow outside. Once you're settled in and melting snow or preparing for the night, limit trips outside to retain as much warmth as possible. Taking these steps will make your tent a lot more comfortable and keep frost at bay.

Cooking Inside or Outside of a Tent

According to manufacturers and safety guidelines, running a stove inside your tent is strongly discouraged. The risks of carbon monoxide poisoning and accidentally catching the tent on fire are significant and well-documented. However, in extreme conditions, such as mountaineering or polar travel, cooking outside may not be a viable option. In these situations, using your stove inside a large vestibule is often the only practical solution.

For polar travel, cooking in the vestibule becomes routine, as being outside for extended periods is simply not safe. Some mountaineering camps prefer to set up an alcove in a snow wall outside the tent for stove use. This can be a safer alternative if the weather permits.

If you choose to use your stove inside the tent, understand the risks and take precautions. Be particularly mindful of:

Carbon monoxide buildup

Flames flaring up, especially when lighting white gas stoves. Unpredictable flare-ups are especially common at high-altitude or in cold conditions.

White gas stoves are notorious for producing large, unpredictable flames during ignition, so extra care is essential. Proper ventilation is critical if you're forced to cook in a tent. Simply opening the vestibule door may not be enough in low-wind conditions—adjusting the tent's vents to promote airflow is essential. Keeping the stove as stable and secure as possible further reduces risks. Understanding these challenges and planning accordingly will help you safely manage cooking in extreme environments.

Rotating Campsites

If you're camping in a single location for multiple days, consider waste management. The following points are some of things you need to think about when planning longer-term campsites:
- Where will you dispose of liquid waste?
- How will you handle body waste over an extended stay?
- What happens if you're stormbound for days?
- For multi-day camps, sleeping on snow will gradually melt the area beneath you, creating a pit. Even with the best insulation, this happens over time. After a couple of nights, you may find yourself sleeping in a depression, making it colder and less comfortable.
- Most people move their tent a few feet to avoid this issue.
- If relocation isn't possible, adding a fresh layer of compacted snow beneath the sleeping area can help restore insulation and level the surface.
- If stormbound, you may have no choice but to deal with the pit—so choosing a site wisely from the start is key.

Establish Your Routine

When setting up your tent and campsite, develop a consistent routine and stick to it. Doing things the same way every day will reduce stress and improve efficiency to keep you moving.

For solo campers: Mentally walk through how you'll handle tasks so you can execute them efficiently.

For groups: Assign roles based on skills and comfort with the cold.

If someone excels at a particular task, let them do it—but don't overburden them. Rotating tasks helps prevent frustration and keeps morale high. If someone enjoys a certain job, let them take it. If roles are interchangeable, rotate tasks for fairness. In extreme cold, minor frustrations can grow quickly, so teamwork is critical. Stick to your routine, but be adaptable. If a more efficient or effective method presents itself, adjust quickly—but make sure the team agrees on the change to maintain efficiency and morale.

Cooking Tents

Some larger expeditions bring dedicated cooking tents to avoid the risks of running stoves inside sleeping tents. Cooking tents like the Mega Mid are designed with a high ceiling, reducing fire risks and improving ventilation. Even if a stove flares up, the flame is unlikely to reach the fabric, and increased airflow helps reduce condensation and carbon monoxide buildup.

One of the key advantages of a cooking tent is the camaraderie it fosters. These tents can be large enough to accommodate the entire team. Everyone can sit comfortably, eat, and discuss the day's events or plan for the next day. A properly set up cooking tent provides a more social, enjoyable space during an expedition.

While cooking tents require extra effort to carry and set up, they are highly beneficial for larger teams. For smaller groups, they may not be as practical, but for big expeditions, a dedicated cooking tent provides an essential gathering space and makes meal preparation far more efficient.

Wildlife Safety

Being outdoors means sharing space with wildlife, ranging from harmless animals like squirrels and marmots to more dangerous ones like grizzly bears and bison. Even seemingly innocuous animals can cause trouble—squirrels and marmots might steal your food or damage your gear, while larger animals like bison can pose significant risks. Although bison may appear calm, if they wander near your camp at night, they could unintentionally trample your campsite or knock over gear.

Bears and wolves are another concern. While wolves are generally not a threat to humans, they may still be curious about your camp and sniff around. It's important not to approach or antagonize wolves, coyotes, foxes, or similar animals, as they can carry rabies and may become aggressive if provoked. Animals are inherently unpredictable, so it's best to give them plenty of space and avoid direct contact.

If you notice signs that animals frequently visit a particular area, move your campsite to a different location. Giving wildlife space is essential, and relocating your tent can help minimize the risk of unwanted encounters.

Daily Tent Checks

If you're camping in harsh conditions and find yourself snowbound or tent-bound for several days, avoid the temptation to skip checking on your tent. Even if your setup includes a sturdy snow wall, it's crucial to suit up in all your gear and step outside to inspect your campsite. Ensure that your guy lines are still in place and that your tent isn't being crushed by wind-driven, packed snow.

It's easy to overlook these checks, but doing so puts you at risk. Taking just half an hour to inspect your campsite can prevent disasters such as a collapsed tent or a broken guy line flailing around at 2 A.M. Regular checks are a small investment in time that can save you from major problems later.

Fire Safety

When deciding where to cook, consider whether you'll use your stove in the vestibule, outside in a contained area like a snow wall, or inside your tent (which is extremely dangerous due to carbon monoxide poisoning and fire risk). Wherever you choose to set up your stove, be aware that placing it near your tent poses a risk. Even though some tents are treated with fire-resistant or fire-retardant chemicals, minimal heat exposure can still cause damage or even ignite the tent, putting you in danger.

If you're planning to use a campfire, think about how you'll set it up. Since your fire will likely be on top of snow, you'll need to create a stable, insulated base to prevent it from burning through. A common method is using a thick platform of packed snow or placing a fire pan or metal sheet underneath. Avoid building fires directly on rocks, as this can leave permanent black marks and may damage the stone.

Ensure your fire is set up far enough from your tent to prevent embers from floating onto the fabric. The same applies to your technical or synthetic clothing—embers can easily damage expensive gear. Avoid leaning over any fire source to minimize the risk of injury. Reducing fire-related risks ensures both your safety and the integrity of your gear.

Frost and Mildew

No matter how much ventilation you have in your tent at night, chances are, frost will still build up. It's simply a part of winter camping. You can expect your own "frost shower" in the morning. That said, you can use a plastic cup with a relatively thin edge to help manage the frost. While still in your sleeping bag, extend your arm out and start scraping the frost off the tent into the cup. Then, you can dump the collected frost into your vestibule, so you don't end up dropping thick chunks of frost into your sleeping bag or down your neck when you sit up. For short trips, this method can be quite nice, but on long winter trips, it's often more practical to simply put on your heavier parka and deal with the frost. The time spent defrosting a tent in the morning is often better used for other tasks, but if you're not in a rush, using a plastic cup to remove frost can improve your morning experience significantly.

Additionally, be aware of mildew and fungus if you're camping for an extended period, especially on long treks. Food crumbs inevitably get everywhere, and even small amounts left on your camp utensils or tent fabric can cause issues. If food residue or saliva comes into contact with synthetic fabric, it can lead to mold or mildew buildup over time. This is particularly common when you pack up your tent while it's covered in snow, which then melts as the day warms. The combination of moisture and organic residue creates the perfect conditions for mildew growth. Clean your tent as quickly as possible to prevent permanent damage or health issues. Be vigilant about keeping your tent clean—neglecting this can lead to unpleasant results.

This is pretty comfortable winter camping weather at 24°F (-5°C).

Chapter 9
Staying Warm and Dry

Staying Warm and Dry

Staying warm and dry during your winter camping trips will be a nonstop challenge—not just from the moment you wake up until you go to sleep, but also throughout the night. Managing your layer system is crucial for enjoying the experience.

One of the goals when you're moving—hiking, skiing, or whatever activity you're engaged in—is often to stay cool rather than warm. It's easy to put on too many clothes, forge ahead, and become overheated to the point of sweating. If you sweat too much and then stop moving, your damp clothing can rapidly cool you down, leading to violent shivering and mild hypothermia.

To avoid this, aim to stay slightly cool as you move. This will reduce the likelihood of sweating into your clothes, soaking them, and eventually developing chills, hypothermia, or worse. One of the hardest moments during winter camping, if you're going to be active, is the first 10 to 15 minutes of transitioning from standing still—preparing your gear—to actually moving. You go from being quite chilled and possibly uncomfortable to overheating quickly if you start with too many layers on.

If the weather is relatively calm and stable, it's often a good choice to remove a layer before you start moving. You want to begin slightly chilled, but not too cold. Then, as you warm up, your body heat will balance out without overheating. Typically, this transition happens within the first 10 to 15 minutes of leaving camp in the morning.

If conditions are too harsh to remove a layer—where you're already shivering violently or it's just too cold—you'll need to focus on venting heat instead. As soon as you start moving, if you can unzip a layer while still maintaining your movement, do so. This takes practice, and due to the variability of winter temperatures throughout the day, sometimes you won't succeed, and you'll need to stop and make adjustments.

Often, you'll see climbing teams marching along, everyone very hot, and they'll be thankful when the guide suggests stopping to remove a layer. As long as you control your own pace and don't disrupt your team's progress, it's fine to call for a quick adjustment if you start to overheat. Just remember, it's easier to vent heat while moving than to stop completely and cool down too much.

Always aim to stay slightly cool when moving. It's easy to pick up the pace a bit and generate more heat, but if you get too hot, stopping to fully take off a layer—removing a backpack harness or whatever else you have on—can be quite the challenge.

Managing Moisture

The ideal goal when traveling away from camp during the day is to stay cool, comfortable, and dry the entire time. Though this is unlikely, it's still the target to strive for. The challenge is that when you sweat and soak your clothes, they not only become wet, but the oils and salts from your body also make them dirty. Once your clothes are soiled, they will remain that way for the rest of your trip, especially on longer outings.

If you're on an extended trip, there's no real way to avoid dirty clothes. You can keep yourself from sweating too much by staying cool, but there's no way to prevent oils and salts from your skin from infiltrating your clothing. It's just something you have to manage.

One trick to help regulate temperature is to carry an extra headband and even an extra hat. These are much easier to remove than a jacket layer and certainly more convenient than taking off pants. It might feel a bit awkward to carry a couple of hats, but your head is one of the few areas where you can easily remove something and stuff an extra hat into a pocket.

There's an old belief that you lose the most heat from your head, but research suggests that heat loss is proportional to the amount of exposed skin, not the head specifically. The head often feels like a major source of heat loss because it is one of the least insulated areas when you're outdoors, but it isn't necessarily where the most heat escapes.

That said, your head and hands are the easiest areas to make thermal adjustments, and regulating these two areas can make all the difference in managing your overall comfort—whether you're too warm or too cold.

Ventilation Techniques

Before removing a layer or jacket completely, use the ventilation features of your clothing. Start by removing a hat; if the wind is too strong and makes you cold, switch to a headband to cover your ears. Even a simple headband can get the job done.

Removing a buff from your neck can also help cool you down. Unzipping your jacket is another easy way to shed heat. If the wind is strong but you're overheating, loosen both your outer and inner jackets to increase airflow, then rezip your outer shell when you need warmth again.

Some jackets have what are called pit zips—zippers that run along the underside of the arm and along the side of your torso. Unzipping these can help cool you down significantly, especially in the underarm area, which has a high concentration of blood flow. Opening these vents can make a big difference in your comfort.

Additionally, if you're wearing shell pants with long side zips, you can unzip them all the way down to your gaiters. Even in breezy conditions, unzipping these ventilation points helps cool you down while keeping your layers in place. When you take a break, you won't need to change out of your jacket to warm up—just zip up your vents. This approach adds a lot of flexibility to your layering system without requiring you to remove clothing entirely.

Adjust Your Glove System

Another layer of your body that you can easily adjust for temperature control is your gloves. Adjusting your gloves requires minimal effort and can have a significant impact. For instance, you might start with a liner glove inside a heavier alpine glove in cold morning conditions. Once it warms up, switch to a thinner pair of gloves that you have ready. This subtle adjustment can make a big difference in your comfort level.

You may notice your hands feeling warm even as they release heat, and adjusting your gloves can help regulate your overall body temperature. If you're traveling on tricky terrain where slipping and falling is likely, avoid putting your hands in the snow, as this will only make things worse. Protect your hands in case of a fall.

Sometimes, conditions allow you to go all the way down to just a quality liner glove. As long as you're not holding an ice axe or doing strenuous activities—if you're simply hiking without trekking poles—liner gloves can be a great way to bleed off excess heat. If you're skiing and the weather isn't too cold, switching to a liner glove can let some heat escape without overly chilling your fingers. A small change like this can make a big difference in staying comfortable while avoiding overheating.

When It Becomes Too Hot

On some winter trips, you may experience drastic temperature shifts. It could go from far below freezing—such as -2°F (-18°C)—all the way up to 45°F (7°C). In the context of winter camping and trekking, these warmer temperatures can feel absolutely stifling.

When it gets too hot, don't hesitate to strip down to your shirt sleeves, even if you're on a polar plateau or deep in the woods. Sometimes, it's necessary. It takes confidence to do this because many people are conditioned to keep all their layers on for warmth. Ignore this instinct as long as it's safe—strip down to your shirt and keep going.

However, be mindful of sun exposure and occasional gusts of wind, which can quickly chill you. Protect your neck and arms from the sun, as well as your head. A lightweight boonie hat is a great option for sun protection, and applying sunscreen is essential. A stick-style sunscreen, such as those from Neutrogena or similar manufacturers, is recommended. This way, you don't get lotion on your hands, which can transfer to your gloves or contaminate your food. Reapply sunscreen multiple times a day, as it tends to wear off.

If the temperature rises further, slow your activity down. Overheating can lead to heat exhaustion, which, if left unchecked, can progress to heat stroke—a serious medical emergency. Pushing yourself too hard in high temperatures can leave you feeling weak and incapacitated for days.

Author's Note

This happened to me in Greenland. I pushed myself too hard, even though the mornings were cold and stormy. By the afternoon, around 2 P.M., the heat became overwhelming. I was stripped down to my shirt and thin liner gloves, but I was still struggling. My companion, Terry, was doing fine because his body metabolized the heat better. I covered my neck to prevent sunburn, but by the end of the day, I was completely depleted.

For the next several days, I felt terrible—low energy and unwell. Not adjusting to or slowing down for the afternoon heat taught me a hard lesson. From then on, we changed our schedule: we woke up at 3 A.M., started moving by 6 A.M., and avoided the heat of the day. That adjustment made all the difference.

Managing Heat with Teams

Adjusting your pace to the conditions is paramount to your health, happiness, and that of your team. Managing heat is a key part of this process—overheating can be as dangerous as getting too cold. Whether trekking solo or in a group, staying cool enough to avoid sweating excessively while maintaining warmth when needed is critical.

If you're traveling solo, you can adjust your pace and clothing as needed, provided you're not under time pressure to reach a destination or falling behind schedule. Set a turnaround time and stick to it—adjust your speed accordingly and focus on both comfort and progress.

When traveling with a team, especially one with varied skill levels, managing heat becomes a group effort. Avoid placing slower members at the back, as they may push themselves too hard to keep up, leading to overheating or exhaustion. Instead, positioning slower members at the front helps maintain a steady, sustainable pace. While faster individuals might feel frustrated, they can manage their emotional response better than the physical toll slower members would endure by overexerting. This approach helps maintain morale and ensures everyone progresses safely.

As a leader or guide, balancing team dynamics with heat management is essential. The primary goal in activities like hiking, climbing, or skiing is to maintain a steady pace rather than frequently stopping, which can disrupt momentum and lead to rapid cooling after exertion, creating discomfort or even health risks.

For example, during a flatland ski trip with a sled, every minute you stop can cost you around 100 yards (or 100 meters) of progress. Over a multi-day trip, unnecessary breaks—if taken too frequently—can add up. Even small delays each day can result in significant lost distance over time.

To manage heat effectively, adjust your layers early when you feel too warm, even if it feels counterintuitive. Protect exposed areas like your neck, arms, and head from sunburn or wind with lightweight gear, such as a boonie hat and sunscreen. Reapply sunscreen frequently, especially on sunny days. Starting earlier in the morning or slowing down during peak heat can help conserve energy and prevent overheating.

By planning stops wisely, adjusting layers proactively, and maintaining a steady pace, you can successfully manage heat for yourself and your team, ensuring a safe and enjoyable trip.

Managing Layers and Draining Heat

If you need to remove layers while trekking, climbing, or hiking, it's crucial to ensure your clothing is fully secured. Many people have made the mistake of stuffing their jacket under a strap or tying it loosely to their pack, only to discover hours later that it's disappeared. Avoid this at all costs.

If you can't pack your jacket efficiently into your backpack, at least secure it with a strap. Run a strap through the sleeves or another sturdy part of the jacket to ensure it's 100% secure and won't fall off. Even in calm conditions, unexpected wind can quickly blow away improperly secured gear. You don't want to look back and see your jacket or gloves drifting toward the horizon. Always take a moment to double-check your gear.

If your clothing gets slightly damp during the day, you can try drying it in the sun if the weather permits. If there's no sun, plan to dry it out at night. The best way to dry your clothes at night, particularly if you're cold camping with minimal heat, is to initially hang them in your tent to air out. For further drying, take slightly damp clothing you wore during the day and place it inside your sleeping bag. Avoid putting in wet clothes, as this can make your bag damp and reduce insulation.

Spread the clothing evenly inside the sleeping bag to maximize drying and prevent cold spots from bunched-up fabric. Placing the clothing you plan to wear in the morning inside your sleeping bag ensures it's warm when you put it on, preventing discomfort from cold gear. This simple practice adds a lot of comfort to your routine.

The human body continuously generates about 100 watts of heat—similar to a 100-watt incandescent light bulb. This is enough to dry slightly damp clothing or boot liners overnight, as long as insulation is sufficient.

This method is efficient, requires zero extra effort, and is the professional way to ensure your gear is ready for the next day. Just remember to zip up your sleeping bag and tuck everything in securely to avoid cold spots or losing items while you sleep. When you wake up, your clothing will be dry, warm, and ready for the next adventure.

Protecting Your Feet and Keeping Them Warm

Keeping your feet warm and protected is one of the most challenging aspects of managing your layering system. Socks and boots require significant effort to remove during the day, so as long as you're not at risk of frostbite, it's better to adjust your upper body layers first to help regulate overall warmth before addressing your feet. The goal is to prevent overheating, which can lead to sweaty feet, blisters, and eventually cold, miserable feet later in the day.

Managing foot warmth can be tricky because removing boots to adjust socks exposes your feet to extremely cold conditions. It's a hassle, and many people avoid it altogether, but failing to manage this properly can lead to discomfort and even health risks.

Some individuals naturally handle foot temperature regulation better than others. People with conditions like Reynaud's disease or poor circulation tend to struggle more with keeping their feet warm. Intuition and experience play an important role in managing this, as everyone's body reacts differently.

One option for managing foot temperature, especially if you're prone to cold feet, is using vapor barrier liners (VBLs). These are plastic or synthetic liners worn over socks to trap heat and prevent moisture from reaching your boot insulation, keeping it dry. This can be particularly effective for people who struggle with cold feet.

However, vapor barrier liners come with drawbacks. Because they completely seal your feet, moisture has no way to escape. Over time, sweat buildup can cause friction spots, blisters, and discomfort. Prolonged use on a long trip may also cause the liners to degrade, compromising their ability to retain heat.

Additionally, the moisture trapped by VBLs can create issues with skin health. Wet feet over long periods increase the risk of hotspots and maceration, which can be painful and make walking difficult. If you choose to use VBLs, monitor your feet closely and adjust as needed.

In general, it's better to avoid relying on vapor barrier liners unless absolutely necessary, such as in emergency situations. Maintaining dry, well-managed socks and boots should be your primary strategy for keeping feet warm. If you use VBLs, reserve them for extreme cold or emergency situations rather than daily use in milder conditions.

By carefully managing your footwear and socks, you can prevent cold, damp feet and ensure a more comfortable and successful outing.

Protecting Your Feet While Traveling

Whether you're skiing, climbing, or trekking, developing what's called a "hot spot" on your feet is a common issue. This typically occurs on the sides or bottom of your feet and feels like a blister might be forming. If you notice this happening, stop immediately—assuming it's safe to do so. Ignoring a hot spot can lead to much worse issues later, impacting both your comfort and your overall trip.

Hotspots often start as a small red area that feels hot to the touch. If addressed quickly, they're usually manageable. Stop to adjust your socks, boots, or foot position, and apply moleskin if needed. Immediate treatment is essential to prevent hotspots from turning into full-blown blisters that make every step feel like misery.

Hotspots can also result from poor technique. If your skiing form causes your foot to slide sideways inside your boot or your cross-country stride is uneven, you're more likely to experience friction that leads to hotspots. These small issues can ruin an otherwise enjoyable trip, so prevention and prompt care are crucial. If you know you have hotspots or blisters in particular locations regularly, it's best to preemptively add bandages.

If conditions are bad—wet, windy, or freezing—it can be tempting to push ahead and ignore the discomfort. However, unless the weather is extremely severe (e.g., winds over 40 mph or 65 km/h), it's better to stop and address the issue. The best approach is to sit on your sled or pack, set up a windbreak if possible, and make your adjustments in a safe, sheltered position.

How to Handle a Hot Spot in the Field:
- Sit on your sled or pack and find a leeward side (protected from the wind) to work.
- Remove your boot and sock, inspecting the affected area for hotspots.
- Address the problem—apply moleskin, adjust layers, or whatever is needed.
- If available, put on clean, dry socks before securing your boot back on.

Some Arctic explorers carry an oversized waterproof bag, like a bivy sack, to create a temporary shelter while addressing foot issues. This can be a lifesaver if you're traveling in extreme conditions with little shelter available. If you're planning a long trip with unpredictable weather, carrying a lightweight, body-sized bag for this purpose can make all the difference.

Even small issues, such as a wrinkle in your sock or a piece of debris rubbing inside your boot, should not be ignored. Stop, take care of it, and ensure your feet stay in good condition. Healthy feet are key to an enjoyable and a safe journey.

Night Sleep Systems

When preparing your sleep system for the night, it's best to have a dedicated change of clothing specifically for sleeping. If you're on a long trip and need to minimize weight, consider cycling or swapping out your least dirty clothes to use as sleepwear. Ideally, you should have at least one set of clean, dry clothes dedicated to sleeping. For longer trips, you might need two or three sets to rotate through, ensuring comfort and hygiene.

Under ideal circumstances, your sleepwear should consist of lightweight, long-sleeve shirts and long-legged underwear. This system works well in most weather conditions. If you find yourself needing to pile on additional layers just to stay warm, it's a sign that your sleeping bag is inadequate for the conditions. This could put your safety and psychological well-being at risk, especially in colder temperatures.

Some people use layering inside their sleeping bags to reduce the bag's weight, but this approach carries risks if temperatures drop significantly below what you expected. The standard advice to sleep in minimal layers (such as just your underwear) remains a valid strategy in well-insulated bags, as it ensures you have extra clothing to add if conditions worsen. This provides flexibility and a safety buffer in your sleep system.

However, if it's extremely cold and you're feeling chilled and unable to sleep, don't hesitate to add more layers. Throw on a fleece jacket or whatever extra clothing you need to stay warm. If your sleeping bag is rated appropriately but you're facing an unexpectedly cold night, it's better to stay warm than to stick rigidly to the idea of only wearing underwear in your bag.

Another benefit of wearing lightweight, long-sleeved shirts and long underwear while sleeping is that it keeps your sleeping bag cleaner on extended trips. Oils from your skin can accumulate in the insulation layer of your bag over time, reducing its efficiency and warmth. Using a clean layer of sleepwear helps protect your bag's performance and keeps it working effectively throughout your trip.

By following these suggestions, you'll stay warmer, more comfortable, and better prepared to face whatever conditions arise during your adventure.

Sleeping Bag Warmth Tips

One of the best ways to ensure your sleeping bag is warm before you get in is by pre-warming it with heated water bottles. When heating water bottles at night, make sure they are safe for this purpose and properly sealed. Seal the bottles tightly and tilt them sideways to check for leaks before placing them in your sleeping bag.

Place the water bottles inside a waterproof sack and then tuck them into your sleeping bag. Over time, the heat from the bottles will warm the interior of the bag. This method not only helps with warmth but can also keep small electronics warm during the night, preventing them from freezing.

Climbing into a sleeping bag with pre-warmed water bottles provides significant psychological comfort, especially in cold conditions. Feeling warmth immediately instead of waiting for your body heat to warm the bag can make a huge difference in how comfortable and relaxed you feel as you prepare to sleep. Additionally, these warm water bottles can retain heat for a long time, keeping you comfortable throughout the night.

It's also a good idea to bring a pair of lightweight down booties in addition to your regular sleeping socks. Dedicated sleeping socks work well, but down booties provide even more insulation and can make a noticeable difference in warmth.

By combining these tips—pre-warming your sleeping bag with hot water bottles and using proper sleeping footwear—you'll ensure a much warmer and more comfortable night outdoors.

Sleeping Bags, Fabric Liners, and Vapor Barrier Liners

It is possible to extend the temperature range of your sleeping bag by using a liner. A fabric liner can add several degrees of warmth to your sleeping bag and, in some cases, even protect it from moisture and dirt, keeping it cleaner and drier over time. In extreme circumstances, a vapor barrier liner can also be used, though it's typically reserved for very cold conditions.

A vapor barrier liner is designed to trap heat by preventing moisture from escaping your body and saturating your sleeping bag's insulation, keeping it dry in extreme cold. This can significantly boost warmth but comes with the downside of retaining all the moisture your body produces. While a vapor barrier liner increases warmth, the lack of ventilation can make it feel clammy or uncomfortable.

Fabric liners, on the other hand, are a more breathable option. They can still add warmth to your sleeping system while helping to keep your sleeping bag cleaner and more hygienic. However, a common drawback of both types of liners is the effort required to use them. Getting into a liner at bedtime and climbing out for a 2 A.M. bathroom break can be inconvenient, especially in cold conditions.

While liners are an effective way to boost your sleeping bag's performance, they shouldn't be relied on solely to compensate for a poorly rated or inadequate sleeping bag. It's tempting to save money by purchasing a cheaper sleeping bag and using a liner to extend its temperature range, but this approach can lead to problems. If the liner becomes ineffective or conditions turn harsher than expected, you may find yourself unprepared and at risk.

Investing in a well-rated sleeping bag is often worth the extra cost in the long run. It ensures reliable warmth and comfort without needing to rely heavily on additional layers or liners, giving you peace of mind and a better night's sleep.

It's going to be a cold night in a single wall tent at -20°F (-29°C).

Chapter 10
Managing Body Heat, Exposure, Travel

Heat Loss Methods

Your body loses heat through four primary mechanisms: **convection, conduction, radiation, and evaporation**.

Convection

Convection occurs when warm air around your body is replaced by cooler air, pulling heat away. Wind accelerates this process, dramatically increasing heat loss. In harsh conditions, do everything you can to get out of the wind. To prevent convective heat loss, seek shelter and improve your insulation. This type of heat loss is especially noticeable in your toes, hands, and exposed parts of your face.

Conduction

Conduction happens when your body comes into contact with a cold surface, such as snow or the ground. These surfaces draw heat away from you. Lying down without proper insulation underneath can result in significant heat loss. Using a foam pad or any insulating layer reduces this dramatically.

Your feet are particularly vulnerable when standing on ice or snow. Even insulated boots won't prevent the cold from creeping in if you remain stationary. To minimize this, stand on foam pads, skis, or snowshoes. Even a small barrier helps. However, be cautious when balancing on skis or snowshoes while performing tasks like setting up a tent.

Radiation

Radiation is the loss of heat as infrared energy. This heat loss can be significant in cold conditions, especially from exposed skin. Mylar blankets or space blankets help reduce this by reflecting body heat. Foam sleeping pads with reflective layers also bounce heat back toward your body. While radiation loss is a factor, it does not account for as much heat loss as conduction and convection in most cold-weather conditions.

Evaporation

Evaporation occurs when sweat turns to vapor, pulling heat away from your body. Staying dry is critical in cold conditions, as wet clothing conducts heat away much faster than dry materials. Manage your layers carefully to avoid excessive sweating.

If you fall into water, heat loss accelerates dramatically—water conducts heat over 25 times faster than air. Wet clothing not only increases conduction loss but also continues to cool you as water evaporates from the fabric. Avoid open water in winter to prevent rapid cooling and life-threatening heat loss.

Body Reactions to Cold

Your body has several natural responses to cold that help regulate temperature. Each physiological response has helpful and detrimental side effects.

Shivering

The first and most familiar reaction is shivering. When your core temperature drops even slightly, your body begins involuntarily contracting muscles to generate heat. While this does produce some warmth, it is not very effective.

If you start shivering while resting, climbing, or skiing, it's a sign that you don't have enough insulation and are entering the early stages of hypothermia. Mild shivering isn't immediately dangerous, but if it becomes violent—or worse, stops while you're still cold—you've entered a critical hypothermic state, which can lead to confusion, poor coordination, and loss of consciousness.

Beyond the physical impact, constant shivering takes a mental toll, making the experience harder to endure. Severe cold exposure can create a negative association with winter activities, leading to discomfort that affects both mind and body.

Vasoconstriction

The second major reaction to cold is vasoconstriction, where blood vessels in your extremities narrow to reduce heat loss. This process prioritizes warmth in your core, brain, and vital organs at the expense of your fingers, hands, toes, and feet.

In extreme conditions, blood flow can be restricted so much that your body sacrifices extremities to maintain core temperature. This is how frostbite occurs—when tissues freeze due to prolonged exposure to subfreezing temperatures. Poor circulation from vasoconstriction increases the risk, but the primary cause is the cold itself. Preventing frostbite is critical.

Environmental Effects of Windchill and Water

Two of the most significant environmental factors that cause heat loss are windchill and moisture conduction. Windchill is the most common. You can feel relatively comfortable in very cold conditions—even around 0°F (-18°C)—but as soon as a mild breeze picks up, it can feel much colder than the actual temperature. Wind increases convective heat loss by stripping away the warm air close to your body. While windchill doesn't lower the actual air temperature, it greatly accelerates heat loss from exposed skin and poorly insulated areas.

What might be manageable temperatures with a decent insulated layer can suddenly require every piece of clothing you have, even in moderate breezes. In stronger winds, the risk of hypothermia or frostbite rises quickly with small increases in speed. If the wind is especially strong and you're stuck in it, you'll need to layer strategically, using air gaps and a windproof outer shell to protect yourself.

Moisture is another major factor. Wet clothing conducts heat away from your body far faster than dry air, even when temperatures are above freezing. When temperatures rise enough to melt snow or bring rain, then drop again, any moisture in your clothing will continue pulling heat away rapidly. Wet materials transfer heat roughly 25 times faster than dry air, leading to rapid chilling and a higher risk of frostbite.

This is why keeping your clothing as dry as possible is critical. Avoid sweating, because once you stop moving, any moisture in your clothing will rapidly pull heat away, leaving you cold and uncomfortable.

Overheating, Sweat, and Dehydration

One of the lesser-understood challenges of outdoor adventuring is overheating. Wearing too many layers for the conditions or your activity level can cause sweating, leaving your clothing damp. Even if you keep moving, this moisture can cool you down through evaporative heat loss, which pulls warmth away from your skin. If you don't replace lost fluids, dehydration further impairs your body's ability to regulate temperature.

As you lose moisture, dehydration reduces blood volume, making circulation less efficient. Combined with the body's natural cold-induced vasoconstriction, this makes it harder to distribute heat effectively. Even though it might not feel necessary in cold conditions, drinking enough fluids is key to staying warm.

Cold air also pulls moisture from your body faster than warm or humid air. Breathing in dry, cold air increases moisture loss from your lungs, while exhaled breath carries away more water vapor in winter. This not only depletes hydration levels but also cools your body further as moisture evaporates from the skin.

Managing overheating and hydration starts with monitoring your sweat levels and breathing rate. If you're sweating too much, you're overdressed for your activity level. When climbing, hiking, or engaging in other exertion, a good rule of thumb is to pace yourself so that you're breathing comfortably. If you're gasping for breath or overheating, slow down to reduce sweating and fluid loss.

Recognizing dehydration in winter is challenging because the cold makes thirst less noticeable. However, staying aware of your activity level, hydration needs, and clothing layers can help you avoid wet clothing, slowed circulation, and moisture loss—all of which increase your risk of hypothermia or frostbite. Managing your pace, hydration, and layers is essential to preventing excessive chilling and the complications it causes.

Protecting Against Frostbite

Protecting yourself from frostbite in winter conditions is a continuous effort. It can sneak up on you unexpectedly when conditions change—whether it's the wind picking up, cloud cover reducing sunlight, or an unexpected fall into water.

Falling into water doesn't directly cause frostbite because water temporarily insulates against extreme cold. However, water conducts heat away from the body 25 times faster than air, which means hypothermia can set in quickly. The real danger comes afterward—if you emerge wet and can't dry off and warm up immediately, the rapid heat loss increases the risk of frostbite, especially in the extremities.

Recognizing the early signs of frostbite is critical. It usually starts with numbness, tingling, and skin discoloration, especially in extremities like fingers, toes, ears, and the nose.

Frostbite Progression

Frostbite progresses in stages. At first, the affected area feels extremely cold, then painful, and eventually goes numb. Numb fingers or toes might feel like wood—rigid and unresponsive to touch.

As the skin cools, nerve function starts to decline near freezing (32°F/0°C), with circulation slowing and dexterity decreasing. While no permanent damage occurs at this point, it marks a threshold where things start going wrong. If the skin continues to cool and drops below 31°F to 28°F (-0.5°C to -2°C), ice crystals begin forming inside cells, tearing tissue apart and leading to swelling and blisters. Severe damage typically occurs below 24°F (-4°C), and frostbite is much more likely below 21°F (-6°C).

Without intervention, frostbite can escalate from superficial damage to deep tissue destruction. The nose, ears, fingers, and toes are the most vulnerable areas. Protecting these areas from exposure is key to preventing severe damage.

Treating Frostbite in the Field

Field treatment for frostbite is challenging. If frostbitten tissue is thawed but refreezes, the damage becomes far worse. If you cannot ensure the thawed tissue will stay warm, it's better to leave it frozen until you reach a location with proper care. Once in a controlled environment, seek professional medical attention immediately.

In some countries without advanced medical resources, severe frostbite may be treated with amputation as a standard response. However, with specialized care, much of the tissue can often recover—provided that infection, like gangrene, is avoided. Early medical intervention within 24 hours is crucial to reduce complications. Recovery can take months, but untreated severe frostbite can lead to infection or tissue death within days. If you're in a remote location, getting home for advanced treatment is critical. In the meantime, focus on preventing infection and managing the injury.

Advanced Frostbite Progression

As frostbite worsens, fingers or toes transition from feeling painfully cold to completely numb and detached, as though they aren't part of your body. At this stage, nerve damage occurs as skin temperatures drop further. Swelling begins as ice crystals form in cells and blood vessels, causing tissue tearing and internal bleeding."

Severe frostbite can progress to:
- **Second-degree frostbite** – blisters and swelling.
- **Third-degree frostbite** – permanent tissue destruction.

At this stage, immediate medical care is critical. This is no longer a minor issue but a serious condition requiring professional treatment.

By recognizing frostbite early, managing exposure, and responding quickly, you can avoid its worst outcomes. Prevention remains the best defense—staying dry, protecting extremities, and acting fast after incidents like falling into water are critical to reducing risk.

Large Temperature Swings and Sudden Storms

When camping in colder months, you'll often face dramatic temperature swings—from sub-zero (-18°C or lower) at night to as high as 40°F (8°C) during the day. Managing these changes is key to staying comfortable and safe.

During the day, the sun might make conditions feel warm, but as soon as it dips below the horizon, behind trees, or clouds roll in, the perceived temperature can drop rapidly as surfaces lose solar radiation.

If you're traveling with gear, plan ahead. As the day transitions, bundle up before the chill sets in. Have your jacket and layers ready so you're not caught off guard. Staying ahead of the temperature drop can make all the difference.

When exploring away from base camp, always prepare for unexpected overnight exposure. Bring insulation—like an emergency blanket or a down jacket—and a shovel to dig into a snowbank or create a windbreak if necessary. A fully built snow shelter takes time and effort, but in an emergency, any protection from wind and exposure can keep you alive.

In environments like glaciers or alpine regions with little cover, storms can develop quickly. One moment, you're hiking in clear conditions; within an hour, fog and mist can descend, followed by sustained winds of 30 to 50 mph

(50 to 80 km/h). These rapid changes can turn routine travel into a fight for survival, especially when windchill, low visibility, and exhaustion set in.

In such conditions, ask yourself: Is it worth pushing on, or should I stop and make camp? Many who choose to push through succeed, but others end up in life-threatening situations. Unless there's an urgent need to continue, it's smarter to stop, make camp, and reevaluate in the morning when conditions may be more favorable. Prioritizing safety over progress can save your life.

Solar Loading and Sun Protection in Winter

In calm, clear skies, even in northern latitudes, the sun's solar load can be surprisingly intense. You can develop a sunburn even in sub-zero temperatures. While the air may feel bitterly cold, the sun's UV rays remain strong and can cause burns or even lead to overheating.

Climbers often experience sunburn in unexpected places, like under their chins, inside their nostrils, or even on the roof of their mouths, due to sunlight reflecting off snow. In high-reflectivity environments, fresh, clean snow can reflect 80–90% of UV radiation, while older or rough snow reflects less—closer to 50–70%.

Consider what type of sun protection to bring on your winter trip. Will you use sunscreen lotion, a solid stick sunscreen, or rely on full skin coverage?

Each approach has advantages and disadvantages:
Lotion sunscreens can cause issues on trips where washing up isn't possible. Handling lotion with gloves on can transfer it to gear, potentially reducing insulation.
Solid stick sunscreens are better for minimizing direct hand contact and keeping gear cleaner. However, even solid sunscreen can leave residue, so bringing glove liners or a small cleaning cloth is a good idea.

Physical coverage alone is an option, but reflected sunlight off snow can cause burns in areas you might not expect. A hat or climbing helmet won't protect everything.

Once you get sunburned, your skin becomes dehydrated and damaged, which can lead to further complications, discomfort, and impaired judgment.

Winter's variability adds to the challenge. Mornings can start bitterly cold, but by mid-afternoon, temperatures may swing 30–50°F (15–28°C). In just six to eight hours, you can go from frostbite risk to overheating and dehydration if layers aren't managed properly.

Managing these extremes is what makes winter travel both fascinating and demanding. Planning ahead to protect your skin, adapt to temperature swings, and stay comfortable is key to making your trip safe and enjoyable.

Hypothermia: The Hidden Danger

Hypothermia occurs when your body loses heat faster than it can produce it, causing your core temperature to drop. Managing body heat during large temperature swings is essential to preventing this dangerous condition. Hypothermia doesn't happen all at once—it creeps in gradually, making it especially insidious if you're alone and unaware of the early signs.

Shivering is the first noticeable response when your body starts to lose heat—a clear signal that you need to act. If addressed early—by adding layers, staying dry, and reducing exposure—you can avoid further problems. However, if ignored, shivering intensifies, becoming violent and harder to control. Fatigue sets in, and thinking becomes sluggish. If the body cools further, shivering stops altogether, a critical danger sign that the body can no longer generate heat on its own.

Hypothermia subtly affects your mental state, making it harder to think clearly or recognize the severity of the situation. In moderate to severe hypothermia, victims may feel falsely confident, become apathetic, or even strip off clothing (paradoxical undressing) due to the brain misinterpreting temperature signals. This is why managing body heat before hypothermia begins is so critical.

Temperature swings during the day can be tricky. Mornings may be frigid, requiring multiple layers, but by mid-afternoon, rising temperatures may cause you to overheat. Sweating in warm periods leads to wet clothing, which dramatically increases heat loss through conduction and evaporation when temperatures drop again later. Wet fabric pulls heat away from the body 25 times faster than air, rapidly accelerating cooling.

To prevent this, adjust your layers frequently—ventilate or remove layers during activity to avoid sweating, and add them back as soon as you cool down or stop moving.

One of the biggest challenges with hypothermia is recognizing it in yourself. As your body temperature drops, you may lose awareness of your condition and fail to recognize your own impairment. This is why staying ahead of temperature changes is crucial.

If you find yourself alone, pay close attention to your physical and mental state. If you're with others, communicate early about how you're feeling and monitor each other for signs of impairment like slurred speech, confusion, or clumsiness.

Hypothermia prevention is about staying proactive:
- Avoid overheating
- Keep dry
- Don't wait until you're already cold to take action

By managing body heat effectively throughout the day, you can navigate large temperature swings and prevent hypothermia before it becomes a threat.

Traveling in Snowy Terrain

When traveling with both a sled and a backpack, it's essential to consider load balance, especially on flat terrain. Aim to load as much of your heavy gear in the sled as possible to reduce strain on your back. Keep only essential emergency items in your backpack, ensuring that if you become separated from the sled, you can still survive and navigate challenges.

Delicate gear, such as electronics, may be safer in your backpack than in the sled, as sleds can tumble and crush fragile items. However, electronics are also highly susceptible to cold, and batteries drain rapidly in freezing temperatures. If stored in a sled, wrap electronics in clothing or foam to insulate them from both impact damage and extreme cold.

Load Management on Steep Terrain

In steeper terrain, the strategy shifts. On climbs like Motorcycle Hill on Denali or similar mountainous paths, pack heavier items in your backpack to reduce the load on the sled. A heavy sled on steep inclines can pull you backward, destabilize your footing, and make climbing much more difficult.

If you stumble, the sled becomes a relentless weight that can drag you down or even off a cliff. The constant backward pull is not only physically taxing but also mentally stressful. On descents, a heavy sled can accelerate uncontrollably, increasing the risk of getting dragged downhill or losing control.

To mitigate stumbling from awkward loads:
- Avoid overloading your sled with heavy items in steep or technical terrain.

- Keep lighter items in the sled and shift more weight into your backpack when necessary.
- Adjust weight dynamically—instead of fully shifting the load to your back, redistribute some weight to the sled when conditions allow, preventing overloading your back and ensuring better control on descents.

Managing Pack Weight and Stability

A backpack exceeding 50 pounds (23kg) can become unwieldy. A heavy, tall pack increases the risk of losing balance, leading to falls or tumbles.

Even though a heavy sled can be frustrating on inclines, it is less likely to shift your center of gravity compared to a top-heavy pack. However, on side slopes, sleds are prone to tumbling, especially if attached with a simple rope. A rigid pole or frame connection provides better control, reducing tipping and dragging risks.

Ultimately, the key is balance. While a heavier backpack reduces sled-related risks, it also introduces its own hazards, such as swaying and instability. Manage your load thoughtfully, keeping both terrain and your physical capacity in mind.

Cold Soaking

One of the things people often don't anticipate when venturing into extremely cold conditions—below -22°F to -31°F (-30°C to -35°C)—is an effect called cold soaking. This occurs when technical fabrics like nylon reach the ambient temperature of the extreme cold environment.

While nylon and similar fabrics don't have the same thermal conductivity as materials like aluminum, they can still feel intensely cold to the touch in these conditions. This happens because cold-soaked fabric prevents the body from retaining heat at the point of contact, creating an effect similar to touching metal. Although this might not always cause frostbite, repeated contact can accelerate localized heat loss, leading to discomfort, numbness, and increased risk of hypothermia over time.

This issue is particularly relevant when handling outer technical fabrics. Repeated contact with cold-soaked materials can be physically draining, reducing dexterity and decision-making ability in extreme conditions.

To mitigate the impacts of cold soaking:
- Wear insulated gloves when handling cold gear.

- Minimize direct skin contact with frozen fabrics.
- Be mindful of cumulative heat loss from frequent exposure to cold surfaces.

Moderately Cold Snow and Soaking Outer Layers

One major challenge in the mountains, even in moderately cold conditions, is wind-driven snow soaking your outer layers. If your outer layer is warm enough, it can melt the snow on contact, leading to a wet jacket.

With a hard shell, this isn't a major issue since it repels moisture. But if you're wearing a heavy down parka as your outermost layer, it may start absorbing water. Some hydrophobic down treatments help resist moisture for a short time, but once down becomes wet, drying it in the field is nearly impossible. The feathers clump together and trap less air, significantly reducing insulation.

Down parkas are typically designed for very cold conditions where snow remains dry and doesn't melt on contact. However, sometimes conditions fall into a middle range where melting happens unpredictably.

When soaking occurs, you may have to decide on your approach:
- Wear your down jacket under a hard shell—reducing its loft slightly but keeping it dry.
- Wear your jacket as an outer layer—risking moisture absorption from melting snow.

To avoid this problem of layering problems:
- Ensure your outer shell isn't too tight—it should have enough room for a down jacket or additional layers without compressing the insulation.
- Consider a layering approach—using a fleece or synthetic mid-layer under a shell for active movement and reserving down insulation for static warmth at camp or rest stops. This balance ensures you stay warm and dry when conditions aren't as predictable as you'd hoped.

Chapter 11
Maintaining Electronics in the Winter

Maintaining and Keeping Electronics Running

Keeping electronics operational in the winter can be a real challenge. The cold rapidly drains battery energy, and once depleted, it doesn't recover easily. Recharging in the wilderness presents another major obstacle—not only is there no plug-in power, but winter solar charging is often ineffective due to dense cloud cover.

Below are some strategies for maintaining communication, navigation, and even entertainment in cold conditions.

Battery Types

Batteries fall into two main categories: primary cells (non-rechargeable) and rechargeable cells.

- **Primary cells** include **lithium, alkaline, and carbon-zinc** batteries. Carbon-zinc batteries are rarely used in electronics because they can't handle high power loads. They may work in basic flashlights or low-power devices, but high-power LED flashlights will drain them quickly.
- **Alkaline batteries** (classic dry cells) are widely available and inexpensive, making them useful for everyday applications like remote controls. However, they perform poorly in cold temperatures. At around 32°F (0°C) or below, they lose their ability to generate electricity and fail quickly.
- **Nickel-metal hydride (NiMH) batteries** are a common rechargeable option, especially in AA size. These require a charger but tolerate cold temperatures poorly unless kept warm. Many rechargeable headlamps and similar devices use NiMH batteries, but they lose power quickly when exposed to freezing conditions.
- **Lithium-ion rechargeable batteries** power most modern electronics,

including cameras and portable devices. However, they do not perform well in extreme cold and can fail when temperatures drop too low. While some lithium-polymer batteries handle the cold better, most lithium-ion rechargeables will need to be kept warm to function properly.

For winter trips, lithium primary cells are the best option. Batteries like Energizer Lithium function reliably in extreme cold, down to -40°F (-40°C), continuing to deliver power when other batteries fail. The downside is they are single-use—once depleted, they cannot be recharged. However, their reliability in frigid conditions makes them a worthwhile choice.

One advantage of lithium-ion rechargeables is that if they stop working in the cold, they may recover some functionality once warmed up. If a camera or GPS battery dies, warming it in an inner pocket can sometimes restore power temporarily.

Other battery types, such as gel-cell or lead-acid, are primarily used in vehicles and off-grid power setups. They are impractical for camping unless you're transporting them in a vehicle or using them with a solar-charging system.

Insulation for Electronics

Insulating electronics can slow heat loss, extending battery life in cold conditions. If you warm a device in your pocket and want to keep it functioning longer, wrapping it in neoprene or fleece can help. However, electronics do not generate enough heat to maintain their temperature independently. Even with insulation, without an external heat source like body warmth or a hot water bottle, devices will eventually cool to the surrounding air temperature, causing the batteries to lose power.

Some storage methods are ineffective in winter:
- **Backpacks or sled bags** may seem convenient but won't protect electronics from the cold. Items stored inside will eventually match the outside temperature.
- **Outer jacket pockets** provide no real insulation. The thin material exposes devices to wind chill and rapid cooling.

The best method is to store electronics in an inner pocket, such as a zippered fleece pocket in your mid-layers. This keeps them close to your body, allowing body heat to help maintain their temperature. If a device generates some warmth while in use, keeping it in an insulated inner pocket will help retain that heat for longer.

Backup Power Supplies

On a long trip, you may need a backup power supply to keep your electronics running. For shorter trips—such as a climb up Kilimanjaro, a weekend in the northern woods of Michigan or Minnesota, or a trek across Yellowstone—battery banks are a great option. They remain reliable when weather conditions prevent solar panels from working, such as under heavy cloud cover. Solar panels also tend to be delicate—if dropped or stepped on, they can break easily. Battery banks, by contrast, are durable and practical.

Modern battery banks recharge via micro USB or USB-C and come in sizes ranging from small, finger-sized units to larger, brick-sized ones. They typically have USB-A or USB-C ports for charging devices, making them compatible with most consumer electronics. However, specialized devices like satellite communication responders may require their own power sources, often using AA batteries. Lithium AA cells are an excellent choice for these, as they perform well in the cold.

While battery banks are versatile, they lose efficiency in cold conditions. A fully charged bank might recharge your phone completely at room temperature, but in the cold, it may only provide a partial charge—sometimes as little as a quarter. This happens because cold battery banks deliver less power, and cold devices don't accept a charge as efficiently.

To maximize performance in the cold, keep both the battery bank and the device warm. Store them in an insulated inner pocket or near your body to maintain functionality. Using additional insulation or hand warmers can also help prolong their effectiveness.

Charging Techniques

When planning to charge your electronics on a trip, consider whether you'll use solar panels while trekking—attached to your backpack or sled—or only when stationary at camp. Think about whether you can manage the panels from inside or outside your tent and how to handle the cabling. Flexible solar panels and cables can become stiff and brittle in extreme cold, so it's essential to test them beforehand.

To prepare, test your solar panels, cables, and devices by placing them in a sealable plastic bag and leaving them in the freezer overnight or for a few days. Once they're thoroughly cold, check their flexibility and usability, simulating camp conditions. While a freezer test at 0°F (-18°C) provides a good baseline, it does not fully replicate extreme cold like -30°F (-35°C).

To keep electronics functional in the cold, warming them with hot water bottles is one of the best techniques. When you get into your tent or shelter, don't immediately turn on your devices. Instead, place them inside your jacket, near your base layer, to let your body heat start warming them up.

After preparing your hot water bottles, dedicate one to warming your electronics. Heat water as hot as possible without risking spills, then pour it into a durable water bottle. Seal it tightly, check for leaks by tipping it sideways, and place it in a waterproof or water-resistant bag. Put the bottle deep inside your sleeping bag, then place your electronics—also inside their own waterproof bags—on or near the hot water bottle. Nestle everything at the foot of your sleeping bag to retain heat.

This "hot water bottle banking" can warm your devices to around 70°F (21°C), even if the air temperature outside is -30°F (-35°C). Once warmed, electronics should function well for a while until they cool down again. Be mindful that repeated warming and cooling cycles can shorten battery life, so use this method primarily for essential devices.

Cold temperatures also affect LCD screens, making them less responsive or completely unresponsive. If your device uses an LCD screen, test it in your freezer to see how it performs in the cold. While newer OLED screens tend to handle low temperatures better, they are not immune to the effects of extreme cold. Testing your setup before your trip ensures fewer surprises in the field.

Waterproofing Your Device

Some devices are built to meet standards like IP67, meaning they are dust-tight and can handle immersion in water up to 1 meter for 30 minutes. However, this does not mean they are waterproof for prolonged exposure or high-pressure water, such as heavy rain or submersion beyond 1 meter. Many electronics, such as cameras, are even more delicate and can only handle light rain at best. If your trip relies on navigation or communication devices, you'll need to carefully protect them from water exposure—water damage could lead to complete failure.

Avoid relying solely on resealable bags like Ziploc-style options. If these bags are punctured or if rain gets inside, water can pool and drown your electronics. Friction, wear and tear, or repeated opening and closing can weaken the seal over time, compromising protection.

For devices without touchscreens, like GPS units, you can often use them without removing them from a sealed bag. GPS units and similar devices typically function fine in this setup. For touchscreen devices, test in advance to see if they still respond through the bag. If they do, you can leave them sealed when referencing maps or tools in wet conditions.

Check your device's water-resistance rating in the manufacturer's specifications to understand its limits. Be mindful of sudden temperature drops, which can cause internal condensation inside your gear. When warm, moist air inside a sealed device rapidly cools, it can lead to electrical shorts or fogging in camera lenses. This often happens when bringing electronics from a warm tent into freezing air.

By properly waterproofing your devices and testing their functionality in protective bags beforehand, you can avoid unpleasant surprises and keep them running in tough conditions.

Smart Devices

How will you handle touchscreen devices in cold conditions? If the temperatures are severely low, your device will be just as cold. Taking off your gloves to use it might not be safe—the screen could be at air temperature (potentially -30°F (-34°C) or colder), which can cause frostbite on contact.

Smartphones are the most common touchscreen devices, but even gloves marketed as "smartphone compatible" often don't work reliably in extreme cold. Capacitive touchscreens rely on skin conductivity, which decreases in the cold. In addition, lithium-ion batteries struggle to provide power in low temperatures, which can cause screens to freeze or become sluggish. Test your gloves ahead of time to see how well they perform. In a pinch, you can use your nose to tap a few keys or icons, though this might not be practical for complex tasks, especially on devices with small or intricate controls.

Some smartphones come with external buttons for features like the camera. Check your device's settings to see if these buttons can be customized for other functions. Using mechanical buttons when possible helps reduce reliance on the touchscreen in cold conditions. Some high-end GPS units and rugged smartphones offer glove mode, which increases touch sensitivity and can improve responsiveness in cold weather.

Keep in mind that devices may glitch in extreme cold, and screen brightness might drop to zero, making it seem like the device has failed. Lithium-ion batteries also drain much faster in freezing conditions, sometimes shutting down devices well before they appear empty. If this happens, warming the device can temporarily restore power.

Conversely, if left in direct sunlight, devices can overheat and dim the screen for thermal protection. In extremely cold conditions, some screens may stay dim even after cooling down, requiring a manual reset or warming to restore brightness. Learn how to adjust screen brightness manually to handle these issues.

Consider using thin liner gloves or touchscreen gloves that fit under thicker gloves. Some people use fingerless gloves or mittens with flip-top covers for quick finger access. While these options can help, frostbite can occur in under a minute at extreme temperatures. No photo or task is worth permanent damage to your fingers—always prioritize hand protection over using your device.

Charging Cables and Interfaces

Whatever devices you plan to use in the field, you'll need to consider the charging cables required for battery banks and solar power systems. Many solar power systems come with adapters ending in a 12-volt lighter adapter, which then requires a USB-C converter. Some solar panels and power stations use proprietary connectors, so check what adapters you actually need before heading into the field.

Be cautious with inexpensive converters, as they may malfunction in extreme cold, especially below 0°F (-18°C). This can be due to poor-quality materials, brittle plastic housings, or weak internal solder joints that fail at low temperatures. Some converters stop working even if they function fine at room temperature. Test these adapters at freezing or subzero temperatures before relying on them in the field.

For longer trips, always carry backup charging cables for all essential devices. Even with care, cables can get damaged from snow, ice, or the wear and tear of trekking. If you rely on a single cable for critical navigation or communication equipment and it fails, you could be stuck. While extra cables and connectors add a bit of weight, they're a worthwhile precaution for mission-critical devices.

Some cables provided with devices are designed for charging only and don't support data transfer. Charging-only cables lack the internal wiring needed for data and can be hard to distinguish from data-capable cables just by looking at them. Some fast-charging USB-PD (Power Delivery) cables are optimized for power but do not support data transfer. Test your cables ahead of time to make sure they meet your needs, especially if you require data connectivity. Don't assume a cable you grab off the shelf or from your pack will work—verify it first.

Thoroughly test all cables, adapters, and backup equipment at home. Check for loose connections or poor performance, as some cables degrade over time, even in storage. Proper preparation ensures your system works seamlessly in the field and helps avoid serious issues caused by equipment failure.

Communication Systems

Whatever communication system you plan to use in the wilderness, thoroughly test it before departure. Satellite phones, GPS messengers, and other systems might work perfectly at home but fail in the field. Cellular service will almost certainly be unavailable in remote areas. For satellite services like Iridium, Starlink, or similar systems, ensure your setup is fully operational. Verify that subscriptions are active and prepay or confirm that your payment method won't expire during your trip to avoid being cut off unexpectedly.

Let people back home know that communication systems are fallible. Missed check-ins due to technical issues or environmental conditions don't always mean there's an emergency. Set clear expectations about how often you'll check in and what delays might mean. This can prevent false alarms and unnecessary rescue calls.

If your trip requires mandatory updates, such as in polar regions or guided expeditions, ensure you fully understand the communication requirements. Backup systems, like a secondary satellite phone or texting service, can be expensive, but they might be necessary to avoid having your trip interrupted or canceled due to miscommunication.

Devices like the Spot Mini or Garmin Mini are rugged and reliable but often rely on Bluetooth connections to a smartphone. While these devices can function independently, their usability varies. Some models have limited message templates or can only send SOS alerts without a phone connection. If your phone resets, loses charge, or breaks, you may lose access to critical functions. Some of these devices have built-in keys for sending messages, but typing on them can be slow and cumbersome. Test their independent functionality before your trip to ensure you can use them without a phone if necessary.

While redundancy in communication devices can improve reliability, relying on interconnected systems (e.g., a phone paired with a satellite device) increases the chance of failure. If redundancy is critical, consider a secondary device that operates on a different satellite network—for example, pairing an Iridium-based device with an Inmarsat or Globalstar system. The cost of extra devices may seem high, but it's often necessary to ensure safety and success on challenging trips.

Condensation on Devices

One of the challenges in cold environments is condensation, which occurs when you move a device from the cold into a warmer space. This is especially critical for electronic devices like cameras and smartphones. When the cold surface of a device meets warm, humid air, moisture can condense on the outside or even inside the device if there's minor damage or a loose seal. Cameras are particularly vulnerable because condensation can form on the internal sensor, potentially causing malfunctions or permanent damage.

To prevent this, make sure the device is fully cold before placing it in a sealed, airtight plastic bag, such as a Ziploc, before entering a warmer area. The sealed bag prevents moist air from directly contacting the cold device. Leave the device in the bag until it has fully warmed to room temperature. Once it's acclimated, you can safely remove it and use it normally.

Even IP-rated waterproof devices can suffer from internal condensation if their seals are compromised or if moisture was already present inside before entering the cold. If condensation occurs inside a sealed device, warming it gradually in dry air rather than immediately turning it on can help reduce potential damage.

The transition period—when the device is warming up—is the most critical time for condensation to form. Larger devices may take longer to warm up fully, so allow extra time for them. Taking these precautions will help protect your electronics from damage caused by internal or external moisture.

Test Electronics Before Leaving Home

Whatever communication device you plan to use in the field, test it thoroughly at home well before your trip. Many people assume a device will work out of the box after purchasing a plan, only to find they missed a critical step, like activating a feature, updating firmware, or adjusting an account setting. This is particularly true for text messaging services and satellite devices like Iridium, which often require additional setup.

When testing, give yourself enough time to resolve any issues. If you need to contact your provider for account changes or troubleshooting, don't wait until the last minute. Testing the night before departure isn't sufficient—get everything squared away well in advance to avoid unnecessary stress.

Satellite phones require even more preparation. Many need SIM cards, which must be purchased, shipped, and installed before activation. Some devices also use prepaid credit systems that require setup and confirmation. Prepaid satellite SIM cards don't always activate instantly—some require manual activation by the provider and may take up to 24 hours to process. If a SIM card or activation service has to be express-shipped, allow at least two weeks to account for weekends or delays. In some cases, you may need to work with a regional satellite provider for activation, depending on your destination.

Satellite services like Iridium and Inmarsat may also require firmware updates before first use, which often need a strong internet connection. Check for and install updates before heading into the field, as some updates require provider assistance and can't be done remotely.

Satellite devices are more complex than standard communication tools, so their setup can take longer than expected. Testing early ensures you have enough time to deal with potential delays, leaving you ready to focus on your trip without last-minute surprises.

It took 3 camera batteries to film my tent setup sequence at -10°F (-23°C) one winter.

Chapter 12
Winter Camping Efficiency

One of the biggest challenges in winter camping is efficiency. Tasks that might take half an hour in warm conditions can take an hour or more in the cold. Cold weather slows you down—it's harder to move with layers on, handling gear with gloves is clumsier, and severe weather can complicate everything.

Breaking down camp, for example, might take 10 minutes in good weather, but in winter, it can stretch to two hours. You may have to dig out your shelter and gear, pack up carefully to avoid damage, and do it all in a windstorm. Staging as much gear as possible inside the tent before stepping out can reduce exposure time and speed up the process.

Plan for these delays. Losing an hour here and there adds up over a long trip. It can seriously impact your ability to make a timed rendezvous or hit an important checkpoint.

Equipment Positioning

Consider how to balance the load between your backpack and sled. Will you use a sled at all or rely entirely on a backpack? Decide where to place your heaviest equipment and what items need to be accessible in case of unexpected weather. Think about how much gear you'll need to retrieve when you arrive at camp, and ensure essentials—like emergency equipment—are ready to grab.

Avoid piling critical or delicate items on top of your pack or sled where they can shift, fall out, or get lost in the snow. Plan ahead so your shovel, tent, snow stakes, and protective equipment are immediately accessible when you reach camp. Also, consider how to access your food, water, and emergency supplies throughout the day without disrupting your load.

Load Balancing

Load balancing is critical for both backpacks and sleds. In a backpack, keep the heaviest, densest items close to your lower back. Lighter, bulkier items should go higher and farther out.

For sleds, place the heaviest items about two-thirds to three-quarters of the way back. On steep inclines, shifting weight slightly forward can prevent the sled from tipping backward or dragging too much.

Placing heavy items too high can make the sled tip over, leading to frustration or even injury. Secure fuel containers carefully to prevent spills that could damage your sleeping bag or food. Liquid fuel bottles should be stored upright to prevent leakage due to pressure changes, and pressurized canisters may need pre-warming before use in subzero temperatures to maintain pressure.

Using smaller, 32-ounce (one-liter) bottles allows for better weight distribution and reduces the risk of leaks. Should one bottle fail, the loss won't be as bad as losing an entire gallon (4 liters) of fuel or water.

Accessible Clothing and Water

Keep your waterproof jacket and extra insulated layers where you can grab them easily. Mornings can be cold and windy, afternoons often warm up, and evenings can bring sudden temperature drops or ice fog. Make sure these layers are accessible without needing to unpack everything.

Water is an exception to general load-balancing rules. While heavy, it needs to be accessible—either at the top of your sled or near the front of your backpack. Burying it too deep wastes time digging it out repeatedly. Even small delays add up over a long trip.

Insulate your water well, especially in extreme cold, using insulated sleeves or, if needed, keeping it inside your coat while traveling or in your sleeping bag at night to prevent freezing.

Time Efficiency

Time efficiency is vital in winter camping. Breaks are short, often just long enough to eat, drink, adjust layers, or take care of basic needs. Minimize fiddling with your gear during stops to maximize travel time.

Small inefficiencies add up. Repeatedly searching for water or supplies can cost miles (kilometers) over a trip. Plan your packing to stay organized and ready for anything.

Backpack vs. Sled Loading

When traveling with a sled and a backpack, focus on load balance. On flat terrain, store as much heavy gear in the sled as possible to reduce strain on your back. Carry only essential emergency items in your backpack in case you become separated from the sled. Delicate items, like electronics, are often safer in your backpack, since sleds can tumble and crush gear. However, if you fall, items in your pack may be damaged, so assess conditions to determine the safest option.

On steep terrain, shift some weight to your backpack to counteract the strain of a heavy sled pulling you backward, but avoid overloading it to the point where you risk falling backward on icy footing. This is especially critical on climbs like Motorcycle Hill on Denali, where a sled can destabilize footing or lead to dangerous situations. A dragging sled not only complicates climbing but also adds psychological stress and fatigue.

Side-hilling poses additional challenges, as sleds are prone to tipping. Pack lighter items in the sled to reduce the risk of tumbling. While it's tempting to rely more on your backpack, overloading it or making it top-heavy can cause balance issues and increase the risk of falls. A backpack exceeding 50 pounds (23 kilos) becomes difficult to manage, especially if the weight shifts unexpectedly. Balance your load to match the terrain, keeping your sled manageable and your backpack stable, while ensuring critical gear remains accessible.

Balancing Sled vs. Backpack

When using a sled and backpack, balance your load based on the trip type—whether it's a weekend outing, long-distance trek, or polar exploration.

For sled travel, consider:
- The weight you need to carry
- Items you'll need during the day
- The terrain

A backpack can double as a sled harness if you lack a dedicated one. If using only a backpack, prioritize accessibility and weight distribution.

Unlike summer trips, winter conditions require careful planning of what must be immediately accessible versus packed deeper. Tubular backpack designs can make access difficult, though lower zippers or hatch-style openings help. Store non-critical items (like next-day food) at the bottom, and keep emergency gear—such as spare snowshoe bindings, crampon straps, or paracord—easily reachable. Quick access to tools can prevent unnecessary delays and maintain safety.

On flat terrain, load the sled heavily to reduce backpack weight. As the terrain steepens, transfer some weight to your backpack to prevent the sled from destabilizing your footing or pulling you off balance. Managing a sled that might tip or slide uncontrollably adds significant physical and psychological strain.

Terrain and Sled Considerations

Side-hilling presents unique challenges. Traditional sleds like the Paris Expedition sled lack stabilizing rails and are prone to tumbling. A long, low-slung load improves stability, while bulky or unbalanced loads increase tipping risks. Use extra straps to secure your gear and prevent shifting during travel, as frequent load tumbles waste time and energy.

Sleds with built-in rails or enhanced side-hill stability can improve performance on uneven terrain. If such sleds aren't available, pack strategically. Avoid tall loads, which increase tipping risks, and position heavier items lower and closer to the sled's center of gravity for better balance. Longer sleds offer better tracking on side slopes, reducing uncontrolled sliding.

On steep climbs, consider using sleds with rigid poles rather than trailing tethers. A rigid connection reduces sled swing and prevents it from slamming into your legs or dragging unpredictably. However, some flexibility in the connection can help absorb shocks on rough terrain, preventing sudden jolts that can throw off your balance.

If using a Paris Expedition sled, consider DIY modifications like side rails or skegs to reduce tipping and improve handling.

Psychological and Physical Challenges

Heavy backpacks make navigating steep or uneven terrain more difficult, increasing the risk of losing balance or falling. Similarly, a heavy sled can pull you off balance or drag uncontrollably, creating a constant struggle.

On steep climbs, shifting some weight to your backpack often improves safety and control, despite added discomfort. However, carrying more than 50 pounds (23kg) in a backpack can lead to unwieldy movements and a higher risk of falls. Consider both physical and mental impacts when distributing your load, adjusting based on terrain and conditions.

Sled mismanagement wastes energy and effort, adding mental fatigue over time. The frustration of frequent tipping, load shifting, or unstable pulls can drain morale, making a difficult trip even harder. Careful load management reduces these problems, helping to maintain both physical stamina and mental endurance.

Pack intentionally, storing less critical items deeper in your sled or pack while keeping essentials accessible. Secure your sled load to prevent shifting or tipping, and be mindful of challenges like side-hilling. Thoughtfully distribute weight to reduce strain and maintain stability, especially on steep or uneven terrain. By managing your sled and backpack loads carefully, you'll enhance efficiency, safety, and enjoyment on your trip.

Adapting to Different Terrain

Adapting to different terrain and weather conditions requires careful consideration of your setup—whether you're using a backpack, a sled, or a hybrid approach. If you're traversing flat snowfields, wooded areas, or mountainous terrain, think about how much load you need to carry on your back versus in your sled. Both setups have advantages and challenges depending on the environment.

On flat terrain, using a sled can help keep weight off your back, allowing for easier travel. However, sleds can complicate gear management and add to your load. If traveling across lakes, rivers, or other open expanses with a sled, keeping your backpack around 25–30 pounds (11–14 kilograms) is ideal to avoid overburdening yourself.

A sled may be impractical in areas with thin or unreliable ice. In such cases, relying on a backpack is the simplest and safest option for short trips with relatively light loads.

For hybrid setups or long-distance exploration, pay attention to how you connect your sled to your harness or backpack. Keeping the sled's pulling cord as long as possible—typically 10-13 feet (3-4 meters)—helps reduce upward force and improves control. However, cord length should be adjusted based on terrain. On steep descents, a shorter cord improves control by keeping the sled closer, reducing whiplash from sudden stops. Conversely, in deep snow, a longer cord helps prevent the sled from plowing into your legs.

Wrapping the cord around a single, reinforced bungee section absorbs shock and improves handling, but too much elasticity can cause the sled to rebound unpredictably on rough terrain. Avoid overusing bungee coils, as this can make the system overly rigid or cumbersome.

Challenges in Deep Snow and Powder

Traveling in deep powder or fresh snow presents unique difficulties. Sleds tend to sink into soft snow, making pulling much harder. Balancing this against the top-heaviness of a backpack requires careful planning.

If traveling in a team, rotate the lead position every 10-15 minutes to prevent one person from bearing the brunt of breaking trail. This strategy reduces physical strain and ensures an even distribution of effort.

Freshly fallen snow may need time to settle and compact. Passing over the trail multiple times or allowing it to sit for a day can make it firmer and easier to traverse. Be prepared for your sled to sink deeply into powder, requiring significant effort to pull it through. Using wider sled runners, a sled skirt, or a lightweight bottom platform can reduce drag and improve flotation over soft snow.

Sometimes, getting through these conditions is simply a matter of persistence.

Glacial Travel and Crevasse Risks

When traveling on glaciers, sleds can help distribute weight across the surface, reducing the risk of breaking through snow bridges. However, they also pose significant dangers.

If a sled falls into a crevasse, its weight can pull you down or cause serious injury. Always maintain secure connections to your sled and avoid overloading it when traversing crevasse-prone areas.

Using rope techniques to secure both the sled and yourself can help mitigate these risks. A chest harness is safer than a hip belt alone, as it prevents the sled from pulling you backward if it drops into a crevasse.

Other Transport Considerations

In deep snow or mountainous terrain, the choice between sled and backpack often depends on:

- Personal preference
- Specific environmental challenges
- Your team's strategy

A backpack offers simplicity but makes you more top-heavy, increasing the risk of falls in deep snow. A sled reduces strain on your back but can add complications, especially in uneven terrain or powder.

By thoughtfully managing your load, alternating responsibilities in a team, and preparing for the specific challenges of your terrain, you can adapt effectively to any conditions. Flexibility and planning are key to staying safe and efficient in varying environments.

Organizing for Efficiency

When packing your gear and equipment, test and organize everything at home. Think through what you'll need in the morning, evening, and during emergencies. Assess whether your gear can serve double duty or if you're carrying unnecessary duplicates. Simplify wherever possible.

Ensure essential emergency items, like a first aid kit, are easily accessible. Keep your heavy parka or shell within reach, as severe windstorms or blinding snow can appear suddenly, especially in mountainous or glacial regions. Always have critical gear ready to grab and consider the sequence in which you'll need items throughout the day.

Using color-coded stuff sacks and pouches can help you stay organized. Assigning colors to categories (e.g., red for emergency gear, blue for clothing) makes it easier to identify what you need quickly. Instead of marking bags with a permanent marker, consider using interchangeable tags to allow flexibility as your gear organization changes over time. Lightweight gear is excellent, but not invincible—handle it carefully to avoid damage.

Managing Large Bags

Large bags simplify packing by reducing the number of separate items to manage, making sled or pack organization easier. However, accessing a single item often requires unpacking a significant portion of the bag's contents, which can become frustrating in cold or challenging conditions. Modular packing—stacking items in the order they'll be used—reduces unnecessary digging and speeds up access.

Plan your system carefully before you leave. Testing your setup at home saves time and reduces frustration in the field. This is especially important in team settings, where well-prepared members can prevent delays and tension. In contrast, unprepared teammates can slow progress and strain group dynamics. A realistic assessment of readiness ensures smoother teamwork.

Flexibility in the Field

No plan survives the first battle. Gear that works perfectly at home may fail or prove inefficient in real-world conditions. Be ready to adapt and adjust as necessary. Share insights with teammates, especially those new to winter camping, to help improve overall efficiency.

Flexibility and communication are essential for maintaining efficiency. What seems ideal in controlled conditions may need modification in the field—stay open to changes and help each other refine approaches as needed.

Daily Gear Setup

Establish a consistent routine for unloading and reloading your backpack or sled each night. When you arrive at camp, ensure your shovel and emergency supplies are immediately accessible. Set up your tent, ground cover, and other essentials without unnecessary digging or unpacking.

If you're using a backpack, keep your tent and setup supplies near the top or in an easily reachable section. Burying them deep inside your pack forces you to unload everything just to retrieve them, increasing the risk of scattering gear and losing items in snow or poor visibility. Loose gear can be easily misplaced in whiteout conditions or darkness, so keeping everything contained is critical.

For sled travel, the "Burrito Roll" technique is highly efficient—folding your tent and ground tarp, rolling them tightly together, and lashing them securely to your sled minimizes unpacking and ensures quick access. However, avoid leaving stakes or delicate components exposed. Instead, wrap them in a reinforced bag or pouch to prevent loss or damage during travel.

In team settings, divide tasks to maximize efficiency. While one person digs a snow pit or builds a wind barrier, another can set up the shelter. If traveling solo or with one other person, balance tasks like constructing a snow wall and pitching the tent to avoid wasted time. Keeping gear organized and accessible prevents unnecessary stress and ensures essential items are always within reach.

Before settling in for the night, take a few moments to prepare for the next day. Lay out emergency layers, pack food that will be needed quickly, and check that your sled or backpack is arranged for efficient loading in the morning. A small effort at night can save significant time and energy in harsh conditions.

Preventing Gear Loss

Losing gear in winter conditions can cause major setbacks, especially at night or in deep snow, where dropped items can quickly disappear beneath the surface. Many essential items rely on small components, connectors, or tools, making their loss particularly problematic.

Attach bright lanyards or cords to small items like pocket knives or tools. A one-foot (30 cm) piece of paracord makes them easier to spot and retrieve if dropped. This small addition adds negligible weight but greatly reduces the risk of losing important gear. Dropped items, especially small, heavy ones, can sink deeper into disturbed snow as you dig, making recovery increasingly difficult and time-consuming.

Carabiners are useful for keeping gear attached and secure, but too many bright cords and lanyards can lead to tangling issues. Bundle or coil cords neatly to strike a balance between visibility and practicality.

Plan how you'll recover small items if they fall into soft snow. Strategies like marking areas systematically or using a small avalanche probe or collapsible trekking pole can save time by gently probing the snow without burying lost items further. Organize your gear to minimize drops, and ensure frequently used tools and connectors are tethered or brightly marked. These precautions reduce frustration and prevent time-wasting searches in the field.

Fast Tent-Pitching Techniques

Before heading out on a winter expedition, practice setting up your tent multiple times in harsh conditions—in the dark, rain, or heavy snow. This realistic testing ensures you can pitch your tent quickly and efficiently when it matters most.

Test how easily you can slide poles into sleeves or clip hangers under challenging conditions. If precipitation starts mid-setup, will the tent fill with water before you get the rain fly on? If so, consider pitching the rain fly first, using a tarp for temporary cover, or reevaluating your tent's design for winter readiness.

Always push tent poles through the sleeves rather than pulling them. Pulling can cause the sections to disconnect, leading to delays and frustration. By pushing, you keep the poles intact and ensure a smoother setup.

For tunnel tents, coordinate with your partner to push poles through simultaneously, speeding up the pitching process and reducing mishaps. In a four-pole tunnel tent, each person can handle two poles, ensuring a, more efficient setup.

In high winds, stake down one side of the tent before inserting poles to prevent it from blowing away during setup. This is especially critical in exposed areas where a loose tent can be lost in seconds.

Allocate enough time to set up camp before dark. If night setup is unavoidable, allow extra time to avoid mistakes or lost gear. Plan for 20-30 minutes in moderate conditions and longer in bad weather. Preparation and practice will save you time and stress when it matters most.

Setting Up on Packed Snow

A solid, packed snow base is crucial for setting up your tent and ensuring a good night's sleep. Loose or unpacked snow does not support weight effectively—it compresses unevenly, causing tent corners or the center to sink. Moving inside the tent worsens the problem, creating holes or unstable surfaces that are difficult to fix.

Upon arriving at camp, start packing down the snow immediately using a shovel, snowshoes, or skis. While this may seem like extra effort, it's essential. Packed snow takes time to harden into a supportive base because compression slightly warms it, allowing it to bond as it cools. If time is limited, focus on evenly compressing the snow to minimize settling issues.

Ideally, give the packed snow at least an hour to solidify before pitching your tent. During this time, handle other camp tasks like building a snow wall, gathering firewood, or setting up cooking gear. This keeps you productive while allowing the snow base to firm up, improving your overall efficiency.

In very cold conditions below -20°F (-29°C), snow bonds more slowly. If temperatures are that extreme, stomping a second time before setting up can improve stability and reduce late-night sinking.

In team settings, divide the work evenly to ensure the entire tent site is properly packed. Alternate between packing and warming up to maintain body heat and prevent fatigue. Using skis or snowshoes to stomp down the snow helps speed up the process while ensuring the site is uniformly compacted. Proper preparation prevents discomfort and ensures a stable base for your tent.

Effective Tent Anchoring

Proper tent anchoring is essential for keeping your tent stable, especially in winter conditions. Tunnel tents, in particular, require properly secured guy lines to remain upright. Even dome tents benefit from securing guy lines in case of strong winds or changing weather. Practice your setup at home to ensure you're comfortable with the process and can adjust to various conditions.

When anchoring your tent, avoid burying items like snowshoes, poles, or other gear too deeply in the snow. Burying these items too deeply can cause increased difficulty during retrieval, especially once the snow hardens overnight. It also risks damaging the gear, particularly plastic snowshoes that may be damaged under pressure. Position these anchors securely but keep them accessible.

For snow anchoring, long snow stakes, such as 12-inch (30 cm) stakes like Hilleberg's, are ideal for providing a firm hold. Smaller stakes often lack sufficient surface area to grip snow effectively, especially in strong winds or packed conditions. If snow stakes are unavailable, use deadman anchors. To create a deadman, bury items like snowshoes or skis horizontally in the snow, ensuring they're packed tightly and have a solid hold.

When tying down your tent, ensure the guy lines are taut and avoid draping them over loose piles of snow. Wind can cause lines to move back and forth, sawing through snow and loosening the anchor. Compact snow firmly around the anchor point and create a straight, stable connection between the anchor and guy line attachment. This prevents the setup from shifting overnight, even in challenging weather.

Proper preparation and thoughtful placement of your anchors will keep your tent secure and stable, allowing you to focus on the rest of your expedition without worrying about unexpected problems.

Striking Camp

Striking camp efficiently in the morning is key to getting your day started smoothly, especially in cold or stormy conditions. Start packing gear inside your tent as soon as possible to save time. Mornings can be challenging—you're tired, hungry, and dealing with low temperatures—so organizing your routine makes a big difference.

Dry out your sleeping bag to reduce moisture from your body and clothing. One method is to drape the sleeping bag over your shoulders like a shawl or jacket while eating breakfast. This keeps you warm and helps dry the bag using your body heat. As you pack, sit on your sleeping pad and deflate your air mattress to stay efficient. Avoid spilling your breakfast while multitasking, as cleaning up a mess will waste time and add frustration.

Warming your boot liners can significantly improve comfort. Place them inside your jacket to warm them before putting on your boots. Avoid wearing boots inside the tent until the last minute to prevent damaging gear. Boot liners like Intuition, known for quick warmth and insulation, are especially helpful, but pre-warming any liners makes the process much easier.

If possible, drag your sled into your vestibule or tent to pack it. Packing inside protects you from the elements and prevents gear from getting lost in blowing snow. Loose items can easily disappear, so keeping everything contained ensures nothing is left behind. Use the available space efficiently to avoid overcrowding or damaging your tent. Once packed, double-check that all gear is transferred to your sled or backpack.

Always keep your shovel handy. Don't pack it away, as you'll likely need it to dig out your tent and stakes in the morning. Store the shovel inside your tent or vestibule for easy access, which avoids exposing yourself to the cold unnecessarily. If traveling with others, ensure everyone knows where the shovels are stored to streamline the process and avoid delays.

Using Skis and Snowshoes as Tent Anchors

Skis, snowshoes, and ski poles can serve as excellent tent anchors, but there are key points to keep in mind to avoid damaging your gear or compromising your setup.

When using skis, always position the tops of the skis away from your tent. This prevents the steel edges on the bases from sawing through guy lines if they move back and forth in the wind. Facing the bases toward the tent can rapidly cut through the lines, leading to significant issues. Similarly, with snowshoes, ensure that guy lines are not wrapped around any sharp edges or decking, as constant movement can fray or sever the lines over time.

To secure skis and poles as anchors, push them into the snow at a steep angle. A 45-degree angle is a good starting point, but adjust based on snow conditions. This increases tension and minimizes slack, preventing the guy lines from riding up and down, which reduces the risk of friction damage. Shallow angles can cause instability and increase wear on the lines.

When using snowshoes as anchors, bury them at least halfway into the snow to ensure they hold firmly against the wind. Be cautious of guy lines rubbing against the decking of the snowshoes. Prolonged friction can damage both the lines and the snowshoe decking, so align them carefully to minimize wear.

Be mindful when inserting skis into the snow. Avoid striking the tails against rocks, frozen tree branches, or hard ice, as this can crack or damage them. If the snow is too hard to insert skis safely, consider using a deadman anchor instead.

By following these guidelines, you can effectively use skis, snowshoes, and poles as reliable tent anchors while protecting your gear and ensuring a secure setup.

Pacing and Movement

Setting a reasonable pace is critical for long-term success on a winter camping trip. Unless you're climbing steep mountains or traversing extreme terrain, aim for a pace where you can maintain a conversation while skiing, snowshoeing, or walking. Pushing past this into higher aerobic levels may feel productive initially but isn't sustainable over time. A conversational pace prevents burnout and keeps you moving steadily without overexertion.

Take scheduled breaks to maintain energy and focus. Avoid stopping too frequently, but also don't push yourself to exhaustion. A common approach for polar exploration or long-distance travel is to move for 75 minutes, followed by a 15-minute break. While shorter breaks may appeal to some, exposure in polar climates often makes them impractical due to the risk of body heat loss or the difficulty of getting back into motion in harsh cold. Maintaining a 15-minute break schedule strikes a good balance between rest and progress.

Using a chronograph watch can help you stick to a disciplined schedule. Break intervals have a significant impact on daily travel distance. For example, taking breaks every 60 minutes instead of 75 can reduce your travel distance by 30-40% over the course of a day, which quickly adds up on longer trips.

In group travel, always set the pace based on the slowest member. Even among highly fit teams, there's usually someone who naturally moves slower. Allowing them to lead prevents fatigue and morale issues from developing at the back of the group. Teams that stretch out over large distances create safety hazards and risk compromising cohesion, especially in harsh conditions.

While slowing down for others may frustrate faster members, remember that success depends on everyone reaching the destination together. Maintaining a unified pace and synchronized breaks ensures safety, efficiency, and a positive team dynamic.

Efficiency on Skis and Snowshoes

When skiing or snowshoeing, maintaining an efficient, repeatable pace is crucial, especially when carrying a heavy load. A common mistake is to take shorter strides, but using a longer stride where possible will conserve energy. Longer strides reduce the number of steps needed, decreasing cycle time and improving efficiency over long distances.

On steep hills, shorter steps may be necessary. Small, deliberate motions like toe-to-heel progressions help manage steep terrain. However, on flatter ground, increasing your stride length by 8 to 10 inches (12 to 16 centimeters) can make a noticeable difference in your energy output. Avoid overextending, as this can disrupt your balance and lead to fatigue. Adjust your stride as needed to stay stable and efficient.

Ski poles are essential for maintaining stability and preventing energy loss, whether you're skiing, snowshoeing, or trekking on foot. Poles help reduce wobbling and stabilize your movements, saving energy that would otherwise go into balancing. On steep climbs or icy terrain, telescoping trekking poles or poles with ice tips provide better grip and support, offering additional contact points to reduce strain and improve balance.

Traveling without poles requires more energy to stabilize forward, backward, and lateral movements, especially when carrying a load. Using poles to create three or four points of contact with the ground significantly reduces the effort needed to maintain stability, making travel more efficient and less tiring.

By optimizing stride length and effectively using poles, you'll conserve energy and maintain a steadier pace, making long-distance travel far more manageable.

Resting Efficiently

As soon as you stop for a rest break, adjust your clothing if needed. Zip up your jacket or add layers—it won't take long to feel chilled.

Drink water—about five or six deep gulps—to rehydrate. Take care of personal needs, then start eating your snack. Eating cold food takes longer because your body has to work harder to break it down in cold temperatures, so be mindful of this. You can't rush it, and it's harder to chew in the cold.

Avoid turning the break into a rushed task, focusing solely on efficiency. Long-term, that's not as enjoyable. Stay aware of the experience and why you're out there in the winter.

When you're done eating, take another five or six gulps of water. It'll help keep your hydration level up. Don't just take a few steps and go. When you're active in the cold, you lose moisture, especially from exhaling in dry air.

You need plenty of water to maintain energy. Proper hydration helps maintain energy levels, as dehydration can cause your blood to become thicker, which makes it harder to circulate oxygen and heat. Also, digestion requires water. Without it, digestion becomes difficult.

Keep fluids in your body as much as possible. Ideally, your urine should be light yellow—not completely clear (which can overwork your kidneys), but not too dark, as that's a sign you're dehydrated.

Shelter Maintenance

Be mindful of your shelter at all times. Check that all the guy lines are taut and that snow hasn't built up too much. If wind starts to loosen your anchor points, whether using stakes, skis, or another method, it can cause problems—especially in extreme cold and deep into the night.

Even though it might be tempting to ignore small issues, over time, especially on longer trips, they can add up and wear out your gear, causing damage. So, don't just hide in your sleeping bag and hope things will be fine. It's better to deal with problems as soon as you notice them.

Regularly inspect your shelter for damage and take care of issues when it's safe to do so. A little needle and thread can go a long way. If you can, push snow off your shelter to avoid a big shoveling effort in the morning. This saves time and energy, making the whole process easier.

Snow Shovel and Snow

When using your snow shovel, make sure to use a "cut and lift" method, not a "stab and pry" approach. At very low temperatures, metals like steel and aluminum can become brittle. Prying on the metal can stress the material, causing it to crack or break, which could leave you without a vital tool.

Instead, use the blade to punch and cut through the snow or rubble. The shovel should be strong enough to handle this along the length of the handle. If the snow is loose, just insert your shovel into the pile and toss it around—no problem. If you're dealing with harder snow or climbing over snowbanks, punch with the edge and cut through the blocks. Once you've cut out what you need, lift the block without applying prying force.

A broken shovel on a winter expedition makes it extremely hard to establish camp, build a snow wall, or dig out snow for water. If your shovel breaks, you'll have to squat down or kneel on the snow, potentially frostbiting your knees, fingers, and toes.

Also, be aware that cheap shovels from online retailers are often not made from hardened aluminum, which is crucial for withstanding the force needed to break through tough snow and ice. Trying to punch through hard snow or ice will cause the edge to chip or fold, or develop metal burrs. These can slice into your tent, pants, or anything else. These shovels can't handle prying loads in the cold and will break easily.

Losing Gear

Make sure any items you have, like gloves or hats, are attached with cords. Never put gloves between your legs or under your armpits, thinking they'll stay secure. It's easy for these items to slip away. Your heavier gloves should also have cords—often called "glove lanyards"—so if you drop them, they won't blow away in the winter or get buried in the snow.

Whenever possible, keep things in your pockets. This makes them easier to access and prevents snow from packing into them, which can create even more problems.

Always think about what might happen if something slips away or blows off. What's your plan if that happens? Keep that in mind at all times.

The faster you can set up camp, the longer you can rest in your tent before continuing on the next day.

Chapter 13
Avalanche Safety for Winter Campers

Avalanches are a serious risk in winter camping, especially in mountainous terrain. While they're often associated with extreme skiing and mountaineering, a collapse of unstable snow can occur unexpectedly, even in areas that don't seem prone to avalanches. Campers who set up in the wrong place or travel through risky terrain without awareness can find themselves in a deadly situation. Understanding avalanche conditions and knowing how to avoid dangerous areas is just as important as knowing how to survive one.

What Causes an Avalanche?

An avalanche happens when a layer of snow loses its grip and slides downhill. Most are triggered by unstable snow combined with a trigger—new snowfall, strong winds, or sudden warming. The most dangerous type, a slab avalanche, occurs when a thick, heavy layer of snow breaks loose all at once. It can reach speeds over 60 mph (97 km/h) in seconds. A loose snow avalanche starts as small chunks of snow but spreads as it falls. It's less destructive but can still knock a person off their feet or push them into dangerous terrain.

Avalanches happen most often when three key factors align:
- **Steep Slopes:** Slopes between 30–45 degrees are the most dangerous. Anything steeper tends to shed snow before it builds up. Flatter slopes rarely produce avalanches, but unstable snow can still crack and shift.
- **Weak Snowpack:** If a soft, weak layer sits under a harder, heavier layer, the snowpack is unstable. A small trigger—wind, weight, or even sound—can cause it to collapse.
- **Weather Conditions:** Heavy snowfall, wind-drifted snow, and rapid warming increase avalanche risk.

Even on mild slopes, unstable snow can be a danger. A higher section can crack and shift unexpectedly, even when the lower part seems solid. A loud, deep "whumph" sound, which occurs when the snowpack collapses internally, is a warning sign. If you hear this, treat the area as hazardous and move out immediately.

It's also possible for a slight slope above a steeper one to crack, triggering a larger slide below, which could catch people by surprise. Even if you're on flat or rolling terrain, if there's a steep drop-off nearby, a collapse above it could set off a full avalanche. Don't assume low-angle snow is safe just because it looks stable.

Wind Slabs and Hidden Hazards

Wind is a major factor in creating unstable snow layers that can lead to avalanches. Strong winds pick up loose snow and redeposit it into wind slabs—dense, compacted layers that form on the leeward side of ridges, gullies, and even mild slopes. These slabs often look smooth but can be dangerously unstable. They can collapse even on nearly flat snow, making for an unsettling experience.

Avalanche debris can also easily cover hidden dangers, like deep crevasses, cliffs, or weak snow bridges, creating an invisible hazard. What looks like a solid surface may be a thin layer over empty space. This is a major risk when traveling in glaciated terrain or across avalanche paths.

Recognizing Avalanche Terrain

Certain features in the landscape can signal avalanche danger. Pay attention to the following signs:

- **Obvious Blocks of Snow:** Large chunks of broken, hard-packed snow at the base of a slope indicate past slab avalanches. These blocks show where the snowpack fractured.
- **Chutes in Steep, Tree-Free Areas:** Open, steep slopes with no trees are natural avalanche paths. If an area looks unnaturally clear, it's likely because avalanches regularly sweep through.
- **Rolling Snow ("Tootsie Rolls"):** Small, rounded snowballs rolling downhill can be a warning sign. This means the surface layer is warming up and starting to move.

A bad campsite choice can put you right in the path of a natural avalanche. Avoid setting up below wide-open slopes, inside gullies, or near cliff edges. Safer spots include ridgelines, dense tree cover, or low-angle terrain away from potential avalanche paths.

Group Travel vs. Solo Travel in Avalanche Terrain

Solo travel in avalanche terrain is risky. If you're caught in a slide alone, survival is unlikely. Even with a beacon, no one will be there to dig you out. Group travel is far safer, but only if done correctly. If an avalanche happens, the group must respond quickly.

The key is moving smart. A group should never bunch up in hazardous terrain.

Safe Travel Techniques in Avalanche Terrain

- **One Person at a Time on Risky Slopes:** If a slope seems unstable, only one person should cross at a time while the rest watch from a safe location. This way, rescuers won't be buried if something goes wrong.
- **Proper Spacing:** Keep 50 to 100 feet (15 to 30m) apart in avalanche zones. This reduces stress on the snowpack and prevents multiple burials.
- **Stop in Safe Zones:** If stopping to assess terrain, pick safe areas like ridgelines or dense tree clusters. Avoid gullies, open bowls, or slopes that lead into terrain traps.

Roped travel is useful in glaciated terrain or across crevasse-prone areas, but it has risks. If not done correctly, a rope can drag multiple people into a slide instead of saving them. Rope use in avalanche terrain should only be attempted by trained teams.

Managing an Avalanche Rescue Without Making It Worse

Rescuing a buried person is critical, but it must be done without creating a bigger disaster. Panicked rescues can turn one burial into a mass casualty event.

Key Principles of Safe Avalanche Rescues:

- **Make Sure the Area Is Safe Before Rushing In:** If the slope is still unstable, more people may get buried. Assess before entering.
- **Don't Let Everyone Rely on Groupthink:** A group in crisis often makes

bad decisions. One trained person should take charge.
- **Keep Group Size Under Control:** Too many people on an unstable slope can trigger another slide. Send in only those needed for the rescue.
- **Stick to the Plan:** Don't make last-minute changes to the rescue approach. Changing tactics in the middle of an avalanche search wastes time and creates confusion.

If the group isn't properly organized, it's easy to lose sight of the buried victim and get caught up in chaos. Stay focused on the goal—find the person, dig fast, and get them breathing again.

Essential Avalanche Rescue Gear
Every person in the group should carry:
- **Avalanche Beacon:** A transceiver that sends and receives signals. This is critical for locating buried victims.
- **Probe:** A collapsible pole used to pinpoint a buried person's exact location before digging.
- **Shovel:** A strong, lightweight metal avalanche shovel for fast digging.

Choosing the Right Shovel
Not all shovels are equal. Do not rely on a plastic shovel. When an avalanche happens, the snow warms up from the force of the slide. As soon as it stops, it cools and hardens. This makes the snow more compact and difficult to dig through. A cheap, lightweight plastic shovel simply isn't adequate for this. In many cases, it will just bounce off the dense, compacted snow. Even though some people rely on them, plastic shovels can't handle the tough conditions that avalanches leave behind. Carry a hardened T-6 aluminum avalanche shovel. It will cut through dense, compacted snow when it matters most.

What to Do If You're Caught in an Avalanche
If an avalanche starts beneath you:
- Move sideways to escape the main flow.
- Ditch heavy gear like backpacks to stay on top.
- Swimming and thrashing can help, but don't rely on it. Avalanches are violent. Snow moves unpredictably. You may be flipped, spun, and unable to control your movement. If you can fight to stay near the surface, do

it—but this is a last-ditch effort, not a reliable plan.
- As the snow slows, create an air pocket with your hands and take a deep breath before it settles.

If someone is buried, act immediately. Time is critical. Use your beacon, probe, and shovel to dig them out as fast as possible. Survival rates drop sharply after 15 minutes.

Avalanches are unpredictable and fast. The best way to survive one is to never get caught in the first place. Safe travel techniques, proper gear, and hands-on training are the best defenses.

Staying safe in an avalanche zone means being prepared and respecting the environment. With the right knowledge and precautions, you can enjoy winter's beauty while minimizing risks.

Chapter 14
Winter Weather

Winter campers face unique challenges compared to summer campers, particularly the unpredictability of the weather. Even though modern forecasts are highly accurate, surprises still happen every year, catching people off guard. This is especially true in the mountains, where forecasts can be right—until they're not. Sudden temperature drops, unexpected polar vortexes, or storms appearing out of nowhere on snow-covered summits can turn a routine trip into a serious situation.

This has happened before and will continue to happen in the future. Understanding how winter weather works, recognizing its variability, and interpreting forecasts for reasonably accurate predictions can improve your chances of having a safe and enjoyable experience—without getting into trouble.

Common Winter Weather Systems

All weather is influenced by high- and low-pressure systems, which dictate cold and warm fronts. The entire planet operates on shifting atmospheric pressure, and even small changes can bring calm, sunny weather or severe storms, depending on the system moving through.

Some pressure systems linger over an area, creating stable and comfortable conditions. However, they can shift suddenly, bringing in cold fronts that cause temperature drops and severe weather.

High-Pressure Systems

High-pressure systems are favored by outdoor enthusiasts. They bring light winds, cold temperatures, and stable weather with minimal storms or blizzards. These systems can be identified using weather apps, pressure maps (such as those from NOAA), or barometric pressure readings from smartwatches or portable barometers.

High-pressure systems often lead to colder temperatures because clear skies allow heat to escape into space. In contrast, overcast skies trap some warmth, keeping temperatures more stable. While clear skies provide better visibility and sunlight, they also mean nighttime temperatures can drop significantly. After a storm, when high pressure returns, temperatures can plummet by 15°F (-9°C) or more in just a few hours, creating unexpected risks at camp. These conditions also encourage frost buildup as rapid temperature changes affect humidity levels.

High-pressure days are easy to recognize: clear skies, minimal wind, and rapid cooling after sunset. Planning for these conditions requires heavier-duty gear for colder temperatures and strategies to manage frost buildup.

Low-Pressure Systems

Low-pressure systems, on the other hand, often bring cloudy skies, higher humidity, and an increased chance of wind, snow, or rain, depending on the temperature. Overcast days tend to keep temperatures steadier, reducing the extreme swings between day and night. This can help prevent overheating during the day and freezing at night, but the stronger winds typical of low-pressure systems create a chilling effect that requires preparation.

Snow, rain, or sleet driven by wind can soak your gear, even in freezing temperatures, as body heat melts precipitation on contact. Proper preparation for low-pressure systems focuses on insulation and wind protection rather than extreme temperature changes. Strong winds and blizzards, particularly with blowing snow or freezing rain, can quickly escalate into serious challenges.

Understanding these weather patterns and planning accordingly will help you navigate the unique demands of winter camping safely and comfortably.

Weather and Cold Fronts

Cold fronts mark the boundary between cold and warm air masses. When a cold front moves through, it signals a sudden and often dramatic change in weather. Temperatures can drop sharply, and the risk of snowfall or even blizzard conditions increases.

One of the clearest signs of an approaching cold front is a sudden shift in wind direction. While most locations have a prevailing wind, changes—sometimes subtle, sometimes more obvious—can indicate an incoming weather shift. In regions where wind patterns are consistent, such as areas where trees lean due to prevailing winds, a shift in direction is a strong signal that a cold front is moving in.

If you notice these changes, it's essential to prepare immediately. Don't wait for worsening weather to set up camp, as this increases the risk of damaging your tent, losing gear, or developing frostbite. The moment you sense the weather turning, take action.

Adopt the climber's mindset: recognize when it's time to stop for the day and focus on staying safe and warm. It's always better to halt early and avoid unnecessary risks than to push yourself into a dangerous situation.

Warm Weather Fronts

Warm fronts, the opposite of cold fronts, bring gradual weather changes. As they move through, skies often remain overcast with occasional light rain or drizzle before clearing. These fronts are typically followed by high-pressure systems, which can cause significant temperature swings between day and night.

During the day, temperatures may rise quickly as the sun comes up, requiring frequent adjustments to your clothing. You might find yourself adding or removing layers at nearly every break as conditions change. While warm fronts generally bring more stable weather compared to cold fronts, they can also create damp conditions with lingering drizzle. The combination of warm days and cold nights presents unique challenges, including increased condensation inside tents.

Preparing for these shifts is key to staying comfortable. The extra cooling at night demands proper insulation, while warmer daytime conditions call for lighter, breathable gear.

Wind Patterns

Under high-pressure systems, winds are usually light and variable. Even mild air movement can cut through clothing and gloves, causing discomfort in cold conditions. Additionally, frost often forms more readily during calm, clear nights as heat escapes into the sky without cloud cover.

Low-pressure systems bring stronger, more unpredictable winds. Wind direction may shift for hours, potentially negating the protection of wind walls or shelters you've built. A sudden reversal in wind direction could expose your campsite to gusts you originally sheltered from. Be prepared to adjust or rebuild your setup to handle wind from any direction, especially at night.

Cold fronts often come with gusty, shifting winds that increase wind chill and make tasks like cooking or traveling more difficult. Setting up your campsite strategically is crucial. In low-pressure or cold front conditions, you'll need sturdier shelters and better wind barriers, while high-pressure systems allow for lighter setups, especially if you use natural features like rocks or trees as windbreaks.

Wind direction is a key indicator of changing weather. Stable winds under overcast skies usually signal calm, predictable conditions. However, when winds pick up or shift suddenly, it often means stronger weather fronts are moving in.

Fog, especially when paired with shifting winds, often precedes significant weather changes. While fog sometimes forms independently of passing systems, its presence in conjunction with wind shifts is a reliable indicator that conditions are about to change. Pay close attention to variable winds and strengthening breezes, as they suggest that current conditions won't last.

Identifying Weather Changes

Certain visual and environmental signs can help predict shifts in weather. Clear skies or thin, high-altitude clouds usually mean stable conditions. However, the appearance of cirrus clouds—those wispy streaks resembling mare's tails—often indicates an approaching weather front. While they don't always mean a storm, they serve as a warning to stay alert for changing conditions.

A sudden shift in wind direction or speed is another key sign. While some areas have consistent wind patterns, mountainous or coastal regions can experience frequent shifts regardless of incoming weather. However, in most locations, a noticeable change in wind strength or direction signals an approaching front.

Temperature changes also provide important clues. If it suddenly becomes warmer or colder than expected, the weather is likely shifting. Rapid warming can sometimes indicate an approaching front, potentially bringing storms or volatile conditions.

A barometer is one of the best tools for predicting weather changes. A drop in pressure, even under clear skies, strongly suggests that conditions may deteriorate. If you don't have a barometer, an altimeter based on barometric pressure can serve the same function. A rising altitude reading on the device—without actual altitude gain—means the pressure is dropping and worsening weather is likely.

Nature often provides its own warnings. In areas with active bird or animal sounds, sudden silence may suggest a drop in atmospheric pressure, as animals can sense changes that humans often miss. This quiet can serve as an early warning sign.

Cloud formations are another valuable indicator. Cirrus and stratus clouds suggest an approaching weather front, while towering cumulus or cumulonimbus clouds—often called anvil clouds—signal atmospheric instability and the potential for storms. These visual clues, combined with temperature and wind changes, can help you prepare for what's ahead.

Sun Effects in the Sky: Predicting Weather

The sun and its effects in the sky can be useful for predicting weather changes. If the sky is clear but you notice a slight haze developing along with a ring around the sun—known as a halo (sometimes called a sunbow)—it's a sign that weather conditions may begin to shift.

This is also true for sun dogs, the bright spots of light that appear about 22 degrees from the sun. Both halos and sun dogs indicate increasing ice crystals in the upper atmosphere, which often signal an approaching weather front, typically bringing a storm or worsening conditions.

Although these atmospheric displays are beautiful to see, they serve as a reminder to prepare for potential weather changes ahead.

Understanding Wind Chill

Understanding wind chill is critical for staying safe and avoiding frostbite or freezing skin. Strong winds make the air feel much colder and increase the risk of hypothermia and frostbite. Weather forecasts often show the actual temperature along with the "feels like" temperature, which accounts for wind speed and humidity.

Wind chill is driven by wind speed and temperature, but local geography influences how winds behave, often intensifying the effect. Katabatic winds occur when cold air at higher altitudes flows downhill, creating extremely strong gusts. These winds are common in polar regions like Greenland and Antarctica but also occur in the mountains, where cold air accelerates as it funnels through valleys.

Geography plays a big role in wind behavior. Mountain passes often act like wind tunnels, turning calm conditions into roaring gusts. For example, at Windy Corner in Denali, air on either side may be still, but the terrain forces wind through at speeds often exceeding 80 mph (130 km/h), with extreme gusts surpassing 100 mph (160 km/h).

Wind chill can have serious effects on your body. It lowers skin temperature rapidly, making the air feel much colder than the actual temperature. Gloves, boots, and face protection must be chosen based on wind-adjusted temperatures. Failing to account for wind chill can result in frostbite and hypothermia, even in conditions that might seem safe.

Become familiar with wind chill charts and plan your gear accordingly. Strong winds can turn otherwise safe conditions dangerous, so always be prepared to mitigate wind chill risks.

Wind Chill Chart

Temperature (°F)

Calm	40	35	30	25	20	15	10	5	0	-5	-10	-15	-20	-25	-30	-35	-40	-45
5	36	31	25	19	13	7	1	-5	-11	-16	-22	-28	-34	-40	-46	-52	-57	-63
10	34	27	21	15	9	3	-4	-10	-16	-22	-28	-35	-41	-47	-53	-59	-66	-72
15	32	25	19	13	6	0	-7	-13	-19	-26	-32	-39	-45	-51	-58	-64	-71	-77
20	30	24	17	11	4	-2	-9	-15	-22	-29	-35	-42	-48	-55	-61	-68	-74	-81
25	29	23	16	9	3	-4	-11	-17	-24	-31	-37	-44	-51	-58	-64	-71	-78	-84
30	28	22	15	8	1	-5	-12	-19	-26	-33	-39	-46	-53	-60	-67	-73	-80	-87
35	28	21	14	7	0	-7	-14	-21	-27	-34	-41	-48	-55	-62	-69	-76	-82	-89
40	27	20	13	6	-1	-8	-15	-22	-29	-36	-43	-50	-57	-64	-71	-78	-84	-91
45	26	19	12	5	-2	-9	-16	-23	-30	-37	-44	-51	-58	-65	-72	-79	-86	-93
50	26	19	12	4	-3	-10	-17	-24	-31	-38	-45	-52	-60	-67	-74	-81	-88	-95
55	25	18	11	4	-3	-11	-18	-25	-32	-39	-46	-54	-61	-68	-75	-82	-89	-97
60	25	17	10	3	-4	-11	-19	-26	-33	-40	-48	-55	-62	-69	-76	-84	-91	-98

Wind (mph)

Frostbite Times
■ 30 minutes   ■ 10 minutes   ■ 5 minutes

Snowfall and Its Implications

Understanding the type of snow in your area is essential for planning. In Utah's Front Range near Salt Lake City and Park City ski resorts, the snow is famously ultra-dry. This light, powdery snow is excellent for skiing but challenging for camping and other tasks. It's difficult to build shelters with and requires a larger volume to melt for water since it has a high snow-water ratio—typically 15 to 20 inches (39–51cm) of snow produce just 1 inch (2.5cm) of water. Collecting enough dry snow can take considerable effort. Camping on powdery snow also demands extra time to pack down your tent site so the snow can consolidate and hold its shape.

Wet snow, common in coastal ranges like the Cascades and Sierras, behaves differently. Influenced by moist ocean currents, this snow is heavier and compacts easily, often earning the nickname "Sierra cement." While this dense, wet snow is ideal for packing tent sites and melting for water, it also increases the risk of wet gear and clothing, adding to your challenges.

Snow type and wind direction are crucial for avalanche prediction. Winds deposit snow unevenly, forming dense slabs on leeward slopes, which are a common avalanche hazard. Long gaps between snowfalls can create weak layers due to frost or faceted crystals forming on the surface. These layers can collapse under new snowfall, increasing the risk of avalanches.

By understanding the characteristics of snow in your area, you can better plan for water collection, shelter building, and avalanche risk management.

Storms and Extreme Weather

Recognizing the signs of an approaching blizzard is critical for staying safe. If the wind shifts direction, strengthens, and the temperature drops quickly, it's a clear signal that bad weather is on the way. A falling barometer confirms that conditions will likely worsen. When you notice these signs, it's better to stop and build camp early rather than risk being caught in a blizzard without shelter.

Preparing your camp in stormy weather takes more time and effort, so plan ahead when conditions begin to change. Winter weather can shift from calm to extreme in just a few hours, with winds often exceeding 40 mph (60 km/h) and sometimes reaching 50–70 mph (80–113 km/h) in severe blizzards. Being unprepared in these conditions can be dangerous, especially if your gear isn't designed to handle the cold and wind.

Your plans should always account for unpredictable weather. Learn basic weather observation skills to stay ahead of changing conditions. If you're camping solo, this knowledge is even more vital. Always aim to find shelter early, stay warm, and have backup plans if you get stuck in a storm. Make sure you have proper communication tools to contact someone if needed and the right gear to handle unexpected situations.

Tragic outcomes often result from failing to check forecasts or observe warning signs. Stories of people caught in freezing weather with inadequate clothing or stranded in vehicles due to sudden storms illustrate how quickly things can go wrong.Shows like *I Shouldn't Be Alive* highlight the consequences of small oversights. A little extra preparation can mean the difference between a successful trip and a dangerous situation.

Weather Awareness

Understanding the weather conditions where you're going is essential. This isn't something you can figure out with a quick search. Studying long-term weather patterns and understanding short-term forecasts are key to planning a safe trip.

If you're heading into the northern woods and see that a severe polar vortex is bringing ultracold temperatures below -30°F (-34°C), and you're not prepared, it's best to reschedule. Even if you've spent money on flights or made other arrangements, your safety—and the safety of those with you or anyone who might have to rescue you—is worth far more than the cost of a trip.

Practice observing the weather at home. Watch for changes when fog rolls in or specific cloud types appear. Compare these with local forecasts from TV, online, or newspapers to see how patterns play out over the following days. With time and practice, you'll start recognizing subtle signs of weather changes, making you more confident and prepared outdoors.

Winter camping is about embracing the challenge and enjoying the experience—not ending up in a dangerous situation. When you're well-prepared and understand the signs of changing weather, you can make smarter choices and have a good time. The goal is to return with great stories to share over a warm meal—stories about how you saw what was coming and knew exactly what to do.

Trekking in winter weather is pretty enjoyable once you get used to it.

Chapter 15
Planning for Short vs. Long Winter Trips

Short Versus Long Trips

Planning for short and long winter camping trips requires different approaches. The basics—food, cold-weather gear, and other essentials—stay the same, but the level of preparation increases significantly for longer trips. Whether you're using a sled, backpack, or pulk sled to carry gear, the time you'll need to spend on food prep, route planning, and logistics will depend on the trip's duration.

Fuel requirements are usually predictable on a daily basis under normal conditions, but extreme cold, altitude, or wind can increase consumption. You'll need to plan where to buy fuel, how to carry it, and how to store it safely both during travel and at camp.

Short trips, such as an overnight or even a three-day outing, require less planning than extended trips but still demand preparation. If something goes wrong, it's easier to get out quickly since you're not far from your starting point. That said, it's still important to be prepared rather than relying on proximity as a safety net.

For long trips—lasting four days or more and stretching into weeks or even months—you'll need to bring backup stoves, spare pumps, repair kits, and additional first-aid supplies. Redundancy is key for extended trips. Longer durations also require more complex planning, particularly for communication. A cell phone might work for a weekend trip, but longer outings often require satellite communication, whether through a GPS messenger or a satellite phone. Modern satellite messengers, such as Garmin inReach, are easier to set up and more affordable. However, traditional satellite phones may require activating a SIM card or setting up a service plan, which can take weeks.

Before heading out, you'll also need to manage responsibilities at home. Whether it's arranging time off from work or handling personal obligations, longer trips require more effort to ensure everything is in place before you leave.

By planning for food, fuel, gear, and communication, and addressing the added logistics of longer trips, you can minimize risks and focus on enjoying the experience.

Gear Considerations for Short Versus Long Trips

For shorter trips, streamline your gear while ensuring you have enough safety and warmth for the conditions. You can often get by with one set of clothes and a sleeping set or just one outfit with an emergency backup. In sheltered areas with mild weather, lighter shelters like tarps or three-season tents can work, as long as no storms are expected. The goal of a short trip is to bring less gear, which can make the experience more enjoyable.

If you need to melt snow for water, you'll still have to bring a stove and enough fuel, even on short trips. For cooking, a minimal setup is usually sufficient unless snow melting is necessary, in which case you'll need to account for extra fuel.

On longer trips, gear must be durable enough to withstand repeated use and versatile enough to serve multiple functions. Items that serve multiple purposes are especially valuable. Essential equipment, like stoves or food storage for areas with wildlife, becomes even more critical. You'll need a plan for handling failures, as small issues can turn into big problems.

Shelters for long trips should be robust. A double-walled tent is a better choice, as long-term forecasts are less reliable, and you'll need protection from unexpected storms.

Thermoses and other insulating items are worth considering on extended trips. They offer both physical and psychological comfort, letting you enjoy warm drinks in the morning or during breaks. On mountaineering trips, carrying hot water during summit pushes can help warm extremities and reduce the risk of cold-related injuries. This reserve water should be saved for emergencies rather than relied on for regular hydration.

Repair kits are essential for long trips. Bring supplies for sewing and patching gear. Small issues, like torn fabric, broken zippers, or damaged packs, can escalate quickly if left untreated. Knowing how to sew can help prevent gear failures that might increase the risk of exposure and frostbite.

Long trips require more preparation, but careful planning and durable gear will help you handle unexpected challenges and enjoy the experience safely.

Packing for Short Versus Long Trips

The key to winter camping is balancing efficiency, safety, and enjoyment. Short trips allow you to cover more ground without overexposing yourself to danger.

For short trips, you might bring fewer layers, relying on predictable weather forecasts and your ability to make quick adjustments or retreat if needed. Lightweight gear is more viable, and shorter outings let you experiment with different cooking or food setups without major consequences if they don't work perfectly.

For longer trips, packing becomes more complex. You need gear that can handle severe weather, even if your route primarily stays in sheltered areas like forests. Sudden exposure to open terrain or a blizzard can catch you off guard, so durable, weather-appropriate equipment is essential.

Food is even more critical on long trips. High-calorie, nutrient-dense, and well-tested meals are necessary to maintain energy and morale. On a short trip, you can get by with less optimized food, but over time, poor nutrition leads to fatigue and declining performance. The psychological effects of hunger also become more pronounced, diminishing the enjoyment of your trip.

Water management is another challenge for long trips. Melting snow requires significant fuel, and filtering or purifying untreated sources is critical to avoid illness. Planning an efficient and sustainable method for long-term water needs is essential.

Efficient packing and storage are key for extended outings. On a short trip, losing half an hour due to disorganization isn't a big deal. But over a long trip, those delays add up to lost miles or even full days of progress. Keeping your gear organized and accessible saves valuable time and energy, allowing you to focus on the experience rather than unnecessary setbacks.

Route Planning: Short Versus Long Trips

Always ensure you have a well-planned route and let others know where you'll be and when you plan to return. This way, if something goes wrong and you don't arrive as expected, they can alert the proper authorities.

On shorter trips, routes are usually less remote, making it easier to retreat if conditions worsen. Navigation is simpler since you're typically covering a limited distance—unless attempting an endurance challenge like the Arrowhead 135 in Minnesota, which follows a well-marked but demanding route.

Short trips also allow for flexibility. If bad weather is forecast before you leave, you can postpone the trip and avoid unnecessary risks. There's less pressure to maintain strict itineraries since your range is limited.

In contrast, long trips require detailed planning. You'll need topographical maps, GPS devices, compasses, and other navigation tools to handle complex terrain. Covering greater distances means encountering varied and challenging environments. Cold significantly reduces battery life, so you'll need backup batteries or a charging method. Solar chargers can work but are unreliable in winter or cloudy conditions.

Weather planning is critical for longer trips. Include buffer days for storms when you might not be able to leave your tent. Accept that some days will be lost to bad weather. You should also plan escape routes or potential rescue points in case of gear failure, injury, or running out of time. Reliable communication devices, such as radios, satellite phones, or personal locator beacons (PLBs), are essential to call for assistance if necessary.

Pacing is vital on long trips. While short trips allow for pushing harder, longer outings require careful energy conservation to avoid exhaustion. Build in rest days to recover, especially if gaining altitude, since climbing more than 1,000–2,000 feet (300–600 meters) per day increases the risk of altitude sickness, which can be dangerous or even fatal.

Unexpected challenges are more likely on long trips. Deep snow, unforeseen terrain, or obstacles not visible on maps can slow progress significantly, sometimes taking an extra day or more to navigate. These factors are part of extended wilderness travel, so plan for delays and remain adaptable.

Short trips prioritize simplicity and flexibility, while long trips require detailed preparation and contingency plans. Both require thoughtful planning, but for extended outings, being ready for the unknown is critical to a successful and safe adventure.

Food Planning for a Long Trip Versus a Short Trip

The fun part of short trips is the freedom to experiment. If a particular food doesn't work well, you can endure some hunger without major consequences. Lightweight, calorie-dense snacks or simple freeze-dried meals work well. You can even get by with minimal or no cooking, relying on energy bars or one-pot meals. On short outings, it's also easier to plan around a reliable water source, reducing the effort needed for water collection.

However, if temperatures drop suddenly, your water source could freeze. Make sure you have a way to chisel through ice, such as an ice chisel (spud bar), auger, or a sturdy tool like an ice axe for thinner layers, and always plan for backup methods to access water.

For longer trips, food planning becomes more critical. You'll need balanced, nutrient-dense meals to maintain energy, protect your immune system, and support muscle recovery. Variety is essential because eating the same food every day for weeks leads to food fatigue, where repetitive meals reduce your appetite and make eating a chore.

Weight is another key factor on long trips. Small increases in weight, like a quarter pound (100 grams) per item, add up over weeks, affecting both storage capacity and travel speed. Fuel requirements also increase. Colder temperatures and higher altitude reduce stove efficiency, and unforeseen delays can further raise consumption. Running out of fuel on a long trip leaves you with few options. Relying on body heat to melt snow is ineffective and can dangerously lower your core temperature.

Aim for at least 4,000 calories per day in cold conditions, though actual needs depend on factors like activity level, body size, and environment. On extreme trips, like polar expeditions or high-altitude climbs, it may be impossible to carry enough food to meet these needs. In those cases, you'll rely on fat reserves, which can be uncomfortable but manageable for a time.

As the old saying in polar exploration goes, "your constant companions will be cold, hunger, and thirst." With proper food planning that balances calorie needs, variety, and weight considerations, you can ensure a safer and more enjoyable experience, even on the longest journeys.

Managing Energy on Short Versus Long Trips

On short trips, conserving energy isn't as critical. With lighter gear and fewer supplies, you can move faster and explore more freely. Minimalist shelters save time on setup and teardown, letting you cover more ground. However, total daily distance is still limited by terrain and altitude gain, so plan accordingly.

For long trips, pacing is essential. Recovery days are especially important in mountaineering, where big moves and altitude gains require time for acclimatization. Skipping these rest periods increases the risk of altitude sickness, which can become life-threatening. If someone in your group is injured, you'll need to allocate additional time to address the situation safely.

Fatigue builds over the course of a long trip as your body burns through fat reserves. This depletes your natural insulation, making it harder to stay warm in later stages of the trip. Cold exposure over time helps with adaptation, but as fat reserves deplete, you may need an extra layer of clothing to compensate for lost insulation. Managing energy carefully helps prevent physical and mental exhaustion, which can impact your ability to make sound decisions.

Time management becomes increasingly critical on extended outings. Small delays, like tasks taking an extra 5–10 minutes, may seem insignificant but can cost valuable daylight and energy, leading to bigger setbacks over time. These inefficiencies can eat into your food, fuel, and progress, potentially affecting your ability to meet objectives or complete the trip.

Short trips allow for more aggressive movement and flexibility, but long trips demand careful pacing, efficient energy use, and strategic planning to maintain endurance and safety.

Safety and Emergency Planning on Short Versus Long Trips

On a short trip, managing evacuation routes is simpler because you can't travel as far. With a shorter window of weather variability, it's easier to predict potential issues and retreat if necessary. Common injuries like blisters or mild sprains can typically be handled with a small first aid kit, though severe sprains may require additional support like an elastic wrap or splint. Communication tools can also be simpler—two-way satellite devices allow you to coordinate assistance without triggering full-scale rescue operations, unlike a personal locator beacon (PLB), which summons significant resources once activated.

For longer trips, a more comprehensive plan is essential. Over time, issues like intestinal problems, severe blisters, or frostbite are more likely, requiring a well-stocked first aid kit. While carrying a heavier kit can feel like a burden, when the need arises, it's invaluable.

Multiple exit strategies are critical on long trips. Consider all potential ways to evacuate if weather turns severe or injuries occur, and be prepared to abandon the trip if necessary—even at a financial loss. Your safety should always take precedence. As they say, "the mountain or destination will still be there for another attempt."

Emergency shelters are a must for extended trips. Learn how to dig snow pits and plan for survival scenarios like snow blindness, frostbite, or broken limbs. These events are common in winter conditions and require preparation and training to handle effectively.

Communication devices on long trips must remain warm and charged to function properly. PLB batteries generally expire after 5–7 years and may require factory servicing or replacement. While maintaining these tools can be costly, they are often essential depending on your destination.

Leave a detailed itinerary with a responsible person at home. Ensure they know your planned check-in times and understand that communication failures may occasionally occur. However, they should also know when and how to escalate to authorities if contact is lost for an extended period.

Before heading out, contact park services, ranger stations, or local SAR organizations in your travel area. They can provide guidance on local risks, resources, and emergency procedures, ensuring you're better prepared for your trip.

On longer trips, comprehensive safety planning, redundancy in systems, and preparation for unexpected scenarios are critical. Always prioritize safety over commitment to reaching your goal.

You may look a bit rough after several months in the field.

Chapter 16
Solo vs. Team Camping

Making the Right Choice

Choosing whether to camp solo or with a team is a personal decision. In winter, many experts strongly advise against going alone due to the increased risks. If you run into trouble, you're solely responsible for getting yourself out—even if you have a communication device, which could fail. Extreme conditions can cause problems to escalate quickly, making self-rescue far more difficult.

In contrast, camping with a team provides a built-in safety net. If someone gets injured or is unable to move, the group can work together to help them. There are also psychological benefits to being with others—if one person is struggling, teammates can offer support and encouragement. Solo campers, on the other hand, must act as their own cheerleader, cook, navigator, and leader—handling every task alone.

This chapter explores the pros and cons of both solo and team camping to help you determine which approach best suits your experience level, comfort, and goals.

Solo Camping: Self-Sufficiency

The greatest advantage of solo camping is complete independence—the freedom to set your own pace, follow your own schedule, and make decisions without consulting anyone else. If you want to change plans or explore a new route, you can do so without negotiation or compromise.

Solo camping is also a powerful test of personal growth. It's where you truly find out what you're capable of and whether you know your skills as well as you think. When you're alone in the wilderness, you quickly discover the depth of your knowledge—or its limits.

Additionally, solo camping strengthens problem-solving skills. Since there's no one else to rely on, you must handle every challenge yourself. This builds mental resilience, forcing you to adapt, overcome obstacles, and face fears head-on. If you've previously depended on others for navigation, decision-making, or survival skills, going solo is an eye-opening experience.

Modern society fosters dependence on others for essentials like food, transportation, medicine, and housing. But in the wilderness, assuming you've packed the necessary gear and know how to use it, you rely only on yourself. You learn firsthand what it takes to survive and, ideally, to enjoy the experience.

Another advantage of solo camping is flexibility. Without a group to coordinate with, you can change plans on a whim without needing consensus. In a group, dynamics can be tricky, and compromises are often necessary. While group decision-making has its benefits, it also requires adjustments. But as a solo camper, you make decisions based solely on your needs, within the constraints of safety and local regulations.

Solo camping also fosters a deeper connection with nature. With fewer distractions and more time for reflection—assuming you're not preoccupied with a device—you become more attuned to your surroundings. The sounds of the wind, the crunch of snow underfoot, and the distant calls of wildlife become more vivid when you're alone.

Solo Camping Challenges

The advantages of solo camping are balanced by its challenges. The most obvious is the increased risk. There's no one to assist in an emergency, whether you're injured, lost, or dealing with a shelter failure—or any number of other problems. If things go wrong, you have to get yourself out unless you can call emergency services or, by chance, someone happens to pass by.

When you go solo, you have to accept full responsibility for any situation. This isn't something to take lightly. You don't want to go out thinking, *"I'll just call for a helicopter rescue."* That's the wrong mindset. Assume the worst—whether it's a broken leg, frostbite, or another serious injury—you are the only one who can get yourself out.

The physical demands of solo camping are also much higher than with a team. You're the only one hauling your shelter, your food, and handling every aspect of the trip, from setting up camp and cooking to navigation and gear maintenance. If an injury occurs, you're also responsible for first aid. The physical and psychological toll can be immense. If you're not used to being in the wilderness alone, or if solitude is difficult for you, be prepared for the adjustment. Start with a light-duty trip, maybe a short outing in warm weather. The isolation of being outdoors can be overwhelming if you're not prepared, sometimes leading to panic or poor decision-making.

Fear is another challenge. When you're with others, the fear factor drops significantly, even if the group has concerns about animals, people, or difficult terrain. When you're alone, the psychological weight of fear and self-doubt can build over time, making it harder to stay focused and make rational decisions.

If you're unsure about going solo, don't start with a long trip. Try overnight trips close to home first. If you enjoy them, gradually push your limits. This is especially important in extreme environments like high-altitude, mountaineering, polar, or deep wilderness travel, where help is far away. There's no immediate support if equipment fails or something goes wrong. If your gear malfunctions, you get lost due to a navigation error, or your compass breaks, you'll quickly realize how critical backup plans are. In solo camping, problems can escalate fast, so preparation is essential.

Solo Camping Skills

When heading out solo, you must have strong map-reading and compass skills. Avoid relying solely on technology—batteries die, devices break, and water can infiltrate your gear. Whatever technology you bring, you need to be able to get yourself out if it fails. You should be proficient with GPS, as modern devices are common in the field, whether on a smartphone, handheld GPS, or other equipment. But always treat them as backup tools. A good old-fashioned map and compass will keep you going, no matter what technology fails. Even if everything breaks down, knowing how to navigate manually is essential.

You also need self-rescue skills to handle hazards like avalanches and crevasses. Escaping both in winter can be challenging, if not outright impossible. If you fall into a crevasse and aren't severely injured, you'll need to figure out how to climb out—possibly by building a Texas prusik, a rope-based self-rescue system. Knowing how to avoid avalanches is just as important as knowing how to self-rescue. The key is to prevent dangerous situations in the first place.

Mental toughness is just as important as physical preparation. You don't want to carry the weight of personal problems into the wilderness. Instead, set small, achievable goals to boost your confidence. Staying organized makes the experience far better. It helps manage stress, keeps you focused in difficult situations, and prevents tunnel vision that could cause you to miss obvious solutions.

Team Camping Advantages

Camping with a team or friends offers significant advantages over going solo. Responsibilities such as cooking, setting up camp, clearing snow, building snow walls, first aid, and navigation can be divided, making the workload more manageable. Some people will have stronger skills in certain areas, so it's often best to let them handle those tasks. However, rotating responsibilities can help prevent overload and ensure that everyone gains useful experience.

Even though a larger group may require a bigger shelter or tent, the ability to distribute tasks remains a clear advantage. Safety is also significantly improved in case of injury, equipment failure, or unexpected emergencies. Beyond that, there's the invaluable benefit of emotional support. When one person is struggling, the group can lift them up. Team members can also monitor each other for warning signs of hypothermia, which can be especially dangerous because the victim is often unaware of their condition. Severe hypothermia can cause confusion or even defensiveness, making it harder for a person to recognize they need help. When you're alone, this can be fatal, but in a team, others can intervene before the situation worsens.

Team camping also allows for skill specialization. If someone in the group excels at navigation, they can take the lead in route planning. If there's a medic or someone with wilderness first responder training, the team benefits from a level of medical support that solo campers simply don't have. This is particularly valuable on longer trips or expeditions where injuries and illnesses are more likely.

Another major benefit is shared gear. Team members can distribute heavy items like tents, cooking equipment, repair kits, and communication devices, reducing the load each person has to carry. This makes movement more efficient and allows for better overall packing compared to a solo camper, who must carry everything alone.

Team Camping Challenges

For all its advantages—strength in numbers, added safety, and shared workload—team camping comes with its own challenges. The biggest issue is group dynamics. Disagreements can arise over route choices, pace, rest breaks, or even meal times. Some people naturally move faster, while others are slower. The slower members may feel pressured to keep up, while the faster ones may grow impatient at frequent stops. Managing this tension is key to maintaining a functional team. Good communication and an understanding of group expectations will make a major difference.

A classic example of strong group cohesion comes from Shackleton's Antarctic expedition. His team was stranded for over a year in brutal conditions, yet they maintained morale through simple but crucial practices—consistently using "please" and "thank you" and showing politeness even in the worst situations.

Another challenge of group camping is slower decision-making. Reaching a consensus on critical choices—such as changing routes or selecting a campsite—takes time. If two skilled individuals have opposing viewpoints, conflict can arise. Planning for this ahead of time is important, and it may help to have a designated leader whose decisions are final, provided they are reasonable and not outright dangerous.

Pace differences are another challenge. Some people want to take in the scenery, snap photos, and enjoy the journey, while others are goal-oriented and focused on reaching the summit or campsite as efficiently as possible. Finding a balance between these mindsets can be difficult, but setting clear expectations beforehand helps prevent frustration.

Groupthink and How to Avoid It

One of the most dangerous risks in team camping is groupthink—a psychological phenomenon where the desire for harmony or conformity results in poor decision-making. This is especially common in avalanche situations. If enough people believe a slope is safe, those who recognize the danger may hesitate to speak up for fear of disrupting the group's momentum. Under pressure, individuals may ignore critical safety concerns rather than challenge the majority. Recognizing and addressing this dynamic is crucial to making sound, independent decisions in a group setting.

One of the most effective ways to prevent groupthink and social pressure from leading to bad decisions is to encourage dissenting opinions. Creating a team culture where members feel comfortable voicing concerns is crucial. Even if those concerns aren't immediately acted upon, acknowledging them ensures better decision-making and helps prevent costly mistakes.

Having a structured decision-making process that weighs the risks and benefits of retreating versus continuing is essential. The **STOP approach—Stop, Think, Observe, Plan**—is simple in theory but can be difficult to implement when cold, hungry, and racing against darkness. Under stress, even the best plans can fall apart.

So, how do you build consensus while avoiding undue pressure? Striking a balance between ensuring safety and reaching agreement—while resisting the push to keep moving forward—is critical. Some people will want to push on, while others will hesitate. Managing these opposing views effectively can mean the difference between a safe trip and a dangerous situation.

Team Skills

The number one skill to develop when camping as a team is effective communication. Clear, open, and non-aggressive dialogue is essential to ensure all group members understand the goals, routes, potential risks, contingencies, and any necessary adjustments. These should be agreed upon before the trip. Once you reach your destination, the original plan may no longer work, requiring on-the-spot changes. Not everyone is comfortable adapting, so it's important to gauge how flexible team members are with making adjustments as needed.

Some people prefer to stick to the plan, while others favor improvisation. If these personalities clash, it can create tension and make the trip unpleasant. To prevent misunderstandings and resentment, ensure that everyone's voice is heard in the decision-making process. If there are too many dominant personalities, they may overshadow those with better judgment or a clearer vision of what needs to be done. Conflict is inevitable, so having a plan to manage disagreements is crucial. The key is to make sure everyone is respectfully heard and that disputes are handled constructively, allowing the group to stay cohesive, effective, and focused on the journey.

Team Role Delegation

Assigning roles based on each person's strengths is key to keeping things running smoothly. If someone is skilled at cooking or navigation, they should have the tools and support needed to succeed. For more physically demanding tasks—such as breaking trails, carrying heavy loads, or digging out snow shelters—rotating responsibilities is essential to prevent both physical and psychological fatigue.

This is especially important when clearing snow or making camp. If some members are doing hard labor while others are resting or focused on less strenuous tasks, resentment can build quickly. Those handling lighter duties must be willing and able to take on heavier work when needed. For example, if a team member struggles with cooking but is assigned an equally crucial task like shelter building, the team could face setbacks.

It's also important to establish a leader or rotate leadership roles to streamline decision-making in critical moments. In an emergency, lengthy debates won't help—discussions can quickly escalate into arguments or shouting matches. When severe weather strikes or another crisis arises, the designated decision-maker must be followed, assuming their choices are reasonable and safe. Having a clear plan for handling disagreements in advance will help maintain order when quick action is needed.

Teams and Decision Points

One of the greatest challenges in team travel versus solo travel is reaching decision points—knowing when to turn around, call for help, or recognize the group's limits. Fitness levels, experience, and mental resilience all need to be taken into account. Some individuals may be physically tough and willing to push forward at all costs, but that doesn't necessarily make them the best choice for leading group decisions. Often, strong communicators are better suited for leadership roles, though more aggressive personalities may resist this approach.

People with military or first responder backgrounds often bring valuable skills, but that doesn't automatically mean they should dictate group decisions. Identifying warning signs—whether it's fatigue, worsening weather, or declining morale—is critical. Some group members may want to push on despite deteriorating conditions, and groupthink—where the pressure to conform leads to poor decision-making—can take over. This can result in injuries, bad judgment calls, and long-term resentment among team members.

To ensure everyone is truly on board with a decision, consider using an anonymous poll if there's disagreement. Establish clear rules for decision-making before heading out—will choices be made by unanimous agreement, majority vote, or a single designated leader? Defining these structures in advance prevents confusion and ensures the group can function smoothly when difficult choices arise.

Handling Emergencies as a Team

Setting clear roles and responsibilities before an emergency occurs is key to an effective response. If one person is handling first aid while others manage communication, shelter, or logistics, knowing who is best suited for each task makes a big difference. For example, someone stronger may be better equipped to haul an injured person, while someone with medical training should focus on treatment. Having roles assigned ahead of time allows the team to act immediately rather than wasting time debating who should do what.

Having a clear decision-maker under pressure is also crucial. This person should be experienced, calm, and able to make decisive choices without causing panic or dismissing input. In high-stress situations—such as injuries, crevasse falls, or equipment failures—teams often default to group decision-making. However, in emergencies, having a designated leader with a team providing input generally leads to faster and more effective action. This doesn't mean ignoring group concerns, but rather ensuring that decisions are made efficiently. A good leader is experienced yet level-headed, avoiding aggression or unnecessary pressure while keeping the group focused.

Team Rope Travel and Safety Practice

One of the biggest advantages of traveling as a team versus solo is the ability to use ropes for glacier travel, steep icy terrain, and hazardous water crossings. On glaciers, rope travel is one of the most critical safety measures for protecting against crevasse falls. It's a fundamental technique for safe travel, but only if everyone understands how to use it properly.

If someone falls into a crevasse, the team has only moments to react before the situation worsens. Training is essential—without proper practice, even an experienced group can struggle in an actual rescue. If ropes are used in steep or icy terrain, everyone must be trained in proper rope techniques, self-arrest, and emergency rescue procedures. Unless the entire team is highly experienced, it's crucial to spend at least half an hour reviewing and practicing a rescue scenario.

People may nod along and say they understand, but in the field, hesitation or mistakes can be costly. Taking time to go over the basics—how to arrest a fall, properly tie rescue knots, and set up an anchor—ensures that when an emergency happens, everyone knows exactly what to do.

The major advantage of team travel over solo travel is its ability to handle more dangerous situations, such as river crossings, navigating steep slopes, or traversing icy ridges. A group has a far greater margin of safety in these scenarios compared to an individual traveling alone.

Overloading Rope Danger

Although traveling in a group is generally safer, there is a significant danger of overloading a rope with too many people. Ideally, a rope team should have three people, but depending on terrain and experience level, teams of two to five climbers are common. Three is often considered optimal, as it provides balance and redundancy while reducing the risk of multiple team members being pulled into a fall. If a group is large, splitting into multiple rope teams ensures that if one team falls into a crevasse or icefall, the others can assist without being pulled into immediate danger.

Practicing techniques for self-safe anchors, setting up for ice and snow rope travel, and maintaining proper spacing between team members is essential. One of the most critical aspects of safe rope travel is ensuring that everyone follows clear signals and commands for movement, stopping, and resting.

Maintaining proper rope tension is another key factor. The rope between team members should droop just enough to prevent unnecessary pulling on the person ahead but not so much that it risks getting underfoot or tangled in crampons, skis, or snow. Keeping the right spacing requires constant awareness and practice. Even experienced mountaineers struggle with this, especially when hauling sleds. It takes discipline and communication to maintain proper rope positioning and ensure safe movement through difficult terrain.

Mount Hood Accident

In 2002, a well-known accident occurred on Mount Hood when a large number of climbers were roped together on a single rope while ascending. At some point, they lost their footing and started tumbling. Several fell into a crevasse or bergschrund, but that wasn't the worst part—the Pave Hawk rescue helicopter responding to the accident was hit by a sudden wind gust, causing it to crash and tumble down the mountain, adding to the tragedy.

The key issue in this accident was the number of climbers roped together.

When too many climbers are tied to a single rope, the forces generated in a fall can exceed what the human body can safely withstand, particularly in dynamic situations. The chances of severe injury—or worse—are significantly higher when a large group is tied together in a fall scenario.

Despite this, some guiding companies still use the practice of tying many climbers together for logistical reasons. However, breaking up the team into smaller rope groups is a far safer approach, even if it requires more guides. While it may seem more efficient to keep everyone on one rope, the risks of multiple climbers being pulled down in a fall make this method a dangerous compromise.

Choosing Solo or Team Camping

There are multiple factors to consider when deciding whether to strike out on your own or go with a team. Experience level is critical, as it may be tempting to bring an inexperienced person on a challenging trip. However, there's a danger that an experienced person may struggle to keep up or lack the necessary skills for the challenges you face.

When going solo, you take on the risks and manage them as you go. If you believe you have the experience, try a two- or three-night trip not too far from your vehicle or home, so you can handle any issues that arise. Use these experiences to build confidence, knowing that if things go wrong, you'll face a tough situation. Also, when you're by yourself, make sure someone knows your plans and when to expect your return.

Terrain plays a big role in deciding whether to go solo. It's never recommended to travel in glaciated terrain alone because if you fall into a crevasse, rescue is nearly impossible without assistance. While some people do it, there are ways to mitigate the risk, such as using extra-long skis, snow pickets, and a leapfrog technique. However, this method is less efficient and more dangerous.

Whether you're on a heavily trafficked trail or in a remote wilderness impacts the decision. While you shouldn't rely on others to rescue you, if you're on a busy trail, going solo might carry less risk because you could lean on passing hikers in an emergency. In remote wilderness, however, there may be no one to help.

Some people value the solitude and self-reliance of solo camping, while others enjoy the companionship and shared workload of a team. Solo camping has the benefit of being more contemplative, allowing you to focus solely on what you're doing and enjoying the experience.

When Solo is Better

Sometimes, solo camping is actually the better choice, especially on shorter trips with easier terrain. Going solo makes the trip more manageable when the terrain isn't too challenging, and you have the freedom to turn around or change your plans. If you have advanced skills, you can venture deeper into the wilderness, confident in your ability to navigate, manage gear, and handle emergencies on your own. There's a significant advantage to going solo when you have the proper skills and equipment.

However, your gear has to be top-notch when going solo. Unlike a team, you don't have much room for error and can't rely on others for backup. Being a soloist means you'll need to invest in reliable, high-quality gear with redundancy built in, as there's no one else to rely on.

Choosing to go as a team is more suitable for challenging conditions or longer trips. The longer the trip, the more important it is to have a team to handle issues. This is especially true in complicated or dangerous terrain, like crevasse fields or mountaineering, where a team provides safety, comfort, and the ability to make better decisions under duress.

A big advantage of a team is that less experienced people can join and benefit from the knowledge of more seasoned individuals. This allows everyone to improve their skills more efficiently, without incurring too much risk.

The downside of going as a team is the need to coordinate everyone. This can be especially difficult on remote or international trips. People may fall out at the last minute due to family or health issues, which could derail your plans if those people are key to the trip. It's essential to have a backup plan in case one or more people drop out. You should also consider any additional costs, as higher expenses can create both financial and emotional strain, leading to hard feelings if someone has to back out.

This is something to discuss beforehand, especially if someone develops a health issue or faces a personal crisis. If someone has to back out, it's important to respect their decision and maintain the relationship for the future.

When you chose to go alone or as a team, there are many considerations. Solo has no backup and teams have interpersonal dynamics. Which you choose will have benefits and drawbacks. Simply consider the old saying, "If you want to go fast, go alone. If you want to go far, go together."

Chapter 17
Dealing with Wildlife in Winter

Wildlife in Winter

One of the major considerations when being outside is wildlife. Although animals are enjoyable to watch from a distance, as soon as they start getting close enough for engagement, the risk increases. With smaller animals, the biggest dangers are bites or having them dig into your food. But with larger animals, the risks are much more substantial, including severe injury or even death.

During the winter, some animals like bears do hibernate, but don't rely on this. Sometimes, those animals can come out and wander around. In many locations where bears hibernate, people think they're tucked away safely, and the risk is minimal, but this isn't always the case. Be mindful, even when it seems like there's no risk.

Author's Note:
One year, while skiing across Yellowstone National Park in January, I came across fresh bear tracks. It was -30°F (-34°C), deep winter, and the park rangers warned me they had seen bear activity, even though it was the coldest, darkest part of the season. So, even when it seems like there's no risk, there always is.

Other animals that are more active in winter include wolves, coyotes, deer, and small rodents. Usually, ungulates aren't a problem, as long as you don't mess with them. But if you're in an area with bison, be cautious—bison can walk over just about anything, and they will. Avoid areas with obvious bison activity.

Smaller rodents can be the real problem in winter. They can get into your food and damage your gear. They may chew on your equipment or tear holes in your gear bag. They're relentless and won't stop. Usually, they aren't a problem until they are. The key is to keep a clean camp. Don't leave a mess behind and avoid spreading your scent more than necessary. Animals have an incredible sense of smell, so don't underestimate it.

Depending on where you are—whether in the high north, northern Canada, Alaska, or Greenland—the bear threat is real. The scarcity of food directly drives animals to be more aggressive or unpredictable. All animals are unpredictable to some degree, but some areas are more challenging than others. Always consider the risks by talking to local authorities and balancing the risks with your desire for enjoyment.

One thing to keep in mind when traveling solo versus in a team is that going solo—or even with just one other person—substantially increases your risk of a negative wildlife encounter. Groups of four or more rarely have problems with larger animals, so traveling in a group can be an advantage.

Changes in Predatory Behavior

One of the challenges in winter is the change in the predatory behavior of larger carnivores. Wolves and mountain lions, for example, tend to become more opportunistic. Usually, a group of people won't encounter problems with wolves or mountain lions, but as civilization pressure increases, it can push these animals to become more opportunistic. They typically won't bother people, but there have been instances where they've become aggressive toward humans.

At the time of this writing, there haven't been many if any substantial wolf incidents with humans, but as time goes on, there's a higher likelihood that could change. Mountain lions are a different story. If you're a smaller person—usually a woman—or if you're alone, you face a much greater risk of a negative encounter. If a mountain lion thinks it can overpower you, it might take the chance if it's hungry and desperate.

If you're a smaller person, it's not recommended to go out alone in winter, as the risk is higher. If local authorities report mountain lion activity or recent sightings, be cautious and take it seriously.

Avoiding Negative Wildlife Encounters

The goal of enjoying wildlife is to respect it and keep your distance. Don't put yourself in a situation where you're near a watering hole or an obvious wildlife trail. If you see tracks through a forest or wilderness area that are clearly animal-made, avoid camping in that spot. Move farther away, because animals tend to follow certain paths—they're well-beaten and efficient for them. Humans often don't realize why one location is more suitable than another for animals, but they need their space to survive, especially in winter when conditions are more stressful. By camping near a known wildlife area, you're putting pressure on them and adding unnecessary risk.

Identifying tracks, scat, and other signs of wildlife activity is something you'll want to learn. The best part about winter camping is that, until the next snowfall or serious melt, the snow leaves a story. You can see exactly what happened. You might find signs of a scuffle—blood or feathers—showing that one predator killed another for lunch. That's one of the joys of winter: it's much easier to see what's going on and be more aware of your surroundings.

Use natural barriers to avoid issues, and avoid natural funnels where animals might pass through. Even though a funnel might provide good protection from the weather, you need to balance the risk. Camping in an area that funnels animals puts you at risk, so consider the dangers of large predators versus the wet conditions when choosing your campsite.

Food Storage

Always follow local regulations regarding food storage and management. There's a reason why different agencies around the world have specific rules—they've developed a solid understanding of what leads to negative animal encounters, especially when food is involved.

If local regulations require food storage, especially with bear canisters or bear-proof storage boxes, there's a good reason for it. Bears and other animals quickly learn to associate humans with food. Tragically, animals are euthanized every year because people feed them or leave food accessible. Predatory animals, like bears and even foxes, can become aggressive. For example, the fox population at Colter Bay in Grand Teton National Park became too aggressive after people fed them sandwiches, leading to the foxes being euthanized.

Even though foxes are cute, they are predators and can become dangerous. Like many mammals, they can carry rabies, so sharing food or being careless with it can put you at risk. If there's a requirement for bear bags or food storage, follow it. Having your food stolen during a long camping trip because you didn't manage it properly can really spoil your expedition.

If possible, cook at least 100 yards (about 90 meters) away from your camp. Unfortunately, during winter, this isn't always practical. If you can, cook away from your campsite, but sometimes that just isn't an option. In the summer, it's easier to cook and clean 100 feet (30 meters) away, or the recommended 100 yards, but winter conditions make that distance harder to manage.

Additionally, dispose of food scraps, trash, and human waste as far from your campsite as possible. Animals are curious, and if they catch the scent of food scraps or human waste, they will dig it up. You don't want to expose yourself to the risk of animals sniffing around or digging up your waste. Protect yourself as much as you're protecting them.

Food and Scent Storage

If at all possible, make sure to store all scented items as sealed as you can. This includes not only food items but also deodorant, sunscreen, lip balm, or anything else that might have a scent, all in relatively odor-proof containers. No container is truly scent-proof unless it is commercially sealed, such as with a heavy-duty foil bag designed for odor containment. Thermal-sealed bags might be effective but can't guarantee complete odor-proofing. Simple resealable plastic bags let scents out and can contact food and other items. The idea is to keep the main item sealed so its scent doesn't float into the air. Humans typically become desensitized to smells quickly and often aren't aware of them due to constant exposure, but animals, living in the wilderness, aren't used to these scents, so they're incredibly attracted to them.

Also, if you can, avoid using cooking clothes that you've worn when handling food. If you spill food on your clothing, make every effort to clean it off and remove it from your campsite. Food smells will attract animals, and you should avoid this risk as much as possible.

Wildlife Encounters: Predators

When dealing with large predators during any camping trip, but especially in winter, it's important to follow specific regulations. If you're in an area with bears and it's legal, carry bear spray. While bear spray is incredibly convenient, being attacked and injured—or worse—is much worse than not having it. Some parks, like Sequoia National Park and Kings Canyon, do not allow bear spray because it is classified as a weapon. However, other areas, like Grand Teton and Glacier National Park, strongly recommend carrying bear spray. Whatever the local regulation is, follow it. But if possible, bear spray is a far better choice than firearms, especially in park areas. With bear spray, your risk of severe consequences is much lower.

That said, I'm not suggesting you shouldn't carry a firearm, but respect local regulations and make sure you're well-trained in the use and consequences of firearms if you choose to carry one.

When encountering bears in winter, make sure to make your presence known and don't be aggressive. Whether it's a brown or black bear will affect how you deal with it. If it's a brown bear or a grizzly, be much more submissive and give them as much space as possible. Their natural instinct is to charge and defend themselves. On the other hand, black bears are less likely to act aggressively but can still become dangerous if they feel threatened or hungry. If the bear is acting predatory—curious, not backing down, and wandering around—be ready for a fight, because it's in a predatory mode.

Animals are always unpredictable, and while they follow certain patterns, you never know how a particular animal will react. With wolves, coyotes, and foxes, encounters are usually more manageable. Wolves, being large and powerful killers, can weigh anywhere from 110 to 140 pounds (50 to 64kg). If you run into a large pack, make your presence known and be as aggressive and assertive as possible. Foxes that have become habituated to humans won't hesitate to approach, so make sure to dissuade them if possible by making noise, flapping your jacket, or using an umbrella to create a larger presence.

The same applies to black bears—make yourself as large and aggressive as possible. With grizzly bears, follow local regulations and suggestions since the interaction is completely different.

Mountain lions are a whole different matter. If a mountain lion decides you're interesting, it may come after you, and it's often very difficult to dissuade them. You'll want to make yourself as large as possible with a stick, rock, shovel, or jacket. Avoid crouching down or doing anything that makes you seem small. Don't set yourself up for a dangerous encounter—if they're hungry and think they can take you down, they will. While mountain lion encounters are rare, video footage has shown how quickly these situations can escalate. You don't want to be caught off guard, flapping your hat in front of a mountain lion's face. Dispel the threat as quickly as possible.

Large Herbivores

Dealing with larger herbivores like deer, moose, elk, and similar animals is relatively easy once you get past the rut season and into winter. They tend to be less aggressive because they're in survival mode. That said, moose are surprisingly dangerous. If you get too close or between them and their offspring, you can put yourself in as much danger as you would with a bear. These are not animals to trifle with. Even though they look silly and seem slow, moose have to fend off predators like bears to survive. And you are nothing to them if you decide to get too close for a selfie. Be prepared to be thrown 15 feet (about 5 meters) into the air—these animals are incredibly powerful.

As long as you maintain a 25-yard (or 25-meter) distance from them, you should generally be safe. The only time a negative encounter might happen is if you get between them and their offspring. Most animals will just walk away, but moose can be more aggressive and can do incredible damage.

If you have a dog with you, be aware that although dogs serve a great purpose, if they're aggressive toward ungulates or bears and then run back to you scared, they might bring that animal right to you. You'll need to be very careful in these situations.

Bison and other large animals should be avoided at all costs. Keep at least 25 yards (or 25 meters) away from them. They may seem silly, unintelligent, and slow, but in just a few seconds, they can reach speeds of up to 35 miles per hour (about 45 km/h), and they can run you over without even knowing it. Bison have charged cars and destroyed vehicles. These majestic creatures can also be ultra-aggressive if you bother them too much, so give them a wide berth.

Defensive Tools

Depending on the area and local regulations, you have several defensive tool options available. One common option in North America and some parts of the world is bear spray. Learning how to properly use bear spray—carrying it, deploying it, and having it ready at a moment's notice—is key. In a pressure situation, if your bear spray is buried deep in your backpack or sled, it might as well be a rock. By the time you get to it, that bear will be on top of you.

While it may be uncomfortable to get bear spray in your face, it will only be debilitating temporarily. You won't end up killing someone with bear spray, and that's what makes it a good defensive option. The effectiveness of bear spray can vary depending on environmental conditions, such as wind or terrain, particularly in areas like Alaska. That's where the game changes, and you need to consider additional measures, like noise deterrents and firearms.

Noise deterrents, such as air horns or other loud devices, are a good choice when warranted. The most important thing when avoiding a negative animal encounter, especially with large predators like bears, is letting them know you're there from as far away as possible. The earlier they hear you, the better your chances are of them wandering away to preserve themselves. Most animals naturally avoid humans unless they're curious.

If you come across an animal carcass in a known active predator area, move away quickly. There's a good chance that carcass is being preyed upon by wolves or bears, and if they sense you are threatening their food supply, they'll react aggressively. Electric bear fences are another option but must be deployed correctly. However, if a bear is determined or highly aggressive, an electric fence may not be sufficient to deter it.

In areas like Alaska, large chain-link camping enclosures are used to protect you from wildlife. If you have the option to use one, it's a good choice, but always respect local regulations. Don't think of yourself as a maverick, because those who did have often ended up injured or killed by a bear.

The question of firearms, where legally allowed, is more complex. Firearms are heavy, dangerous, and should be your last resort, especially with grizzlies. Grizzlies are large, powerful animals, and a small handgun won't be effective against one. You'd need a much more powerful weapon. There are stories of people using a .300 Win Mag rifle on a grizzly in Montana, where a man had to fire four rounds to stop the grizzly from attacking. Your handgun won't compare to that.

In the United States, grizzly bears are a federally protected species at the time of publication, and shooting one—justified or not—can result in serious legal consequences. Even in self-defense, authorities will conduct a thorough investigation, and you must be prepared to defend your actions in court and to game wardens. Simply claiming a bear was a threat is not enough. Evidence must clearly support that lethal force was the only viable option. Penalties can include heavy fines, loss of hunting privileges, and potential legal charges. Other countries, such as Canada, have their own regulations regarding bear encounters, which may differ significantly from U.S. laws. Understanding local wildlife protections, carrying bear spray, and knowing how to respond in an encounter are essential to avoiding legal trouble and ensuring a safe outcome.

Before carrying a rifle, pistol, or shotgun, or using slugs, consult with local authorities. This is a more complex issue than this book can cover. Just know firearms are an option, but it's a much more complicated and high-consequence choice for self-defense in the outdoors.

Wildlife Safety During Travel

One of the great things about traveling in winter is the ability to move quietly, aside from the swishing sound of your synthetic fabric pants and jacket or the crunch of your snowshoes. The snow absorbs much of the noise in the winter environment. However, this increases the chance of unexpectedly coming upon an animal and having a negative encounter.

Traveling in groups is always the safest option for wildlife safety. Going solo increases the risk of a surprise encounter with a moose, grizzly, bison, or other animals. Making noise by talking, singing, or making other racket as you go along can help, though it can get tiring and mentally exhausting. Yelling isn't as effective as clapping, whistling, or making other noises that don't require as much physical energy. If you're using trekking poles, clacking them together can be an effective option, but doing that constantly can also become exhausting.

The best option is to simply travel in a larger group in active wildlife areas. The most important thing to do is avoid startling animals, especially around blind corners, hollows, or hills where you can't see far ahead or into dense brush. In dense forests, make every effort to announce your presence. This way, animals, like moose, will be aware that something is nearby and may want to avoid it.

If an animal starts to look unhappy or aggressive—clacking teeth, flapping ears, or bobbing its head—this means you've entered their discomfort or safety zone, and you need to back away quickly. Always follow local regulations when doing so. If possible, keep facing the animal while backing up. However, this will be very difficult with skis or snowshoes, as backing up is nearly impossible. If you turn and run, even when on skis, it can trigger the predatory response of the animal, causing it to pursue you.

There's no easy way to handle this once you're too close to the animal, so making lots of noise whenever possible is the best approach. Don't put yourself in a situation that forces you to get yourself out of.

Polar Bears

If you're traveling in winter conditions where polar bears are a potential risk, the rules are a bit different. This typically applies to the far north of Canada, Alaska, or Greenland. Bear spray won't be effective, as it will put you far too close to these animals. Polar bears are predatory and agile, unlike grizzly bears, which, while also agile, have a different predatory and attack style. Grizzly bears can charge from 100 yards (about 90 meters) away, but polar bears are known for their speed and strength in close quarters. While this isn't the case with polar bears, be aware that any animal can act unpredictably.

Understanding polar bear behavior and foraging in these regions is key. Talk to locals and do plenty of reading. Typically, people use polar bear dogs to help protect themselves and announce a bear's presence. Some people set up electric fences as a defensive barrier. However, rifles and shotguns are the most common methods for defense in the high Arctic latitudes.

Though you'd generally want to avoid a polar bear encounter, sometimes there's no way around it. This is a risk that people living in these climates face. Some may argue you shouldn't be there, but that perspective often comes from those unfamiliar with life in remote areas. For people in remote wilderness areas, carrying a firearm is simply a reality.

In Alaska, people often carry heavy-duty firearms, like a more powerful rifle or shotgun, when going berry hunting or polar bear spotting. On guided trips where polar bear encounters are a risk, guides always carry rifles, usually at least a .30-06, if not something heavier. Polar bears are massive, and if they decide to go after you, there's no other solution.

Some guides have had success using bear spray, but be aware that if you're within 20 feet (7 meters) of a polar bear, you won't have time to switch to a firearm. This happens quickly. So, if at all possible, avoid traveling alone, and consult guides about what to do before you go. In some areas, carrying a firearm is required. Be prepared for this, both for travel and use.

At the time of publication, polar bears in the United States are protected under the Marine Mammal Protection Act (MMPA) and the Endangered Species Act (ESA), making it illegal to harm or kill them except in cases of legitimate self-defense. Any defensive shooting must be reported and will be investigated by federal authorities, and failure to justify the action can result in fines or legal consequences. Other countries with polar bear populations, such as Canada, Norway, and Greenland (which is part of the Kingdom of Denmark), have their own regulations, which may differ significantly. Rules regarding polar bear protection are subject to change, so it is essential to stay informed about local wildlife laws, carry proper deterrents, and avoid encounters whenever possible to ensure both safety and legal compliance.

Local Regulations and Approaches for Handling Dangerous Animals

When traveling in areas where wildlife encounters are a real risk, it's crucial to follow local regulations and adopt the regional approach for dealing with dangerous animals. Always respect the rules in place, as they have been developed to ensure both human safety and the protection of wildlife.

Local authorities and wildlife experts will provide the most accurate information on how to handle specific animals in your area of travel. Many regions have strict guidelines regarding wildlife safety, including what defensive tools can be carried, such as bear spray or firearms. Some places may restrict firearms altogether, while others, like those in polar bear territory, may require them. Always check local regulations well in advance to avoid surprises.

In addition to regulations, it's important to adopt the local mindset regarding how animals should be treated. If the area promotes non-interference with wildlife and encourages avoiding dangerous encounters rather than confronting animals, follow this guidance. Local guides and residents will know the safest practices, and it's essential to respect their experience. Avoid putting yourself in a situation that could lead to an encounter, and if you find yourself at risk, follow the local recommendations for dealing with the situation.

By staying informed and respecting the regulations and local customs, you can reduce the risks and safely enjoy your outdoor adventures.

Dealing with a Negative Wildlife Encounter

If you end up in a negative wildlife encounter, whether with a small or large animal, and sustain scratches or bites, you'll need to seek medical help. These injuries are not something to ignore, especially if caused by a large predator. If you're not severely injured, your next step is to start working your way out for help. The danger with mammal bites and scratches is the high probability of both infection and diseases like rabies.

Be aware that rabies is nearly always fatal in humans if left untreated. If you get rabies—even from the tiniest scratch or bite from a small animal like a bat—and start showing signs, your life is at risk. Rabies is one of the few diseases nearly 100% fatal in humans.

Tick-borne diseases are less of a concern in winter, as ticks are typically frozen and buried under the snowpack. However, even a bite from a small animal like a fox, coyote, or squirrel should prompt you to seek medical treatment immediately. The risk of mammal-transmitted diseases is high, and capturing the animal for investigation is often unlikely or impossible.

If you're injured by wildlife, you may need to end your trip and seek professional medical help right away. It may not always require evacuation unless you're seriously injured, but keep in mind that you only have a limited amount of time to treat these infections or bites before they become life-threatening.

Bison grazing during moderate snowfall in Yellowstone National Park. They look slow and tame from a distance but don't be fooled.

Chapter 18
First Aid

Having some first aid knowledge is essential for any wilderness outing, whether you're visiting a local park or traveling to a remote destination abroad. Sooner or later, especially during winter travel, someone may get injured or become debilitated. Knowing how to handle such situations can make all the difference—whether you're treating a manageable injury or preventing a tragedy.

This chapter covers the basics of first aid to help you get started. However, taking a professional wilderness course is strongly recommended. NOLS (National Outdoor Leadership School) offers an excellent Wilderness First Aid course. For those with more time, the Wilderness First Responder course provides more comprehensive training, though it requires a greater time commitment. For most adventurers, the NOLS Wilderness First Aid course is an excellent place to start.

Challenges of First Aid in Winter

One of the biggest challenges of dealing with first aid situations in winter is managing the cold. Once an injury occurs, everyone—including the victim and responders—has to stop moving, which increases the risk of getting cold quickly. Staying warm, active, and clear-headed is critical. One of the most important rules in an emergency is not to become part of the problem—stay part of the solution.

Freezing temperatures make bandaging and wound care more difficult. Medical adhesives don't work as well in the cold. Removing gloves in cold weather increases the risk of frostbite and reduces dexterity. Even with training, delicate tasks like applying bandages or using tools become much more challenging in winter.

Winter conditions can also delay evacuations. Fog, storms, or dangerous weather may ground flights or prevent rescue crews from reaching you. Pilots, rescue crews, and first responders won't risk their own safety if conditions are too dangerous. You'll need to handle the situation until it's safe for them to evacuate you. Always remember: the cavalry won't come if it puts them in serious danger.

Limited Access to Supplies

Traveling in winter naturally limits how many supplies you can carry. You're already carrying substantial extra weight from food and cold-weather gear. To manage this, pack minimal, multi-use, and cold-resistant first aid items.

Most supplies work fine in cold conditions, but bandages that rely on adhesives can fail. Adhesives may become brittle or lose stickiness in freezing temperatures. Inexpensive bandages from local stores might not work at all.

If your first aid kit includes medications, check their temperature requirements, as some liquid medicines can freeze or become ineffective in extreme cold. This is something you need to plan for when packing.

Cold Weather Specific Injuries

Hypothermia

Hypothermia is the number one danger in winter camping. It progresses through five stages, from mild symptoms to death. Early signs include shivering, mild confusion, and slurred speech. As it worsens, shivering becomes extreme. When shivering stops, the situation becomes critical. Speech becomes more slurred, coordination is lost, and the person may feel sleepy and apathetic. In advanced stages, they may appear dead, with body systems functioning at minimal levels. The final stage is death, where the heart and brain stop functioning.

First Aid for Hypothermia

The first step is to stop what you're doing and focus on warming the person. Add insulation, use warm water bottles, and share body heat. In severe cases, you may need to snuggle skin-to-skin in a sleeping bag or combine sleeping bags. This may feel awkward, but saving a life takes priority.

Preventing hypothermia is critical. Manage moisture by avoiding sweating and keeping layers dry. Overdressing can lead to sweat-soaked clothing, which causes rapid cooling once you stop moving. At the first signs of uncontrollable shivering, stop and address it immediately. Staying dry and layering properly can prevent serious issues.

Hypothermia Psychological Challenges

Recognizing and addressing the psychological effects of hypothermia can be difficult. A person with hypothermia may feel embarrassed, defensive, or aggressive. As confusion sets in, they might insist nothing is wrong, even while losing coordination.

If you're traveling alone and notice violent shivering or confusion, stop immediately. Solo travelers face greater risks, as confusion can lead to dangerous decisions. "Paradoxical undressing," where a person sheds clothing because they mistakenly feel overheated, is a common cause of fatal hypothermia.

The danger of hypothermia isn't just the drop in body temperature. The psychological and social challenges of dealing with it can make it even harder to manage. Recognizing the signs early and acting quickly is essential.

Frostbite

Frostbite is a localized problem compared to hypothermia. Once skin freezes, the damage can range from minor to severe, potentially leading to amputations. Recognizing frostbite early is critical. In the beginning stages, skin may turn white, hard, or numb—this isn't severe yet, but it needs immediate attention.

If your toes or fingers are cold, quick action can help. Try doing jumping jacks, skiing, or climbing harder to restore circulation. If these situations continue, though, and the skin temperature drops below 15°F (-9°C), skin cells begin to freeze, forming ice crystals that can cause irreversible damage.

The first stage of frostbite involves numbness where toes or fingers feel wooden, like tapping on a block of wood. You can still manage it here without permanent damage, but nerve damage has already started. Pay special attention to toes—if they're cold and numb, then start to burn, and the balls of your feet hurt, it's a sign the damage is progressing. The cold pain is shifting because the body is prioritizing its core, pulling blood away from extremities to keep vital organs alive.

As frostbite worsens, the skin may blister and eventually turn black, sometimes in a short time. Stop all activity when safe and treat it immediately. The most important thing during rewarming is to avoid re-freezing at all costs. Re-freezing will do far more damage than the initial freeze, as ice crystals that form inside the tissue can cause further destruction. As the skin thaws, the pain can be extreme, and you may need painkillers or anti-inflammatories to help.

Once thawed, make sure the skin cannot freeze again. If frostbite has progressed to blistering or blackened tissue, you'll need medical attention. Be aware that some doctors, especially in international settings, may lack experience with frostbite and recommend amputation too quickly. Seek a modern medical center with professionals trained in treating frostbite. Severe cases can sometimes recover over six months if infection or gangrene doesn't set in. Even with serious frostbite, it's often possible to minimize permanent damage.

Keep checking your extremities and stay aware of how your body feels. People may hide injuries out of embarrassment, poor planning, or bad luck, but delaying treatment only makes things worse. In groups, encourage open communication and deal with problems as soon as they arise.

Trench Foot

Trench foot, or immersion foot, is a unique problem in cold-weather travel. It happens when your feet stay wet for too long, whether from sweat or getting dunked in water. This can lead to skin damage, severe blistering, and potentially frostbite if not addressed.

Symptoms include numbness, swelling, and discoloration. In the early stages, discoloration may appear as red or purple hues, and the skin may look pale or blotchy in more severe cases. Treating it outdoors can be tough. You may need to stop, set up a shelter, or at least get your feet into a sled bag if possible. Letting your feet stay wet for long periods increases the risk of painful blisters and infections.

To prevent trench foot, keep your feet warm and dry. Change socks regularly and, if possible, elevate your feet. Sweaty feet are common during activities like climbing or skiing, but letting the issue go unchecked can cause unnecessary pain and injuries. Address any signs of trench foot quickly to avoid serious complications.

Chilblains: Cold-Weather Skin Damage

Chilblains, also known as perniosis, are an unpredictable reaction to cold exposure that causes painful, swollen red or purple patches on the skin. Unlike frostbite, chilblains don't involve freezing tissue but result from small blood vessels constricting in the cold and then reopening too quickly when warmed. This can lead to itching, burning, and, in severe cases, blisters or ulcers. While often linked to damp conditions, they also occur in extreme dry cold, like in Antarctica, making them a concern for winter travelers.

Though chilblains are most common on fingers and toes, they can appear in unexpected places. Polar thigh is a well-documented version affecting the outer thighs, usually from wind-chilled fabric pressing against the skin. The stomach and lower back are also vulnerable where tight clothing or backpack waist belts restrict circulation. Buttocks can be affected from prolonged sled pulling or sitting on frozen surfaces. In severe cases, chilblains can break open, creating deep sores that heal slowly and risk infection.

It's important to distinguish chilblains from frostbite. Chilblains cause red, swollen, or itchy skin that stays warm to the touch, while frostbite involves numb, pale, or waxy skin that feels hard and frozen. Frostbite sets in suddenly, while chilblains develop over time. Preventing chilblains means keeping skin warm, avoiding pressure from tight clothing, and using windproof layers. Treatment includes gradual rewarming, avoiding direct heat, and using skin-protecting creams. Severe cases may require medication to improve circulation, but prevention is the best defense.

Snow Blindness

Snow blindness is a common but preventable injury in winter environments with high snow exposure. It's caused by ultraviolet (UV) light, which comes directly from the sun and is also reflected off the snow, surrounding you from all angles. This exposure damages the cornea's surface cells, creating tiny pits that lead to pain, temporary blindness, and long-term vision issues if untreated. The condition feels like having sand thrown into your eyes and can be debilitating, especially if it happens on a summit or in an exposed area.

Modern protective glasses usually shield your eyes from UV light, but cheaper models may not provide full protection. Make sure your goggles or glasses are rated to block 99–100% of UV light. Some manufacturers don't label their products clearly, and those should be avoided. High-quality brands rarely have this issue, making them a reliable investment.

Proper glacier glasses or full wraparound goggles are essential in snowy conditions. Cheap goggles or glasses that don't wrap around allow reflected light from the snow to reach your eyes, causing damage. Light-colored or white frames can reflect UV light internally, worsening the problem. Regular summer sunglasses with flat lenses don't offer enough protection, and even wraparound sunglasses may let light in from below.

Even briefly removing your goggles or glasses to work on gear can expose your eyes to harmful UV light. If you need to take them off, shield your eyes with your arm so they're only exposed to light from the sky. UV light from the sun is direct, but snow reflects UV from all directions, significantly increasing exposure.

If snow blindness starts, it can feel like there's sand in your eyes, combined with extreme burning or redness. Stop immediately if it's safe, set up camp, and rest your eyes in complete darkness. Use cold compresses if possible. Recovery can take several hours to a few days, depending on the severity of the injury. Taking precautions with proper eye protection is the best way to avoid this painful and preventable condition.

Other Mechanical Cold-Induced Issues

One challenge of traveling in the cold is muscle stiffness. Even though your core temperature stays regulated, the cold causes the temperature in your blood and extremities to drop. This makes your muscles and ligaments stiffer, increasing the risk of injury.

Before starting activities like skiing, warm up properly. Do jumping jacks, high steps, or light jogging to get your blood flowing. It's crucial to warm up before strenuous physical activity to avoid injuries.

Using trekking poles can also help. They provide four points of contact (two poles and your feet), improving stability and reducing strain. This simple step can make a big difference in preventing injuries.

Falling Injuries in Winter Camping

One of the most common winter camping injuries is slipping, tripping, and falling. Using crampons, microspikes, snowshoes, or skis in icy conditions is essential for safety, but these tools increase the risk of snagging your foot and falling. Be mindful of your footing, even though it can be tiring to focus on every step. It only takes one misstep to fall into a dangerous situation, and fatal accidents happen to climbers every year.

Crampons, while helpful, come with their own risks. A stumble can cause you to accidentally step on the spikes of your own crampon, potentially puncturing your boot or injuring your foot. If your back foot kicks out, the front points of your crampons can drive into your calf, causing serious injury that will likely end your trip.

If you experience a minor sprain, you may be able to work through it. However, fractures or concussions require you to stop and stabilize the injury. Use poles or other gear as splints if needed. Concussions can occur if you hit your head on ice. Watch for symptoms like nausea, dizziness, or confusion, which indicate a more serious issue.

Always wear a helmet when skiing, climbing, or traveling at speed. A helmet is inexpensive insurance to protect your head from serious or permanent damage. Take precautions and stay aware to prevent falls and manage injuries effectively.

Burns from Stoves and Heaters

It's easy to get burned by a hot stove or heater when melting snow or cooking food in winter. The bulkiness of clothing and gear makes handling things awkward. This is especially true with gloves, which reduce dexterity and enlarge your hands, making precise movements harder. Close quarters only add to the challenge.

When pouring hot water from a snow pot into a water bottle, wear waterproof, heavy-duty gloves. It's easy to lose control of hot or boiling water and spill it onto your hands, which can lead to serious burns. Be especially careful during these transfers.

For minor burns, cool the area immediately. Snow can be used if available, but cold water is a safer alternative. Don't overdo it, but ensure the burn is cooled quickly. For moderate burns, wrap the area to protect it. Severe burns covering larger areas require sterile dressings. Keep the victim warm to prevent shock and wait for help to arrive.

Synthetic clothing is a hazard around stoves. It can catch fire or melt if exposed to heat, sticking to the skin and causing severe burns. Be mindful when lighting stoves or handling pots to avoid this risk. Always handle stoves with care to protect yourself and your gear.

Blisters

Blisters are a common injury in winter camping and trekking. Properly fitting boots and moisture-wicking socks can help prevent them during long hikes or skiing in cold conditions.

The best way to avoid blisters is to address a hotspot immediately. A hotspot feels like a localized warm spot on your foot. If you notice one, stop as soon as it's safe and deal with it right away. Acting quickly can usually prevent a blister from forming.

Use moleskin to treat a hotspot. Cut a square large enough to surround the affected area and cut a hole in the center, ensuring the sticky part does not come into direct contact with the hotspot itself. Apply the moleskin around the area and cover it with a bandage to reduce friction. Blisters typically form from repeated friction, so wearing multiple socks or moisture-wicking socks is also helpful.

If a blister has already formed, where the skin separates and fluid builds up, you'll need to treat it carefully. Moleskin and bandages are still effective. Keep your feet dry, warm, and free of friction to prevent it from worsening. Certain boots may not fit some foot types naturally, which can increase the risk of blisters, especially around problem areas like the heels, ankle bones, and forefoot.

If you know you're prone to blisters in specific spots, pre-treat those areas. Durable bandages like Johnson & Johnson Tough Strips work well because their adhesive is strong. Avoid touching the sticky surface when applying, and place them over known problem areas before hiking or skiing.

Severe blisters can cause significant damage. In extreme cases, large sections of skin can peel off, making every step feel like walking on broken glass. This kind of injury can be debilitating and ruin your trip. Proper preparation, good-fitting boots, and quick action to address hotspots are your best defenses.

Basic First Aid Kit

A proper first aid kit is critical for winter camping. Cold-resistant bandages and medical tape are essential. While a couple of band-aids and a gauze pack can cover many needs, cheap, standard duct tape often fails in extreme cold below 0°F (-18°C), so it's better to use high-quality medical tape or durable bandages designed for cold conditions. Band-Aid Tough Strips are a top choice—they stick reliably even in sub-zero temperatures.

An infrared thermal blanket is a lightweight and effective emergency tool. It can be used for signaling or re-warming yourself or someone else. These blankets are inexpensive and take up very little space but can make a significant difference in an emergency.

Include hand and foot warmers for cold-related injuries or emergencies. However, if you find yourself relying on them often, it's a sign that your outerwear isn't sufficient and should be improved.

A multi-tool with scissors and tweezers, along with a pocket knife, is a must. Scissors are particularly important since using a knife for tasks like cutting medical tape or bandages can lead to accidental cuts, which could worsen the injury. A simple folding pair of scissors can handle many tasks safely. Needles are effective at removing splinters and repairing gear with thread as well.

Store your first aid supplies in a strong, waterproof container. The cheap cases that come with basic kits often don't hold up in harsh conditions. Wet supplies are often ruined, so upgrading to a durable case is worth it.

Avoid overpacking your kit, but make sure it contains the essentials. A compact, well-prepared kit with cold-resistant supplies can make all the difference in an emergency.

First Aid Communication

Always carry a remote communication device for emergencies in remote areas. Options include satellite phones, personal locator beacons (PLBs), or SOS-enabled GPS devices. Have an evacuation plan in place—know who to call, what the local authorities' procedures are, and the basic steps to take while waiting for help. This is especially important for air rescues, where visibility from the air is limited.

If an air rescue is needed, make sure your location is highly visible. From above, even a group of people can be difficult to spot. Assign roles if you're with others—one or two people can care for the injured while others create a landing area or signal for help. Build a fire, stomp out "SOS" in the snow, or use bright gear to make your position obvious. Make signals as large as possible; something only a few feet long (around one meter) will be nearly invisible from the air.

Activating a PLB or emergency SOS device is a serious action and should only be used in genuine emergencies, as it alerts rescuers to your exact location, potentially wasting valuable resources if misused. Use them only for severe injuries, hypothermia, frostbite, or other life-threatening situations.

Be realistic about emergencies. Some hikers call for helicopter rescues when they are tired or scared, even though they aren't in danger. Such non-emergency rescues are costly, dangerous for the crew, and can delay critical responses to those in actual need of help. Helicopter evacuations are costly, pose a significant risk to the crew, and are not guaranteed, especially in bad weather or dangerous terrain. Depending on the situation, a ranger may assist instead. Don't assume you'll automatically be flown out. Plan carefully, know your limits, and use emergency tools responsibly.

Knowing When to Evacuate or Turn Around

Knowing when to evacuate or turn back is one of the hardest decisions in the outdoors. Minor blisters, burns, or mild injuries can often be managed, and you might decide to continue. This requires careful attention to group dynamics since not everyone has experience dealing with medical issues. In remote locations, reactions can be unpredictable. Assign jobs and responsibilities to help maintain focus and morale during an evacuation.

Group morale is especially important on trips where significant time and financial resources are invested. People may feel frustrated or upset if the trip is disrupted, so it's critical to stay attentive and address issues before they escalate. Many accidents can't be avoided, but recognizing warning signs early can prevent minor problems from becoming severe.

For serious conditions like deep frostbite, advanced hypothermia, or severe fractures (such as those involving bone displacement), the trip is over. Recovery in the field isn't realistic, and your priority must shift to evacuation and getting everyone home safely. When injuries or conditions reach this point, the focus needs to be on evacuating the injured and getting out of the dangerous area as quickly and safely as possible.

Preventative Measures

One of the most important ways to prevent problems in the outdoors is to build physical endurance, strength, and flexibility. Warm up before any activity, like hiking or skiing, and watch for early signs of fatigue or injury. Pay attention to your group—if someone is slurring their words or stumbling, it could indicate a serious issue like hypothermia. Adults may feel embarrassed or defensive when confronted, so addressing the problem can be difficult.

Preparing properly for outdoor winter adventures takes effort. Some people may decide not to go because of this, and that's okay. If someone isn't capable or responsible enough, they could become a liability. The same applies to you—if you're not mentally and physically prepared for the rigors of winter adventures, it's better to postpone the trip than to risk creating problems for yourself or others.

Overuse and Poor Form Injuries

When using snowshoes, crampons, or skis, make sure your gait is smooth and even. If your foot slides out or shifts awkwardly, it can lead to ankle injuries or blisters.

Adults often dismiss this issue. Some feel embarrassed about their technique and may insist it's just their natural gait. But ignoring it can lead to serious blisters or more severe injuries down the line.

Managing this with adults on trips can be tricky, as they may resist feedback or feel self-conscious about adjusting their movements. Kids are usually more receptive since they're used to taking instructions in school. Adults, however, may resist feedback and end up with avoidable injuries later.

Use proper backpacking and sled-towing techniques to avoid friction injuries and repetitive stress, especially on long hikes. Stay hydrated and eat well—pushing yourself too hard without proper nutrition can lead to fatigue, injury, or impaired decision-making.

Mental Health and Psychological Effects

Learn to recognize the signs of mental fatigue. Isolation, cold, and physical exertion can wear down your mental state. Symptoms like irritability, anxiety, and decision fatigue (the mental exhaustion that comes from making many decisions) are common in winter conditions. Constant decision-making takes a toll because, in daily life, most adults operate on autopilot. When every action requires thought, it can quickly wear you down, sour your attitude, and cause conflict with teammates.

A positive mental attitude is critical. Humor, even dark humor, is often a coping tool for those in high-stress professions like military, police, or first responders. But not everyone is used to this style of humor, and some may find it upsetting. Get to know your team's personalities and stress responses before a long trip, so you can anticipate how individuals may react under pressure. Friction can escalate in tough environments. Simple courtesies, like saying "please" and "thank you," are crucial for maintaining group harmony and mental balance when people are exhausted.

Exhaustion, fear, and cold reveal true character. People may lash out, but this is often a passing reaction. In emergencies, staying calm and proactive is key. Develop techniques to manage panic, especially during injuries. Blood or serious trauma can rattle those who aren't used to it. Staying calm helps everyone focus on the situation and provide support to the injured person.

Use group support during emergencies. Avoid finger-pointing or blaming—it's not helpful in the moment. Focus on solving the problem and getting everyone home safely. There's time to analyze and review later. In the moment, stay clear-headed, avoid panic, and focus on the next immediate steps.

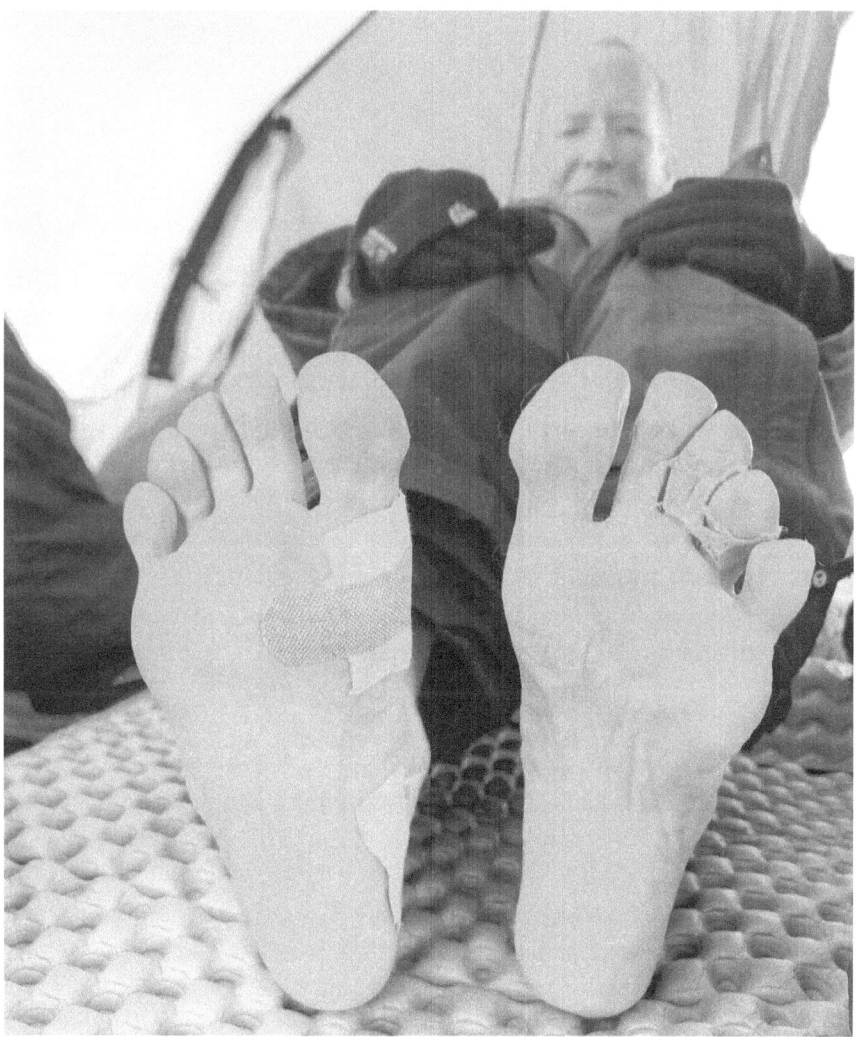

After a week skiing across the Greenland icecap, Dr. Terry Williams needed some first aid for his feet.

Chapter 19
Training and Fitness

Introduction

Winter camping is far more physically demanding than summer camping. The cold, snow, and ice slow everything down, requiring more effort to hike, set up camp, and even complete basic tasks like melting snow for water. A hike that would be simple in warm weather becomes exhausting in deep snow, especially when carrying a heavier pack or pulling a sled. Without proper conditioning, fatigue sets in quickly, as exhaustion reduces endurance and impairs focus, making every task more difficult.

Physical fitness isn't just about making things easier—it's about safety, efficiency, and enjoyment. A well-conditioned body can handle the cold better, recover faster, and move through the terrain more effectively. Training for winter camping doesn't require extreme workouts, but it does need to be specific to the challenges of snow-covered landscapes.

Why Fitness Matters

One of the biggest challenges in winter camping is simply moving through the environment. Snow creates drag, forcing you to lift your feet higher with every step, especially if you're wearing snowshoes, which help distribute your weight and reduce sinking. Ice and uneven terrain demand balance and core strength to prevent falls. On top of that, your gear is heavier—winter packs carry extra layers, a more robust sleeping system, and additional fuel for melting snow. Those who aren't physically prepared will find themselves struggling early, and exhaustion makes every task harder.

Physical training doesn't just improve strength and endurance—it also builds mental resilience. A strong body allows for better decision-making in emergencies. Fatigue and weakness can lead to rushed, panicked choices, whereas a well-trained body can handle stress and maintain focus under pressure. The better your fitness, the more energy you have to enjoy the trip instead of just surviving it.

Training for Winter-Specific Strength and Endurance

Training for winter camping is about functional strength rather than raw power. The goal is to prepare the body for long days of movement, carrying weight, and handling unexpected challenges like shoveling out a tent platform or climbing a steep, snow-covered slope.

One of the most important areas to focus on is leg strength. Snow, ice, and deep drifts require much more effort than walking on solid ground. Squats and lunges build the strength needed for these conditions. Step-ups onto a bench or stairs mimic the motion of climbing with a pack, especially useful for trekking through hilly or mountainous terrain.

Endurance is just as crucial. Winter conditions can turn a short hike into a long, grueling effort, so the body needs to be conditioned for sustained movement. The best training for this is carrying a weighted backpack on regular hikes, gradually increasing both the weight and the difficulty of the terrain. Running, cycling, or stair climbing help build cardiovascular strength and endurance, ensuring that you don't burn out quickly when breaking trail through fresh snow.

Core strength is another major factor. A strong core helps with balance, especially on icy or snow-covered surfaces, preventing falls. It also plays a role in carrying a heavy pack or pulling a sled across long distances.

Key training exercises for winter camping strength:
Squats and lunges: Build leg power for snow travel.
Step-ups: Mimic climbing with weight.
Planks and side planks: Strengthen core muscles for balance.
Loaded pack hikes: Simulate real-world conditions with a heavy backpack.

Training with Gear and Real-World Preparation

Gym workouts and basic strength training provide a foundation, but nothing replaces real-world practice with actual winter gear. Training should include time spent moving with snowshoes, skis, and backpacks to get used to the extra weight and movement patterns. If pulling a sled, it's a good idea to train with a loaded sled on snow, sand, or grass to develop the strength needed for long hauls.

Another essential skill is snow shoveling. In deep snow, even setting up camp requires heavy physical effort. Digging a tent platform, carving out a windbreak, or building an emergency shelter all require upper body and core strength. Practicing with an avalanche shovel, even in your backyard, helps condition the muscles for the real thing.

Cold-weather exposure, such as spending several hours outdoors in freezing temperatures while carrying weight and wearing full winter clothing, is also part of training. Moving through the cold is different from training in a warm gym. Testing gear in realistic conditions, such as in cold and wet environments, helps ensure your equipment works as expected and prevents surprises on the trip.

Gradual Training Progression

Fitness doesn't happen overnight. Training should start gradually, building up from basic endurance to more challenging exercises that simulate winter conditions.

A beginner training plan should focus on cardiovascular endurance, basic strength, and balance. Brisk walking, cycling, or stair climbing will build cardiovascular endurance, while bodyweight squats, lunges, and planks strengthen the legs, core, and stabilizing muscles. Adding a backpack with increasing weight helps simulate real conditions, allowing your body to adapt gradually without overloading it too soon.

As fitness improves, training should shift to hiking with a loaded pack on uneven terrain, practicing with snowshoes or skis, and incorporating resistance training like weighted squats and sled dragging. The goal is to prepare the body for sustained activity in winter conditions.

For those planning longer or more difficult winter expeditions, training should include high-intensity workouts to improve stamina, along with steep hikes carrying full winter gear. Cold-weather acclimation becomes even more important at this level, as exposure to extreme cold for extended periods can strain the body and require proper adaptation.

Example training progression:

Beginner: Walking, cycling, or stair climbing for endurance; bodyweight squats and lunges; light pack hikes.
Intermediate: Hiking with a loaded pack; snowshoe practice; weighted squats and lunges; sled-pulling on easy terrain.

Advanced: Heavy pack hikes in rough terrain; high-intensity interval training (HIIT); dragging a weighted sled; cold-weather exposure training.

Training for winter camping doesn't have to be extreme, but it must be specific to winter conditions, focusing on functional strength, endurance, and the use of specialized gear. Building leg strength, endurance, and core stability makes it easier to move through snow and ice without exhausting yourself. Practicing with real gear—snowshoes, backpacks, sleds, and shovels—ensures that your body is ready for the extra effort that winter conditions demand.

Being willing to train by dragging a heavy truck tire while carrying a 40-pound (18kg) backpack will make all the difference on your winter trek.

Part 3
Stoves, Cooking, and Water Management in Winter

Cooking in winter presents unique challenges that require different approaches than warm-weather camping. Cold temperatures affect stove performance, fuel efficiency drops, and handling gear with gloved hands makes even basic cooking tasks more difficult. Liquid fuel stoves (white gas) are the most reliable in extreme cold, while canister stoves require special handling to function well in freezing temperatures. Protecting your stove from wind, keeping fuel warm, and cooking efficiently are essential skills for winter camping.

Once your cooking setup is dialed in, selecting the right food becomes the next priority. In freezing conditions, your body burns significantly more calories just to stay warm, so high-fat, high-calorie meals are key for sustaining energy. Some foods freeze solid and become impossible to eat, so planning meals that cook quickly and packing ready-to-eat options will reduce hassle. Eating at regular intervals—even before you feel hungry—helps keep your metabolism working efficiently, preventing cold-related fatigue.

Water management is just as critical. Dehydration is a major risk in winter, even if you don't feel thirsty. Cold air pulls moisture from your breath, sweat evaporates unnoticed, and relying on snow for water can be a slow, fuel-intensive process. Insulating your water supply, storing bottles upside-down to prevent freezing, and staying consistently hydrated are all essential.

This section covers everything you need to know about winter cooking, from choosing the best stove and fuel to packing the right food and preventing dehydration. Whether you're on a short overnight trip or a multi-day expedition, a well-planned system will keep you fueled, hydrated, and prepared for the challenges of winter camping.

Chapter 20
Stove Use in the Winter

Choosing the right stove for winter camping is critical—cold temperatures affect fuel efficiency, stove performance, and how easily you can cook in the field. A stove that works fine in summer can fail completely in freezing conditions if it's not suited for extreme cold. Liquid fuel stoves (white gas) are the most reliable choice in subzero temperatures because they maintain consistent pressure regardless of temperature, while canister stoves require pressure regulators or inverted canister setups to function in winter.

Beyond stove type, knowing how to operate your system efficiently in winter is just as important. Wind, snow, and altitude all affect burn rate and fuel consumption. Small adjustments—like using windshields, pre-warming fuel, and optimizing heat transfer—can make a major difference in cooking success. Safety is also a top concern, as winter campers often cook inside vestibules or enclosed spaces, increasing the risks of carbon monoxide buildup and fire hazards.

This chapter covers everything you need to know about stove selection, fuel choices, cold-weather modifications, and efficient cooking techniques to ensure your stove works reliably when you need it most.

Choosing the Right Stove for Winter Camping

Not all camping stoves work well in extreme cold. Liquid fuel stoves (white gas) are the best choice for winter because they maintain consistent fuel pressure, burn hot, and function reliably even in subzero temperatures. They require priming and maintenance but offer the most dependability in harsh conditions.

Canister stoves (isobutane/propane mixes) can work in winter if they have a pressure regulator or use an inverted canister design to feed fuel in liquid form. However, standard upright canister stoves struggle in extreme cold because fuel pressure drops as temperatures fall.

Alternative options like alcohol stoves, solid fuel stoves, and wood-burning stoves are usually too inefficient for serious winter use. Alcohol burns poorly in the cold, Esbit tablets take too long to heat water, and wood is often buried under snow or too damp to burn.

When choosing a stove, consider cold-weather performance, ease of operation with gloves, fuel availability, and efficiency. The following sections cover fuel choices, efficiency tips, and essential modifications to ensure your stove performs when you need it most.

Fuel Choices

When deciding what fuel to use for your winter expedition, consider the benefits of each option. The two primary options are pressurized canisters or liquid fuel.

ISO-Butane Canisters: ISO-butane canisters are convenient for shorter trips and some mountain expeditions. However, at higher altitudes and in cold temperatures, the pressure drops, making it harder to vaporize and melt snow. ISO-butane is less efficient than liquid fuels, so it's better suited for moderate conditions rather than extreme winter camping.

Propane: Propane doesn't burn efficiently at high altitudes or in cold temperatures, making it unsuitable for winter or high-altitude expeditions. It works well for mid-to-low altitude camping but isn't reliable for extreme conditions.

White gas: Liquid fuel white gas is the standard for winter camping. It's easy to calculate how much you need, and it doesn't require heavy canisters like ISO-butane. White gas is the most common choice because it burns cleanly and efficiently. In places like Greenland, where white gas can be hard to find, heptane is a great alternative. It has a higher energy content than white gas, burns cleanly, and is often available in bulk. White gas comes in many names in each country.

Denatured Alcohol: Denatured alcohol isn't ideal for winter camping. It's unpressurized, inefficient compared to white gas stoves, and has a high vaporization temperature. In the cold, it often won't ignite without being warmed first, even with an open flame. This adds risk, especially when dealing with gloves and winter gear.

Other Fuel Types

There are other fuel options for liquid fuel stoves, such as kerosene, gasoline, diesel, and heptane. However, not all fuels perform equally, and some should only be used when no other alternatives are available.

Heptane: Heptane is an excellent and very viable fuel for liquid fuel stoves. It burns cleanly, hot, and reliably, even in extreme cold. Its high vapor pressure makes it easier to ignite than kerosene, making it ideal for winter expeditions. Unlike some fuels, heptane doesn't leave residue, which reduces maintenance issues.
Kerosene: Kerosene is harder to ignite in cold temperatures and doesn't burn as hot as white gas. It leaves an oily residue that can clog the stove's jets more quickly, requiring more frequent cleaning. It often needs a starter gel to ignite, making it less practical in extreme conditions.
Gasoline and Diesel: Gasoline and diesel are emergency options, but they require swapping the stove's jet to handle their specific burn characteristics. Gasoline contains additives that produce noxious fumes, which can make indoor use hazardous. These fuels burn less cleanly and create more carbon buildup, so cooking outside is strongly recommended when using them. Some stoves come with multi-fuel kits to handle these fuels, but make sure your stove is compatible.

While many international fuel stoves can burn a variety of liquid fuels, this doesn't mean all fuels will burn efficiently. White gas and heptane remain the best options for winter camping because they burn cleaner, hotter, and more reliably in extreme cold. For winter expeditions, liquid fuel stoves, especially those using white gas or heptane, remain the most reliable and efficient choice.

Author's Note

I've used heptane for over a month in Greenland with zero problems. It performed flawlessly in subzero conditions, making it a trusted option when white gas wasn't available. Heptane is often found in bulk at industrial fuel depots, which is a great resource for expedition planning, though availability may vary by location.

Flame Control

There are two main types of liquid fuel (white gas) stoves for winter camping with different applications:

Expedition-Style Stoves: Stoves like the MSR XGK are designed to put out maximum heat quickly. They're primarily for melting snow and boiling water, not simmering. These stoves are difficult to adjust for lower heat for cooking. Once you turn them up beyond a quarter, they increase heat rapidly, producing intense flames.
Simmer-Capable Stoves: WhisperLite-style stoves are designed for more precise simmer control, making them better for cooking in the field. However, unless you're using a winter-specific model like the WhisperLite Universal (where the fuel line passes through the flame), these stoves can be harder to start in cold conditions.
Fuel Line Design in Cold Weather: On stoves like the MSR XGK, the fuel line runs near the flame, which helps vaporize the fuel before combustion in very cold temperatures, ensuring the stove runs efficiently.
Choosing the Right Stove: Your choice depends on your cooking needs. If you're focused on covering distance and mainly melting snow or boiling water for freeze-dried meals, expedition-style stoves like the MSR XGK are the better choice. For more extensive cooking, a simmer-capable stove like the WhisperLite can work well, provided it's suitable for winter use.

Fuel Use While Cooking in Winter

Fuel consumption can vary widely depending on conditions, efficiency, and technique. While 5.9 oz (175ml) of white gas per day is often quoted as a standard amount for an MSR XGK stove, this is only sufficient if you are efficient and careful with your use. Factors like using heat exchangers, stove reflectors, keeping out of the wind, and minimizing unnecessary heat loss can significantly reduce fuel usage.

In colder or more demanding conditions, or if you need to generate larger quantities of water, you may require 6.7–7.6 oz (200–225ml) of fuel or possibly more. This extra fuel may also be needed for tasks like filling hot water bottles to place in your sleeping bag for additional warmth.

Fuel consumption depends on several variables, including your stove's efficiency, the temperature of the water, wind or breezes that might disperse heat, and your pot setup (e.g., whether you use a heat exchanger).

A day's fuel usage can range from 5.9-8.5 oz (175–250ml), depending on factors such as temperature, humidity, wind, and exertion. It's essential to test and budget for your fuel usage before heading out. Conduct tests in the coldest temperatures you expect to encounter, and, if possible, practice melting snow to gauge your stove's performance.

For planning purposes, aim for approximately 7.6 oz (200ml) of fuel per day, but be prepared for fuel consumption to vary based on the conditions you face, and work to improve efficiency with experience and practice.

Maximizing Cooking Efficiency

When melting snow, consider pre-warming it if possible. Leaving snow in the sun or packing it into your tent can start the melting process using body heat. Always cook or melt snow in one session. Repeatedly turning the stove on, bringing it to temperature, and then cooling and cleaning it wastes both fuel and time—two key resources in winter camping.

Think about whether the water needs to boil or just be lukewarm. In pristine areas like the Arctic, Greenland, or Antarctica, freshly wind-driven snow is usually pure and free of contaminants. But in areas where people camp often, like mountaineering or expedition sites, you'll need to boil water or heat it to pasteurization temperature (149°F or 65°C) to avoid contamination from human waste.

Use insulated containers for your food and water to retain heat and lower fuel use. Non-insulated containers cool quickly, which might lead you to heat food and water more than necessary. Insulated options help reduce this need.

For shorter trips, insulated food containers may not be worth the extra weight—about 1 pound (0.5 kilograms). On longer trips of a week or more, they can make a big difference, saving fuel and effort while improving overall efficiency.

Flame-Out Prevention

One of the main challenges during startup with liquid fuel stoves is the tall yellow flame that can occur. When you pressurize the stove to the manufacturer's specifications, open the fuel bottle, and turn on the valve, liquid fuel spreads into the combustion chamber. If lit immediately, it can produce flames over a foot or even two feet (30–60 cm) high. Inside a tent, this can easily damage or destroy the fabric—or worse, start a fire.

To prevent this, follow the correct startup sequence for your stove in winter conditions:

Pressurize the Fuel: Pump your stove to the appropriate pressure.

Prime the Stove: Open the valve slightly to let a small amount of fuel enter the combustion chamber. Ensure the fiberglass wick inside catches the fuel. The stove should be in an upright position during this process.

Preheat the Diffuser: If it's very cold, dribble a little fuel onto the flame diffuser at the top. This will help it ignite more easily.

Shut the Valve: After priming, immediately close the valve to prevent additional fuel from flowing into the chamber.

Ignite the Fuel: Use a striker to vigorously ignite the fuel. Strike it on the sides or directly on the flame diffuser. In windy conditions, use a windscreen or other protection to help light the stove.

As the fuel burns, the heat will begin vaporizing the fuel in the line. You'll start to hear the stove "wake up" with the characteristic burner sound. Let the flame burn as hot as possible until the fuel in the cup is nearly gone. Timing is critical here.

Open the Valve Gently: Just before the fuel in the cup burns out, slowly open the valve about one-sixth to one-tenth of a turn to let a small, controlled amount of fuel flow. This prevents large flames. You may get a small puff of flame, but it will be manageable.

Let the Stove Heat Up: Allow the stove to run for 30–60 seconds or longer until it's fully heated. Once it burns with a steady, blue flame, you can open the valve fully for maximum heat output.

Additional Stove Tips

No Pot During Startup: Don't place a pot on the stove during this process. Flames during startup can coat your pot with soot and make it hard to see what's happening.

Add Water First: Once the stove is running, add some water to your pot (at least a finger's height). Never start melting snow directly in a dry pot, as this can damage the pot. Gradually add snow to the water as it melts to avoid overheating or warping the pot. By following this method, you can safely start your stove inside a tent, even during severe storms, without risking flame-outs or uncontrolled flames.

Making Your Stove Work Better in the Cold

Before starting your stove, preheat your fuel bottle if the temperature is below -22°F to -31°F (-30°C to -35°C). This step is critical in extreme cold, as colder fuel doesn't vaporize as easily, making the stove harder to light and less reliable. Preheating helps ensure consistent performance.

The best way to preheat the fuel bottle is to place it inside your jacket. Avoid putting it directly against your skin to prevent frostbite. Instead, tuck it against an insulating layer like a mid-layer or fleece. This warms the fuel gradually and safely. You don't need to pressurize the bottle before warming it. Raising its temperature by 18–27°F (10–15°C) improves fuel vaporization, which is essential for starting and maintaining a steady burn.

For added efficiency, use a windscreen around your stove to retain heat and protect the flame when igniting the stove. In extreme conditions, these small steps improve initial fuel ignition and reduce frustration or the danger of an initial flare-up.

Preventing Carbon Buildup

Preventing carbon buildup is important for keeping your liquid fuel stove running smoothly. After turning off the stove, let the fuel burn out completely. As the last of the fuel burns, you'll see a small yellow flame, which can leave a bit of carbon inside the stove.

Once the stove has cooled, pick it up, turn it upside down, and shake it. Many stoves have a small needle with a brass weight inside the jet, called a shaker jet. Shaking the stove causes the needle to rattle around and clear out carbon deposits. If your stove doesn't have a shaker jet, you'll need to manually clean the jet.

Always pack a proper cleaning needle with your expedition kit. Regular needles won't work—you'll need a super-fine wire needle specifically designed for clearing carbon from the jet. Without this tool, carbon can eventually clog the valve, causing the stove to lose performance or stop working entirely.

By using the shaker jet regularly (or manually cleaning the jet when necessary) and carrying the right cleaning tools, you'll keep your stove reliable and avoid frustrating issues in the field.

Safety and Efficiency Setup

Make sure wherever you're using a stove, nothing flammable is directly above it—especially your tent. If you have to cook inside a vessel or even in your tent, place the stove as far from the fabric as possible. Even if the flame isn't near the tent fabric, the constant heat rising can weaken or distort it over time. Nylon is especially prone to damage from heat. Never let a hot flame or metal touch the tent fabric—this can ruin it or, worst case, cause a fire.

Always use a base under your stove. This prevents it from melting the snow below, which can cause the stove to tip, spilling fuel or water and creating a fire hazard. Tipping stoves are also hard to handle safely, especially with gloves in winter. A solid, larger base, like a tough aluminum pan or reflective material, improves stability and helps bounce heat back into your pot, improving cooking efficiency.

Some people use custom stove bases made from carbon fiber or fiberglass. A simpler and more reliable option is a disposable aluminum roasting pan, like a 9 x 13-inch (23 x 33 cm) turkey pan. These are cheap, easy to find at most grocery stores, and will last for a month-long trip. For longer trips, bring a second pan as the first might get damaged from repeated packing in a sled. These pans are recyclable and can also be repurposed in emergencies.

Stove holders like the MSR Trillium are lightweight but can let heat melt the snow underneath, causing instability. Over time, even these bases may allow the stove to tilt. A tough, larger aluminum base is a better choice for consistent stability.

For safety, you must be able to quickly move the stove if it catches fire or fuel spills. Always position the stove so it can be tossed out of the tent if necessary. If you must run a stove in your tent, open the top flap for ventilation to prevent dangerous carbon monoxide buildup. Carbon monoxide is odorless and deadly, especially when first lighting the stove. To minimize risk, light the stove as far away as possible and make sure the tent has good airflow until the flame stabilizes.

The stove base is essential for efficiency, stability, and safety.

Stove Wind Protection

All stoves need some form of wind protection. White gas and canister alcohol stoves are particularly vulnerable to air currents, which can carry heat away and even extinguish the flame. This can happen quickly. Manufacturers usually provide a sheet of aluminum foil that you can wrap around your stove to create a wind barrier. This keeps the stove from going out and prevents wasting fuel by allowing heat to escape.

Another useful tool is a heat exchanger. It's a corrugated piece of aluminum that clamps to the outside of your pot. The heat exchanger keeps the heat close to the pot, improving heat transfer. It also adds thermal mass, helping stabilize the pot.

Heat from the stove can melt the ground or snow beneath it. You need a stove base to prevent uneven melting, which can make the stove tilt. Over time, the stove can sink into the snow, creating a dangerous situation.

Some people use stove boards, which are typically made from reflective metal like aluminum. These are useful because, if the stove gets out of control or there's a fuel leak, you'll need to grab it and throw it out of your tent. Yes, in extremely cold conditions, you may need to cook inside your tent. While not ideal, cooking outside isn't always an option in severe weather. Mountaineers, like those on Denali, often set up outdoor kitchens, but in bad weather, cooking outside is far from pleasant.

Another option for stove bases is dedicated stove holders, like the MSR XGK or WhisperLite Trillium Base. The Trillium Base is compact and helps stabilize the stove, but the holes in it can still allow heat to melt the snow, making the stove unstable. A good solution is to use aluminum turkey pans or cooking pans. These disposable or recyclable pans provide a lightweight base that prevents snow from melting beneath the stove. They also contain spills, preventing fuel from leaking onto the snow. In an emergency, you can pick up the pan with the stove and throw it out of your tent.

This simple design is also helpful when cooking outside, providing the same protection while serving as a container for your windscreen around the stove.

Transferring Fuel into a Fuel Bottle and Stove Turn-Off

When transferring fuel into a fuel bottle, use protective gloves, like nitrile or chemical-resistant ones, to keep fuel off your hands. Avoid using your regular camping gloves, as they can absorb fuel, become a fire hazard, and may be damaged by the fuel. Once soaked, they'll retain the fuel smell for a long time, and they can pose a fire risk if exposed to a spark.

When pumping your fuel bottle, don't exceed the recommended pressure. Follow the manufacturer's instructions or pump only until firm resistance is felt. Over-pumping can break the neck of the pump.

After using your stove, be careful when depressurizing the canister. Fuel can spray out, and the rapid evaporation can cause frostbite due to the cooling effect. Keep your hands clear and depressurize slowly.

Pay attention to the pump's small filter stone at the bottom. If it falls in the snow, it will absorb water and stop drawing fuel. To fix this, carefully drip a small amount of fuel over the stone to displace the water. Be cautious while handling spilled fuel to avoid accidents. Always take care when handling the pump to prevent drops or damage.

Which Fuel Bottle

MSR fuel bottles and others come in various sizes, typically ranging from 11 oz (325ml) to around 27 oz (800ml). Smaller bottles are easier to handle, and if they tip over, there's less fuel at risk of spilling. They also require less effort to pump. However, smaller bottles need refilling more often, especially if you're melting snow daily for water. Larger bottles are more efficient for extended use since they hold more fuel, reducing the need for frequent refueling.

The downside of larger bottles is that they're heavier. For long trips, it's smart to bring a backup fuel bottle. Even though the chances of damaging or cracking a fuel bottle are low, accidents can happen on long expeditions. A good setup is to carry a midsize bottle as your primary and a smaller one as a backup. Decide if the backup should be full or empty based on your trip length and fuel needs.

When using a fuel pump, make sure the flexible straw with the white filter stone is pointing down into the fuel. If it's positioned upward, it won't draw fuel properly when the bottle is partially empty. This can happen if the pump is twisted incorrectly during setup. Fixing it requires depressurizing the stove, removing the pump, adjusting the straw, repressurizing, and restarting the stove. To avoid this hassle, double-check the straw's orientation during setup. It may take some practice to get it right, but it'll save time and frustration later.

Most expedition travelers replace the standard childproof fuel bottle caps with simpler, more functional expedition caps. The childproof versions can be difficult to operate in extreme cold, becoming stiff and nearly impossible to open with gloves. In subzero temperatures, struggling with a stubborn cap isn't just frustrating—it wastes time and increases exposure to the elements. Expedition caps offer a more practical solution, allowing quick, reliable access to fuel while still keeping it secure.

That said, be mindful if traveling with children in winter, as fuel bottles require careful handling. For home storage, it's best to transfer fuel into proper, sealed containers designed for long-term storage rather than keeping it in a stove fuel bottle. Ideally, don't store fuel in stove bottles when not in the field, as these are meant for active use, not prolonged storage. Respect local fuel storage laws, but in the backcountry, function takes priority—proper handling and awareness remain the best safety measures.

Spare Stove Pump

On a winter camping trip, always bring a spare pump and a stove repair kit, especially if you rely on melting snow or ice for water. If your stove fails on a multi-day trip, you'll have no way to get water, which can put you in serious trouble. At a minimum, bring the mini repair kit designed for your stove and, if using a liquid fuel stove, carry an extra fuel pump. For longer expeditions, take the full field repair or expedition repair kit along with two fuel pumps. Broken fuel pumps are common at winter camps on Denali or similar locations.

Make sure to clean carbon buildup from your stove every night after use. Carbon can clog the jet where fuel sprays out and ignites, especially at higher altitudes or in cold temperatures. Follow your manufacturer's instructions for cleaning. Many liquid fuel stoves have a shaker needle system—turn the stove up and down and shake it for a minute until you hear clicking. Don't skip this step, as carbon buildup can choke the stove and cause it to fail. Canister stoves don't suffer from this issue as much, but they don't perform well in cold temperatures or high altitudes due to pressure loss, making them harder to ignite and maintain.

Over the years, I've helped many people whose stoves failed on expeditions. Once, on Denali, a couple approached me with a clogged stove. They couldn't make water and would have had to abandon their trip. Using my expedition repair kit, I cleared the jet with the cleaning needle, took the stove apart, and got it working again. Without a functioning stove, they wouldn't have been able to continue. Always carry the right tools and spares—you don't want to rely on someone else's preparedness to keep your trip from falling apart.

Stove Repair Kit and Spare Pump

On a winter camping trip, always bring a spare pump and a stove repair kit, especially if you rely on melting snow or ice for water. If your stove fails on a three-day or longer trip and you can't get water, you'll be in serious trouble. At a minimum, carry the mini repair kit designed for your stove, and bring an extra fuel pump if you're using a liquid fuel stove. For longer trips, bring the full Field Repair or Expedition Repair Kit and two fuel pumps. Broken fuel pumps are common at winter camps on Denali and similar locations.

You also need to clean carbon buildup from your stove every night after shutting it off. Carbon can clog the jet, where the fuel sprays out and ignites. Most liquid fuel stoves have a shaker needle. Turn the stove up and down and shake it until you hear the clicking. Don't skip this step, especially in cold temperatures or at high altitudes, where carbon buildup can be substantial and cause your stove to fail. Canister stoves don't struggle with this as much, but they don't perform well in the cold or at high altitudes due to pressure loss and difficulty maintaining a steady flame.

Author's Note

Over the years, I've helped many people whose stoves failed during winter trips. On Denali in 2024, a couple approached me because their stove was completely clogged. They couldn't make water. Their expedition was over if they couldn't get their stove functioning. Using my expedition repair kit, I cleared the jet with the repair needle. Being prepared with the right tools and spares can make or break an expedition.

Stove Repair Kit

Always bring a stove repair kit, no matter the type of stove you're using. This is especially important for liquid fuel stoves, as they require more maintenance. Manufacturers sell small kits for short trips, but for longer treks, you'll need a full expedition repair kit. These kits include spare gaskets, nuts, bolts, jets, and other essentials. Canister stoves typically need less maintenance, though they come with their own drawbacks.

If you're using a liquid fuel stove and plan to melt snow for water, bring at least one spare pump. If your pump breaks and you can't get water, you're in trouble. After using your stove, once it's cooled, turn it upside down and shake it thoroughly if it has a shaker jet (common on white gas stoves). This will help prevent clogs and keep your stove in good shape.

Make sure you know how to use the repair kit and have the necessary tools to disassemble your stove in the field if needed. You don't want to figure this out at 8 P.M. when you're trying to get water. If your stove fails in the wilderness, you need to know exactly what to do. In extreme cold, components can freeze, or moisture on the fuel pump (especially in the inlet stone or check valve) can freeze the pump's action. Be careful handling the stove and always wear nitrile gloves to avoid frostbite when transferring fuel.

Before heading out, always check your stove to ensure the jet is tightly screwed down. It can loosen during heating and cooling cycles. Follow the manufacturer's maintenance recommendations.

Author's Note

Over the years, I've helped countless people with stove issues. On one Denali expedition, a man asked me for help with his stove. I wondered why he didn't go to the guided group, but maybe he felt more comfortable with me. I inspected his stove and found the fuel jet clogged with carbon. Using the special tool from my MSR-XGK repair kit, I cleared the jet and got the stove working again.

I also remember an Australian friend I met on Denali who broke his stove pump. At the time, I only had one spare pump, and I didn't think much of it. After that, I learned my lesson. Fuel pumps are delicate and can break easily due to pressure or freezing temperatures. The weight of an additional pump is negligible, but it could be the difference between making it home and not.

Dealing With Fuel Line Clogs in the Field

A clogged fuel line can turn a reliable stove into dead weight, especially in winter when you can't afford delays in melting snow for water. If your stove is sputtering, burning weakly, or failing to pressurize, the issue is often carbon buildup or near-frozen fuel residue in the jet or line.

For white gas stoves, many models have a built-in shaker jet cleaning system. To use it, turn off the stove, invert the fuel bottle, and shake gently to dislodge any debris inside the fuel line. If that doesn't restore performance, try manually clearing the jet with a stove cleaning wire, usually stored inside the repair kit.

If you suspect a clog in the fuel intake tube, avoid blowing into it—introducing moisture into the line in freezing conditions can make the problem worse. Instead, warm the stove and fuel line by holding it inside your jacket for a few minutes to loosen any frozen residue. If the clog persists, carefully detach the fuel line and run a thin cleaning wire through it to clear any blockages.

For canister stoves, fuel clogs are less common, but in deep cold, the fuel inside the line can freeze, especially if there's any moisture present. Warming the canister in your jacket for a few minutes can help restore pressure. If an inverted canister stove still burns weakly, the jet may be partially clogged with dirt or fuel residue—gently tapping the burner head or clearing the jet with a cleaning tool may help.

What to Do If Your Stove Fails in the Field

Even the best stoves can fail, and in winter, losing the ability to melt snow for water is a serious survival issue. If your stove won't light, run through a quick troubleshooting checklist:

Check for pressure issues: If using a liquid fuel stove, the pump may need re-lubrication. Every time you insert the fuel line, lubricate the o-ring to ensure a good seal. Lip balm works well, as does any petroleum-based lubricant. Pump cup oil is the best, but it's messy and not always practical in the field.
Wind exposure: A weak flame is often due to wind, so double-check your stove placement and windshield.
Cold fuel or low vapor pressure: In extreme cold, fuel vapor pressure drops, meaning your stove may not generate enough power to sustain a proper flame. Warm the fuel bottle inside your jacket for a few minutes before trying again. Canister stoves struggle in deep cold unless used in inverted liquid-feed mode or pre-warmed.
Flame sputtering or surging: The jet may be partially clogged with carbon buildup. If the stove has a cleaning needle, use it. You should be able to see light through the stove's jet—if not, it's likely clogged. Prevention is key: shaking the stove upside down every time you shut it off helps keep carbon deposits from accumulating.
Stuck check valve: The check valve in the pump can get stuck, preventing proper pressurization or causing dangerous fuel leaks. Test your stove at home to learn the normal pumping sound—if it sounds different in the field, something is wrong. If the valve sticks, try adding a drop of fuel into the pump tube, then pump slowly to free it.
Cold-starting trick: If the stove isn't getting hot enough to stay lit, carefully add a few drops of fuel to the flame diffuser and ignite it. This can give the burner enough warmth to vaporize fuel properly, but be extremely cautious, as too much fuel can cause a dangerous flare-up.

Avoid Snow Extinguishing the Stove Flame

If you set a hot pot directly on the snow, snow can freeze to the bottom of the pot almost instantly. When you place it back on the burner, melting snow can dislodge and fall into the stove, extinguishing the flame. This can be dangerous because the stove may continue releasing fuel vapor, creating a fire hazard when relighting.

If this happens, the safest action is to immediately shut off the fuel valve, wait for the vapor to clear, and then relight the stove. However, in the field, many experienced travelers simply relight the stove immediately to avoid the extra effort of repressurizing the system. If you do this, be mindful of the risks—if too much vapor has built up, a flare-up is possible. Always be ready to pull back quickly when lighting to avoid burns.

To prevent this problem altogether, never set your hot pot directly on the snow. Instead, use a stable, non-combustible surface like an upturned shovel to keep the pot off the snow. This method prevents snow from sticking to the bottom, reduces the risk of burns, and keeps a hot pot from melting through your tent floor or other gear. Before placing the pot back on the stove, always check and brush off any moisture to avoid flameouts.

Avoiding Ice in the Stove Burner

Ice buildup inside the burner head is primarily an issue with canister stoves, but in rare cases, it can affect liquid fuel stoves if moisture gets trapped and freezes before the next use. This happens when water vapor from melting snow or steam condenses inside the burner, and if temperatures are low enough, this moisture can freeze. For canister stoves, this can block fuel flow or burner ports, reducing performance or preventing proper ignition.

When Ice Buildup Happens
- Most common in canister stoves when the burner cools rapidly in extreme cold, trapping moisture that later freezes.
- Possible in liquid fuel stoves if moisture collects inside the burner before storage and freezes overnight.
- More likely in humid conditions inside a tent vestibule or snow shelter, where steam can condense inside the stove.

How to Prevent and Fix Ice Buildup
Let the stove cool completely before packing it away—this prevents

moisture from freezing inside. Keep the burner dry by avoiding excess steam or condensation around the stove when cooking.

For canister stoves, if the burner is frozen, warm it slightly before lighting—hold it inside your jacket for a few minutes or gently heat the burner with a lighter.

For liquid fuel stoves, check for moisture before storage and dry the burner if necessary. If ice is suspected, preheat carefully before lighting.

While ice buildup in the burner is mainly a canister stove problem, liquid fuel stoves can experience it in rare cases if stored wet in extreme cold. Keeping the burner dry and storing the stove properly will prevent issues and ensure reliable performance.

Know How to Disassemble Your Stove Before You Need To

If troubleshooting in the field isn't working, you may need to take apart your stove to clean a clogged jet or fuel line. This is not something you want to figure out for the first time in subzero temperatures. Before heading into the field, practice disassembling and reassembling your stove at home so you know exactly where each part goes and how it fits together.

Work in a controlled space—tiny parts are easy to lose. Many stoves use a small shaker jet needle or a fine cleaning wire, and if you drop it in the snow, it's gone forever. If you must work on your stove in the field, never do it directly over snow. Instead, work over your stove board inside the tent, making sure the stove is completely cool and depressurized before disassembly.

If you cannot repair the stove, switch to emergency water collection methods. Cold-soak food if necessary and pack snow into a bottle and let it warm against your body to generate small amounts of liquid water. It won't be fast, but it can keep you hydrated until you reach safety.

Cooking in a Tent Vestibule

In extreme winter conditions, cooking inside a tent vestibule is standard practice in polar travel and mountaineering, where exposure to wind and severe cold makes outdoor cooking impractical or even dangerous. While widely used by experienced winter travelers, it comes with serious risks of carbon monoxide poisoning, fire hazards, and moisture buildup, requiring careful attention to safety.

Proper ventilation is essential—always keep the vestibule partially unzipped or a vent open to allow airflow. Never cook in a fully sealed tent, as carbon monoxide buildup can be lethal. Instead of relying on gadgets like carbon monoxide detectors, experienced travelers use proper airflow and awareness to manage this risk.

Fire safety is just as critical. White gas stoves, in particular, can flare up during priming, and if a flame catches the synthetic fabric of a tent, it can melt or ignite instantly. Always place the stove and fuel bottle together on a stable, heat-resistant surface, such as a stove board or a disposable aluminum baking pan. This prevents the fuel bottle from sinking into snow, keeps it stable, and helps insulate it from the cold.

Since melting snow for water can take hours, pumping the fuel bottle while the burner is running is a necessary risk. As pressure drops in the bottle, the flame weakens, requiring occasional pumping to maintain steady output. This must be done carefully and steadily to avoid sudden surges of fuel that can cause flare-ups or erratic burning. If possible, use slow, controlled pumps to keep pressure stable rather than waiting until the flame weakens significantly. Always keep your face and hands clear of the stove while pumping, and be aware that any fuel leaks or malfunctions could result in a dangerous fire inside the tent vestibule.

Never lean over a running stove. Synthetic fabrics from jackets, gloves, and sleeping bags can melt or catch fire instantly if they come too close to an open flame. This is especially dangerous inside a tent, where even a small fire can spread rapidly. Always work from the side, keeping loose clothing and insulation well away from the burner. If adjusting the stove, kneel or crouch at a safe distance rather than hovering over it.

Another major risk is excess moisture buildup from steam. Letting water boil to the point of heavy steaming can coat everything inside the tent with condensation, which then freezes, soaking your sleeping bag, clothing, and gear. This is especially dangerous for down insulation, which loses warmth when wet. Keep pot lids on, heat water just until hot, and minimize steam to keep your sleeping area dry.

While vestibule cooking is a necessary skill for serious winter travel, it demands discipline and careful execution. With the right precautions, it allows for safe, efficient meal preparation in the harshest conditions—but a single mistake can have serious consequences.

Packing & Storing Your Stove in Winter

Packing a stove for winter travel is about protecting the stove from damage while preventing fuel contamination in your cookware. Stoves are fragile in the cold—small parts can snap, fuel pumps can crack, and pressure seals can fail if not handled properly. At the same time, fuel contamination is a real risk, but one that can be managed with proper precautions.

Many experienced winter travelers, including those on polar expeditions, store their stove inside their 2-liter pot for protection. This keeps the stove from getting crushed in a pack, prevents small parts from breaking, and consolidates gear efficiently. The trade-off is the potential for hydrocarbon contamination from residual fuel in the fuel line. To mitigate this, shake out all excess fuel from the line before packing the stove. This simple habit reduces the chance of contamination while keeping the stove safely stored.

For the fuel bottle, practicality outweighs unnecessary safety features. Removing the pump before packing prevents it from breaking under pressure in a tightly packed sled or backpack. Using expedition fuel caps—instead of the cumbersome childproof models—makes opening the bottle easier in extreme cold, where gloves and frozen fingers make fine motor tasks nearly impossible. These caps are more practical, more reliable, and don't fail at the worst moment.

Ultimately, winter stove packing is about smart risk management. Protecting the stove without compromising usability, preventing contamination without overcomplicating things, and ensuring your fuel system is both secure and accessible in extreme conditions. Calculated trade-offs—like properly purging fuel lines, using gear in a way that prioritizes function, and relying on field-proven methods—are what matter most in real-world conditions.

Efficient Camp Cooking

One of the biggest challenges with winter travel is efficiency. Everything takes more effort in the cold. Moving is harder, clothing is bulkier, and walking on ice is risky. Making camping and cooking as efficient as possible makes the experience far more enjoyable.

If you're moving constantly during the day, the best cooking method is simply boiling water and melting snow. This minimizes effort and eliminates cleanup, assuming you're eating from a foil bag of dehydrated food or pre-packaged meals.

If you do want to cook something more complicated, cleanup becomes the challenge. For longer trips, reserve some hot water at the end of your meal to rinse food residue from your thermos or food container. Swishing hot water through the container helps remove food scraps and reduces the need for wiping.

Drinking Your Dishwater

In winter camping, consider a different use for your dishwater. Assuming there's no contamination (e.g., leftover oils or food scraps), consider drinking it. This serves two key purposes:

Hydration: Cold weather makes it harder to stay hydrated. You sweat less but urinate more, and dry air pulls moisture from your body. Drinking rinse water helps replace lost fluids.

Nutrient Retention: A surprising amount of salts and nutrients remain in food residue. Pouring rinse water onto the ground wastes those valuable nutrients.

Hygiene in Winter Camping

One of the biggest challenges in winter camping is staying clean and handling dishwashing in freezing conditions. If you're cooking instead of using pre-packaged meals, you'll need to figure out how to clean up without wasting water or exposing your hands to freezing temperatures.

Running water is usually unavailable unless you're near a creek or river, but that comes with its own risks—falling in could be life-threatening. Washing dishes in cold conditions means exposing your hands to freezing water, which can be painful and dangerous unless you bring dish gloves or protective liners.

Cleaning cloths, sponges, or scrubbers need to be maintained too. In freezing temperatures, they can develop bacterial loads due to temperature fluctuations (warm days and cold nights), which create condensation that provides a breeding ground for bacteria. If you can't properly clean them, they can freeze solid and become unusable.

For food waste disposal, always pack out your trash unless regulations allow burning. The best approach is to use resealable plastic bags to store food waste and trash without taking up extra space. Sealing waste properly also reduces smells that attract animals. If burning is allowed by regulations, be sure to do so safely, following Leave No Trace principles.

Chapter 21
Food for Winter Camping

Winter camping food is a completely different animal compared to summer camping food or your regular diet at home. In warm weather, you can eat just about anything—carb-heavy meals, heavier proteins—without much trouble. But in winter, food freezes solid, and your body burns more calories just to stay warm.

At high altitudes (10,000–16,000 feet / 3,000–5,000m), digestion becomes more difficult. Burning fats requires more oxygen, followed by proteins, while carbohydrates are the easiest to metabolize. This makes carb-heavy meals more efficient for energy at altitude, though balancing calorie intake with your body's ability to digest and metabolize at high altitudes is key.

You need food that is lightweight, high in calories, and still edible when frozen or freeze-dried. Some freeze-dried foods require hot water to prepare, which can be a challenge in extreme cold, so having pre-packaged, high-energy foods that don't require cooking is a smart backup. These are some of the challenges explored in this chapter.

Macronutrient Needs

There are three fundamental energy sources for the human body, and in winter camping, balancing them correctly is critical:

Fats: The Highest-Calorie Fuel

Fats have the highest calorie density, providing nearly twice the energy per ounce compared to proteins and carbohydrates. They burn slowly, offering long-lasting warmth and endurance in cold conditions. Good sources include butter, coconut oil, nut butter, olive oil, cheeses, and certain nuts. Adding butter to oatmeal, mixing whole powdered milk into cereals, or snacking on high-fat foods can help maintain energy levels.

At altitudes above 10,000 feet (3,000m), fats become harder to digest because high altitude reduces appetite and oxygen availability, making it more difficult for the body to process them efficiently. While they provide sustained energy, they aren't ideal for quick bursts of fuel. If you need immediate energy, carbohydrates are the better option.

Proteins: Essential for Endurance

Proteins support muscle maintenance and long-term energy, making them essential for sustained activity. Good sources include jerky, freeze-dried meals, protein bars, powdered shakes, and certain nuts and legumes. Since proteins take longer to digest than carbohydrates, they work best when combined with carbs to create a steady energy release.

Protein contributes less significantly to immediate energy needs and is better suited for recovery and endurance over long periods. Relying too much on protein, especially in high-protein diets like keto or carnivore, won't give you the quick energy needed for a summit push or a long trek. It takes time for the body to break down protein, meaning you might feel sluggish for the first hour until your body starts burning the fuel.

Carbohydrates: The Fastest Energy Source

Carbs provide quick, easily accessible energy, making them ideal for short breaks and high-output activities. Good sources include instant rice, pasta, granola, dehydrated fruit, and freeze-dried meals high in carbs. Complex carbs like oats, whole grains, and pasta offer steady, long-term energy, while simple carbs like sugary snacks, dried fruit, and granola give fast bursts of fuel when needed.

Balancing All Three for Maximum Performance

The best way to start your day is with a balanced meal containing carbs, proteins, and fats. Eating only carbohydrates burns through energy too fast, leading to an early crash. Relying solely on fats or protein can leave you feeling sluggish in the morning. A well-rounded breakfast fuels your body for the long haul and prevents early hunger before your first break.

Freeze-Dried and Dehydrated Food

Freeze-dried foods are staples for backpackers, adventurers, campers, hunters, and anyone heading into the backcountry. If you're traveling away from a vehicle where weight matters, dehydrated food is one of the best ways to carry lightweight, space-efficient meals.

The main advantage is that moisture is removed without losing much, if any, nutrition or energy content. This makes dehydrated food compact and efficient. A meal that starts at 10 to 15 ounces (280–425g) can drop to just 4 to 5 ounces (110–140g) once the water is gone. Water is the heaviest component of most foods. Without it, the food isn't edible, so hot water is needed to rehydrate it.

Another big advantage is shelf life—think 25 years or more. Most other foods don't last that long because they still contain moisture. Even dried beans, lentils, or pasta in bags can lose their ability to rehydrate properly over time.

Sealed, foil-packed dehydrated foods prevent moisture and oxygen from getting in. Many also contain oxygen absorbers to remove any leftover oxygen, which helps keep the food from degrading.

The best part? All you need is hot water. Whether you use the original pouch, a food thermos, or another sealed container, keeping it covered is key. If the food is exposed to air while rehydrating, the water cools too fast, and the process won't work as well. Hot water and a sealed container make all the difference.

Meal Ideas for Dehydrated Food

The variety of dehydrated foods from different manufacturers is substantial. Whether you go with Mountain House or another brand, the options stay mostly the same—soups, stews, pasta, lasagna, chicken with rice, beef teriyaki, and more.

One big advantage of dehydrated meals is that you can also make your own. You can go all in and buy a dehydrator to create custom meals, so you know exactly what's in them, including the nutrition and energy content. The biggest challenge with this is getting a proper foil-sealed bag, which is usually only available in commercial manufacturing. But for shorter trips, a vacuum sealer with plastic bags can keep food safe from moisture and oxygen for several months.

A hybrid approach is to buy pre-dehydrated ingredients from a supplier and mix them into your own meals, skipping the need for a dehydrator. This skips the time and expense of dehydrating while still letting you control what goes into your food. Some store-bought dehydrated meals are high in salt, or they might contain ingredients—like bell peppers—that don't sit well with everyone.

No matter what method you use, test every meal in the field before a long trip. Even if the ingredients seem fine, you might find that a particular meal doesn't sit well or is difficult to manage in the field.

Another challenge is meals with milk-based ingredients, like turkey tetrazzini or other creamy dishes. If you eat from a bag or use a food thermos, milk residue can spoil fast. Even if the food was fine when you ate it, any leftover milk product can turn overnight. This is especially tricky when winter camping, as cleaning equipment can be more difficult in cold conditions.

Meals with cheese, like lasagna, are another thing to watch for. They taste great but can stick to your spork, fork, or food container and be surprisingly hard to clean. If melted cheese coats everything, getting your container ready for the next meal can be a hassle. Keep that in mind if you're using a food thermos instead of eating straight from the bag.

Suggested Rehydration Techniques

Using an insulated container instead of the original pouch is one of the best ways to rehydrate food. Insulated containers hold heat better than foil pouches, keeping meals warm longer and making the rehydration process more effective. Hot water has more energy, allowing it to penetrate and soften dehydrated food faster. Trying to rehydrate with cold water can work, but it's much slower—hot water is almost essential for efficient rehydration.

You also need to plan for water use. In addition to drinking water, dehydrated meals take a good amount—sometimes 11–17 ounces (a third to a half liter) per meal. Make sure to factor this into your water supply. The water should be fully boiling or close to it before adding it to food. In camping conditions, heat loss happens fast, so once the water is poured in, seal the container immediately to keep as much heat as possible.

Keeping Food Warm While Rehydrating

A trick to improve rehydration, especially in extreme cold, is to put the sealed food pouch or thermos inside your sleeping bag. Make sure there are no leaks first. At -30°F (-34°C) or colder, the outside air will pull heat from your food fast, slowing or even stopping rehydration. Keeping the pouch inside a sleeping bag or insulated layer helps maintain heat, which is especially important for meals with rice or pasta since they take longer to absorb water. Do not put your food directly on snow or frozen ground. It will suck the heat out immediately, making rehydration much slower or even impossible.

Preventing Spills and Pouch Failures

Be careful when pouring boiling water into a food pouch. Many pouches are semi-rigid and can flop over unexpectedly, spilling your entire meal. Most rely on a Ziplock-style seal, but because of the fine powder inside, they don't always seal properly. Some Ziplocks can even tear, making them useless for resealing.

When opening a pouch and removing the oxygen absorber, wipe dust off the Ziplock strip before sealing. This helps reduce the chance of leaks. If you're placing the pouch inside your sleeping bag, be careful—any small puncture or tip-over can result in spills, leaving you with frozen food in your sleeping bag.

Using a Food Thermos for Rehydration

A food thermos keeps meals warm longer but comes with a trade-off—it must be cleaned thoroughly after every use. Any leftover food can spoil quickly, especially with temperature changes throughout the day.

If food spoils inside the thermos, your next meal could be contaminated with bacteria, leading to potential foodborne illness. To avoid this, always rinse with hot water and scrub it clean. A dry piece of toilet paper can help wipe out residue before rinsing. Pay extra attention to the threads of the lid, where food can collect and start to smell.

Pouches vs. Insulated Food Containers

Pouches require no cleanup—just eat and toss them in your trash bag. Insulated food containers like thermoses or food jars keep meals warm longer but must be cleaned thoroughly after every use.

Both methods work, but keeping everything clean is critical to avoid contamination, bad smells, or worse—bacteria in the next meal.

Dealing with Frozen Food

One of the challenges of winter camping is frozen food. What's easy to eat at room temperature or in summer can turn into a rock-hard, inedible mass in the cold. Even an overnight trip can freeze your food solid unless you go to great lengths to keep it warm, like storing it in your jacket or near a heat source. But insulation alone isn't enough—without direct heat, food will eventually match the outside temperature.

Managing Frozen Food

During the day, temperatures may warm up and thaw food slightly, only for it to refreeze overnight. This thaw-freeze cycle can cause food to go rancid, which is something to watch out for. If a food isn't edible at subzero temperatures (0°F/-18°C)—like butter, coconut oil, beef jerky, or cheese—you'll need a plan to thaw it.

One of the best ways is to pre-thaw food for the next day, keeping it in a warm place so it doesn't freeze again. As soon as you set up camp, take out what you plan to eat tomorrow and store it in your jacket, sleeping bag, or a hot water bottle. This will give it time to soften overnight. You'll want to crush or break it up while it's warm so it's easier to eat the next day. What seems edible at home can become teeth-breaking hard in the cold.

A good way to test your food before a trip is to freeze it solid in a standard freezer for two days and then try to eat it after 15 minutes—about the length of a typical break in the field. You'll quickly find out what works and what doesn't.

Some foods stay edible even when frozen solid. Chocolate, nuts, and gummies may get firmer but won't become impossible to eat. However, foods with a taffy-like consistency, protein bars, sandwiches, or anything chewy will turn rock hard.

A trick is to pre-crumble food inside its package while it's warm. If you have a protein bar, for example, warm it up inside your jacket, then squeeze and break it into small pieces while it's still soft. The next day, even when frozen, those small crumbles will melt in your mouth quickly, making it much easier to eat.

Arctic Trick: Using a Nalgene Bottle for Food

Arctic explorers often use a mix like GORP (a trail mix traditionally made of Good Old Raisins and Peanuts) because it doesn't freeze solid and isn't sticky. One way to store it is by packing it inside a 1-liter Nalgene bottle, letting you easily eat directly from the bottle without dealing with wrappers. This saves time, keeps your hands warm, and reduces the hassle of fumbling with packaging in extreme cold.

A Nalgene bottle is easy to open, even with heavy mittens, and prevents handling food with cold hands, which can lead to contamination or freezing. This method saves time, prevents frostbite, and cuts down on frustration. Food size matters—small grains may pour out too quickly, while larger pieces could be more difficult to eat quickly or on the move. Finding the right balance between size and edibility is key. Test this method at home before relying on it in the field.

Best and Worst Foods for Extreme Cold

Even if a food works fine at room temperature, cold temperatures can change how it behaves. You'll have to eat quickly, handle food with gloves, and accept that sanitation won't be perfect. Planning ahead for frozen food can make or break your winter trip.

Best frozen foods: Butter (still edible at -50°F/-45°C, though very firm unless kept warm), hard cheeses, nuts, freeze-dried meals, and dry grains.

Difficult foods: Soft cheese (can develop mold if not sealed properly), cooked grains (if they retain moisture), fresh fruit (freezes solid), and bread (usually gets ruined, though tortillas stay flexible).

Meal Ideas

Coming up with winter food can be a challenge. Below is a compact list of potential meal ideas. The approach depends on whether you'll be constantly mobile during the day or staying in a base camp.

If you're mobile, everything needs to be easy to eat and manageable when frozen. At base camp, you have more flexibility and variety in meals.

Base Camp Meals

For breakfast, consider granola or instant oatmeal with dried or freeze-dried fruit and butter. Butter is key—it provides sustained energy after the carbohydrates and proteins from the grains and milk have burned off.

For lunch, tortillas with cheese and jerky or sausage are a good option. Sausage is great, but in subzero temperatures, it can become nearly inedible. If you need protein, jerky is a better choice. Just be aware that some jerky contains additives like MSG, which some people react to. Always test foods before a trip.

For dinner, look for pasta with freeze-dried meat and vegetables, dehydrated chili, or a curry-style dish with instant mashed potatoes. These give you a good mix of nutrients and warmth.

During the day, snack on trail mix, nuts, seeds, energy bars, protein bites, and freeze-dried fruit. GORP (Good Old Raisins and Peanuts) is a classic high-energy mix. Choose snacks that won't freeze too hard and damage your teeth.

Meals for Mobile Days

On long-distance travel days, foods that require handling, like tortillas, are less practical. Choose a high-calorie breakfast that provides both fast and sustained energy.

A great option is granola with whole powdered milk (avoid non-fat versions). Nido Fortificada, a full-fat powdered milk from Latin American or Mexican brands, is an excellent choice. Add three tablespoons of raw cane sugar instead of refined white sugar. The sugar gives an immediate energy boost, while the complex carbs and proteins in the granola provide longer-lasting fuel.

The fat in whole powdered milk also increases endurance, and the calcium supports muscle function and neurotransmitters. It's not just for bone health—it directly impacts physical performance throughout the day.

Lunch and Snack Options for Mobility

For lunch, good-quality food bars that have been pre-crushed overnight are easier to eat in the cold. Super dry foods like granola or oat bars can be tough to eat because they require extra water for rehydration. Soft, chewy bars are better for quick eating.

Chocolate bars are an excellent high-calorie option. Salted almonds and energy chews like Clif Shot Bloks are also good for steady energy.

Be careful with too much sugar as your main food source. A better option is 70% dark chocolate, which has a higher fat content and a lower glycemic index, meaning energy is released gradually instead of causing a spike and crash.

Other good options include shortbread cookies—they're high in fat, provide a mix of protein and sugar, and remain edible even at temperatures as low as -50°F (-45°C). Examples include Keebler shortbread or Walkers-style butter cookies.

In extreme cold when traveling long distances, you don't have time for elaborate food prep. Choose foods that are easy to eat with gloves on, require minimal handling, and won't freeze solid. The right mix of fast energy, long-lasting fuel, and warmth will keep you moving efficiently.

Wildlife Safety & Food Storage

Proper food storage is critical to avoid attracting wildlife. If you're in an area with bears—brown or black—you'll need bear-resistant food containers.

Never store food in your tent. A bear trying to get to your food at 2 A.M. could easily become a life-threatening situation.

Dumping food scraps or residue near camp attracts animals, which is a serious problem in any environment. Rinsing with water and drinking it afterward reduces food smells that could attract unwanted visitors.

By minimizing waste and maximizing efficiency, you'll save energy, stay hydrated, and reduce environmental impact—all critical for a successful winter camping trip.

Food should be stored at least 100 yards (91m) from your tent. In winter, this can be a challenge, especially when conditions make it harder to manage, but it's far better than dealing with a bear tearing through your camp.

Smaller animals can be just as much of a nuisance. Squirrels, chipmunks, raccoons, and rodents will chew through your tent to reach food. If an animal bites or contaminates your food, it should be considered unsafe due to the risk of diseases like rabies.

Even non-food scented items like toothpaste, deodorant, and lotion should be stored in bear-resistant containers if regulations require it.

Many people don't realize that animals can smell food through plastic bags even when you can't. Their sense of smell is far stronger than ours. Never assume food is safe just because it's sealed—store it properly.

By following strict hygiene and food safety practices, you'll reduce risks, protect your food supply, and keep wildlife at a safe distance.

Winter Food Final Thoughts

Planning food for winter camping takes more effort and experience, but it's not impossible to figure out. The best way to test everything is to freeze it at home first. Put your food in the freezer for two days until it's solid, then take it out and test if your methods work—all while you're in a comfortable setting.

Doing this before you're out in deep cold is critical. You'll already be dealing with gear, weather, and exhaustion—food shouldn't add to that struggle of managing everything.

Make sure whatever food you bring is easy to eat and manage. Avoid relying on dishes that need cleaning. On an overnight trip, you can get away with more traditional cooking, but on longer trips where weight matters, efficiency is key.

Expedition-style cooking with pots works for larger trips, but you'll need a way to clean them. If food freezes inside your pot, even hot water may not be enough to clean it out. Have a plan for handling food waste so it doesn't become a problem.

It's critical to test all your food before your trip. Try eating only the freeze-dried meals and snacks you plan to bring for a couple of days at home. Make sure it doesn't cause stomach issues, which can become a serious problem in extreme cold.

Be well-prepared, and winter camping will be a challenging but rewarding experience.

Prepare food well ahead of your winter camping departure date. Repackaging and preparing food takes a surprisingly long time.

Chapter 22
Water Management in Winter Camping

Managing water in winter is crucial for staying hydrated and conserving fuel. Melting snow requires constant attention—you can't just set your stove and let it go. If you're careful with fuel, 5.9-6.7 oz (175–200ml) can produce 4–5 quarts (4–5 liters) of water under optimal conditions, though factors like wind, stove efficiency, and snow density can affect this.

If you're collecting wind-driven snow, it's usually clean and free of contaminants. However, light, dry snow has low density and takes up more space. Packing it down slightly before melting helps, but compressing it inside the pot as it melts is more effective for improving density and water yield.

Melting Snow Efficiently

Always start with at least one or two fingers of liquid water in your 2-liter pot before adding snow. Avoid 1-liter pots—they're too small to efficiently melt snow. Add packed snow gradually rather than dumping in fluffy snow, which takes longer to melt.

If you're in an area with fresh, uncontaminated snowfall, you don't need to boil all your water. Boiling to 212°F (100°C) consumes unnecessary fuel and time. For drinking water, lukewarm is usually sufficient if you're confident in the snow's purity. However, near cities, lower elevations, or industrial areas, snow may contain contaminants, so boiling or chemical treatment is recommended. For dehydrated meals, use the hottest water possible, near boiling—hotter water improves rehydration, softens food better, and enhances taste.

Water Purification in Cold Weather

Filtering water in freezing conditions is a major challenge. Most filters freeze easily, and once frozen, they're useless. To prevent this, store your filter in a sealed plastic bag inside your sleeping bag at night.

A better winter option is chemical purification, like Aquamira. It works well in the cold, but keep in mind that cold water slows the reaction time, so allow extra time for the treatment to be effective.

Preventing Water from Freezing

Keeping liquid water from freezing is just as important as melting it. Most thermoses are steel, which cools quickly when exposed to cold air or surfaces. Instead, fully insulate your thermos by wrapping it in a fleece jacket, down jacket, or extra clothing to retain heat overnight.

The most efficient approach is to heat all your water in the evening while setting up camp. Mornings in winter are slow—getting out of a sleeping bag, heating water, and packing up takes time. Having water ready saves fuel and energy.

Using Water Bottles in Freezing Conditions

If you're using Nalgene bottles, keep the threads dry to prevent freezing. Never put your lips directly on the threads—moisture will freeze instantly, making the bottle impossible to open.

To prevent bottles from freezing:
- Tap off excess water before sealing.
- Store the bottle upright unless you are confident in your setup. Some people store bottles upside down to keep the lid from freezing first, but this can cause leaks or ice buildup in the threads, making it impossible to open. If you do store it upside down, check for leaks first. If the bottle does leak you will have a substantial problem. Storing the bottles upright is lower risk. Simply chisel through the ice to get at the water.
- If the lid freezes shut, place the bottle under your arm or inside your jacket for a few minutes to loosen the ice.
- Purchase quality water bottle insulators like the Outdoor Research SG Water Bottle Parka. Neoprene sleeves offer minimal insulation in extreme cold.

Water bladders are unreliable in winter. Even with neoprene sleeves, the hose and valve will freeze solid. Unlike a bottle, you can't chip away ice inside a bladder without damaging it. Some wide-mouth hydration reservoirs with insulated sleeves and heated hoses work in extreme cold, but they require careful management and aren't foolproof. Rigid water bottles remain the most reliable choice for winter camping—they're easier to fill, won't collapse, and can be thawed if necessary.

Melting Snow

When melting snow, always make sure there's liquid water in the pot first. Without it, the snow can scorch the pot or damage the stove. Once you've added snow, close the pot immediately to retain heat. This helps the snow melt faster and reduces fuel use. The more you open the pot, the more heat escapes, slowing the process.

Don't let the water reach a full boil or start steaming over. Boiling wastes fuel since water won't get hotter than its boiling point—it just vaporizes. Excess steam can contribute to condensation inside your tent, though most condensation comes from breath and ambient moisture. A quick peek is enough to check progress—look for small bubbles forming but not a rolling boil.

While full boiling is often recommended for water sterilization, research shows that pasteurization—keeping water at 170°F (77°C) or higher for a sustained period—can effectively kill pathogens. However, some pathogens require longer exposure at this temperature, and at high altitudes (above 10,000 feet / 3,000m), water boils at a lower temperature, which may not be hot enough for quick sterilization. When in doubt, boiling remains the safest option. Check with reliable sources like the USDA, CDC, or WHO for the latest guidelines.

Snow Sources for Water

When gathering snow for water, use the cleanest source possible. Avoid snow near campsites, trails, or animal tracks, as it may be contaminated with food waste or human and animal waste products. These contaminants are often invisible but can make you seriously sick, turning your winter camping trip into a real challenge.

Dense, compacted snow melts more efficiently than light, powdery snow. Fluffy snow takes up more space, melts slower, and sticks to your stove and shovel, creating a mess. Use a shovel or another clean tool to transfer snow into your pot instead of your gloves. Handling snow with gloves compresses the insulation, making them colder overall, even if they don't get wet.

Avoid using solid ice unless necessary, as it takes much longer to melt, though it provides more water per unit volume than snow. A good technique is to mix ice with snow for better efficiency. The best snow is dense, "styrofoam-like" packed snow. Fluffy snow requires more effort to melt and wastes heat, as you'll have to open the pot frequently to add more. For efficiency, pack the snow down in your shovel before scooping it into the pot, then continue compacting it inside the pot as it melts. This reduces air gaps, saving time and fuel while ensuring a clean water source.

Plan for at least one hour a night to melt snow to make enough water for the next day's activities.

Chapter 23
Specialized Diets

The easiest and most practical approach to winter camping nutrition is a well-rounded diet that includes a variety of foods. If you're not particular about what you eat, you have the advantage of flexibility, making it much easier to adapt to winter conditions.

Eating a mix of fats, proteins, and carbohydrates ensures you get both quick-burning and long-lasting energy. Carbs provide immediate energy, fats sustain endurance, and protein aids in recovery. A balanced diet allows you to pack fast, easy-to-eat foods along with more substantial meals for when cooking is possible. A well-rounded diet allows for the most variety, ease of preparation, and adaptability to different conditions. If one type of food freezes solid or becomes difficult to eat, you still have other options.

For most winter campers who aren't following a specialized diet, this means:
Carbs for quick energy: Granola, oatmeal, dried fruit, crackers, or trail mix.
Fats for long-lasting fuel: Cheese, nuts, peanut butter, coconut oil, or olive oil.
Proteins for strength and recovery: Jerky, canned fish, freeze-dried meats, or protein bars.

Challenges of Specialized Diets in Cold Conditions

For those following a specific diet, winter camping presents unique challenges. Some diets make it easier to grab and eat food without stopping, while others require more planning to maintain energy levels. Cooking isn't always practical in extreme cold, especially in bad weather when setting up a tent or stopping for long periods isn't an option.

Additionally, many foods that people eat at home freeze solid in the backcountry, making them difficult or impossible to eat unless they're broken into smaller pieces ahead of time or kept warm inside a jacket.

Vegan and Vegetarian Considerations

A vegan or vegetarian diet can work for winter camping, but it requires careful planning. You need to ensure adequate protein, calorie density, and food usability in extreme cold. Many plant-based foods are lightweight and shelf-stable, making them easy to pack. However, freezing temperatures create serious challenges, especially when it comes to accessing fats on the move. One of the biggest concerns for plant-based winter campers is the lack of calorie-dense fats. Olive oil is a good fat source but a spill can be disasterous. These are critical for sustained energy, warmth, and satiety.

Vegetarian/Vegan Key Challenges:
Protein sources often require cooking: Foods like lentils, quinoa, and beans provide excellent protein but need long cooking times, which may not be practical in extreme cold.
Energy bars and nut butters freeze solid: Pre-crushing bars or keeping them inside a pocket makes them easier to eat.
Lower calorie density: Many plant-based foods are lower in fat, requiring larger portion sizes to meet energy needs.
Freezing affects usability: Some foods that are easy to eat at home become rock-hard in subzero temperatures, making them impractical unless warmed first.

Vegetarian/Vegan What Works Best:
Pre-cooked grains (quinoa, rice, oats): Can be eaten cold if needed.
Nut butters and trail mixes: High in fat and protein, but must be managed to prevent freezing.
Oil-based meals (olive oil, coconut milk-based curries, high-fat plant spreads): Help boost calorie intake.
Freeze-dried meals: Some plant-based options cook quickly with hot water. Instant powdered foods (mashed potatoes, couscous, polenta, powdered hummus): Rehydrate quickly in hot water, making them easy to prepare in a tent, but impractical to make while actively moving.
Fortified foods: B12, iron, and vitamin D are nutrients to watch, but for short trips, deficiencies are not a major concern.

Vegetarian/Vegan Energy & Practical Considerations:
One of the biggest challenges of a plant-based diet in winter travel is caloric

efficiency. Fat provides 9 kcal per gram, while carbohydrates and protein only provide 4 kcal per gram. This means that if your diet relies mostly on carbs and protein, you'll need nearly twice the food weight and volume to match the same energy output as fat-based foods. On a multi-day winter trip, every ounce matters, and bulkier food means less room for other essentials.

Plant-based fats like chia, flax, olive oil, and nut butters seem like good solutions, but they don't always work well in freezing conditions. Oils solidify. Nut butters turn rock-hard. Seed and nut bars become frozen bricks that can be impossible to eat without warming them up first. These foods might be fine in camp, where you have time to heat them. On the move, however, frozen fats are nearly useless unless kept warm inside your clothing. Even high-calorie food bars freeze solid, making them difficult to eat unless pre-cut into small chunks or kept in an inside pocket to thaw.

Vegan and vegetarian diets can work for winter camping, but testing food in freezing conditions is essential. Some plant-based staples that seem great at home become completely inedible in the cold. To stay fueled in extreme cold, choosing calorie-dense, cold-resistant foods and planning for easy accessibility will make all the difference.

Keto and Low-Carb Considerations

Keto and low-carb diets rely on fat and protein for energy, but in high-exertion activities, they present unique challenges. Fat provides long-lasting fuel, while protein supports muscle repair, but neither breaks down as quickly as carbohydrates. This can lead to energy crashes if you need an immediate fuel source for intense activity, especially if you're not fully fat-adapted. Over time, fat adaptation can mitigate this issue. Those new to keto should plan for it.

Keto Challenges:
Reduced Glycogen Availability: Without carbohydrates, glycogen stores are low, which can lead to slower recovery after high-exertion activities like breaking trail, shoveling snow, or extended uphill climbs.
Cold Adaptation Issues: Some people on keto report feeling colder, as the body relies on fat metabolism instead of easily accessible carbohydrates for heat generation.
Lower Burst Energy: Quick, high-output activities (like sprinting or sudden exertion) rely on glycogen, which isn't readily available on keto, making it harder to sustain short bursts of high intensity.

Limited Food Options: Many standard camping meals (like oatmeal, freeze-dried meals, and energy bars) don't fit keto, requiring careful meal planning and custom food preparation.
Electrolyte Imbalance: On keto, sodium, potassium, and magnesium get depleted faster, increasing the risk of fatigue, muscle cramps, and headaches, which can be dangerous in extreme cold.
Digestion Issues in Cold: Some people struggle to digest high-fat foods in very cold conditions, as fat metabolism is slower than carbs, which can lead to stomach discomfort or low energy if the body isn't fully adapted.

Keto What Works Best:
Prioritize Easy-to-Digest Fats: Some fats digest more easily than others. MCT oil, coconut oil, and butter are faster-burning fat sources that provide quicker energy compared to hard cheeses, nuts, and heavy meats.
Use Protein for Recovery: While keto is high in fat, moderate protein intake is key for muscle recovery. Freeze-dried meats, jerky, and hard cheeses work well as compact, calorie-dense options.
Supplement Electrolytes: To prevent fatigue and muscle cramps, add extra salt to meals and consider carrying electrolyte tablets or bouillon cubes to replenish sodium and potassium.
Test Keto Adaptation Before Your Trip: If you aren't already fat-adapted, don't start keto in the middle of a winter expedition. Keto adaptation can take weeks, and low energy in extreme cold can be dangerous.
Use Keto for Base Effort, Not Sprints: Keto works well for steady, low-to-moderate exertion, like long snowshoeing days at a controlled pace. However, for short bursts of intense activity (climbing, running, escaping a bad situation), having some fast-burning carbs as backup (like a small amount of dried fruit or a gel) is smart.

Keto Key Considerations:
Keto campers may need to include small amounts of fast-digesting fuel, like dried fruit or nuts, to avoid bonking during high-exertion moments. While the body can generate glucose through gluconeogenesis, this process is slow and inefficient for immediate energy needs. Relying solely on lean protein won't sustain energy levels—fat remains the primary fuel source for endurance. However, fat metabolism takes time, which can be a disadvantage when sudden bursts of energy are needed, such as climbing a steep section,

breaking trail, or responding to an emergency.

Not all fat sources are practical in extreme cold. Coconut oil becomes a rock, and olive oil is difficult to consume directly without causing digestion issues. Ghee stays semi-soft longer, making it a better option, but it still requires a container that won't crack in freezing temperatures. Hard cheeses, nuts, and cured meats provide more accessible fat sources, though frozen cheese can become difficult to chew. Fat-based energy needs to be portable, easy to consume, and not require extra effort to prepare in the field.

Keto and low-carb diets can work for winter camping, but they require careful planning. It's essential to ensure energy needs are met without relying on impractical fat sources or foods that freeze solid. Unlike carbohydrates, which can be absorbed quickly, fat takes several hours to be broken down and converted into usable energy. If you need an immediate energy boost, fat alone won't help—you'll have to rely on stored reserves or a quick-burning fuel source.

Author's Note

One of my friend's sons attempted a one-day ascent of Mt. Whitney while following a keto diet. By the time he reached the top of the switchbacks on the main trail, he was stumbling, nearly vomiting, and on the verge of passing out from exhaustion. He had completely bonked. His legs barely worked, and the altitude only made things worse.

He had keto protein bars and ate them, hoping they'd give him a boost. But because fat and protein take hours to convert to usable energy, they did nothing to help him in the moment. His only real backup plan was descending, but he had pushed his body to the limit without fast-access energy. His climbing partner realized how serious the situation was and considered calling for help, but they hadn't planned for trouble—their cell phones had no signal, and there was no way to get outside assistance. Fortunately, his partner was able to help him descend before things got worse, but it was a serious lesson in how quickly energy depletion can turn into an emergency in the mountains.

I've also seen climbers on the Grand Teton rely solely on protein bars, refusing to bring fast-digesting carbs. Some run out of energy at the Lower Saddle, already exhausted before reaching the real technical sections. A few push on to the Upper Saddle (~13,200 feet / 4,023 m), where they face a junction—either committing to the technical, exposed route to the true summit or taking the less committing scramble to the Enclosure.

By the time these climbers reach the Upper Saddle, they're visibly shaking from exhaustion, realizing they don't have the energy to continue safely. If they stop to eat a protein bar hoping for a boost, it won't help them in time—by the time that bar starts providing meaningful energy, they'll already be back at the car.

At that point, thankfully, many turn back—if they didn't, they'd be risking a fatal fall on dangerous, exposed sections with 1,000 feet (300+ meters) or more of air below. Attempting those moves while shaking from exhaustion is an incredibly dangerous situation with no room for error.

Protein is not an immediate energy source, and relying on it alone can lead to critical energy crashes in high-exertion situations. In technical mountaineering, where exhaustion affects judgment and safety, having a fast-burning fuel source isn't just about reaching the summit—it's about making it back down safely.

Carnivore Considerations

A strict carnivore diet can work in winter camping, but it requires significant planning and food management. While shelf-stable options like pemmican, jerky, and hard cheeses provide portable protein and fat, cooking fresh meat in the winter in the field and on the move can be extremely difficult.

Carnivore Key Challenges:
Cooking logistics: A single-pot setup means melting snow for water first, and dealing with fat drips and cleanup can be a major hassle in freezing conditions.
Temperature fluctuations: Tent interiors can warm significantly during the day, causing bacon and butter to spoil, even in subzero environments.
Frozen meats: Raw meat freezes rock-hard overnight, making it tough to prepare without extended cooking time.
International travel restrictions: Many countries prohibit the import of meats, and local options may differ (e.g., bacon in Chile is different from American bacon).

Lack of quick energy: Carnivore lacks fast-burning fuel, making high-exertion activities like breaking trail more taxing.

Carnivore What Works Best:
Pemmican: Long shelf life, high-fat, high-protein, but should be stored in a sealed, cool container to prevent spoilage from heat fluctuations.
Freeze-dried or shelf-stable meats: Easier to manage than fresh meat.
Hard cheeses (if tolerated): More resistant to spoilage, but may freeze solid in extreme cold.
Rendered fats (tallow, lard, MCT oil): Energy-dense but tricky to store and use in fluctuating temperatures.

Carnivore Energy & Practical Considerations:
Carnivore provides steady energy for low-intensity activity, but both fat and protein take significantly longer to digest and convert into usable energy compared to carbohydrates. Carbs can be digested and used for energy within 30-60 minutes, while fat takes around 6-12 hours to become fully available. Protein can take 4-8+ hours to contribute meaningfully to energy through gluconeogenesis, a slow and inefficient process for immediate fuel needs. This means that if you need quick energy for physically demanding moments like climbing a steep section, breaking trail in deep snow, or reacting in an emergency, your body won't be able to deliver it as fast as a diet that includes some carbohydrates.

For moving expeditions, carnivore presents specific challenges with spoilage, cooking logistics, and border restrictions on meat products. Repeated thawing and refreezing of fatty meats can lead to rancidity or bacterial growth, even in cold weather. Hard cheeses and cured meats are more stable but can freeze solid, making them difficult to eat without warming. If you rely solely on carnivore, you'll need to account for food accessibility and cold resistance to ensure you can sustain energy throughout the trip.

Since high-output activities demand fast energy, it's worth considering a backup option for emergencies. Some carnivore dieters tolerate honey, which provides a quick, digestible energy boost when needed. Planning ahead for both steady endurance and higher exertion needs will help make this diet more functional in extreme conditions.

Testing Your Diet in a Freezer Technique

Regardless of diet, test your food choices ahead of time in a home freezer before heading into extreme cold. Foods that seem fine at room temperature may become impossible to eat after freezing all day in your pack. Keep in mind that home freezers are typically around 0°F (-18°C), while outdoor winter conditions can be much colder (-20°F to -40°F / -29°C to -40°C). Some foods that pass a home test may still freeze rock solid in extreme backcountry conditions.

A good test is to freeze your food for a few days, then try to eat it within five minutes after pulling it out. That's about how much time you'll have on a short break while traveling. If it's too hard to chew, takes too long to soften, or requires warming up first, it's not a good option for quick energy on the move.

Another issue to watch for is thawing and refreezing. During the day, sun exposure and body heat can partially thaw food, only for it to refreeze at night. This cycle increases the risk of food spoilage, especially for keto and carnivore diets, where high-fat and protein-rich foods can turn rancid or develop bacteria. Be mindful of how you store perishable items, and if something smells off or has a slimy texture, don't risk eating it. Freezing preserves food, but temperature fluctuations can ruin it.

Key Testing Steps:
- Freeze your intended meals and snacks overnight.
- Try eating them directly from the freezer without warming them up.
- Assess which foods are still practical and which need adjustments.
- Be mindful of thawing and refreezing cycles. Food that partially thaws during the day and refreezes at night can spoil, turn rancid, or develop bacteria, especially high-fat and protein-rich items like meat, cheese, and butter.

This simple test can prevent unpleasant surprises in the field and help refine your packing strategy, though nothing fully replaces real-world cold exposure.

Author's Note

> During my three-month solo expedition to the South Pole, which I wrote about in *Antarctic Tears*, I brought pre-cut salami. After a few weeks, I pulled it out to eat and noticed ice crystals inside the

package. I realized the meat had likely thawed and refrozen multiple times as my sled bag warmed in the sun on windless days. I decided not to eat it—and I was glad I didn't.

Explorer Vilborg Arna Gissurardóttir, who was traveling the same year as I did, brought a similar meat product with her. She didn't notice the ice crystals and ate it. She developed food poisoning and spent an entire day vomiting, a dangerous situation in an extreme environment.

Even meats like salami, which are considered shelf-stable, can spoil if they go through repeated thaw and refreeze cycles. Be aware of this risk, especially with high-fat and protein-rich foods, and store them carefully to avoid a potentially serious problem in the field.

Final Thoughts on Winter Food

Winter camping requires more energy than summer camping, and not all diets are easy to maintain in extreme cold. The best diet is the one that keeps you fueled, allows you to eat in freezing temperatures, and doesn't require impractical cooking methods in harsh conditions.

Test your food in the cold before your trip. Many home-friendly foods become rock-hard in freezing conditions. If possible, test them in real winter conditions, not just in a home freezer.

Consider energy balance. Fast-burning carbs provide quick energy, while fats burn slower but sustain warmth and endurance—both play a role in maintaining exertion levels.

Think about practical cooking limitations. If stopping to cook isn't an option, food choices need to be ready-to-eat or require minimal preparation.

With proper planning, most diets can be adapted for winter camping, but some require more effort than others.

Author's Note

This section is not an endorsement of any particular diet. I eat a wide variety of foods and have experimented with different dietary approaches in various conditions. My goal isn't to advocate for any specific way of eating, but to highlight practical considerations for winter camping, especially in extreme cold.

I have known people who have used all the diets mentioned here, and they have all faced specific challenges in winter environments.

Specialized Diets

Some solutions exist, but not every approach works the same for every person or every trip. There may be better strategies or new solutions that were not known at the time of publication. The best approach is to talk with your doctor or dietitian if you have specific dietary needs and, most importantly, test everything in real winter conditions before committing to a long expedition.

For those following a medically necessary or religious diet, it's important to seriously consider the demands of winter expeditions before heading into extreme conditions. Long expedition winter camping trips don't leave much room for trial and error, and strict dietary restrictions can quickly become a survival risk if things don't go as planned. While some people swear by their chosen diet, others adjust their eating to match the physical demands of extreme conditions.

Outside of the U.S., many outdoor enthusiasts seem to take a more flexible or traditional approach to nutrition, focusing on a mix of whole foods rather than strict dietary regimens for performance. That doesn't mean a particular diet won't work, but in the face of a dangerous situation, your life and the safety of your teammates matter most. If dietary adherence is absolute, strongly consider what you will truly do in an emergency or when you need to push beyond your limits. Be very honest with yourself and your choices before you are in a dangerous situation.

Diets are a highly personal topic. People feel strongly about their choices. My goal isn't to debate what's right or wrong but to encourage realistic assessment of whether a diet will keep you warm, fueled, and functioning in the harshest environments. When conditions turn unforgiving, adaptability is often the key to staying safe and making it home.

Short test trips will reveal potential food issues before they become serious problems on an extended winter journey. Being adaptable in the field can mean the difference between a successful trip and a dangerous situation.

Chapter 24
Shopping and Packaging Food

Buying and packing food for winter camping requires careful planning to ensure you have enough calories, the right foods for cold conditions, and efficient packaging for transport. In extreme cold, food choices matter—high-calorie, dense foods help maintain body heat, while poorly chosen foods can freeze solid or become difficult to prepare. Packaging is equally important; bulky containers waste space, excess trash adds unnecessary weight, and fragile packaging can tear in a pack or become brittle in the cold.

Choosing lightweight, durable, and compact packaging makes a huge difference in efficiency, especially for multi-day trips. Thoughtful meal planning also reduces waste, streamlines cooking, and ensures you can eat easily in freezing temperatures without unnecessary hassle.

Buying the Right Foods

For long expeditions, it's best to shop several weeks in advance to ensure you get everything you need. However, for a short overnight trip, a quick shopping run is usually enough. The key is choosing high-calorie, cold-weather-friendly foods that won't become impossible to eat in freezing temperatures.

Prioritize calorie-dense foods: Nuts, cheese, jerky, chocolate, and high-fat energy bars offer sustained energy.

Check calorie count per ounce: Some diet or protein bars are filling but low in fat, making them less energy-dense and unsuitable for high exertion in winter.

Choose foods that handle freezing well: Hard cheeses, chocolate, and cured meats remain edible even in subzero temperatures.

Avoid foods that freeze into rock-hard blocks: Nut butters, fresh fruit, soft bread, and some energy bars can become inedible unless pre-portioned or

kept warm. Denser breads like bagels or tortillas handle freezing better and remain chewable when warmed in a jacket or sleeping bag.
Bring 10% more food than expected: This provides a buffer in case of delays or increased exertion without overloading your pack.

Repackaging for Efficiency

Once you have your food, repackaging helps reduce bulk, prevent freezing issues, and make meals easier to access in the cold.
Remove unnecessary packaging: Store-bought foods often come in bulky boxes or wrappers that take up space.
Use vacuum-sealed bags for high-risk trips: These protect against moisture and punctures, which is critical in extreme environments. However, vacuum-sealed food can be stiff and difficult to open when frozen, so plan for accessibility.
Balance security vs. weight: Vacuum-sealed bags are durable but heavier than Ziploc-style bags. For most trips, using double-layered Ziplocs for low-risk foods and vacuum-sealing only critical items is a good compromise.
Portion food into single servings: This makes meals and snacks easier to grab without unnecessary handling in freezing conditions.
Label everything: Include cooking instructions and calorie counts for quick reference in camp.
Use insulated storage: Prevents certain foods from freezing too quickly or keeps them at usable temperatures longer. Be aware that insulated storage also adds weight and bulk which present their own set of challenges.

Author's Note

I had a food bag failure on a Greenland tundra expedition, where I only lost a small amount of food, but it could have been much worse. I've read stories about northern Alaskan expeditions where bags failed and entire food supplies were compromised, resulting in the loss of tens of thousands of calories—more than a week's worth of food. The group returned much thinner than when they left, and in one case, a missing bag led to severe malnutrition and exhaustion, forcing the climbers to cut their trip short.

It's a reminder that even minor failures in food storage can have catastrophic consequences in the field. Having a backup plan for food protection is essential when you're relying on it for survival.

International Travel Considerations

If traveling internationally, check food import laws before packing. Many countries restrict fresh meat, dairy, and certain packaged foods, so you may need to purchase perishables locally.

Customs laws vary: Some allow sealed, commercially packaged foods, while others ban them entirely. Processed options like canned fish or freeze-dried meats may be accepted where fresh versions are not.

Plan for local sourcing: If bringing food isn't an option, research where to buy suitable items at your destination.

Check restrictions on meat, dairy, and processed foods: Bacon, jerky, and cheese are common items that may not be allowed.

For domestic trips, repackaging food for space, weight, and accessibility is the best approach. For international trips, research import laws to avoid losing food at customs and adjust your packing strategy accordingly.

Shopping for 70 pounds (32kg) of butter for a three month expedition.

Part 4
Terrain and Environmental Considerations

Winter camping isn't just about staying warm—it's about understanding and working with the landscape to move efficiently and camp safely. Snow, ice, wind, and extreme temperatures shape every decision, from where you set up camp to how you navigate the terrain. When you learn to read the environment, you can use it to your advantage—setting up a wind-protected camp, using firm snow for easy travel, or taking advantage of frozen lakes and rivers as natural highways. But a miscalculation can turn an otherwise manageable trip into a dangerous situation. Choosing the wrong spot for a tent can leave you exposed to avalanches, collapsing snow bridges, or high winds that will rip your shelter apart. Understanding how snow and ice behave underfoot can mean the difference between an efficient trek and exhausting postholing through deep drifts.

The environment itself is a constant challenge, but also an incredible part of the experience. High-altitude winter travel offers stunning, wide-open views and crisp, clear air, while frozen lakes and rivers can provide smooth, fast travel if you know how to assess the ice safely. Even something as simple as a clear, calm day can be deceptive—cold sinks into valleys at night, and an open area with no wind protection can leave you dangerously exposed. But with the right knowledge and preparation, you can turn these conditions to your advantage, making your winter trip smoother and more enjoyable.

This section breaks down the key environmental factors you'll face—from snow types and avalanche risk to navigating ice and handling extreme weather. By learning how to read the terrain and adapt to changing conditions, you'll make better decisions, stay safer, and move through the winter landscape with confidence. Mastering these skills not only keeps you out of trouble, but also allows you to fully appreciate the unique beauty and freedom that winter travel offers.

Chapter 25
Navigating Winter Terrain

Understanding Winter Terrain

When heading into the wilderness for winter camping, there are plenty of terrain options—forests, mountains, large open fields, or even polar regions. Each has its advantages and disadvantages, but the number one challenge is always the weather. Even with modern forecasting, winter conditions can change instantly, and that's just the nature of it.

Below is a breakdown of different terrains and what to consider when selecting your first or fiftieth winter camping spot:

Forests: The biggest advantage of forest winter camping is the natural windbreak, available firewood, and insulation from trees. One of the unsung benefits of trees is that they radiate infrared energy, making the area around them several degrees warmer than open spaces. Camping 100 feet (30 meters) deeper into a forest instead of an open meadow can make a big difference in temperature.

Valleys: Valleys offer natural shelter and often have access to water since creeks and rivers tend to run through them. However, temperature inversions can create a surprising difference of 5–15°F (2–8°C) between the valley floor and the slopes above. Cold air settles in valleys, pushing warmer air out and displacing it to higher elevations. Additionally, winter flooding can be a risk. Ice dams can form on creeks, unexpectedly causing water to rise or break through.

Mountains: Mountains are naturally appealing for their views and remoteness, but they come with hazards. Avalanche risk increases significantly on slopes between 30–45 degrees. There are also crevasses on glaciers, steep drop-offs, and deep snow accumulation. While forests and valleys usually experience

a more predictable snowfall and melt cycle, mountains can generate rapid and extreme weather changes. Heavy snowfall of three feet (one meter) or more overnight is possible, increasing the risk of entrapment or exposure.
Large Open Fields: Wide, open spaces provide easier navigation since landmarks like hills or mountains are often visible. However, exposure to wind can be severe, and there is little to no natural shelter. Wind chill becomes a major factor, increasing heat loss and the risk of frostbite.
Polar Travel: The most extreme terrain, polar travel allows camping anywhere with an unlimited supply of snow for water. There's typically no concern for contamination unless traveling over the Arctic Ocean, where sea ice may contain salt and other impurities. However, there are hidden crevasses, brutal weather, and extreme logistical challenges. Traveling in these areas requires careful planning and higher costs.

Navigating in Winter Terrain

When planning a route, your number one tool should be a topographical map. It helps you assess terrain steepness and identify avalanche hazards or unstable snow conditions.

In mountainous regions with relatively shallow slopes, you have more flexibility. But once slopes exceed 30 degrees, the risk of avalanches rises significantly, with the highest risk occurring between 30–45 degrees. Snow can become unstable, either sliding onto you or breaking away as you cross. Avalanche terrain is one of the biggest dangers because conditions can change without warning.

Avalanche forecasting services track recent and long-term weather patterns, snowpack stability, and risk factors. Learning to read an avalanche forecast is critical if you're traveling in high-risk areas.

Another challenge is that snow can conceal hazards. You might unknowingly be crossing over a creek, thin ice, or a hidden snow bridge covering a gap or crevasse. If that bridge collapses, you could drop through unexpectedly. Overhead hazards are also a concern—trees can fall, and high winds can make conditions worse. Even established roads, like those in Yellowstone, can become impassable due to drifting snow and ice.

When climbing or descending, consider whether you need crampons, ice axes, or avalanche safety gear. The steeper the terrain, the more technical your equipment must be. Snowshoes aren't always ideal for steep slopes—sometimes, switching to crampons and ice axes is necessary. Some travelers use skis or snowshoes for the approach, then switch to ropes and crampons for steeper climbs.

The most critical skill in winter travel is assessing snow stability. A basic or advanced avalanche course teaches you how to identify shear layers, weak points, and overall snowpack risks. These courses range from single-day intros to multi-day advanced training, depending on how deep you want to go.

In winter travel, making the tough call to turn around when conditions are unsafe can save your life. The more informed and prepared you are, the safer and more confident you'll be in the backcountry—especially in the mountains.

Snow and Ice Travel Techniques

Knowing which tools and methods to use for traveling on snow and ice can make all the difference. Choosing the right gear improves efficiency and safety.

On snow, it's rare to travel without some kind of traction aid. Even on well-packed trails, snow can be slippery. Microspikes or light-duty crampons help prevent slipping. Microspikes provide decent grip and have less risk of causing stumbles but don't offer as much traction as crampons. Light-duty aluminum crampons provide more stability but can snag on snow, increasing the risk of tripping.

If the snow is deep, microspikes and crampons won't be enough unless you want to posthole your way through—an exhausting workout. Snowshoes are the next step up, allowing easier movement through deep snow. They fit almost any boot and come in a variety of styles, from aluminum rail types to traditional wood-frame models. However, without a heel lifter, climbing steep slopes is difficult. Snowshoes also perform poorly on sidehills, twisting your feet into awkward angles, which can lead to fatigue or injury.

Skis allow for efficient long-distance travel but require a bigger investment in gear and skill. Cross-country skis work best on relatively flat terrain. They're cheaper and require less technical ability. Backcountry skis are wider, handle deep snow better, and can be fitted with skins for uphill travel or pulling a heavy sled. Regular cross-country skis have built-in traction patterns but struggle on steep terrain. If you're hauling a sled, track skis can be frustrating since each step requires extra effort to maintain grip.

On steep or glaciated terrain, skis and snowshoes become impractical. This is where crampons and rope techniques come into play. Proper rope spacing and snow anchors are critical for safety. Rope travel provides a safety net if someone falls into a crevasse, allowing teammates to arrest the fall and attempt a rescue. However, rope travel has risks—if the fallen climber accelerates too quickly, an unprepared partner can be pulled in as well.

A two-person rope team presents significant challenges. If one person falls through a weak snow bridge, the other must react instantly to stop them. If they don't, both could be pulled in. Ideally, three or more people should be on a rope team for better stability. There have been real cases where a single person fell into a crevasse and dragged their partner in with them.

Rope travel also requires climbing gear, harnesses, and proper tie-in techniques, which add complexity. While rope travel is essential in some conditions, it's not always the best choice. Evaluating the terrain, team skill level, and proper tools is key to safe winter travel.

Crossing Frozen Lakes and Rivers

There's a huge advantage to traveling across frozen lakes and rivers in winter—you can bypass routes that would normally take hours or even a full day to detour around. Frozen waterways allow for direct travel, cutting substantial distance off your route.

However, crossing ice comes with significant risks. Ice thickness isn't always consistent, so you need to constantly evaluate conditions. This is especially true in thermally active areas, where weak points can form. On large lakes, strong winds can force the ice to break apart unexpectedly, creating a dangerous situation.

Always test the ice thickness as you go. Use an ice auger, chisel, or drill to measure depth, and tap the surface with trekking poles to check for cracks or hollow sounds. If you notice thinning ice, stop immediately and reassess.

Frozen rivers are even more dangerous. Ice tends to build up along shorelines but can be significantly thinner in the middle, where the current runs strongest. Areas near underwater springs, fast-moving sections, and confluences can also have weakened ice, even along the edges. A river crossing may appear solid at first, but stepping onto weaker ice in the center or near these areas can lead to an unexpected breakthrough.

The biggest danger of falling through river ice is being swept under by the current. If the ice remains unbroken downstream, getting back to the surface may be impossible. Even in a lake or slow-moving creek, self-rescue is extremely difficult. Ice near the break may continue to crumble as you try to pull yourself up, and if the water is deep, you may have no solid ground to push against. A heavy backpack or sled makes escape even harder.

Cold shock and hypothermia set in fast. The gasp reflex caused by cold shock can lead to drowning within seconds. Hypothermia develops more gradually, typically over 10–30 minutes, depending on water temperature. If crossing ice is necessary, distribute your weight by using skis or lying prone if needed. Knowing how to self-rescue and assist others is critical. Never run straight toward someone who's fallen through—stay at a distance and spread the load. If you fall through too, you'll be in just as much trouble.

Winter Map Reading

One of the biggest challenges of winter travel is simply reading the map. Terrain features that are easy to see in summer—ridges, mountain valleys, and rivers—can be completely hidden under snow. Overcast skies, snowfall, or flat light can make visibility so poor that even if mountains are nearby, the landscape may appear featureless due to low contrast. Flat light occurs when the sky and ground blend together, making it difficult to see surface features and depth changes. This is especially common in polar and high-altitude environments.

Sometimes, you need deductive reasoning to figure out your route, especially when trails become obscured or completely invisible. In flat terrain like open plains or northern tundra, there may be few or no landmarks, making navigation tools like compasses and GPS devices essential. This is even more critical in winter, since many land features that help with summer navigation are buried.

When identifying terrain features, confirm with others in your group to ensure your interpretation matches the map. Using contour lines to estimate elevation and distance is more difficult in winter because travel speed is naturally slower. Deep snow, rough terrain, and extra gear weight can slow movement by 50% or more, and in extreme conditions, up to 80%.

When reading a topo map, note that closely spaced contour lines indicate steep terrain, which also increases avalanche risk. Slopes between 30–45 degrees are the most prone to avalanches, but concave slopes and wind-loaded areas are also high-risk zones. Some trails cut along steep hillsides may still be passable, but they can hide dangerous washouts buried under snow. Snow can also conceal trail edges, and stepping onto a weak patch could cause a sudden slide.

Cornices—overhanging snow formations along ridges—are another hidden hazard. They can collapse underfoot without warning, leading to a sudden and unexpected fall. If you're following a narrow ridge or traversing steep terrain, always be aware of snow breakaways that could send you sliding.

Identifying these hidden hazards early can mean the difference between a safe journey and serious trouble.

Compass in Winter

Using a compass in winter travel is especially valuable because cold conditions drain GPS batteries fast. Gloves make touchscreens difficult to use, and in extreme cold, electronics can fail. A compass has no batteries, no software, and works anywhere on Earth.

Make sure you get a global compass if you travel across hemispheres, but also check that your compass has an adjustable declination feature. Magnetic declination varies depending on location, and if your compass doesn't allow for adjustment, you'll have to manually calculate it every time.

When traveling in snow, trails often become obscured or completely invisible, making navigation a challenge. You'll rely more on off-trail navigation. Using visible landmarks and triangulation, you can confirm your position and stay on course.

In wide-open terrain, it's also possible to navigate using sun shadows and snow formations. The sun moves in a predictable arc, so shadows can serve as a reference throughout the day. Wind-sculpted snow formations (sastrugi) are more reliable than wind direction itself since they indicate prevailing wind patterns over time, rather than shifting day-to-day conditions.

For long-distance travel in open terrain, a chest-mounted compass is a great option. Instead of pulling out a handheld compass, you can check it at a glance while skiing or snowshoeing without stopping. This saves time and keeps you moving efficiently in harsh conditions.

Compasses can develop air bubbles inside their liquid-filled housing due to altitude changes or rapid pressure fluctuations, which often occur at high elevations. These bubbles can interfere with the compass's accuracy, making it difficult to get a precise reading. While some bubbles may dissipate once the pressure stabilizes, others can become permanent, especially after prolonged exposure to altitude or extreme conditions. In these cases, shaking or tapping the compass won't help, and the accuracy may remain compromised. Additionally, some compasses, including those designed to work globally, can suffer from sticky needles. This issue, where the needle drags or sticks against the housing, can occur even in models that are supposed to perform well in all conditions. This is particularly noticeable in cold environments, like Greenland, where both bubbles and needle drag can disrupt navigation. Once these issues arise, there is no easy fix, and it's important to be aware that certain compasses may be prone to these issues at high altitudes or in cold conditions.

Author's Note

I've experienced compasses developing bubbles due to extreme altitude fluctuations, and unfortunately, these bubbles never seem to disappear, even after descending to sea level. This issue has occurred with compasses from different manufacturers.

Global compasses are excellent for high-latitude or southern hemisphere travel, but some manufacturers have altered their designs over time, seemingly to cut costs. As a result, the needles can become sticky in the cold, developing a heading error of up to 30°. I encountered this problem during my Greenland icecap crossing—both Terry and I faced it. It's detailed in my book *Two Friends and a Polar Bear*. What works perfectly at home can become a real challenge in the field, even with compasses that are specifically designed for these conditions.

GPS Navigation

Choosing a GPS for navigation can be a challenge because there are so many on the market. Handling your GPS with gloves is tricky, and taking them off risks exposing your hands to the cold and even frostbite. Granted, you might not use your GPS for long, but in winter conditions, even short exposures can be dangerous. A GPS with glove-friendly buttons and long battery life is usually a better choice.

It's tempting to rely on a touchscreen smartphone, but in the cold, batteries drain quickly, and touchscreens can stop responding due to reduced electrical conductivity. Many gloves claim to have touchscreen capabilities, but they don't always work reliably, especially when wet. If gloves or screens become wet or frozen, they may fail completely.

Some GPS units offer a button interface, while others connect to your phone via Bluetooth. In winter conditions, the bigger the screen, the better—even though a larger screen adds a few ounces (56–85 grams), the improved usability is worth it.

One of the more ideal GPS devices today connects to the Iridium satellite network, allowing two-way communication—like the Garmin inReach Explorer+. The Spot device only allows one-way check-ins and emergency messages, which limits communication if conditions change.

Some GPS devices include built-in topographic maps, while others require an aftermarket purchase. If possible, choose a model with built-in maps to avoid extra hassle. Many modern GPS units use internal rechargeable lithium-ion batteries, which perform better in extreme cold than older AA-powered models. If your GPS does use replaceable batteries, always choose lithium AAs and carry spares—they last far longer in the cold. Alkaline batteries fail in subzero conditions (below -18°C). Nickel-metal hydride (NiMH) batteries lose charge quickly in cold storage but work well if kept warm before use.

Before you depart, set your waypoints, load offline maps, and use a compass—relying on the GPS only for quick check-ins so you can follow your trail. Keeping a GPS running for eight or nine hours straight is difficult and may drain the battery in a single day.

As GPS technology evolves, consider that your current device might be tougher to use in the future. Even basic GPS units from a decade ago still work, though they lack modern features. While they can be expensive, the temptation to rely on a smartphone for navigation in winter comes with risks—battery life and touchscreen issues make them far less reliable than a dedicated GPS unit.

Whiteout Navigation

One of the most challenging aspects of winter travel is navigating in a complete whiteout. When you're camping or traveling in a wide-open space with overcast skies and dense fog, it can be impossible to see the sun or any landscape features. Whether you're in a large open field, a polar plateau, or a treeless plain, the disorientation can be extreme. It often feels like you're floating in a pool of milk with scuba gear on—completely detached from the world around you. The loss of spatial awareness can cause proprioceptive disorientation, where your brain struggles to determine up from down, making you feel unsteady or even causing you to fall.

The best technique for navigating in a whiteout is using a chest-mounted compass. This method, called micro-navigation, involves small, continuous course adjustments when there are no visible landmarks or clear wind direction. Without a fixed reference point, it's easy to walk in circles or corkscrew since most people favor one leg over the other.

Instead of stopping every few steps, keep moving while glancing at your compass every 15 seconds to correct your course. Keep your head level and use only your eyes to look down, briefly glancing below the edge of your glacier glasses. This is easier with glasses than goggles, as goggles often restrict downward vision. If you drop your chin, you can lose spatial awareness and balance, compounding the disorienting effect of a whiteout.

A key technique to reduce disorientation is keeping the tips of your skis in your lower peripheral vision. This helps maintain proprioceptive feedback and prevents the tilting sensation that occurs when looking straight into the featureless void. Without a reference point in your field of view, you can tilt wildly as though you're intoxicated, even falling over without realizing it until you hit the snow or ice. Keeping ski tips or even trekking poles in sight gives your brain an anchor, allowing you to balance more effectively.

The key is to make small course corrections while still in motion, rather than stopping to adjust. This creates a slight snaking pattern instead of a perfectly straight line, but it's far more efficient than repeatedly stopping and restarting. While intuitively it feels like stopping would improve accuracy, it actually wastes energy and momentum—especially when pulling a sled or skiing. Restarting after every adjustment requires extra effort, making the overall journey harder. It's much easier to maintain forward movement and continuously adjust as you go, even if it means sacrificing a perfectly straight path.

Wind can also be a useful secondary reference, particularly in gentle, steady conditions where you can feel subtle shifts. However, a tailwind is much less helpful for sensing directional change, since it moves with you rather than against you. Wind should be used as a reinforcement rather than a primary navigation method, as it isn't always accurate and can shift unpredictably.

Counting is key to staying on course. In whiteout conditions, you mentally count to 15, then glance down at your compass to verify your heading before looking back up. A 60-second count is too long, as it allows too much drift before correction. The robotic nature of counting and correcting can help keep you focused, pulling your mind away from the ethereal experience of whiteout navigation—where the endless, featureless landscape can make you feel detached from reality. Instead of fixating on the void, the repetition of count, glance, correct, repeat becomes a rhythmic process, grounding you in movement and keeping you from getting lost in the overwhelming nothingness.

If traveling with a partner, they can provide feedback when you're off course, but constant corrections from others can become distracting or frustrating. The mental load of continuously navigating blank terrain—effectively blind to the landscape—is exhausting. Many people experience mental exhaustion and decision fatigue, leading to errors or even the urge to sit down and stop moving. Travel speed can drop by 30 to 70 percent, depending on experience and conditions. The more you practice micro-navigation, the less your efficiency suffers, whether you're skiing or snowshoeing.

If you're traveling short distances or under extreme pressure, it's sometimes better to stop and wait out poor conditions. Some routes and guides recommend waiting until visibility improves to avoid accidentally walking into a crevasse or off a cliff. If conditions force you to continue, micro-navigation is the best way to stay on course.

Whiteouts tend to be worse in the afternoon as rising temperatures increase fog or cloud cover, though this varies by region. However, on the Greenland icecap, the exact opposite can occur—whiteouts in the morning that clear up by late morning as the sun burns off the clouds. In these situations, experience with local conditions is crucial for making safe travel decisions.

Assign navigation duties to whoever is most mentally stable and capable of handling the stress. People unfamiliar with this type of navigation often struggle, becoming irritable or losing focus under pressure.

Short vs. Long-Distance Navigation

The tools and techniques you use depend on whether you're navigating short or long distances.

In a dense forest, constant route adjustments are necessary to avoid trees, rough terrain, and natural obstacles. The trick is to balance left and right adjustments to stay on course. A compass works best for this because you can make continuous heading corrections. A GPS is less useful in dense forests since it shows your position but not your real-time course adjustments. Under a cloudy sky, without a compass, it's easy to drift off course or travel in circles.

For short-distance navigation to a known camp or landmark, the offset method helps. Instead of aiming directly at your target, travel 5 to 10 degrees left or right of it if there's a linear feature like a road or river nearby. That way, if you hit a barrier, you'll know which direction to adjust. If you aim straight at your destination and end up slightly off, you won't know which way to turn. GPS can correct for this, but if it fails, the offset method provides a reliable backup.

For long-distance travel, keeping a steady heading is critical. One technique is to take a sighting on the farthest visible object—a hill, rock formation, or even a distinctive tree. Check your compass for alignment, then lock onto the target and drop your compass without looking away. Keeping your eyes fixed on a distant landmark prevents drift, especially in winter, where everything can look the same.

Chest-mounted compasses allow for quick course corrections, but for long distances, the "sight and go" method is more effective. Find a distant object, sight it with your compass, then travel toward it without looking down again. In whiteout conditions where distant landmarks aren't visible, this method isn't as effective—short-range sighting, picking features 50–100 feet away (15–30m), is better.

Travel as far as possible during the day using your compass, then check and correct your position with GPS at night in your tent. This reduces GPS battery drain while keeping navigation efficient. Keeping the GPS warm inside a jacket or insulated pouch helps extend battery life. Many winter travelers use external battery packs with insulated cords to recharge their GPS in emergencies.

Running a GPS all day isn't practical. Cold temperatures drain batteries, and screens can be difficult to use while traveling. Instead, take a bearing to your next waypoint, then use terrain features to guide you. The key is balancing precision with speed.

Here are some considerations of different navigation tools:
- How accurate do you need to be?
- How fast can you travel while maintaining course?
- What's your margin for error?
- Can you adjust your route based on available terrain features?
- How long can you rely on your GPS before needing to recharge?

If you move too quickly and end up a mile (1.6 km) off course, you'll waste time correcting it. Slowing down and making more frequent course corrections may be the better approach, depending on terrain and conditions.

The climb up Motorcycle Hill on Denali seems steep. That is, until your team reaches the saddle and starts up the even steeper Squirrel Hill toward Windy Corner.

Chapter 26
Dealing with Altitude

Dealing with Altitude

When heading out on a winter camping trip, unless you're in a far northern location with snow at low elevations, you'll likely be in the mountains. One of the dangers of mountain travel is altitude sickness. There's no way to predict who will get it, who won't, or when it will strike, but common risk patterns exist.

Altitude sickness happens due to reduced oxygen at higher elevations. It can cause acute mountain sickness (AMS) and, in more severe cases, high-altitude pulmonary edema (HAPE) or high-altitude cerebral edema (HACE). Mild AMS symptoms include dizziness, nausea, and persistent fatigue. More severe symptoms include shortness of breath, confusion, and fluid buildup in the lungs or brain. If that happens, the only solution is to descend at least 1,000 to 2,000 feet (300 to 600 meters) as quickly as possible. Symptoms usually improve with descent. If they don't, seek medical help immediately.

Altitude sickness can occur as low as 5,000 feet (1,500 meters) but is more common above 8,000 feet (2,400 meters). The best way to prevent it is to limit altitude gain to 1,000 feet (300 meters) per day above 8,000 feet (2,400m). You can climb higher during the day, but it's critical to descend lower to sleep. Stay well-hydrated—your urine should be light-colored. Avoid alcohol, as it worsens symptoms, and eat plenty of high-carb meals to keep your body fueled.

Some people take acetazolamide (Diamox) to help acclimate. Others use aspirin or Viagra, though their effectiveness varies. Dexamethasone is an emergency treatment, not something to take while ascending—it's a last resort if symptoms become severe.

If you start experiencing mild symptoms, rest, hydrate, and descend if needed. If you develop a severe headache or a wet cough, descend immediately. Bad weather can make evacuation difficult, so always have an escape plan and check forecasts. In extreme cases, supplemental oxygen may help, but it's usually used under medical supervision.

Acclimating to High Altitude

The best way to prevent or reduce altitude sickness is to climb high and sleep low, scheduling acclimatization days to give your body time to adjust. Some assume that if they live at high altitude—like in Colorado or certain areas of Europe—they can fly somewhere and immediately start ascending. The problem is that acclimatization fades over time. If you descend for too long, your body loses its adaptation, and you'll have to start the process over.

Spending time at intermediate elevations helps ease the adjustment. The higher you go, the lower the oxygen pressure, which increases fatigue and physical strain. It's not always easy to tell if you have AMS. Being in good shape helps, but even elite athletes can be caught off guard by altitude sickness.

Hydration is one of the most critical factors in acclimatization. Dehydration can worsen AMS symptoms and increase fatigue. Drink enough fluids so your urine stays light-colored. Avoid alcohol, as it interferes with acclimatization and worsens symptoms. Eating plenty of high-carb meals also helps by keeping energy levels up.

Controlled breathing and pacing techniques can also make a difference.

One method is pressure breathing:
- Take a deep breath into your belly, expanding your stomach.
- Purse your lips like you're blowing out a candle and exhale forcefully.

This helps remove carbon dioxide, signaling your body to take in more oxygen. It works, but it takes practice and can make you lightheaded if you're not used to it.

Altitude affects everyone differently, so staying aware of your body's signals is key. Adjust your pace, focus on hydration, and give yourself time to adapt.

Balancing Activity and Safety

It's difficult to balance the desire to climb higher and push farther with the limits of the human body. People see grand adventures—trekking up Everest looks like a challenge but not an insurmountable one. What they don't see is the 4 to 6 weeks required just to acclimate at base camp, which sits at around 17,600 feet (5,364 meters) on the Nepal side. That's the key to avoiding AMS, HACE, and HAPE—pacing yourself, avoiding overexertion, and recognizing early signs of fatigue before they become serious.

If you suddenly notice your coordination slipping, you're stumbling, or you're struggling to eat, those are warning signs that altitude is affecting you. You need to make adjustments. The higher you climb, the harder it is to eat because digestion requires oxygen. Fat is a great fuel for cold-weather trekking, but at high altitude, it takes far more oxygen to break down than carbohydrates or protein. The higher you go, the harder it gets to process fats, then proteins, until you're mostly relying on simple carbohydrates.

Even though modern diets discourage high-carb intake, at altitude, carbs are the easiest fuel for your body to use. There's no way around it. Also, maintaining electrolyte balance is critical to avoid hyponatremia, which can occur when excessive urination leads to sodium loss without proper replacement. Rehydration salts or something like Pedialyte (or a generic version) can help.

Stay warm and manage sweat levels to prevent overloading your system. Plan rest stops in sheltered areas if possible to conserve energy and warmth. Some people can climb much faster than others, but you only discover your pace through experience. Training by climbing 1,000 feet (300 meters) at mid-elevation helps, but it won't fully prepare you for high-altitude conditions until you experience them firsthand.

Fitness Requirements

Another factor that affects acclimatization is fitness level. Simply put, the fitter you are, the better your body handles stress under load. If you've spent time running, climbing, hiking, biking, rowing, towing a tire, or training in any endurance sport, your body is likely better prepared. That said, fitness doesn't make you immune to altitude sickness. Some people, no matter how strong, just have to climb slower. And that's okay. In some cases, highly fit people may even be at higher risk of AMS because they push too hard and ignore symptoms.

It's hard to accept that sometimes our bodies aren't as adaptable as we'd like them to be. If you see someone pushing on despite clear signs of distress, they may not even realize there's a problem. Poor coordination or brushing off symptoms can be early signs of AMS. Normally, you wouldn't intervene, but sometimes it's worth asking, "Hey, are you okay?" Some people are touchy about it, so you have to be careful how you say it. At the same time, ignoring it completely could lead to a rescue situation, risking your summit bid, your team's safety, and their health.

Author's Note

One time on Denali, I was resting at the pass before heading around Windy Corner. A team of climbers came up, led by a woman who was clearly struggling. She was stumbling left and right as though she'd been drinking, but she brushed it off, saying she just needed a snack and some water. She looked pale and weak—classic altitude sickness symptoms. She hadn't vomited, but she was visibly in bad shape.

She was with a large team, so I didn't involve myself further, but I asked, "Hey, are you okay? Do you need any help?" She dismissed it quickly. I later found out she was leading a disabled climbing team and may have felt pressured to push on. I'm not sure if they made the summit or how she fared, but sometimes just speaking up is the best you can do.

That said, you have to be careful speaking up to people in the mountains. You don't always know the full situation, and egos can be at stake. Asking if someone is okay is one thing, but pushing too hard or making accusations can turn a bad situation worse. If a team feels insulted, they may get defensive, and the last thing you want is to create tension—especially if you later find yourself in trouble and need their help. It's a delicate balance, but at the very least, a simple "Is everyone doing alright?" can sometimes make a difference.

Flying to base camp in Alaska is an adventure in itself. As soon as you step off the plane, you'll feel the altitude as you struggle to drag your gear away from the landing strip.

Chapter 27
Reducing Impact

Leave No Trace Camping

One of the surprising advantages of winter camping is that it's often easier to follow Leave No Trace principles. Packing out waste, minimizing camp impact, and respecting natural features are all part of this ethic. In warmer seasons, moving through the environment leaves a more lasting impact. But with snow cover, your presence has far less effect—if you handle things correctly. A key part of this is packing out your own waste, including toilet products.

Understandably, this can seem unpleasant, but in many areas—like Mount Whitney—pack-out is required. Some locations even provide wag bags for containment. In winter, the ground is often frozen, making burial impossible. If waste is left behind, animals will dig it up and scatter it, creating a mess for others. The Leave No Trace principle follows the old saying:

"Take nothing but photographs, leave nothing but footprints."

The idea is simple—the more people who visit, the heavier the impact. Land managers struggle with balancing public access and environmental protection. The deeper implications of this are beyond the scope of this book, but the best mindset is to leave no evidence you were ever there. Snow provides a temporary, durable surface that protects fragile ecosystems beneath.

When snow is deep enough, traveling on it has minimal impact compared to camping directly on the ground, where you could crush plants or damage delicate environments. However, compacted snow from heavily used routes or campsites can accelerate melting and expose vegetation, so it's important to be mindful of where you set up. The goal isn't to stay home—it's to be conscious of your impact. That way, the next time you return, the land looks just as beautiful and rugged as before.

Water Management

One of the biggest challenges with human waste in winter is that it freezes quickly, making standard disposal methods ineffective. The usual practice is to dig a cat hole at least six inches (15 cm) deep, bury waste, and cover it. But in winter, with several feet (a meter or more) of snow, this becomes impossible. The temptation is to dig a small hole and let the snow cover it. That may seem contained, but animals are curious—even if it grosses us out, they will dig it others. The bigger issue is toilet paper waste. Ideally, you should haul it out or burn it if it's legal in your area. Carrying used toilet paper isn't pleasant, but it's far better than returning in spring to find waste scattered everywhere.

Food waste is another problem. The goal is to leave no food scraps behind and pack out all trash. One efficient way is reusing food packaging—using the same resealable plastic bags that held your food to contain your garbage. This way, you don't need extra trash containers, and everything stays sealed. Never burn plastics—they release toxic fumes, harm the environment, and leave a mess when the snow melts.

When camping, stay at least 100 feet (30 meters) from any water source, including streams, rivers, and lakes. This helps prevent contamination. Gray water—the rinse water from food containers—should never be dumped near water sources. Even if the water is frozen, food residue left behind will contaminate it when everything melts in spring. The best practice is to dispose of gray water far from water sources, where bacteria and the natural environment can break it down. That said, don't leave large amounts of food waste. A small amount of rinse water is manageable, but anything more should be packed out.

Traveling Camp Practices

When selecting your route, stick to established paths or durable snow surfaces to avoid damaging vegetation. When the snowpack is deep, you can travel almost anywhere since the snow protects the plants underneath. But when the snowpack is thin, frozen plants become brittle due to lack of moisture and can be permanently damaged. In summer, plants may spring back due to their moisture content, but in winter, once they're crushed, they often don't recover.

Be mindful when choosing a campsite, especially in alpine tundra, where delicate plants take years to decades—sometimes longer—to recover. Even if you need to pack down some snow, it's better than resting directly on fragile ground. Above the tree line, the soil is easily disturbed, and plants aren't adapted to heavy foot traffic. If possible, stay on dedicated trails or already impacted areas to minimize damage. Prioritize using stoves over campfires whenever possible. Campfires are great in winter, but avoid blackening rocks, scorching the ground, or leaving burn marks. If you do build a fire, the best practice is to use a raised platform on the snow to prevent lasting impact.

Also, be cautious around technical clothing—sparks from a fire can easily burn holes in synthetic fabrics, tents, and sleeping bags. Many materials melt or ignite quickly, even if treated with fire-retardant coatings. This isn't about avoiding the outdoors or being afraid to explore—it's just about being mindful of where you step and camp so the landscape stays as rugged and wild for the next person as it was for you. The goal is to leave no trace, so when spring comes, no one can tell anyone was ever there.

Respecting Wildlife

In winter, it's important to avoid feeding animals or disturbing their natural habitat, especially near nesting or denning areas. Wildlife is adapted to surviving outdoors year-round, managing their own challenges, but human presence can disrupt their natural behavior, stress them, or even kill them by introducing foods they aren't meant to eat.

One of the biggest problems with feeding wildlife isn't just that the food may be harmful—it's that animals quickly learn to associate humans with food. Even feeding an animal once or leaving behind food scraps can teach it that people are an easy food source. Instead of foraging as they should, animals will start seeking out humans and becoming more aggressive over time. This is especially true with foxes, coyotes, deer, and bears. It may seem fun to feed wildlife, but it's a mistake. There is saying:

"*A fed bear is a dead bear*"

This is unfortunately true. Every year, bears are put down across the U.S. and other countries because they've learned to rely on human food. Once that happens, they stop searching for their natural food sources and start raiding homes, trash cans, and campsites. When they become a threat, wildlife officials often have no choice but to euthanize them. This also applies to animal dens—especially for hibernating species. Disturbing a den in winter can be devastating. That den is its only shelter, just like your home is for you. Walking over or collapsing a den can happen without you even realizing it, leaving an animal exposed to the elements, which can be fatal.

To avoid disturbing critical winter wildlife habitat, research the area before you go. Contact local land agencies to find out if there are known sensitive zones. Some species, like bighorn sheep, have high energy demands in winter. If they're forced to relocate from their natural habitat, they can quickly become malnourished or dehydrated, which can be fatal. Wildlife may look tough, but winter is hard on them. The best thing you can do is give them space, avoid stressing them, and let them survive without interference.

Winter is hard on wildlife. Give them the space they need to survive.

Part 5
Planning and Executing Your Winter Adventure

A successful winter trip doesn't begin the moment you step into the snow—it starts with comprehensive planning long before you leave. Winter travel comes with its own set of challenges that demand detailed preparation. Weather extremes, difficult terrain, limited daylight, and the need to stay warm and safe are just a few of the elements that make winter expeditions uniquely complex. Proper planning lays the foundation for a safe, comfortable, and efficient experience, ensuring that you're ready to handle the unexpected when it inevitably arises.

The further off the beaten path your winter adventure takes you, the more planning is required. Remote and challenging environments demand careful consideration of every detail, from the gear you use to the food you carry, how you transport your equipment, and developing contingency plans for any situation. What works in the summer, where conditions are milder, won't necessarily hold up when you're facing sub-zero temperatures, unpredictable weather, and potentially hazardous terrain.

Adapting to the winter environment means understanding the specifics of the season. Winter trips aren't just about packing your gear and hitting the trail—they require anticipating potential risks, planning for the worst-case scenarios, and being prepared for all eventualities. Preparation is the difference between a smooth, exhilarating journey and a trip cut short by unforeseen obstacles. This section will guide you through every aspect of planning and executing your winter adventure, so you can navigate the cold, snow, and ice with confidence, ensuring that you're not only ready to face the challenges, but to thrive in them.

Chapter 28
Preparing for Your Trip

Gear, Food, and Logistics

Winter camping requires more gear, more calories, and more preparation than warm-weather trips. The first decision is the scale of your trip. If it's a local outing, you have the advantage of knowing the terrain and being able to cut the trip short if something goes wrong. A regional trip, where you're driving four to eight hours, requires more commitment. Weather conditions may differ significantly from where you started, and mistakes in packing become harder to correct.

National and international trips bring even more challenges. At this level, you need to consider permits, transportation logistics, and fuel availability. Weather can disrupt flights, gear can get lost, and essential supplies like fuel and food may be unavailable at your destination. The best approach is to start planning early—six months to a year in advance, depending on permit requirements and destination logistics. Some permits and paperwork take months to process, and agencies don't operate on your timeline.

Regardless of the trip's scale, a thorough gear checklist is non-negotiable. Missing one key item—like insulated gloves or an extra fire-starting method—can cause serious problems. Pack efficiently to avoid digging through a disorganized bag in freezing temperatures.

Checklists matter: A detailed gear checklist ensures nothing critical is forgotten—clothing, navigation, cooking equipment, and emergency supplies all need to be accounted for.
Packing strategy is key: Distribute weight evenly and keep essential gear within easy reach. Items like gloves, headlamps, and navigation tools should be in quick-access pockets.

Redundancy matters: Have backups for critical gear. That doesn't mean carrying duplicates of every item, but ensuring you have multiple methods to accomplish essential tasks like fire-starting, water purification, and navigation.
Test your setup before leaving: A backyard overnight can expose gear flaws and food problems before they become real issues in the field.

Food and water require careful planning. Winter burns far more calories than summer hiking, and dehydration happens quickly because cold weather reduces thirst cues. Melting snow takes time and fuel, so carrying insulated bottles pre-filled with water can save energy. Bring at least 10% more food than you think you'll need to cover unexpected delays.

Traveling and Flying with Winter Camping Gear

Flying with winter gear adds complications many people don't anticipate. Airlines restrict stoves, fuel, sharp tools, and lithium batteries, so know the rules before you go.

Stoves and fuel bottles must be completely dry and free of fuel residue: Airlines won't allow them otherwise.
Fuel cannot be flown with: Plan to purchase it at your destination and confirm availability ahead of time. Some countries may not stock specific fuel canisters or liquid fuel types, so research stove compatibility before arrival.
Sharp items go in checked baggage: Ice axes, crampons, and knives should never be packed in carry-ons.
Bring essentials in your carry-on: Boots, gloves, and base layers should stay with you in case of baggage delays.
Lithium batteries have restrictions: Devices like avalanche beacons, GPS units, and headlamps may need to be carried on rather than checked—check airline regulations before flying.

Once you arrive, getting to your actual starting point can be another challenge. Many winter destinations require additional transport beyond the airport, whether it's a rental car, a shuttle, or even a bush plane. Some locations may require winter-specific transport like snowmobiles, sled dogs, or tracked vehicles to reach the trailhead. If you plan to rent gear at your destination, confirm availability in writing. Many people assume they can rent what they need, only to hear *We're sold out* when they arrive.

For international trips, customs restrictions can complicate things further. Some countries ban the import of freeze-dried food, dairy, and meats, so research restrictions before packing. Fuel types also vary by location—white gas, propane, and kerosene go by different names, and stove compatibility can differ.

If your trip requires shipping gear ahead, plan for delays. Freight to remote areas like Greenland or Antarctica can take five weeks or longer. Even within North America, gear shipments can get held up, so have a backup plan if your shipment doesn't arrive on time.

Adapting to Changing Conditions

Winter weather is unpredictable. Forecasts help, but storms, whiteouts, and deep snow can force last-minute changes. Flexibility is key.

Monitor conditions before and during your trip. A satellite communicator or weather radio can provide real-time updates.
Be ready to reroute. If an avalanche zone, unexpected ice field, or extreme cold makes your planned route unsafe, find an alternative or wait for conditions to improve.
Build in buffer days. If weather delays you, having an extra day in your plan—especially for key travel legs—can prevent risky decisions.

Food and water management must also be adaptable. If a trip stretches longer than planned, rationing may become necessary. However, having that 10% extra food buffer prevents unnecessary risk.

Most importantly, know when to turn back. If conditions become too dangerous—whiteout, avalanche risk, exhaustion—retreating is the smart move. Many winter disasters happen because people ignored warning signs, thinking they could push through. A failed attempt is always better than a life-threatening situation.

Transportation and Handling Gear in Harsh Environments

Winter travel, whether by car or plane, demands special attention to logistics.

If driving, winter tires are mandatory. Chains alone won't be enough if your vehicle isn't built for snow and ice. All-wheel drive is helpful but doesn't make you invincible—sliding on ice at 30 mph (45 km/h) is still dangerous.

For remote areas, renting a four-wheel-drive vehicle with winter tires is often the best choice. Many rental agencies in southern states don't stock vehicles with winter tires. Even in colder regions, confirm that rentals have proper winter-rated tires before booking. If coming from a warm climate, attempting to drive through snowy roads with the wrong tires is asking for trouble.

For those shipping sleds or large expedition gear, air freight and cargo transport require advance planning. Airlines will transport skis and standard winter gear, but polar sleds or oversized pulks often need separate shipping arrangements. Freight services take time, so always confirm transit policies before departure.

Handling Delays and Unexpected Challenges

Delays are almost guaranteed in winter travel—bad weather routinely cancels flights, ferries, and shuts down roads. Expect it and plan accordingly.

Fuel availability isn't guaranteed. In remote areas, stored fuel may be old or degraded—white gas lasts longer than gasoline, but always check before you leave civilization.

Acclimation takes time. If traveling across multiple time zones, expect fatigue. If heading above 8,000 feet (2,440m), give your body a few days to adjust before exerting yourself to reduce altitude sickness risk.

Have an emergency contact plan. Make sure someone knows your itinerary and has specific instructions on who to call if you don't check in.

Winter camping is rewarding, but success depends on preparation and flexibility. The better planned you are, the safer and more enjoyable your trip will be. Test your gear, plan for the unexpected, and stay adaptable. Winter travel is unpredictable, but that's part of what makes it such a great adventure.

Budget well and have spare money in your bank account in case you need to take a helicopter ride to start your winter expedition.

Chapter 29
Long Trips

Packing Strategies for Long-Distance Travel

When traveling long distances—whether by plane or road—you have to be strategic about packing. Whether you're heading to a remote Arctic outpost, a mountain range, or just driving across the country for a winter trip, how you organize your gear matters. Airlines have strict baggage limits, and small aircraft used for remote flights often have even tighter weight restrictions due to fuel and cargo capacity limits. If you're driving, space and weight distribution become the main concerns. Either way, you need to think through what goes where, how you'll handle repacking at your destination, and what absolutely cannot be lost or buried under other gear.

If flying, keep your checked luggage under 50 pounds (23kg) if possible. This reduces the risk of injuring yourself while carrying it. Airlines limit the number, weight, and size of checked bags, and smaller aircraft may impose even stricter rules. If driving, be mindful of weight distribution. Heavier gear should go low and toward the center to prevent unnecessary strain on your suspension and avoid dangerous shifts in weight on icy roads.

Planning for Longer Winter Trips

On a longer winter trip, organization is key. Whether you're out for five days or a few months, careful planning makes the difference between success and suffering. You need to balance essentials with weight to keep your load manageable.

For extended trips, hauling gear with a sled or pulk reduces strain. Fuel is critical since you'll need it to melt snow or ice for water. White gas is the most reliable option in extreme cold, as propane may struggle to vaporize in subzero temperatures. If you have access to liquid water, you'll still need to filter large volumes over time. Water filters like the Sawyer work well in summer but are a liability in winter—if they freeze, expanding ice can damage the filter membrane, rendering it useless. Chemical treatments like Aquamira work in the cold but require enough supply and a way to keep them from freezing.

If you're driving to your starting point, plan for breakdowns, road closures, and extreme weather. Bring extra fuel, traction devices, a shovel, and enough food and water to last if you get stuck. In remote areas, a satellite communicator or emergency beacon is a smart backup. Pack so that essential items like boots, gloves, and emergency supplies are easily accessible—not buried under everything else.

Managing Food and Caloric Needs

On long trips, you can't cut calories too much without losing too much weight. In polar travel, you're always running a calorie deficit. Hunger is constant, and you have to accept that. If you can't hit 4,000 calories per day, you'll start shedding weight fast. Food is heavy, so you have to carry enough while knowing you'll still lose weight over time.

Author's Note:

On the Greenland expedition Terry and I did—featured in *Two Friends and a Polar Bear*—we each lost nearly 30 pounds (14kg). We carried as much food as possible, about 2 pounds (900 grams) per day, but it wasn't enough. That was the absolute weight limit we could fly with and manage to haul. Terry felt the hunger early, but for me, it didn't hit until the third week. The last two weeks were tough, but we made it through.

Packing and Repacking

Pack your gear in phases: one setup for camping, cooking, and emergencies, and another for travel. If you're flying to your starting point, you'll likely need to repack when you arrive. Set aside at least a full day for this so you're not rushing. If driving, pack in a way that allows quick access to critical items, especially if you'll be sleeping in your vehicle along the way.

Some gear should never go in checked luggage:
- Electronics and anything with batteries

- Essential medications
- Critical gear, especially boots

Climbing boots and ski boots are a priority. You can often replace skis or snowshoes if needed, but finding the right boots can be nearly impossible. Many skiers and mountaineers carry their boots over their shoulders through airports rather than packing them, as heavy boots can be difficult to manage at security. Some travelers wear their boots during flights to avoid baggage issues, though this can be uncomfortable on long-haul trips. Packing them in carry-on ensures they arrive at the destination. Some airlines have strict carry-on rules, so packing efficiently is important. Climbers and polar travelers sometimes wear extra layers on the plane to reduce baggage weight, keeping essential gear with them while traveling. If driving, store extra layers, gloves, and emergency gear where they're easy to reach in case you need to stop in extreme cold.

Redundancy

For critical items like your stove, communication, and navigation, you need backup equipment. If any of these fail and you have no way to navigate, communicate, evacuate, or make water, you're in serious trouble. This is especially true if you're deep in the backcountry with no easy way to get back or signal for help. If you can't communicate and no one's around to pick you up, you've set yourself up for a bad situation.

Make sure critical systems, especially your stove, have a backup. On a long trip, bring a second stove. Even with a repair kit, if your stove is damaged beyond fixing, you're stuck. Without a way to melt snow and make water, things get dangerous fast. In a dry, cold climate, you can dehydrate and die in a couple of days.

If you need water purification, have a backup. For long winter travel, fresh snow is usually your best bet—just make sure it's clean. A water filter isn't always practical on extended trips, so plan on melting snow. If you use open water sources, you'll need to boil or chemically treat it. Keep in mind that some chemical treatments work more slowly in freezing temperatures. Water filters can freeze, rendering them useless, so if you rely on one, keep it insulated and carry a backup purification method.

Have practical redundancy in your system. A spare pair of liner gloves, a sewing kit, and a few key tools can keep small problems from becoming big ones.

A backup GPS and compass are a good idea. They're tough but not indestructible. If they get smashed, lost, or stop working, you'll need a way to navigate.

Emergency communication is a must. There are too many good options now to justify going without it. For long trips, satellite phones, InReach, and Iridium networks make a huge difference. Make sure you have two-way communication, not just a one-way device like a SPOT tracker. A SPOT is useful for sending non-emergency check-ins, but you won't know if anyone received your message or if help is on the way.

PLB (Personal Locator Beacon) are strictly for true emergencies—like a debilitating injury or total equipment failure where you can't move and need rescue. Unlike a SPOT, a PLB transmits a distress signal on 406 MHz and doesn't require a subscription. It's the most reliable one-way distress signal, but since it's only for life-threatening situations, it shouldn't replace a two-way device for routine communication.

Field Repairs

Make sure you have at least an essential repair kit. Include duct tape, a multi-tool, a needle and thread kit with lots of strong thread, a spare tent pole section or extra connector, zip ties, aluminum wire, and cold-resistant adhesives like Gorilla Tape—regular duct tape won't stick in extreme cold.

A 50-foot (15-meter) or 100-foot (30-meter) section of 550 paracord can mean the difference between keeping your expedition going or calling for rescue. It's light, versatile, and strong.

Have a comprehensive first aid kit and know how to use it. Just as important is a sewing kit. Bring heavy-duty outdoor thread designed for upholstery and a good needle set. It's all you need to fix a tear in your jacket, pants, sleeping bag, or tent. A needle and thread that costs just a few dollars or euros can make the difference between continuing or turning back.

Know how to sew before you leave. In extreme cold, stiff fingers and bulky gloves make field repairs even harder, so practice beforehand. Spend 20 minutes watching a tutorial or ask someone who knows. Actually practice on fabric so you get the process down. If the damage isn't too bad, you'll be able to stitch things back together and keep moving.

Gear repair tape is also useful. Duct tape can be messy on gear, so having proper repair tape helps. Things rip, wear out, or snag—whether it's your technical pants catching on ski poles or something unexpected.

Supply Conservation

Calculate your daily caloric and fuel needs based on activity and weather. As your expedition stretches from one week to two, three, or more, your caloric needs will increase. Water intake stays relatively stable, and fuel consumption should remain fairly consistent.

Plan for at least 5.9 oz (175ml) of fuel per day, up to 7.6 oz (225ml) in extremely cold conditions. It takes a lot more fuel to melt snow at low temperatures, so factor that in. If you can hit 4,000 calories per day, you'll have plenty to eat—that's about 2.4 pounds (1,100 grams) of food daily. On longer trips, food weight adds up fast, so you'll need to thin it out where possible.

Use the most fuel-efficient cooking techniques. Insulated pots, windshields, and avoiding overboiling all help. A little wasted fuel here and there adds up, and once you're out, there's no replacing it in the field.

Portion meals carefully to avoid waste. Test everything before your trip and track how much food and fuel you actually use. Pre-packed daily rations help track consumption and prevent overuse, avoiding the risk of running low too soon. There's nothing to think about—just grab a pack and eat. If you rely on large containers, you might over-portion and run out too soon.

Bulk food containers come with risk—if one spoils or is contaminated, you could lose a significant portion of your supply. Pre-packed rations keep food safer and more secure while simplifying portion control.

Customize Gear

Be ready to customize your gear. Sometimes seams need to be removed, straps added, or zippers checked and reinforced. Bring an extra toothbrush, fine brush, or a dedicated zipper cleaner to remove ice from zipper teeth. Ice buildup can jam zippers, and forcing them when frozen can cause permanent damage. If your tent's outer zipper fails, sealing the door becomes a serious problem.

If you need extra guy line points or attachment loops for stability in harsh conditions, add them. Even if your tent is expensive, unless it's a heavy-weather expedition model like those from Hilleberg or The North Face, it may not be built for extreme conditions. Be ready to modify it.

For extremely cold conditions, make sure your water bottle insulation actually works. Thin neoprene sleeves won't cut it—you'll need to keep bottles in your sleeping bag or use a fully insulated cover. If your bottle leaks, it could soak your sleeping bag, so be careful.

Modify your sleeping pads if needed. Adding grip dots stops sliding. Use paracord, hook-and-loop straps, or adhesive grip strips to secure a foam pad to an air pad for backup insulation and extra warmth.

If you're constantly in low-light conditions, add visibility tape to your gear. Adaptability is key. If you're on a long ski expedition but might hit varied terrain like Greenland's icy hills, bring crampons. Skis alone won't always work. On smooth, hard ice, bare boots can be dangerous, and switching to crampons quickly can make a big difference.

If you use crampon adapters for ski boots, know that they often need solid engagement depth to function properly. On hard ice, ski-mounted crampons can be unstable, putting strain on your ankles and gear. Be ready to switch as needed.

Additional Thoughts

Knowing you need extra planning, redundancy, and adaptability for long trips is key. You can get away with some things for a while, but on an extended trip, you don't want to struggle nonstop beyond the already tough challenge of winter travel and covering long distances.

The joy of completing a long trek in winter is immeasurable, but you want to do it with as much style and enjoyment as possible. Check your gear regularly. A small tear caught early is an easy fix. Ignore it, and it could become a major problem—like a torn tent or a massive hole in your jacket or pants.

On long trips, flexibility is everything. Be prepared. If you have critical gear that isn't easily replaceable—like ski boots or telecommunications equipment—you need to keep it with you at all times, especially when flying or traveling between locations. Think ahead. If a key piece of gear got lost or damaged, how would you recover or repair it? Plan for that, and you'll be able to keep moving forward.

Expect to have piles of gear for a winter trip. The colder it is and the farther away your destination, the more you will likely need.

Chapter 30
Polar Camping

The biggest challenge of polar camping is not just getting there, but adapting to the harsh environment and extreme conditions once you do. The environment, the isolation, and the extreme conditions make it unlike anything in lower latitudes. Reaching these places takes extra effort, but it feels like stepping onto an alien planet.

The severe cold, harsh weather, and their effects on the body are only part of the challenge. Just getting to a polar environment is difficult. Few people travel there, making it an expensive and demanding endeavor.

The reward is in the experience. In places like the Arctic, the Greenland Plateau, the Arctic Ocean, or Antarctica, you'll face continuous extreme cold. Stay long enough, and your body starts to adapt. After a couple of weeks, you'll feel relatively warm, changing how you experience the cold.

Polar terrain is vast, featureless, and often disorienting, making navigation and survival particularly difficult. Yet, in the Arctic, polar bears and birds survive in this harsh world. These exposed spaces offer no natural wind breaks or landmarks, making survival far more challenging. But once you learn how to live in them, it becomes the ultimate test—like stepping onto Planet Hoth from *The Empire Strikes Back*.

Few places on Earth feel this alien.

The biggest mental challenges are monotony, isolation, and the endless daylight or darkness, depending on the season. Whiteouts can last for days, completely obscuring the landscape and creating serious risks, such as falling into crevasses or losing all sense of direction. If you're not prepared, they can be disorienting and dangerous.

Even clear days present challenges. The endless white snow and blue sky create a sameness that can wear on the mind, leading to feelings of isolation, anxiety, or depression due to the lack of visual variety and contrast. This isn't a place for everyone. But for those seeking the ultimate challenge, polar terrain is the final frontier.

Unlike well-known mountains such as Everest, some believe there's no perceived glory in crossing a polar region compared to reaching a summit. However, the act of being in the location is often the value. Polar regions are more exotic, not as trafficked, and have never-ending dangers. The reward isn't in reaching a destination. It's in the journey itself.

Snow and Ice Conditions

Navigating hard-packed, uneven snow surfaces in polar regions is incredibly difficult. One moment, the surface is relatively smooth. The next, you encounter sastrugi—sharp ridges of wind-sculpted snow. These formations can range from 3 feet (1 meter) to 9 feet (3 meters) tall and are often impassable.

Traveling across these surfaces is the ultimate test of long-distance skills. The snow is as hard as packed dirt, making falls brutal. Skis help bridge some of the gaps in sastrugi, but only if you're moving in the right direction.

One of the biggest challenges in polar climates is how snow behaves. In Antarctica, the wind, not the sun, packs the snow. Even a thin layer can make a sled feel like you're dragging it through sand. In contrast, Greenland sees significant snowfall each year. The surface starts out firm, but as the sun rises and temperatures warm, it softens into slush. By midday, what was once a solid surface can turn into a challenging slog.

This shift in snow conditions affects efficiency. In places like Greenland, where daylight transitions are extreme, the best strategy is to travel early. By afternoon, the sun becomes intense, causing overheating and slowing progress. Waking up at 3 A.M. every day is mentally tough and physically taxing, but if you push through, the experience is worth it.

Featureless Terrain: A Deceptive Landscape

One thing to be aware of in polar climates is the prevalence of sastrugi and ice ridges. In Greenland, particularly along the Arctic Circle, sastrugi typically reach heights of about 1 foot (30 cm). However, in the northern reaches, taller sastrugi can be encountered. Additionally, Greenland generally receives more snowfall than Antarctica, influencing its ice dynamics. The surface of the ice is impacted by the higher snowfall, making it more variable than the drier conditions in Antarctica.

The Greenland Ice Sheet appears flat from the air, especially when flying to Europe, but on the ground, it's different. Glaciers spilling off the ice sheet form towering walls of ice, sometimes hundreds of feet (over 30 meters) high, creating massive barriers between the interior and the coast. The summit of the ice sheet rises over 8,000 feet (2,400 meters). From a distance, it looks like a smooth, rolling expanse of snow, but it's not as featureless as it seems. East Greenland is even more dramatic, with mountains rising sharply from the frozen coastline.

Antarctica is even more extreme. The South Pole sits at 9,301 feet (2,835 meters). Most of the continent is above 5,000 feet (1,500 meters). Titan Dome, one of the high points of the plateau, feeds katabatic winds—cold, dense air that flows downhill with force. The Transantarctic Mountains stretch over 2,200 miles (3,500 km), making them one of the longest ranges in the world. Across Antarctica, nunataks—exposed peaks of mountains buried in ice—rise above the frozen expanse, breaking up the white horizon.

Despite these massive features, maps make polar terrain look empty. Sastrugi, ice ridges, and subtle elevation changes barely register on satellite views. What seems smooth on a map can be a maze of obstacles in reality.

Liquid Water, Moulins, and Ice Hazards

As the season progresses and liquid water pools form at the edges of the Greenland Ice Sheet, the situation becomes even more dangerous. Along with the water pools, moulins can open up where water drains into deep chasms beneath the ice. These chasms are often hidden beneath the surface, with the soft ice giving way to the massive cracks below. If you fall into one of these holes, the chances of survival are slim without a rope team, proper crevasse rescue training, and quick access to rescue equipment.

The sheer depth and darkness of these chasms make them deadly. Even if you manage to survive the fall, getting out without assistance is virtually impossible. This is why, in later-season travel, having a rope team is essential. You need constant vigilance and safety protocols in place to avoid falling into these treacherous traps. The ice may look solid, but in reality, it hides dangerous structural weaknesses beneath its surface, often caused by meltwater infiltration or ice flow, making it far more unstable than it seems.

Ice Floes and Arctic Ocean Hazards

In the Arctic Ocean, broken ice can create chaotic ridges that rise up to

10 feet (3 meters) or more. These formations, driven by shifting ice floes, can pose significant obstacles to travel and navigation. The dynamics of the ice floes are constantly changing, influenced by ocean currents and wind patterns. Even if these ridges seem like a minor challenge, their unpredictable nature can create dangerous situations.

The ice floes on the Arctic Ocean are often compacted and rugged, with areas of thin or cracked ice that can break away unexpectedly, forming leads of open water. These open water leads are cracks or openings that form in the sea ice, providing access to the ocean but also creating significant risks. The constant changes in ice conditions, including sudden openings and the shifting of floes, require constant monitoring and careful navigation.

Understanding Ice Dynamics

The ice dynamics in Greenland and Antarctica are influenced by local factors like snowfall, wind, and the underlying topography. While Greenland's ice is shaped by the heavier snowfall, Antarctica's ice is shaped by its cold and dry conditions, leading to a drier, firmer surface. However, both regions are prone to ice movements and shifts that can create crevasses, hidden moulins, and unpredictable conditions for those navigating across them.

Wind Patterns and Navigation

Wind direction matters. Sastrugi form along the predominant wind, so even if a storm shifts the wind temporarily, it will return to its usual pattern. In Greenland and Antarctica, wind follows a katabatic flow, shaped by the landscape. It pours down from the high plateaus toward the coast.

Closer to the coast, the wind can get violent. In places like Isortoq, East Greenland, where many Greenland icecap crossing expeditions start and end, winds often hit 100 mph (160 km/h), making travel impossible in storms. Similar conditions occur in Antarctica near the coastal ice shelves.

Greenland crossings follow predictable wind patterns, but conditions shift depending on the route. An east-to-west crossing will face a lateral wind from the north, blowing toward the spine of the ice sheet. Past this high point, the landscape undulates, then drops over 100+ miles (160+ km) along the Arctic Circle. The wind shifts to a tailwind, making travel easier.

A west-to-east crossing is tougher. Teams face a headwind most of the way to the spine. After crossing the summit, the steeper descent on the East Greenland side brings a lateral north wind on the left. That's just along the

Arctic Circle—further north or south, the patterns shift but still follow the katabatic flow shaped by the ice sheet.

For expeditions launching from East Greenland, taking a helicopter from Tasilaq to the 1,000-meter (3,000-foot) ice plateau can be a smart move. It avoids brutal terrain and unpredictable coastal storms, making for a stronger start at elevation.

Efficient Travel in Polar Terrain

On clear days, navigation is easier. If you can see sastrugi ridges or unmoving clouds ahead, take a compass reading, set your sight on a distant landmark, drop the compass, and start skiing.

A chest harness for your compass makes travel more efficient. It eliminates the need to stop and check your direction constantly. Whether in bright sunlight or a total whiteout, a chest-mounted compass makes quick corrections and keeps you moving.

Group Travel

Most people travel in polar climates as a group. Managing how far apart or close together you stay is critical. Keeping slower members or guides at the front sets a steady pace that everyone can maintain. It can be frustrating for faster people, but for slower ones, it makes a huge difference. The stress of trying to keep up over time can wear people down, leading to frustration and group tension.

Spacing matters. In polar environments, getting too spread out is dangerous. If a storm suddenly rolls in and you're a mile (1.6 km) or more apart, visibility can vanish in minutes. Tracks blow away fast, and if one person has a tent and the other doesn't, the situation can become serious.

Even if you can see each other from a long distance, that can change fast. The moment a whiteout hits, wind-driven snow erases visibility. A travel companion who was in sight seconds ago can disappear completely.

Some guides let stronger team members push ahead, expecting the group to regroup later. This can work, but it's a risk. Sometimes, staying closer together is the smarter choice.

Preparing for Polar Conditions

One of the key aspects of traveling in polar climates is dealing with vast, open spaces. To move through them, you need to be adaptable and prepared for anything. Crevasses are a constant danger, especially near the coast or in high-risk zones like Antarctica. Even when they seem invisible, they're always a possibility.

A tragic example is Dixie Dansercoer, author of *Polar Exploration*. In 2018, while crossing Northern Greenland on skis, he fell into a hidden crevasse and lost his life. The ice is constantly shifting, and snow bridges, formed by accumulating snow and pressure over crevasses, can collapse without warning.

This risk isn't limited to Greenland. Massive crevasses exist throughout the polar regions, often hidden until someone breaks through. You always need to be aware of the dangers and ready to set up camp at a moment's notice.

Help isn't always close. In bad weather, it could take hours, days, or even a week for rescue. In Greenland, travelers have been stranded at DYE-2 for five days during a severe storm. DYE-2 is an abandoned Cold War radar station, part of the old DEW Line (Distant Early Warning System) built to detect incoming Soviet bombers. While it's long been decommissioned, it still provides a solid structure for shelter in emergencies. Those stuck there were lucky to have a building to retreat into—without it, 100 mph (160 km/h) winds would have made survival a fight just to keep a tent from being crushed under drifting snow. The cold alone can leave you frostbitten if you're not constantly managing your gear and shelter.

Traveling in polar regions is the ultimate test for a winter camper. It's expensive, rescues are difficult, and the environment is harsh. If you're thinking about going, test your skills many times before committing.

Even on guided trips, you need to have experience skiing in polar conditions. Skis are the only practical way to cover long distances in these environments. Crampons are a backup for sections of hard ice where skiing isn't possible. Snowshoes work for shorter distances or deeper snow, but they are too slow and inefficient for the long distances required in polar travel.

Polar travel demands commitment, but the experience is unmatched.

A finished moderate weather snow block wall for wind protection. It starts off with a rubble base with cut blocks added on top. Total height: 4 feet (121 cm).

Part 6
The Daily Experience of Winter Camping

Winter camping isn't just about theory—it's about real experiences in the field, where conditions dictate every decision and survival depends on preparation, adaptability, and mindset. In this chapter, I've included excerpts from two of my expeditions:

- A 35-day polar journey across Greenland, where cold, isolation, and relentless ice tested every decision. We ran out of food, with only some snacks remaining. We're one of the oldest teams ever to cross Greenland unaided and unsupported. To avoid the dangerous coastal start, we took a helicopter from Tasilaq to the 3,000-foot mark on the icecap. This move saved us a lot of stress and potential scheduling issues, as it would have been expensive to fly to Isortoq anyway (though the scheduled flight there would have been far cheaper). The half-hour helicopter ride to the ice cap cost $5,200 USD, but it was worth every penny. This expedition is chronicled in *Two Friends and a Polar Bear,* co-authored with Terry Williams. The book presents our experiences in raw, immediate journal entries, offering an unfiltered look at the challenges, triumphs, and mental battles of polar travel.

- The psychological challenge of moving above 11,000 feet (3,400m) on Denali as a solo climber. Denali brings a unique set of mental hurdles—doubt, motivation, and the weight of every decision. The isolation and extreme conditions make it a trial of both body and mind. During the climb, every choice has massive consequences. The higher you go, the more the mountain tests your resilience. This story is drawn from *Lost at Windy Corner,* which takes a narrative-driven approach, putting you inside the headspace of climbing one of North America's most formidable peaks. It's a journey of perseverance and mental endurance, as I navigated the mountain alone, pushing through whiteouts and near-lethal weather.

Both books explore the realities of extreme cold, mental endurance, and the raw beauty of winter landscapes. If you want the full story, these books put you in the thick of it. For now, enjoy these glimpses into what winter camping and high-altitude travel feel like when you're deep in the moment, facing both the elements and yourself.

Listening to a pack of wolves howl as the sun rises in a purple sky makes all the cold, hunger, and thirst worth it.

Chapter 31
Expedition Experience: Greenland and Denali

Two Friends and a Polar Bear (Greenland Icecap Crossing)

Editing Note: These journal entries are lightly edited to give a sense of what it's like to travel in the polar regions. They are transcribed from our handwritten journals in the field, preserving the raw experience of each day while streamlining some of the details for clarity.

(Aaron's Journal)
Camp 15, Ice cap
66° 19.564'N 43° 12.889'W @ 8,034 feet (2,449m)
11.3 miles (18.2km) from camp 14
Total 122.3 miles (196km)
86.5 (138km) miles to DYE-2
Day 15 (Aaron's Journal)
Saturday, May 6, 2023
We started skiing at 5:45 A.M.

DYE-2 is 86 miles (138km) away. It should be 8 days of travel. The summit is 22 miles (35km), so it should be 2 days away. Point 660 is 194 miles (312km) away. At 11 miles (18km) per day, it should be 18 days away. That's going to be really close to our pickup date. Nothing like a little bit of stress.

Terry is a great speed manager. He's always fine-tuning where he applies effort and where he holds back. It's probably smarter than me going at 80–85% all the time. It's a challenge to figure out the right balance.

He follows me at his 95% speed (since I'm faster), so when he leads, he's running at a 70% power rate, according to him. For the first 20 minutes, I'm slower than him, recovering from my shift. But by the end, I'm tailing pretty close. It's a tough balance.

I swapped to colder weather clothes and poured on the throttle today, covering 10.2 miles (16.4km) by 6 P.M. We added our 35 minutes of extra time and got it to 11.3 miles (18.2km).

I called it "paying the Piper"—putting in the extra effort now will pay off at the end of the trip.

Our schedule today was me on shift 1, Terry on 2, me on 3, Terry on 4. Once the sky turned to a whiteout in shift 4, he started going in circles and almost fell over while looking at his compass. He was a good sport about it and enjoyed the experience. We learned that I was to take over when it was 100% whiteout. He did okay as long as he could see something.

I started getting cold burns on my face. A storm of wind and snow came up after a completely calm morning. We survived and built an extra-big snow wall. It was worth it.

We're 20 miles (32km) and 2 days from the summit. And then it should be all downhill!

We decided to have me lead for speed and Terry lead to let me recover.

Both Terry and my lips are DESTROYED. They hurt so bad I couldn't hardly sleep last night.

(Terry's Journal)

Saturday, 6 May, 2023 (Terry's Journal)

[The wind shifted to southeast.]

Eventful day. Aaron asked me at 2 A.M. if we should get an earlier start. I reminded him of how "sticky" the snow often is that early, so we slept until 3 A.M. He suggested it because there's no wind. It was overcast and flat light when we got out to ski at 5:45. Mild temperatures of ~0°F (18°C).

1st shift, Aaron led. We crossed a sled track only 1–2 days old, heading in a more North-South direction. Aaron skiing fast & strong.

2nd shift, I led off. It started to snow lightly, okay so far. Eventually deteriorated to "inside the ping pong ball." Conditions were very disorienting. I slowed so much that Aaron took over & led the rest of the shifts, keeping us moving fast. He wants to make the mileage we need.

A weak storm seemed to blow through, but the wind picked up and changed 180° from the usual. We had stripped off layers because we were skiing so hard, but had to armor up for the rest of the afternoon.

Cold winds blowing at our backs from the southeast (back left). Aaron had me lead for 25 minutes in the last shift so he could recover. We then did a 30-minute "bonus round" and did an additional mile! Great total for today. I couldn't keep up, but he's determined to keep us moving!

At camp, we built the best wind wall yet & made extra protection for my windward vestibule. To keep us moving faster, Aaron has been hauling the shotgun. Now, he's got the first aid kit & the morning thermos also.

My feet are improving. I took the bandages off for the night so they can dry. We were in bed by 8 P.M.

Aaron & I talked about other strategies to move faster. He's willing to lead much more. I told him I didn't want to resent me for not pulling my weight. We slept great despite the wind noise in the tent. Must be exhaustion.

Our constant companions, cold, hunger, and exhaustion.

***

Lost at Windy Corner

Chapter 7

The next day would be my first above 10,000 feet (3,048m). I was now living at real altitude. And I felt it. Even when I arrived the previous evening, I knew that it would catch up with me. Single-hauling up the mountain had pushed my body to the limit. Climbing to camp with an eighty-pound (36 kg) sled and a fifty-pound (23 kg) pack guaranteed that I would be worn out. But in my mind, I had felt it was better to advance as long as I was able, even if it was tough. I would rather be higher on the mountain when poor weather moved in.

My nose was stuffy all night, making sleep nearly impossible. Had I slept better, I might have felt better than I did. But that was a pile of "what-ifs." I was dealing with "what-dids" and "what-are-you-going-to-do-about-its?" It had been a long time since I had camped on a glacier with congestion. Even though I had a cold and bronchitis in Antarctica, it was easy to sleep with a runny nose.

This was different. The symptoms were like I had caught a cold, though I didn't think I had. I was forced to breathe through my mouth the whole night, which meant I became badly dehydrated. I chugged water at regular intervals, but that caused its own problems. I had to relieve myself several times during the night, further cutting into my sleep. My body had gone haywire. I had never thought of bringing a nasal decongestant on a trip like this. I had cold medications to help with a runny nose, but those wouldn't help here.

I didn't want to waste a half roll of toilet paper trying to clear my nose. Those little squares of industrial paper were a critical resource—run out of them and, well, things would be much rougher on the mountain. Instead, I used the polar nose-clearing technique. That is, I grabbed a handful of icy snow, balled it up, jammed it into my face, and blew. Then I hucked the disgusting clump as far away from camp as I could. I repeated the process until I could breathe again. And this repeated planting of my face in the snow worked.

Though the process sounds unpleasant, it relieved the discomfort. The supply of icy snow was infinite, so I never had to worry about running out. Plus, there was the distinct advantage of not chaffing my nose with rough toilet paper. I had suffered on previous winter trips with bleeding and raw nostrils. Once I figured this out, many treks ago, I permanently eliminated a significant source of stress. Minor annoyances at home can turn into major infections in the wild, but I never wasted my valuable toilet paper on my nose. Being careful with resources and my health made the difference between an enjoyable expedition and a painful escapade.

Swallowing two aspirin to reduce the effects of altitude, I wondered what I would do with myself today. I hadn't had a rest day on an expedition not forced by weather or health in years. They were necessary for success on Denali, but it felt strange. It was as though I was wasting time not climbing.

The great danger on high-altitude mountains is climbing too quickly. Coombs's *West Buttress* book warned that climbers have developed serious high-altitude sickness at 11k camp. I took the warning seriously. Though I'd been training to 10,000 feet (3,048m) in Jackson, prematurely advancing higher could result in altitude sickness. Patience was a climber's best friend on this mountain.

After eating breakfast and consuming two liters of water, I felt marginally better.

"Did I make a mistake by moving from 9k to 11k camp in a single haul?" I asked myself. Many other teams climbed up and down to reduce the workload. The idea of going back and forth was utterly unappealing. My only desire was to move forward and do so quickly. This was the first moment of doubt I had about what I was doing here.

Knowing how dangerous doubt was, I immediately set out to eliminate the feeling. I donned my outer gear and jumped out of the tent. Knowing that action and motion helps humans to acclimate to the altitude, I set out to walk back and forth toward Motorcycle Hill. I took twenty fast steps and nearly passed out. I saw sparkling stars. Leaning over with my hands on my knees, I remembered where I was—near the Arctic Circle.

One of the reasons Denali is difficult to climb is because the atmosphere is thinner near the polar regions. At an equivalent altitude in the lower forty-eight states, there is more oxygen. This mountain is closer to the pole and the altitude I was at felt more like 12,000 feet (3,700m).

Chastising myself for not walking more slowly, I rested a minute.

"That was dumb," I scolded myself. "Come on, practice your high-altitude techniques."

When I climbed in Mexico with a team lead by Randall Peeters, an Adventure Grand Slam climber and author of *Journeys to the Edge*, imparted wisdom I couldn't figure out by myself. Now, I had to self-regulate my speed. Fully standing up, I practiced pressure breathing to recover my senses. It's a similar action to blowing out a candle. In a few moments, the lightheadedness dissipated.

After letting the annoyance stew for a moment, I washed it off with laughter. I knew to acknowledge my emotions, let them run their course, then cut them off. They are a natural human experience after all. The trick is not to let them run away with you. Visualizing a shower of laughter to scrub off the grime of irritation, a smile returned to my face. The technique is easy to write about but it's another matter to put it into practice. It takes time and patience to master. Sometimes negative emotions still overwhelm me. Staying upset is difficult, though, if you are wearing a smile.

Walking two hundred yards back and forth from camp to the base of Motorcycle Hill made me feel better. My headache subsided and a natural smile returned. I told myself, "Here I am on Denali, climbing solo. Have a good time with it."

Thrusting my hands into the air in triumph, I repeated the mantra, "You will succeed. You are a careful and strong climber. You will make it and return home safely." This positive reinforcement seems goofy but it works. It plants a vision of safety and success in my mind. When climbing alone on a mountain, I need all the positive vision I can muster.

While climbing back and forth, I watched the snow stream off Squirrel

Point. Long tails of snow flew off the cliff, hundreds of yards long. That meant climbing up higher was dangerous. If anyone was on the ice plateau or at Windy Corner, they were enjoying 50 mph (80 km/h) winds or worse. Hot though 11k camp was being up there in that windstorm would be far worse. Even though it was zero degrees at night, the camp turned into a solar oven by the afternoon. With three large walls of ice surrounding the glacier, there was nowhere for the air to go. This geography caused the air temperature to skyrocket.

Later in the day, I thought I heard a bird chirping in camp. Wandering around, I found a black-capped chickadee flitting around the tents. Here was another diminutive songbird far away from the tundra. It disappeared behind a snow wall, chirping a few more times. Then it went silent.

"Strange," I thought. Hoping nothing was wrong with the poor beast, I looked to see if it was injured. Walking around the wall, I was greeted by a surprise. There was nothing there but snow. I walked about, looking to see if it was hiding somewhere. No, it was gone. I heard no chirping or flapping going on. Frowning, I looked into the sky. Had I imagined this flying visitor? I had hallucinated about ravens in Antarctica in my peripheral vision, but I was sure this bird was real.

Yet, it was gone.

"Maybe Alaskan birds have cloaking devices," I teased myself. I thought about asking my neighbors about the bird. Then I thought better of it. There was no need to bother anyone with a trivial question like that. People already looked at me like I was crazy when they heard I was climbing alone. I didn't want to encourage the notion.

I pondered the question of how best to deal with transporting my supplies up to 13.5k camp. How was I going to haul enough emergency supplies in case I was caught in conditions like today without hauling everything? At the minimum, I would need a sleeping bag, shovel, and sleeping pad if I became stuck for a night. But what if a big storm came in, trapping me for several days? Then I would need my stove, fuel, pot, and food.

I didn't want to carry an unnecessary thirty-pound (14 kg) load up the mountain. I saw other teams climbing up with fully loaded packs and sleds, then returning completely empty with sleds lashed to their backs like turtle shells. What a joy that must be, to walk with only a liter of water and little else. These climbers were tethered together in a group. Should conditions turn dangerous, they had each other to rely on. Guides likely carried emergency supplies for the group, too.

Last year several people were trapped at Denali Pass at 18,000 feet (5,500m) due to a sick climber. Their guide had to abandon them to get help. This broke the unwritten rule of guiding—never leave your clients. The problem was, he didn't carry a sleeping bag or steel shovel in case they had to bivouac.

I didn't want to end up like them, stuck without shelter and no way to dig a cave. Death was certain in a storm without shelter and a sleeping bag on Denali. As a solo climber, carrying overnight gear was mandatory. The cache run would take six to eight hours. If I wasn't willing to carry the gear to survive a surprise storm, what was I doing here?

Later in the evening, the wind calmed down and quit dragging long tails of snow off Squirrel Point. Snow was still blowing off the cliff, but it looked like the windstorm was dying out. I hoped that tomorrow conditions would be calm enough for a cache run. After a long, hot day at 11k camp, I was ready to move out.

Looking across a wintry landscape after a month on the Greenland icecap.

Chapter 32
Conclusion

Embracing the Adventure of Winter

Being able to lie in your tent, warm and comfortable, nestled deep in your sleeping bag—it's a feeling few will ever understand. The cold is pressing against the walls, the wind whispers outside, but inside, you are prepared. Your stomach is full, your body is hydrated, and the day's efforts have paid off. There's a deep satisfaction in knowing you did everything right.

Then, in the dead of night, you hear a sharp crack followed by a deep, resonating boom. You wonder what it could be. At extreme temperatures—as cold as -30°F (-35°C)—trees can shatter and explode. The freezing sap inside expands, splitting the tree apart in a sudden rupture of sound. It's a rare experience, one few people will ever witness.

You wave your hand outside your sleeping bag, and it's like plunging your arm into ice water. The tent is still. The night stretches on, silent except for the occasional groan of shifting ice or the distant howl of wind against the peaks. These are things you can't buy or simulate. They don't exist in videos, books, or forums—they have to be lived.

Maybe you're someone who enjoys winter in your local mountains or frozen lakes. Maybe you've ventured into the deep wilderness, where the cold dictates everything. Wherever you go, winter has a way of showing you something new. You don't have to push for Arctic extremes or seek out the most remote destinations to find meaning in the experience. The simple act of stepping into the cold, embracing the silence, and challenging yourself in nature is what winter camping is all about.

Winter is not just a test of gear, planning, or endurance. It's a mindset. It's about being adaptable, prepared, and open to learning—because even the most experienced campers know that winter always has new lessons to teach.

Final Takeaways for Safe and Enjoyable Winter Adventures

Every trip adds another layer of understanding. The first time you camp in the cold, everything feels like an experiment. You're figuring out how to keep your fingers warm, how to light a stove in subzero temperatures, how to pack a sleeping bag without losing heat. By your fifth, tenth, or fiftieth trip, the routines become second nature.

Winter never stops offering challenges:
- No matter how much you prepare, winter will throw something unexpected at you. The forecast will be wrong. The snowpack will be deeper than expected. A lost or forgotten piece of gear will force you to improvise. This is part of the adventure.
- Flexibility is just as important as preparation. Being ready doesn't mean having the perfect checklist—it means knowing how to adapt when the unexpected happens.
- Winter camping is about problem-solving. No one gets it perfect every time. Mistakes happen and they are often the best teachers.

If there's one truth to winter camping, it's this: you will never master it completely. There is always another experience waiting to challenge you, to refine your skills, and to push you to be a better traveler in the cold. That's why we keep coming back.

Encouragement to Keep Exploring and Learning

Winter camping is not about perfection—it's about progress. Each trip refines your skills. Each experience builds confidence. Whether you're exploring new regions or simply perfecting your system in a familiar place, every time you venture out, you gain something valuable.

Challenge yourself, but also enjoy the moment. Not every trip has to be a test of endurance. Some of the best winter trips are the simplest ones—a quiet night in the woods, watching the snowfall. Explore new winter destinations. Maybe you've mastered local winter camping—now it's time to try snowshoeing in a mountain range, skiing into a frozen valley, or even planning a longer multi-day trek. Connect with others. The winter camping community is full of knowledge. Forums, social media, and local clubs are great ways to exchange tips, learn from experienced campers, and share your own insights. Keep pushing your skills forward. Try a longer trip, test a new shelter system, or refine your packing strategy. The more you practice, test, and learn, the more winter becomes a place of comfort rather than challenge. Winter is a world of discovery, and it belongs to those who embrace it.

Final Words

Imagine standing outside your tent as the sun sets, casting deep blues and purples across the sky. Snowflakes gently begin to fall, and the world around you is still, save for your breath and the soft crunch of snow beneath your boots. You step inside, zip up your sleeping bag, and let the warmth envelope you.

This is winter—raw, untamed, and unforgettable. To truly experience it, you must step out into the cold, breathe in the crisp air, and awaken your senses. No amount of reading or preparation can compare to that moment.

Whether you're just starting out or have years of experience, there's always more to learn. Engaging with others—through local clubs, formal training, or online communities—helps you grow as a winter camper. Use these resources, expand your knowledge, and most importantly, get out there. Every journey, every lesson, every challenge will make you stronger and more skilled in the cold.

Winter camping is for those who thrive on challenges. The question is, where will you go next?

The adventure is waiting.

Appendices

Appendix 1
Author Resources for Winter Camping

Winter camping is a skill that improves with experience, but learning from others can fast-track your progress. Whether you're a beginner looking for guidance or an experienced camper wanting to push your limits, there are organizations, courses, and communities that provide valuable resources. From avalanche training to multi-day expeditions, these groups offer education, mentorship, and connections to the broader winter outdoor community.

Learn More from My YouTube Channel and Website

For practical winter camping tips, gear reviews, and expedition insights, check out my YouTube channel:

YouTube: @ALinsdau

I share firsthand experiences, tips, and gear breakdowns from real-world winter adventures. Whether you're new to winter camping or planning an extreme cold-weather trip, my videos provide insights into staying warm, efficient packing, survival strategies, and real-life problem-solving in winter conditions.

Website: www.aaronlinsdau.com

Visit my website for articles, books, and additional resources on winter camping, survival, and expedition planning.

Appendix 2
Training and Education

If you're serious about winter camping, mountaineering, or backcountry travel, these organizations provide formal training in safety, navigation, and survival skills.

American Alpine Club (AAC): A nonprofit organization dedicated to advancing mountaineering and alpine climbing. Offers access to resources, training programs, and networking opportunities for winter climbers and outdoor enthusiasts.
Website: www.americanalpineclub.org
American Alpine Institute (AAI): One of the premier mountaineering schools in North America. Offers courses on winter camping, avalanche safety, glacier travel, and expedition planning.
Website: www.alpineinstitute.com
National Outdoor Leadership School (NOLS): A top-tier outdoor education provider that runs wilderness survival and winter skills courses. Their winter backcountry expeditions focus on leadership, risk management, and self-sufficiency.
Website: www.nols.edu
American Avalanche Association (AAA): A key resource for avalanche education and safety training. If you're venturing into avalanche terrain, a Level 1 avalanche course is essential.
Website: www.americanavalancheassociation.org
Avalanche Canada: The leading resource for avalanche forecasts, courses, and training programs in Canada. Provides real-time avalanche bulletins and educational materials for backcountry travelers.
Website: www.avalanche.ca
European Avalanche Warning Services (EAWS): A network of avalanche warning centers across Europe, providing forecasting and safety guidance for alpine regions.
Website: www.avalanches.org

The British Mountaineering Council (BMC): Offers training courses in winter mountaineering, ice climbing, and expedition planning for UK-based adventurers.
Website: www.thebmc.co.uk
Norwegian Trekking Association (DNT - Den Norske Turistforening): Norway's leading outdoor organization, providing guided winter tours, backcountry hut access, and winter safety courses.
Website: www.dnt.no
Swiss Alpine Club (SAC - Schweizer Alpen-Club): A fantastic resource for hut-to-hut skiing, mountaineering, and winter trekking in Switzerland. Their website provides route guides, weather conditions, and safety tips.
Website: www.sac-cas.ch

Local Clubs and Community Groups

Many local ski and Nordic clubs offer winter survival courses, group outings, and opportunities to connect with experienced campers. Check for clubs in your area—these groups are often the best way to get hands-on experience and find people to camp with.

Local Nordic Ski Clubs: Nordic skiing and backcountry touring clubs often host winter skills workshops, avalanche awareness courses, and group outings.
Local Mountaineering Clubs: Many alpine clubs have winter camping meetups and overnight snowshoeing trips where you can gain experience in a safe setting.
Meetup and Facebook Groups: Many winter camping and backcountry skiing groups organize events through Meetup.com and social media. Find local groups to join outings, swap tips, and get real-world advice.

Winter Camping Events and Courses

If you want hands-on experience with gear, navigation, and winter survival, attending a course or event can be a great way to learn from professionals and practice in real conditions.

REI Winter Camping Courses: Some REI stores offer winter backpacking classes and guided trips. While these tend to be more beginner-focused, they are a great way to ease into winter camping.

Website: www.rei.com/learn

Winter Mountain Festivals: Some regions host winter outdoor events that include avalanche safety courses, winter survival workshops, and gear demos. Look for events like:

Ouray Ice Festival (Colorado, USA): Focuses on ice climbing, but offers winter mountaineering and avalanche workshops.

Banff Mountain Film and Book Festival (Canada): Includes talks and workshops on winter exploration.

Guided Winter Expeditions: Companies like Alaska Mountaineering School, Jagged Globe (UK), and Expeditions Unlimited (France) offer guided multi-day winter treks and expeditions where you can learn skills in a controlled, real-world setting.

Hoarfrost coating trees in West Thumb geyser basin. Experiencing Yellowstone National Park in the winter is an unmatched experience.

Appendix 3
Online Resources and Reading

For those who want to deepen their knowledge, these resources provide expert insights into winter travel, survival, and expedition planning.

Books on Winter Camping and Survival
Mountaineering: The Freedom of the Hills: The ultimate guide to mountaineering and winter travel, covering navigation, survival, and high-altitude skills.
NOLS Winter Camping: Buck Tilton & John Gookin: A solid introduction to cold-weather camping, covering gear, techniques, and safety.
Complete Guide to Winter Camping: Kevin Callan: An excellent introduction to hot tent camping.

Websites and Forums
Backpacking Light (backpackinglight.com): Great resource for ultralight winter gear and techniques.
Mountain Project (mountainproject.com): Forum with discussions on winter climbing, mountaineering, and backcountry skills.
SummitPost (summitpost.org): A user-generated resource with trip reports, route descriptions, and winter conditions for mountains worldwide.

YouTube Channels with Great Winter Camping Content
@ALinsdau: The author's channel, where I share firsthand experiences, tips, gear breakdowns, and expedition insights for winter camping.
Joe Robinet: Covers winter bushcraft and cold-weather survival.
MyOwnFrontier: Features winter solo backpacking trips and gear breakdowns.
The Outdoor Gear Review: Reviews winter camping gear and cold-weather survival tips.

Appendix 4
Author Gear: Winter Overnight

Note that these overnight items depend on location and activity. I don't carry all items listed; it serves as a checklist to review what might be necessary, allowing me to make a decision based on location and weather.

Consider each item and make a decision on what you plan to do. Are you going to ski, snow shoe, climb, base camp, or otherwise? That will decide what you need.

Jackets
☐ Shell jacket or parka (eVent)
☐ Fleece Jacket
☐ Heavy or light down jacket
☐ Fleece vest

Pants (Activity Dependent)
☐ REI Climbing pants
☐ Eddie Bauer Fleece Pants
☐ Shell pants
☐ Gerry Ski Pants (Costco)
☐ Super gaiters
☐ OR Crocodile regular
☐ OR Crocodile custom insulated

Underwear
☐ Icebreaker: boxer-brief, 150, 200 weight
☐ Ex-Officio: synthetic boxer-brief, long weekend trips
☐ Sports boxer-brief: synthetic like Reebok, whatever is available at the local big box store

Long Underwear
☐ Icebreaker: wool full-length legging 150, 200, 260 weight
☐ Sleeping long underwear

Socks
☐ Smart Wool: wool weights: hiker, heavy hiker, hunter, summit, expedition
☐ Wrightsock: crew length

Shirts
☐ Icebreaker: wool long sleeve 150, 200, 260 weight, all trips
☐ Ex-Officio or Eddie Bauer: synthetic button down shirt
☐ 32° Heat (Costco) or other no-name brand: synthetic t-shirt
☐ Medium weight REI shirt
☐ Featherweight REI shirt
☐ Sleeping shirt

Gloves
☐ Light gloves

- ☐ Medium gloves
- ☐ Heavy gloves
- ☐ Mittens
- ☐ Poggies

Headwear
- ☐ REI windproof fleece hat
- ☐ REI windproof fleece headband
- ☐ Balaclava
- ☐ Cold Avenger mask
- ☐ Neck warmer
- ☐ Buff (regular, Arctic)
- ☐ Bug head net
- ☐ Baseball cap
- ☐ Boonie hat

Eyewear
- ☐ Goggles
- ☐ Glasses
- ☐ Spare glasses

Boots
- ☐ Light Duty - Not recommended for winter
- ☐ Med - Shoulder season
- ☐ Heavy - Vasque boots
- ☐ Insulated - Danner 400g boots
- ☐ La Sportiva Nepal Cube
- ☐ La Sportiva Baruntse
- ☐ Millet Everest and Olympus Mons

Cross country boots & liners
- ☐ Rosignol BC boots - good to 0°
- ☐ Light ski boots
- ☐ Heavy insulated ski boots
- ☐ Intuition liners
- ☐ Touring boots
- ☐ Hybrid boots
- ☐ Alfa Mordre Pros
- ☐ Wool Kartankers
- ☐ Neoprene Inferno liners
- ☐ Intuition liners versus wool kartankers. Go with the intuition liners if available.

Other boots and foot items
- ☐ Forty Below Overboots
- ☐ Custom toe caps
- ☐ Forty Below camp booties
- ☐ Western Mountaineerin down booties

Travel Gear
- ☐ Skis
- ☐ Telescoping trekking poles
- ☐ Glob stop
- ☐ Glide wax
- ☐ Snow Shoes

Boots Grip Gear
- ☐ Boot chains
- ☐ Microspikes
- ☐ Crampons: instep or full
- ☐ Crampon extender bars
- ☐ Multitool & Crampon tool

Snow camping equipment
- ☐ Ice axe
- ☐ Backpack
- ☐ Paris expedition sled
- ☐ Tow hardness & rope
- ☐ Helmet
- ☐ Snow shovel
- ☐ Steel shovel for hard conditions

Tent Items
- [ ] Hilleberg Nammatj 2
- [ ] Ground tarp
- [ ] Tent tarp
- [ ] Guy lines for tent tarp
- [ ] Stakes for tent tarp
- [ ] REI Mesh bags for gear

Sleeping bag
- [ ] Sleeping bag -20 deg lower than lowest expected temperature
- [ ] Sleeping pad(s) + patch kit
- [ ] Foam sleeping pad

Stove & cooking equipment
- [ ] XGK Stove
- [ ] Spare fuel pump
- [ ] Fuel (white gas)
- [ ] Fuel funnel
- [ ] Fuel bottle (325mL or bigger)
- [ ] Nalgene water bottles x 4
- [ ] Nalgene insulation (OR SG) x 4
- [ ] Water thermos
- [ ] Food thermos
- [ ] 2L titanium cooking pot
- [ ] Ferro steel strikers
- [ ] Lighter/matches
- [ ] Utensils
- [ ] Aqua Mira

Electronics & navigation
- [ ] Map
- [ ] Compass
- [ ] GPS
- [ ] Smartphone
- [ ] Battery banks
- [ ] Charging cables
- [ ] Head lamp + spare batteries
- [ ] Camera, film, batteries,
- [ ] Spare batteries for all, Battery banks
- [ ] Tripod, selfie stick, Eddie Bauer mini-tripod

Repair items
- [ ] Gorilla duct tape
- [ ] Sewing kit
- [ ] Multitool
- [ ] Knife

Food
- [ ] Breakfast
- [ ] Bars
- [ ] Snacks
- [ ] Freeze-dried dinners

Toiletries
- [ ] Toothbrush/paste
- [ ] Toilet paper
- [ ] Wet wipes
- [ ] Hand sanitizer
- [ ] Nitrile gloves
- [ ] Deodorant
- [ ] Pee bottle
- [ ] Tylenol/aspirin/Advil
- [ ] Ear Plugs
- [ ] Clippers, snippers, nail file
- [ ] Lip balm
- [ ] Sunscreen
- [ ] Hand lotion
- [ ] Stingeze

Other items
- [ ] Thermacare hand warmers

Appendix 4 Author Gear: Winter Overnight

- ☐ Firestarter - petro jelly + cotton ball
- ☐ Bug repelent
- ☐ Watch
- ☐ Bear spray

Vehicle gear
- ☐ Spare keys
- ☐ Ice scraper
- ☐ Tire chains & tools
- ☐ Tow strap
- ☐ Return home clothes
- ☐ Sandals
- ☐ Socks
- ☐ Maps
- ☐ Local/destination map
- ☐ Foldable truck shovel
- ☐ Jumper cables
- ☐ Blankets
- ☐ Road flares

Free Downloads

Looking to take your winter camping skills to the next level? Download Aaron's exclusive Winter Camping Gear List and Greenland Expedition Gear List—packed with essential gear recommendations based on his own expeditions. These lists will help you tackle the toughest winter conditions with confidence. Plus, when you sign up for the Sastrugi Press newsletter, you'll receive a free ebook—*How to Keep Your Feet Warm in the Cold*—to help you stay comfortable and safe during your winter adventures.

You'll also receive occasional updates about Aaron's fiction stories including the *Grant Colson Adventure Thriller Series*—a heart-pounding journey in the SERA (Strategic Exploration and Recovery Agency) universe, where lost history holds the key to the future. Follow Grant Colson as he uncovers hidden secrets and races against time.

Don't worry, your privacy matters. You can opt-out at any time, and your information will never be sold. We are committed to keeping this partnership safe and valuable for you—no spam, just the content that matters. This is a double opt-in email, so you're in full control. Sign up now, and get prepared for your next adventure—whether in the wild or through the pages of an exciting thriller!

www.sastrugipress.com/winter-camping-download/

Author's Review Note

I hope you enjoyed this book. Please consider giving it a rating and add a few words about your reading experience at your favorite online retailer.

The link below with a QR code will take you to the book's web page. From there, you can follow links to various online retailers.

Giving our book rating and a short written review about why you enjoyed it will help me immensely.

Thank you!
Aaron Linsdau

www.sastrugipress.com/books/the-motivated-amateurs-guide-to-winter-camping/

Use your smart device to scan the QR code for the book's webpage.

Other Books by the Author

Black Ice

Some missions don't have a way back. When a hypersonic drone crashes in northern Finland, Grant Colson races against the elements and unseen dangers before the mission—and his team—are erased by the Arctic. *Free download.*
www.aaronrlinsdau.com/sera/black-ice/

50 Jackson Hole Photography Hotspots

This guide reveals the best Jackson Hole photography spots. Learn what locals and insiders know to find the most impressive and iconic photography locations in the United States. This is an excellent companion guide to the *Jackson Hole Hiking Guide*.
www.sastrugipress.com/books/50-jackson-hole-photography-hotspots/

Adventure Expedition One
by Aaron Linsdau M.S. & Terry Williams, M.D.

Create, finance, enjoy, and return safely from your first expedition. Learn the techniques explorers use to achieve their goals and have a good time doing it. Acquire the skills, find the equipment, and learn the planning necessary to pull off an expedition.
www.sastrugipress.com/books/adventure-expedition-one/

Antarctic Tears

Experience the honest story of solo polar exploration. This inspirational true book will make readers both cheer and cry. Coughing up blood and fighting skin-freezing temperatures were only a few of the perils Aaron Linsdau faced. Travel with him on a world-record expedition to the South Pole.
www.sastrugipress.com/books/antarctic-tears/

Lost at Windy Corner
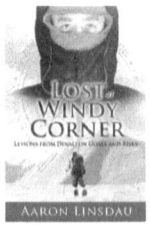
Windy Corner on Denali has claimed fingers, toes, and even lives. What would make someone brave lethal weather, crevasses, and avalanches to attempt to summit North America's highest mountain? Aaron Linsdau shares the experience of climbing Denali alone and how you can apply the lessons to your life.
www.sastrugipress.com/books/lost-windy-corner/

The Most Crucial Knots to Know

Knot tying is a skill everyone can use in daily life. This book shows how to tie over 40 of the most practical knots for virtually any situation. This guide will equip readers with skills that are useful, fun to learn, and will make you look like a confident pro.
www.sastrugipress.com/books/the-most-crucial-knots-to-know/

The Motivated Amateur's Guide to Winter Camping

Winter camping is one of the most satisfying ways to experience the wilderness. It is also the most challenging style of overnighting in the outdoors. Learn 100+ tips from a professional polar explorer on how to winter camp safely and be comfortable in the cold.
www.sastrugipress.com/books/the-motivated-amateurs-guide-to-winter-camping/

Two Friends and a Polar Bear
by Terry Williams, M.D. & Aaron Linsdau

This story of friendship is about two old friends who plan to ski across the Greenland Icecap along the Arctic Circle in hopes of becoming one of the oldest teams to succeed.
www.sastrugipress.com/books/two-friends-and-a-polar-bear/

Use your smart device to scan the QR codes for website links.

Visit www.aaronrlinsdau.com/subscribe/ and join his email list. Receive updates when he releases new books and shows.

Visit Sastrugi Press on the web at www.sastrugipress.com to purchase the above titles in bulk. They are available in print, e-book, or audiobook form.

Aaron Linsdau at the South Pole

About the Author

Aaron Linsdau is the second-only American to ski alone from the coast of Antarctica to the South Pole (730 miles / 1174 km). He set the world record for surviving the longest expedition ever for the Hercules Inlet to the South Pole route.

Visit Aaron's YouTube channel:
www.youtube.com/@alinsdau
or scan the QR Code:

About the Author

Aaron Linsdau is the second-only American to ski alone from the coast of Antarctica to the South Pole, setting a world record for surviving the longest expedition ever for that trip. He has walked across Yellowstone National Park in winter, crossed the Greenland tundra alone, lead one of the oldest teams ever across the Greenland icecap unsupported, has trekked through the Sahara Desert, climbed on Denali solo multiple times, and successfully climbed Mt. Kilimanjaro and Mt. Elbrus.

Aaron is an Eagle Scout and has received the Outstanding Eagle Scout Award. He holds a bachelor's degree in electrical engineering and a master's degree in computational science. Aaron wrote the book and produced the film *Antarctic Tears* and the show *World Beyond*. He also wrote best-selling guidebooks for the 2017 and 2024 total eclipses. Several of his books have been best sellers in their Amazon category.

Visit Aaron's website: www.aaronlinsdau.com

Visit Aaron's YouTube channel:
www.youtube.com/@alinsdau
or scan the QR Code:

www.ingramcontent.com/pod-product-compliance
Lightning Source LLC
Chambersburg PA
CBHW030133170426
43199CB00008B/54